PAYING THE HUMAN COSTS OF WAR

PAYING THE HUMAN COSTS OF WAR

AMERICAN PUBLIC OPINION AND CASUALTIES IN MILITARY CONFLICTS

CHRISTOPHER GELPI

PETER D. FEAVER

JASON REIFLER

PRINCETON UNIVERSITY PRESS

PRINCETON AND OXFORD

Published by Princeton University Press, 41 William Street, Princeton, New Jersey 08540
In the United Kingdom: Princeton University Press, 6 Oxford Street, Woodstock, Oxfordshire OX20 1TW

ISBN: 978-0-691-13902-9
ISBN (pbk.): 978-0-691-13908-1
Library of Congress Control Number: 2008937647
British Library Cataloging-in-Publication Data is available

This book has been composed in Sabon Typeface
Printed on acid-free paper ∞
press.princeton.edu

Printed in the United States of America

10 9 8 7 6 5 4 3 2 1

Dedication

TO ALL THOSE WHO BEAR FIRST-HAND THE HUMAN COSTS OF WAR: THE MEN AND WOMEN WHO HAVE SERVED IN THESE WARS, AND THEIR FAMILIES, ESPECIALLY THE FAMILIES OF MATTHEW LYNCH '01 AND JAMES REGAN '02

CONTENTS

ILLUSTRATIONS

TABLES

ACKNOWLEDGMENTS

THE AUTHORS are indebted to very many friends and colleagues who have helped to shape our work in a variety of ways throughout the development of this project. We could not possibly express our gratitude to all of those who have helped us in some way over the four years that we have been developing this research. We would, however, like to thank some of those who were especially important in completing this work. In particular, this book would never have been possible without generous support from the Carnegie Corporation. Thanks go especially to Stephen Del Rosso, who was instrumental in securing the funding for our initial wave of surveys as part of the "Wielding American Power" project at Duke University. Thanks also to the National Science Foundation and especially Frank Scioli and Jim Granato who supported our 2004 surveys through an SGER grant.

Thanks also go to those who helped us gather the data that are the centerpiece of this book. Tony Parker of the Parker Group was instrumental in helping us to field our initial phone survey in October 2003. Bill McCready and Michael Dennis of Knowledge Networks were also very supportive of our research and made it possible for us to continue our polling throughout the 2004 election year. In addition, thanks to Peter Hart of Hart Research Associates and David Petts of Bennett, Petts and Normington. Hart's fielding of our "success" question was important in validating that measure.

We would also like to thank our many friends and colleagues at Duke University from whom we learned so much as we conducted this research. John Aldrich, Kathryn McNabb Cochran, Scott de Marchi, Alexander Downes, Joseph Grieco, Ole Holsti, Bruce Jentleson, Emerson Niou, Renee Richardson, and Kristen Sharp all provided comments, critiques, and suggestions that have improved our work. Janet Newcity provided important comments and suggestions on the survey instruments, and constructed the design for the cover.

In addition, we have received tremendously helpful support from the comments and suggestions given by colleagues across our discipline who have endured innumerable presentations of this research in progress. Many have served as commentators on panels, provided comments on draft versions of our work, or have responded in print to our previously published work relating to this project. Adam Berinsky, Bill Boettcher, Steve Biddle, Mark Blumenthal, John Brehm, Michael Cobb, Alexandra Cooper, James Druckman, Philip Everts, Scott Gartner, Paul Gronke, Eric Larson, Louis Klarevas, Amy McKay, John Mueller, Michael O'Hanlon, Robert Pape, and Jay Williams were among those who provided helpful comments and critiques.

This book also benefited tremendously from the opportunities that we had to present our research at various workshops and conferences. Participants at the "Wielding American Power" conference hosted by the Triangle Institute for Security Studies and the Monday Seminar Series at the Duke University Social Science Research Institute provided early guidance to our work. In addition, comments from participants in the PIPES workshop at the University of Chicago, the Olin Seminar Series at Harvard University, the Workshop in International Relations at Stanford University, the "Wartime Election of 2004" conference at Ohio State University, and the "Casualties and Warfare" conference at Duke University made important suggestions and contributions to our research.

Throughout this research project we have sought to produce work that would be of interest both to those in academia and those who reside outside the ivory tower. Toward that end, we would like to thank the numerous members of the Fourth Estate who helped us understand this issue from their unique vantage point: Mike Abramowitz, Peter Baker, Fred Barnes, David Brooks, Ron Brownstein, Dan Froomkin, Michael Gordon, Nick Kristoff, Bill Kristol, Doyle McManus, Susan Page, Tom Ricks, David Sanger, Sheryl Stolberg, Shankar Vedantam, and Bob Woodward. Our discussions with them helped us understand how our work could connect to the "real world."

We would also like to thank those policymakers and policy advisors from both parties who invited us to present our research to them. Their perspective helped us understand the applicability, and the limits, of our argument. In particular, we thank Tim Adams, Anthony Blinken, Kurt Campbell, Matthew Dowd, Aaron Friedberg, Clark Murdock, Richard Myers, Barry Pavel, Mitchell Reiss, Joel Shin, Nancy Stetson, Jim Thomas, Pete Wehner, and Paul Wolfowitz.

Finally we would like to thank our families— Janet, Mitchell, and Grace; Karen, Samuel, Ellie, and PJ; and Amy—for their support throughout this process. Without their love and patience we surely never would have brought it to completion.

While the help and support that we have received from many different sources has undoubtedly improved our work a great deal, any remaining errors are, of course, our own.

CHRISTOPHER GELPI
Durham, N.C.

PETER D. FEAVER
Durham, N.C.

JASON REIFLER
Atlanta, Ga.

Chapter One

THEORIES OF AMERICAN ATTITUDES TOWARD WARFARE

PERHAPS the most important task that American citizens entrust to their elected officials is the decision to deploy the country's military forces in combat. In making such decisions, leaders place the lives of American citizens—and the citizens of other nations—in the balance. For decades scholars and politicians have sought to understand the conditions under which Americans are willing to support their leaders' decisions to use military force. In this book, we show that many conditions are important for shaping the public's willingness to bear the human costs of war, but most important of all is the public's expectations that the military operation will be successful.

Initially, scholars believed that the public was not capable of placing constraints on the use of force either because Americans would reflexively "rally 'round the flag" (Verba et al. 1967), or because their attitudes toward foreign policy lacked structure and content (Lippmann 1955; Converse 1964). Later work examining the reaction to the Vietnam War continued to see the public's reaction to the use of military force as reflexive and unthinking, but drew the opposite conclusion about the direction of that reaction, seeing the public as unwilling to tolerate any use of military force that resulted in even a few American deaths (Luttwak 1996; Klarevas 2000).

Ever since the Vietnam War, policymakers have worried that the American public will support military operations only if the human costs of the war, as measured in combat casualties, are trivial.[1] The general public, so the argument goes, is highly sensitive to the human toll, and this sets severe constraints on how American military power can be wielded. Political leaders who engage in costly military ventures will face their own sure demise at the ballot box. Americans stop supporting military operations that produce casualties, and voters punish political leaders who deliver

[1] Except where otherwise noted, we will use the term *casualties* to refer to *deaths*. We recognize that in military parlance, *casualties* means both the dead and the wounded, a much higher number in any conflict. In popular usage, however, *casualties* has generally meant *dead*. In our own polling, except where noted, we used *deaths* in all relevant question wordings so that our claims are not contaminated by any public confusion about the terms.

such policies. Indeed, ever since the rejection of the Versailles Treaty and the rise of isolationism in the United States, but especially since the Vietnam War, the conventional wisdom has cited public reluctance to bear the costs of global leadership as the Achilles heel of American foreign policy.[2] The conventional wisdom is so strong that it is enshrined in Army doctrine and regularly invoked by U.S. leaders.[3]

In this book, we argue that the American public is more discerning and deliberative than most pundits and policymakers expect, and thus American foreign policymakers are less constrained than the conventional wisdom implies. Casualties do not produce a reflexive collapse in public support. Under the right conditions, the public will continue to support even relatively costly military operations. In a similar way, casualties are not as toxic for public support of the president as popularly believed; combat deaths do not translate directly into political death. To be sure, the public is not indifferent to the human costs of American foreign policy, but the constraints placed by American public opinion are not as limiting as popularly believed. Instead, the public appears to take a reasonably level-headed cost-benefit approach in forming attitudes toward military missions.

Our central argument is that—within this cost-benefit framework—when it comes to supporting an ongoing military mission in the face of a mounting human toll, expectations of success matter the most. Many factors—the stakes, the costs (both human and financial), the trustworthiness of the administration, the quality of public consensus on the foreign policy goal in question, and so on—affect the robustness of support. But the public's expectation of whether the mission will be successful trumps other considerations. When it comes to voting on a president who has led the country into a costly war, the relative weights of factors shift; expectations of success still matter, but the most important factor appears to be whether the public views the initial decision to start the war as correct.

Of course, actual success, let alone perceptions of success, are not entirely under the control of policymakers; nor are public judgments about the rightness or wrongness of the initial resort to military force. The president has neither a free hand nor a blank check. But the image of the American public as a paper tiger—a mirage of strength that collapses in the face of casualties—is as incorrect as it is popular.

[2]While each presents this view in a different way with distinctive emphasis and insight, this is the bottom line of the following authors: Bernstein and Libicki (1998); Coker (2001, 2002); Eikenberry (1996); Gentry (1998); Huelfer (2003); Hyde (2000); Klarevas (2000); Kober (2003); Lane (1998); Luttwak (1994, 1995, 1996, 1999); Moskos (1995, 1996/97); Mueller (1994, 2002); Sapolsky and Shapiro (1996); Sapolsky and Weiner (1994). Of course, the conventional view is also ubiquitous in media commentary, too numerous to list. For illustrative examples, see Brown (2000); Kilian (2002); Knickerbocker (2003); McManus (2003). For a good critical review of the conventional wisdom, see Lacquement (2004).

[3]Unattributed (1993); Kull and Destler (1999).

We show that our argument makes the best sense of the voluminous survey data that are now available on this subject. We make wide-ranging use of surveys administered by others, but the centerpiece of our book is data from proprietary national surveys that we designed and conducted from October 2003 through November 2004. These data, representing the results of some 8588 interviews with adult Americans, are an unmatched resource of information, the most extensive and detailed compilation of public attitudes toward casualties of which we are aware. The coincidence of our field research with the ongoing war in Iraq provided an unprecedented, albeit tragic, opportunity to gauge public attitudes toward casualties as events on the ground evolved—and also allowed us to reshape our research focus accordingly.

Indeed, it is impossible to investigate a topic like this today without having the ongoing conflict in Iraq uppermost in mind, and we do look very closely at public opinion on the Iraq war. Concern, however, for what might be called "the public's stomach for costly military action" predates the Iraq war (as does our initial research design).

The issue, in fact, is as old as the Republic. General George Washington and the Continental Congress worried about the willingness of the American colonists to continue to pay the costs of war with Britain. "There is a danger," the general wrote to the Congress, "that a commercial and free people, little accustomed to heavy burdens, pressed by the impositions of a new and odious kind, may not make a proper allowance for the necessity of the conjuncture, and may imagine that they have only exchanged one tyranny for another."[4] President Lincoln likewise confronted the issue in the Civil War. From Lincoln's vantage point, the mounting human toll of the war seemed on a collision course with the 1864 election.[5] His concerns seemed justified, moreover, in light of the impact that war casualties had on Republican candidates in the 1862–63 midterm elections.[6] President Wilson spoke eloquently about the wastefulness of war, opining that "never before have the losses and the slaughter been so great with as little gain in military advantage."[7] The terrible human toll of World War I left what one scholar called a "dark shadow" on the American public, and enshrined the "casualty issue" as a crucial constraint on American foreign policy.[8] Concern over casualties drove U.S. efforts in the 1930s to avoid involvement in another major European war, and shaped the way the war was ultimately fought.[9] Of course,

[4] Washington (1937:107). See also Fisher (1908:244–45) for a discussion of ebbing public support for the Revolution in the face of mounting costs.

[5] Parish (1981:346).

[6] Carson et. al. (2001).

[7] Quoted in Hughes and Seligmann (2000:69).

[8] Huelfer (2003).

[9] Huelfer (2003:181–211).

World War II proved to be the bloodiest American war (not counting the Civil War) and, compared with every military operation since, World War II is held up as the exceptional instance of the American public having a strong stomach for war. At the time, however, President Roosevelt and his military commanders worried greatly about public casualty tolerance and went to extraordinary lengths to manage the public's reception of adverse news.[10] On the other side, both Adolf Hitler and Japanese leaders were convinced that the ethnic composition of the American public, and the democratic government's responsiveness to that public, meant that the economic and military potential of the United States would not be realized in combat; the United States might look tough on paper but, once bloodied, it would collapse.[11]

Concern over the public's tolerance for casualties was arguably a defining feature of the major military operations of the Cold War: Korea and Vietnam. Vietnam, in particular, is remembered as the war that established beyond dispute that the American public will not support a "long and bloody conflict in a faraway land," as one North Vietnamese leader put it.[12] Each of the leaders who brought the United States into these wars saw his political headaches multiply with the mounting combat toll, and each was denied a second term as a result. America's enemies drew the predictable inference about the United States: In the words of Chairman Mao, "[I]n appearance it is very powerful but in reality it is nothing to be afraid of, it is a paper tiger."[13] Vietnam thus raised the question, "Why do big nations lose small wars," and the answer lay in the difficulty of sustaining popular support in the face of mounting costs.[14]

Since Vietnam, of course, the issue has only grown in prominence. The hasty exodus from Beirut after the tragic Marine barracks bombing in October 1983, the hasty retreat from Somalia after the infamous "Black Hawk Down" Ranger raid in October 1993, the force protection mindset in the Bosnia and Kosovo missions—all reflect a conventional wisdom that the American public will reflexively turn on any military mission that involves a human toll. Political leaders' fears of public casualty phobia further help explain decisions against U.S. military intervention in such places as Rwanda, Congo, or Sudan. Edward Luttwak summarized the conventional wisdom well: "The prospect of high casualties, which can rapidly undermine domestic support for any military operations, is the key political constraint when decisions must be made on which forces to

[10] Giangreco (2004).

[11] Friedlander (1967:10); U.S. Strategic Bombing Survey Summary Report (Pacific War), July 1, 1946; and Donald Chisholm, "The Risk of Optimism in the Conduct of War," *Parameters* 33, no. 4 (2003):114–32.

[12] Quoted in Lewy (1978:432).

[13] Mao (1977:310).

[14] Mack (1975).

deploy in a crisis, and at what levels."[15] The Weinberger/Powell doctrine further enshrined the view that public support for military operations was a scarce resource—difficult to mobilize and easy to lose.[16] The view that public resolve was easily overcome was further reinforced by the fact that three influential groups bought into the idea: determined enemies of the United States, media elites, and policymakers. Thus, Saddam Hussein premised his strategy in the first Gulf war on the idea that casualties would defeat the U.S. popular will, even if it did not defeat the military.[17] Slobodan Milosevic knew that he could not directly defeat NATO's military might in the Kosovo war, but believed that inflicting even modest attrition on NATO forces would be sufficient to prevail politically.[18] And in his infamous November 1996 *fatwa*, Osama Bin Laden quite explicitly invoked American casualty phobia in Somalia as evidence for his strategic premise that the United States could be defeated with only a relatively modest level of damage: "[W]hen tens of your soldiers were killed in minor battles and one American pilot was dragged in the streets of Mogadishu, you left the area carrying disappointment, humiliation, defeat and your dead with you. Clinton appeared in front of the whole world threatening and promising revenge, but these threats were merely a preparation for withdrawal."[19] As Steven Kull and I. M. Destler show persuasively, American media elites and policymakers agreed.[20]

The terrorist attacks of 9/11 did not erase the issue from public commentary. Indeed, within a few weeks, pundits were fretting about the bleak prospects for the military operation in Afghanistan and warning that victory would require an unacceptably high military commitment.[21] Even with the Taliban routed and al Qaeda in full retreat, the question of casualty tolerance continued to dog the war, most famously in disputed allegations that a fear of casualties drove the administration to withhold American troops from the assault on Tora Bora in December 2001.[22]

Pundits were once more invoking the "lesson of Vietnam" as the war with Iraq loomed, arguing that the public simply did not have the stomach for the kind of bloody fighting required in Iraq.[23] Based on reports of interviews with former Iraqi commanders, Saddam Hussein himself evidently thought as much, specifically invoking the Somalia incident as proof

[15] Luttwak (1996:36).

[16] Campbell (1998:357).

[17] Lacquement (2004).

[18] Lacquement (2004).

[19] Bin Laden (1996).

[20] Kull and Destler (1999:88–92). For a particularly poignant version, see Thomas Friedman's (2001) pre-9/11 oped on this subject—a column in which he pretends to be Bin Laden celebrating American casualty phobia.

[21] Mearsheimer (2001).

[22] Franks (2004).

[23] Schmitt and Shanker (2002); Ricks (2003a); Boyer (2003).

that the American public was casualty phobic.[24] The war was barely a week old, when observers began to worry that news of combat fatalities would cause public support to collapse.[25] As the security problems in Iraq persisted long after "major combat operations" had ended, the daily reminders of a mounting human toll were carried in grim headlines, often paired with analyses that warned that public support was eroding precipitously.[26] The bloody toll in Iraq featured prominently in the 2004 electoral campaign, and countless observers speculated that President George W. Bush, like Presidents Johnson and Truman before him, would find his electoral hopes lost in a far and distant war. Bush did defy the expectations and win reelection, but the political toll of the Iraq war remained a preoccupation for political observers of all stripes—and for the administration as well.

The relative popularity of the war ebbed and flowed, but as this book went to press (fall of 2008), public opinion had turned sharply negative according to a number of measures, and we could observe some substantial public pressure to begin withdrawing U.S. forces from Iraq. In January 2007 the president increased the number of U.S. troops in Iraq in response to the continuing civil violence there. The president's policy was widely unpopular, but the intensity of public pressure to withdraw troops remained somewhat difficult to gauge. Surveys demonstrated substantial shifts in opinion about the conditions for withdrawing U.S. troops depending upon the specific phrasing used in the question. For example, CBS surveys done in both April and May 2007 asked respondents a simple "yes or no" question regarding whether they support setting a specific timetable for withdrawing American forces from Iraq and found that nearly 65 percent of the public favored such a timetable. Questions that allowed respondents to express support for a specific withdrawal timetable, or for a more flexible policy that would link funding of the war to specific "benchmarks" of progress by the Iraqi government, indicated that "benchmarks" was the median position. Specifically, a Fox News poll indicated that 39 percent supported setting a timetable, 32 percent supported "benchmarks," and 24 percent supported giving the president's policies more time to work. Thus while the public has become increasingly dissatisfied with the Bush administration's handling of this conflict, the public pressure to end U.S. participation in the war has been remarkably slow to materialize. At first blush, then, the Iraq war did not settle the question of whether or not the American public was casualty phobic.

The effect of casualties on American public opinion, whether measured in terms of support for the military operation or support for reelecting the

[24] Zucchino (2003); Shanker (2004).

[25] Ricks (2003b); Purdum (2003); Elder and Nagourney (2003).

[26] Morin and Deane (2003); Matthews and Bowman (2004). Louis Klarevas (2003) even speculated that "the public's KIA threshold could be as low as 500 deaths."

leader who opted for war, is thus both an enduring and timely issue. It is also a question of great importance. Concerns about casualties drive both American foreign policy and American electoral campaigns. It also drives the behavior of America's most determined foes. In short, the issue is worthy of the sustained attention we give it here, and so we proceed as follows. In the rest of this chapter, we contrast the conventional wisdom with the existing scholarly literature in two separate areas: first, public opinion on casualties; and second, the role of foreign policy in elections. We finish the chapter by laying out a summary of the theoretical argument that we will test in the rest of the book.

Chapter 2 assesses our argument in light of aggregate data on public opinion from surveys conducted by others during times of military conflict. We begin by focusing on five military operations that are most often invoked by the conventional wisdom—Korea, Vietnam, Lebanon, Somalia, and Kosovo. Then we look in-depth at the most recent military operation in Iraq, through the U.S. presidential election in 2004. In chapter 3 we argue that many of the debates and issues raised in chapter 2 cannot be definitively answered through an examination of aggregate data alone—as is most commonly done. We examine individual belief systems about the use of force and demonstrate that key arguments in this literature can be measured and tested at the level of individual attitudes. In chapter 4 we return to the theoretical debates described in this chapter and test them at the individual level with a series of survey experiments about hypothetical military missions. Chapter 5 builds upon the results of our survey experiments by applying our argument to an ongoing real-world conflict—the Iraq War. We examine a series of proprietary surveys completed between October 2003 and October 2004. Chapter 6 extends our argument by examining the impact of the Iraq War on the 2004 presidential election and shows how our argument can help explain the Bush victory. Chapter 7 investigates the question left hanging by our argument: If the key attitudes in support for war and vote choice are "expectations of success" and "belief in the rightness of the war," what deeper factors explain those key attitudes? Chapter 8 is a brief conclusion, summarizing our results and identifying questions for future research.

Scholarly Research on Public Attitudes toward Casualties: Logarithmic Decline, Cost-Benefit Calculi, and the Elasticity of Demand for Military Missions

Casualty tolerance is a difficult concept to study, but over the years a fairly substantial body of scholarship addressing the issue has accumulated. Following our own earlier work, we distinguish between a variety of terms that are often treated as synonymous in popular discourse, but that are analytically quite distinct.[27]

By the noun forms of *casualty tolerance*, *casualty sensitivity*, and *casualty shyness*, we mean the overall willingness of the public to continue to support a military operation even as the human toll is rising; in theory, the public's tolerance/sensitivity/shyness could be absolute, high, moderate, limited, or nonexistent. By the adjectival forms of *casualty tolerant*, *casualty sensitive*, and *casualty shy*, we mean specific claims about how casualties affect public support. Thus, the claim that the public is casualty tolerant is a claim that casualties do not substantially undermine public support for a mission; the opposite claim that the public is casualty shy means that casualties do substantially undermine public support. The claim that the public is casualty sensitive is simply a claim that the public views casualties as a negative, preferring less if possible. Virtually all research—including ours in this book—assumes that the public is casualty sensitive in this minimal sense. This is another way of saying that casualties are a human cost of war; we would prefer the same benefit, the goals of the war, at lower cost if possible.

The conventional wisdom described earlier, however, goes a step further, and claims that the public's casualty tolerance is so low that even historically low numbers of casualties will undo public support for a military mission. We call this extreme form of casualty sensitivity "casualty phobia."[28] Casualty phobia is different from pacifism. Pacifism is opposition to any use of force; casualty phobia involves initial support for the use of force, but the support evaporates rapidly and irrevocably at the sight of body bags.

Finally, for the sake of clarity, we will use the terms *casualty averse* and *casualty aversion* to refer to the policies and behaviors that political leaders and the military implement with regard to this issue. Thus, the military can adopt casualty averse rules of engagement, depending on their understanding of the casualty aversion policies of the political leadership; these policies are themselves at least partly in response to political leaders' personal casualty tolerance and also their beliefs about whether the general public is casualty shy or even casualty phobic.

The conventional wisdom is that the public is casualty phobic, but the scholarly consensus is otherwise. The scholarly consensus has evolved over time, partly in response to the growing sophistication of methods of assessing public opinion and partly in response to perceived changes in

[27] The following section draws on and refines the parallel section in Feaver and Gelpi (2004:98–102).

[28] Others have called it the "body bag syndrome" or the "Dover factor" (referring to the airbase in Delaware that serves as the port of entry for the remains of American military personnel killed abroad), or other similar names.

the nature of public opinion as technology and America's role in the world itself have evolved. The literature is best understood as three layers of interlocking (and not necessarily successive) debates.

The first debate concerns whether casualties affect public support for the war according to a fixed pattern of inexorable decline or whether the public views casualties and the use of force through a rational cost-benefit calculus. Early research during the Vietnam War emphasized what came to be called the "rally 'round the flag" effect—the way public support spikes during crises—and the degree to which determined political leaders can reinforce public resolve through decisive action; viewed this way, public casualty sensitivity was not a debilitating constraint on American military power.[29]

As the Vietnam War continued and public support eroded, the scholarly consensus shifted. Jeffrey Milstein was a pioneer in applying the sophisticated techniques of the McNamara "whiz kids" to the problem of public support for Vietnam. He found a variety of strong correlations: As the U.S. military commitment increased and as casualties increased, public support dropped, whereas public support climbed when the burden was shifted to the shoulders of the Vietnamese themselves.[30]

John Mueller built on this work with a landmark study of public opinion in the Vietnam War (with a comparison to the Korean War).[31] Mueller is famous for arguing that public support for the Vietnam War dropped in proportion to the log of casualties: "While [the American public] did weary of the [Korean and Vietnam] wars, they generally seem to have become hardened to the wars' costs: They are sensitive to relatively small losses in the early stages, but only to large losses in later stages."[32] Viewed in toto, Mueller's finding cuts *against* the casualty phobia thesis. Public support for an ongoing military operation did not drop catastrophically with mounting casualties. On the contrary, casualties drained public support only slowly. Mueller, however, was arguing that public support dropped reflexively, and more to the point, inexorably. Mueller's oft-quoted study thus fixed in the public mind the idea that support for Vietnam buckled as the body-bag toll mounted, and this gradually hardened into the conventional wisdom that the public is reflexively casualty phobic.

Mueller later reinforced the "inexorable decline" view with his analysis of public opinion during the first Iraq war, which emphasized that public support was far more precarious than the euphoria over the quick victory might indicate.[33] Scott Gartner and Gary Segura revised this argument

[29] See Verba et al. (1967); Waltz (1967)

[30] Milstein and Mitchell (1968); Milstein (1969, 1973, 1974).

[31] The central thesis is available in Mueller (1971), but the full compilation of polls is found in Mueller (1973).

[32] Mueller (1973: 62).

[33] Mueller (1994)

somewhat, noting that support for the Korean and Vietnam wars declined with logged casualties during periods when the casualty rate was low, but in periods of high casualty rates, then public support drops with marginal casualties, not logged cumulative casualties.[34] Other research also showed that there was a direct link between mounting casualties, antiwar protests, and then subsequent changes in U.S. governmental policy.[35]

This view of a fixed pattern of declining public support with rising casualties was challenged in a series of studies that showed that public support did not inexorably decline. On the contrary, Benjamin Schwarz showed how the rally 'round the flag effect not only inured political leaders from the negative impact of casualties early on in a military operation, but also might even have driven the public to favor escalation of a military operation rather than the withdrawal suggested by the "body bag syndrome."[36] Moreover, several major scholarly investigations assessing public opinion and national security during the Cold War painted a collective picture of a "rational public," one very capable of responding to elite debates and weighing the complexities of foreign policy. [37] The public, in this way, went through what Alvin Richman called a simple "ends-means" calculus.[38] Eric Larson applied this argument to the surveys originally analyzed by Mueller, as well as public opinion from subsequent wars, and found, contra Mueller, that the complex cost-benefit calculation fit the data better than a reflexive, logarithmic response.[39] Today, the scholarly consensus is nearly unanimous in favor of the "rational cost-benefit" model, and Larson's oft-cited version serves as a point of departure for most subsequent research in the field.

The cost-benefit model, however, is not necessarily a rebuttal of the casualty-phobia thesis, and, indeed, the model raises what can be considered the second big debate in the academic literature: If the public applies something like an economistic rational calculation about war, how inelastic is the public's "demand" for war? [40] It is at least theoretically possible for the public to have such an elastic demand—to be so "price sensitive"—

[34] Gartner and Segura (1998).

[35] Lorell and Kelley (1985).

[36] Schwarz (1994).

[37] Holsti and Rosenau (1984); Russett (1990); Wittkopf (1990); Hinckley (1992); Page and Shapiro (1992); Sniderman (1993); Zaller (1994); Richman (1995); Holsti (1996). For a more skeptical view, but not one that dismisses polling altogether, see Althaus (2003).

[38] Richman (1995).

[39] Larson (1996).

[40] In fact, the protagonists in this first wave of debate are not quite as sharply contradictory as the literature implies. Part of what Mueller found in the gradual decline of public support for the Korea and Vietnam missions may simply be a result of the fact that as the casualty toll mounted, the "costs" for securing the goals went up, lowering the net cost-benefit calculation.

that even marginal numbers of casualties cause public support for the war to collapse. Thus, in more recent work, Mueller explicitly accepts the cost-benefit model, but, writing before 9/11, he argued that the public saw so little benefit in most military missions that in effect the cost-benefit calculation was functionally equivalent to a casualty-phobic posture.[41] Likewise, Louis Klarevas endorses the cost-benefit model, but then elsewhere argues that for some key categories of missions the public sensitivity to casualties is so high that trivial numbers of casualties can produce a "Somalia Syndrome."[42] Most scholars who have examined public opinion polls closely come down on the other side, however, concluding that the demand, while not completely inelastic, is nevertheless not as price sensitive as to approximate casualty phobia.[43]

The third debate, which our work engages head on, takes the issue of elasticity a step further: What factors shape the "elasticity of demand" for military missions? Put another way, under what conditions will the casualties cause public support for a given mission to decline more rapidly or more slowly?

For instance, there is a wide scholarly consensus that stakes do matter. The more vital the public views the military mission, the higher the price the public is willing to pay to achieve it, other things being equal. This insight, however, borders on a tautology, since the way you can be sure that the public considers the military mission to be more vital is that the public shows a willingness to tolerate more casualties in conducting it.

There is also a wide scholarly consensus that multiple factors may be at work at the same time.[44] What distinguishes different authors in this third wave of debate, however, is the pride of place they give to certain factors. One can identify in the existing debate, five different claims that argue, in effect, that "other factors may also matter for driving casualty tolerance but this is the factor that trumps the others."[45]

[41] Mueller (2002).

[42] Compare Klarevas (2002) with Klarevas (2000).

[43] This is the bottom line of the following poll-based analyses: Jentleson (1992); Richman (1995); Kull (1995/96); Larson (1996); Strobel (1997); Jentleson and Britton (1998); Burk (1999); Kull and Destler (1999); Feaver and Gelpi (1999, 2004); Everts (2000, 2001, 2002, 2005); Erdmann (1999); Eichenberg (2004).

[44] Larson (2000); Klarevas (2002).

[45] Here we list only the factors that might vary from case to case in the current era. There are a number of other arguments emphasizing different factors that would explain changes in the underlying casualty tolerance from what it might have been in previous generations. Thus, Luttwak (1994, 1996) argues that the public is more casualty sensitive now than in the time of the World Wars because of the lower birth rate. Moskos (1995) argues that the public is more casualty sensitive now because they see that children of the elite are not at risk in most military missions. Sapolsky and Shapiro (1996) argue that casualty phobia has driven changes in technology that have, in turn, reinforced casualty phobia by fostering

First, Bruce Jentleson argues that the "pretty prudent" public bases its casualty tolerance on "the principal policy objective (PPO)" envisioned by the military operation.[46] PPOs involving "foreign policy restraint" will be accepted by the public as important and thus worth even a serious price; these included the traditional military tasks of using force to coerce an adversary engaged in aggressive action against the United States or its allies. Missions deemed "humanitarian intervention" enjoy public support only if the costs are relatively low. Still other missions, dubbed "internal political change," are viewed as inherently dodgy adventures by a skeptical public; public support for these missions is hard to come by and easy to lose as costs mount.

Second, Eric Larson argues that public casualty tolerance follows domestic elite casualty tolerance.[47] When domestic elites line up in a consensus behind the mission, public support will be robust even in the face of mounting costs, but when domestic elites are divided, then even small amounts of casualties will be highly corrosive of public support. By domestic elites, Larson primarily refers to potential political rivals in Congress.

Third, Steven Kull and his colleagues argues that public support for a military mission will be more robust if the public sees that other countries likewise support the mission and thus the United States is not obliged to bear the costs all by itself.[48] Multilateral support may function as an elite cue—"this mission must be justified because lots of other states are sup-

unrealistic expectations as to what extent human toll is unavoidable in war. Numerous people (Stech 1994; Neuman 1996; Livingstone 1997), have argued that the advent of near-real-time television coverage of military operations has heightened public casualty sensitivity by giving the deaths a vividness and immediacy that makes them more shocking. Logically, these works belong in the first or second wave because they are claiming that the public is, in fact, highly casualty sensitive and are blaming a factor that is largely unavoidable and so should apply with equal force to every military mission we might consider. In fact, some of these factors may well be at work; a variant of Moskos argument shows up in the social contact variable described in the text and we will give emphasis to the role of technology in the concluding chapter. Moreover, as we discuss in the concluding chapter, there has been an order of magnitude shift in the public's casualty tolerance. Whereas in previous wars, casualty concerns arose after tens or even hundreds of thousands of fatalities, now the concerns are arising even when the death toll is only in the tens or hundreds. The generational factors may help explain this phenomenon, but they do not help explain the conditions under which the public is willing to continue to support particular military missions given the environment we face today.

[46] Jentleson (1992); Jentleson and Britton (1998). See also Eichenberg (2005).

[47] Larson (1996, 2000). Larson applies Zaller's (1994) model of how elites cue public opinion. Larson (2000) offers a model for weighing multiple factors at the same time, including various indices that attempt to measure the public's perceived utility in a given military mission, expectations of success, and leadership cuing. He gives pride of place, however, to leadership cuing.

[48] Kull, Destler, and Ramsay (1997); Kull and Destler (1999); Kull and Ramsay (2000); Kull et al. (2002, 2003a, 2003c).

porting it" [49]—or the public may simply prefer to have the burden distributed more evenly.

Fourth, a variety of scholars and pundits have identified what might be called the "contact" factor in shaping robustness of the public's stomach for costly military ventures. One of the earliest systematic studies of the question was Donald Rugg and Hadley Cantril's analysis that compared the views of person's with draft-age family members versus those without such members to the prospect of war *before* the United States entered World War II; Rugg and Cantril concluded that there was no difference and, at least at that time, opposition or support was not a personal matter.[50] On the other hand, Scott Gartner, Gary Segura, and Michael Wilkening showed that individuals from counties with higher casualty rates had greater opposition to the Vietnam War than individuals from counties with lower casualty rates; in other words, local losses increased casualty sensitivity.[51] Similarly, Karol and Miguel (2005) looked at county-level aggregate data and found casualties within some counties reduced the proportion of the vote for Bush relative to its level in 2000, though they find that casualties had no impact in other counties. This argument is another way of understanding the popular claim advanced by Charles Moskos, Charles Rangel, and others that the general public, whose children are at risk in military combat, are more sensitive to casualties than are elites, whose children by and large do not serve in the military.[52]

Fifth, our own prior research identified expectations of success as the crucial factor.[53] If the public believes the mission will succeed, then the public is willing to continue supporting the mission, even as costs mount. When the public thinks victory is not likely, even small costs will be highly corrosive. Note that the critical attitude specified here is expectation of eventual future success, not necessarily assessments of how the war is

[49] In Grieco (2003) this mechanism is hypothesized as the critical factor behind a public preference for multilateralism.

[50] Rugg and Cantril (1940).

[51] Gartner, Segura, and Wilkening (1997). See also Gartner (2004).

[52] Moskos (1995, 1996/97). Rangel (2003). Our own research confirmed that social contact does affect casualty sensitivity in this way, but simply being a parent did not; we were unable to assess the impact of being a parent of someone in the military (Feaver and Gelpi 2004:166).

[53] Feaver and Gelpi (1999, 2004); Feaver (2001). Kull and Ramsay (2001:223–24) reach a similar conclusion: "Americans do not and are not likely to respond reflexively to losses by wanting to withdraw from a military operation...provided that the public has support for the operation in the first place and believes that it is likely to succeed." Richard Eichenberg (2005) likewise agrees, noting that "successful military operations enjoy high support, regardless of other factors that may be present." And van der Meulen and Konink (2001), in their analysis of Dutch public opinion surrounding the Bosnian operation, concluded that expectations of success were the best predictor of Dutch casualty tolerance. See also Kull (1997).

going right now or most recently. Of course, recent experience can shape expectations of the future, but our claim was that the future judgment was the one that matters. It is the difference between how the patient feels right now versus how optimistic the patient is that he will get well eventually; the latter is the more crucial attitude for determining one's tolerance for enduring pain.[54]

Beyond these five factors are a host of demographic factors that research has shown affect casualty sensitivity. Race is a significant factor, with African Americans being more sensitive to casualties than Caucasians.[55] Gender is also significant, with women more sensitive than men.[56] Education and age likewise matter, though they do not have a consistent effect; depending on the case in question, sometimes education and age are positively correlated with casualty tolerance and sometimes they are negatively correlated.[57]

Each of these studies establishes convincingly that the favored factor matters (and most also show that other factors matter, too). It should be noted that the cost-benefit approach does not preclude the possibility that in the very long run—something like the decade-long involvement in Vietnam—time may itself shape the calculation.

Every factor that is given pride of place in analyses—whether external multilateral support, or domestic elite consensus, or prospects of victory—is likely to be negatively affected to some degree if the war drags on indefinitely. But from a policymaking perspective, the inexorable decline is slow enough to provide a window for military operations, provided the other factors are favorable. Of these other factors, the demographics are less policy-relevant; policymakers seeking to shore up public support for a military mission as costs mount—or war protestors seeking to undermine public support—are not able to do much about changing demographics. The other factors—how the mission's purpose is framed, the degree of elite or international consensus, the perceived likelihood of victory—are indeed in play for policymakers. Accordingly, we single them out for special attention.

The existing scholarly literature makes one further observation relevant to the shaping of our current project. Most pundit commentary treats public opinion in the aggregate with sweeping statements about overall casualty phobia or overall robustness of support. In fact, however, it makes

[54] In this way, "expectations of success" is different from the attitude that Gartner and Segura favored in their use of marginal casualty rates. In their words, "[R]ecent casualties send a signal that the war is not going well—a signal that dominates other cost measures when the marginal casualty level is increasing." Gartner and Segura (1998:295).

[55] Verba et al. (1967); Wilcox et al. (1993); Gartner, Segura, and Wilkening (1997); Gartner and Segura (2000); Nincic and Nincic (2002); Feaver and Gelpi (2004).

[56] Wilcox et al. (1993); Bendyna and Finucane (1996); Gartner, Segura, and Wilkening (1997); Nincic and Nincic (2002); Eichenberg (2002); Feaver and Gelpi (2004).

[57] Compare Gartner, Segura, and Wilkening (1997) with Feaver and Gelpi (2004).

more sense to view public opinion as an aggregation of different pockets of opinion, each with different responses to casualties. Our own review of public opinion on the use of force identified a quadripartite pattern that seemed to recur across a variety of different cases. The public was made up of solid hawks (roughly 30 to35 percent) who will support virtually any military mission virtually regardless of the costs; solid doves (roughly 10 to 30 percent) who will oppose essentially any mission regardless of costs; casualty-phobics (roughly 15 to 20 percent) who support a mission provided it is extremely low cost; and defeat-phobics (roughly 15 to 40 percent) who support a mission, despite mounting costs, provided that the mission is likely to succeed, but who turn on a mission provided that it looks like it is doomed to failure.[58] With such a distribution, the public reservoir of support in the aggregate is adequate even for low-stakes missions that involve the cost of human lives. The exact percentages on any given mission vary with the stakes and a host of other factors, but in broad-brush terms one inference is that a resolved president can count on at least 45 percent support for any successful mission; this degree of support is adequate to carry on even as casualties mount, given the executive branch's privileged position on foreign affairs and the likely nature of military conflicts that the United States would face.

In sum, we glean from the existing literature four key insights that serve as the point of departure for our study:

- Public attitudes toward casualties are very difficult to assess and may change over time.
- The public is not casualty phobic, but casualties do affect public support for military operations by counting as the costs in a cost-benefit calculus.
- A range of factors shape the elasticity of demand for military operations—the rapidity with which casualties might undermine public support in any given mission. At present, however, no study is able to show how much one factor matters compared to the other relevant factors.[59]
- While judgments are possible about public opinion in the aggregate, in fact individuals respond to casualties differently.

Foreign Policy and Elections

In this book, we also examine the way that casualties and attitudes toward the war in Iraq affected the 2004 election results, and in so doing we encounter yet another bit of conventional wisdom—this time about

[58] Feaver and Gelpi (2004: 186).

[59] Gartner, Segura, and Wilkening (1997) do offer multivariate analysis that pits their contact variable against other demographic variables. They do not, however, compare it with the other factors that the literature has deemed significant: the nature of the mission, the degree of domestic elite cuing, multilateral support, and expectations of success.

the link between foreign policy and elections.[60] The conventional view is summarized by the pithy aphorism attributed to then-candidate Clinton's campaign advisors in 1992: "It's the economy, stupid." Public opinion in general has been considered to be ill informed and unsystematic.[61] Foreign policy evaluations in particular have been suspect and not considered likely to shape vote choice. When forming attitudes about the performance of the economy, citizens have their personal experience to fall back on. But foreign policy is so removed from the everyday lives of most citizens, it was argued, that it is simply unreasonable to think that what happened beyond U.S. borders would have a large impact on Americans' political behavior. In support of this claim, many studies showed, at best, only weak evidence that foreign affairs affects the voting decision.[62]

This skeptical view was gradually challenged by scholarship that identified a "rational public," capable of making reasonable or competent decisions from limited amounts of information.[63] Indeed, research showed that citizens have reasonably structured attitudes concerning foreign policy; attitudes of foreign policy affect political evaluations; and citizens respond in understandable ways to changing world events.[64] The public may not be very good at quiz bowl questions about international current events, but the public as a whole has stable and reasonable opinions that change in response to changes in the real world.[65] Public opinion may be "latent" on many issues, but when activated by news events and especially by prominent debates within the elite over foreign policy options, it becomes a factor that policymakers must address.[66]

If the public has rational views about foreign policy, it is not so unreasonable to think that the distant world of foreign affairs can have a meaningful impact on political behavior like vote-choice. Voting, as Morris Fiorina has argued, involves both retrospective and prospective judgments, as shaped by an individual voter's political predispositions.[67] How well have these candidates performed in the past and which is likely to do the best job in the future, are questions to be measured against an individual's own ideology, especially in terms of defining phrases like "how well" and "best job."

It has long been known that economic evaluations have an effect on presidential approval and vote choice.[68] An increasing amount of evidence

[60] This section draws on material published in Gelpi, Reifler, and Feaver (2005).

[61] Campbell et al. (1960); Converse (1964).

[62] Almond (1950); Stokes (1966).

[63] Popkin (1991); Page and Shapiro (1992); Sniderman (1993); Lau and Redlawsk (1997); Lupia and McCubbins (1998).

[64] Hurwitz and Peffley (1987a, 1987b); Peffley and Hurwitz (1993).

[65] Shapiro and Page (1988); Wittkopf (1990); Holsti (1996).

[66] Sobel (2001). For an extensive review of this literature, see Powlick and Katz (1998).

[67] Fiorina (1981).

[68] Kinder and Kiewet (1979, 1981); Kiewet (1983).

has emerged showing that foreign policy judgments matter as well as, and in roughly equal magnitude to, economic evaluations. In an analysis of the 1980 and 1984 presidential elections, Aldrich, Sullivan, and Borgida find that foreign policy issues were just as powerful a vote determinant as domestic issues.[69] Likewise, in a time-series analysis of aggregate quarterly presidential approval data, Nickelsburg and Norpath show that the president is as much "commander-in-chief" as "chief economist."[70] Adding major foreign policy events as predictor variables to their model, these international events matter at least as much as economic evaluations. Using individual-level data from several national random sample surveys conducted from 1983 to 1987, Wilcox and Allsop (1991) find that approval of Reagan's foreign policy is consistently a good predictor of his overall approval, though, as a predictor, the strength of foreign policy approval relative to domestic issues does depend on the salience of economic or foreign policy issues at a given time.[71] Nincic and Hinkley (1991) and Annand and Krosnik (2003) also show that foreign policy attitudes affect the evaluation of presidential candidates. One intriguing study even found a link between the casualty rates at the district level and the electoral fortunes of members of Congress running in the 1862–63 congressional elections; the higher the level of casualties in a specific congressional district, the worse the incumbent fared in the election, though the substantive effect was quite small (an incumbent lost less than 1 percent of the two-party vote for every one hundred casualties in his district).[72]

The precise impact of foreign policy on electoral choice does appear to wax and wane with the flow of current events. Survey responses regarding the nation's "most important problem" suggest that the economy is nearly always salient in the minds of voters, while concern about foreign affairs varies substantially, depending on world events. Foreign affairs will play a less prominent role in elections during a relatively quiet time internationally, say 1996, than they will in an election during the middle of a controversial war, say 2004.

In sum, we glean from the existing literature four key insights that serve as the point of departure for our study:

- Foreign affairs in general, and political salient matters like war casualties in particular, do affect vote-choice.
- Both retrospective and prospective judgments come into play when individuals make a vote-choice.
- Behavior seen in the aggregate—for example, elections won or lost—are a function of individual-level choices, that is, individual voters choosing one candidate over another based on a host of factors, including foreign issues.

[69] Aldrich, Sullivan, and Borgida (1989).
[70] Nickelsburg and Norpath (2000).
[71] Wilcox and Allsop (1991).
[72] Carson et al. (2001).

- These effects are likely to be pronounced when foreign issues are salient, for instance, during wartime.

Our Approach and Argument: The Interaction of Expectations of Success and Perceived Rightness of the War

The foregoing review of the scholarly literature has five implications for the research design of this book. First, because the vast majority of the scholarship evaluating public attitudes toward casualties is based on aggregate data, we will emphasize analyses of individual-level opinion. Where appropriate we will also assess aggregate opinion, but aggregate data by itself cannot settle the debates that remain. Second, because casualty sensitivity is such a difficult concept to measure, we will use a variety of measures—aggregate versus individual-level opinion, hypothetical versus real-world scenarios, and direct versus experimental question designs—to ensure that our findings are robust and not an artifact of question wording or ephemeral survey context. Third, for these same reasons, where possible, we will draw on surveys designed explicitly to tap into attitudes toward casualties; relying on surveys where the casualty question is an afterthought may be misleading. Fourth, where possible, we will use appropriate multivariate statistical techniques to isolate and compare the separate (or interactive) effects of different factors on casualty attitudes; in this way we can to make a more confident assessment about the relative weights. Fifth, our model will incorporate both backward and forward-looking questions, since the attitudes of direct interest—whether to support a military mission and which candidate to elect as president—involves both retrospective and prospective judgments.

The centerpiece of our project is proprietary opinion survey data from nine original surveys that we designed and administered to different random national samples from 22 September 2003 through 1 November 2004. The first survey was administered by telephone by the Parker Group from 22 September 2003 through 12 October 2003, and consisted of 1203 interviews with adults drawn from a Random Digit Dialed (RDD) U.S. national sample.[73] The next eight surveys were all administered via the Internet by Knowledge Networks: Wave 1 (6–20 February 2004, 891 respondents), Wave 2 (25 February–4 March, 870 respondents), Wave 3 (5– 18 March, 930 respondents), Wave 4 (19 March–2 April, 889 respondents), Wave 5 (2–16 April, 881 respondents), Wave 6 (17–29 April, 899 respondents), Wave 7 (18–28 June, 900 respondents), Wave 8 (21

[73] The survey instrument is from us, the authors.

October–1 November, 1125 respondents). The Knowledge Networks data is equivalent to a national RDD sample.[74]

These data have three distinct advantages over other casualty-related opinion data.[75] First, the data come from surveys designed explicitly to measure casualty tolerance and to probe the determinants of that attitude. As we explain in more detail in chapter 3, casualty tolerance is very difficult to measure, and previous measures, including our own, were not well-suited to the kinds of comparative analyses that make up the heart of this project. Second, the surveys sampled opinion over the span of a year in the midst of a war during which the combat toll more than tripled, and during which the public was exposed to countless news reports and commentaries about the human costs of war. The most sophisticated previous work in this area, including our own, was primarily based on hypothetical scenarios asked during peacetime, and this naturally raised doubts about the robustness of any findings. Third, the last survey wave was conducted just on the eve of the 2004 presidential election and is the only nationally representative casualty-related survey ever conducted in such close proximity to an election. As we will show in chapter 5, our poll is a very good proxy for a survey of the electorate, and we are thus able to probe the electoral implications of casualties in an unprecedented way.

Our goal in conducting this research is to extend our empirical grasp of how Americans structure their understanding of foreign affairs in the area of military conflict. We seek to build upon existing theoretical models and empirical evidence to improve our knowledge of how Americans respond to seeing their fellow citizens die in combat on behalf of their country and how their attitudes toward war influences their voting behavior. We fully understand, however, that ours will not be the last word on this topic. In fact, as we discuss in chapter 7, we believe that our research raises important questions for future work in political psychology regarding

[74] For more information on the Knowledge Networks methodology, see http://www.knowledgenetworks.com/. For an analysis of the representativeness of the Knowledge Networks panel and their sampling methodology, as well as an analysis of mode effects and panel effects, see Dennis et al. (2004). The full survey instruments are available from us, the authors.

[75] One study that approximates ours in design used a well-crafted series of survey experiments administered to 251 undergraduates at Ohio State University. The survey, conducted in February and early March 2003, used hypothetical questions about casualties in an ongoing operation in Kosovo, but manipulated the level of casualties (none versus 15), the frame ("genocide" versus "bandits, thugs, and warlords"), and the putative effectiveness of the Kosovo operation to date (no report, successful, and unsuccessful). The findings of the study are largely consonant with our own. Mentioning casualties reduced support by about 17 percent; the "successful" frame increased support by about 10 percent, whereas the "unsuccessful" frame reduced support by about 20 percent. Contrary to our findings, however, the study found that the effects were additive and not interactive. See McGraw and Mears (2004).

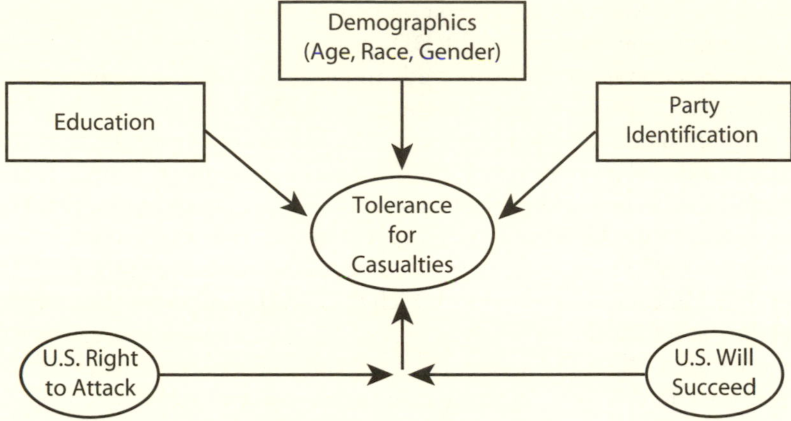

FIGURE 1.1. A Model of Tolerance for Casualties

information processing and belief formation. We recognize that the answers to these questions of information processing and public "rationality," cannot be fully answered without further theoretical and empirical work in political psychology.

Nonetheless, we believe that our research sheds important new empirical light on the way that Americans structure their understanding of foreign policy and how they respond to America's experience of war. Our detailed findings are too varied to enumerate here, but we can provide a snapshot of our overall argument and the main results from the analyses presented in the chapters that follow. Our basic model of casualty tolerance is reflected in figure 1.1.

We argue that support for continuing a military operation (or, for that matter, starting such an operation) in the face of mounting combat casualties is a function of the interactive effect of two underlying attitudes: expectations about the likelihood that the military operation will be a success and belief in the initial rightness of the decision to launch the military operation.[76] The more likely you think the operation will be a success and the more correct you think the original decision was, the more you will be willing to pay a higher cost in the form of mounting combat fatalities. The relationship is interactive, meaning that if one believes that the operation is doomed to failure, then also believing that the decision was the "right thing" does not have so big an effect; likewise, if you believe that the decision was wrong, then also believing that the operation will be suc-

[76] This argument is anticipated in Kull and Ramsay (2001:224), who conclude after reviewing a wide range of aggregate poll data on peacekeeping missions in the 1990s, that "support for continuing an operation is likely to be sustained provided that the public has support for the operation in the first place and believes that it is likely to succeed."

cessful does not have so big an effect. But, following our own earlier research, we argue that expectations of success will be the more important of the two factors.[77] That is, varying expectations of success have a more substantial effect on one's stomach for war than do varying beliefs about the rightness or wrongness of the war; the support of people who believe that the war can still be won but think that the war was wrong is more robust in the face of a mounting human toll than is the support of people who believe that the war is lost but think the war was the right thing to do in the first place.

Of course, other factors contribute to expectations of success and a belief in the rightness or wrongness of the decision to use force. Real-world developments intervene, such as the capture of Saddam Hussein or the failure to find stockpiles of weapons of mass destruction. The public resolve of leaders can reassure publics that success is still likely despite adverse developments on the battlefield. Presidential rhetoric can likewise serve to reinforce public conviction in the rightness of the cause. As Larson and Kull and others have argued, the endorsement of actors not directly implicated in the decision can also reinforce beliefs about the appropriateness of war. For that matter, as we explore in chapter 7, perceptions of the rightness of the decision may itself be shaped by expectations of success, and vice versa. Viewed this way, however, success still trumps other factors; the causal arrow running from perceptions of success to belief in the rightness of the war is stronger than the causal arrow running in the other direction. Moreover, demographic factors like gender, race, age, partisan affiliation, and so on, all have a separate influence on the key attitudes we are studying. Importantly, however, we find that partisan attitudes, which the conventional wisdom tends to treat as dominant, has most of its effect early on in the causal chain; that is, controlling for the influence of partisan affiliation on belief in the rightness of the initial decision to use military force, we find that partisanship has only a very modest effect on casualty tolerance.

When it comes to the electoral decision in wartime, the same basic framework operates. Attitudes about the rightness of the war and the likelihood of success interacted to shape the voter's choice between President George W. Bush and challenger Senator John Kerry. The relative weights, however, were reversed. Whereas the prospective attitude of expectations of success was dominant in shaping casualty tolerance, it was the retrospective attitude about the rightness of the war that dominated in shaping vote choice. Individuals who believed that the decision for war was

[77] As we explain in some detail in subsequent chapters, we have modified our understanding of casualty tolerance from what we first presented in Feaver and Gelpi (2004). The bumper-sticker version of our argument stays the same: expectation of success trumps other factors. But the way in which we integrate that insight with other findings has changed.

wrong but believed that we would win were willing to continue the military mission despite mounting casualties; in the choice for president, however, they were more likely to favor Kerry over Bush. Individuals who believed that the decision for war was right but believe that we would lose are not willing to continue the mission in the face of mounting casualties; they were, however, far more likely to prefer Bush over Kerry.

Throughout we are able to confirm the modest form of the claims made in the existing literature. As Jentleson has argued, individual attitudes about the rightness or wrongness of certain categories of missions in the abstract does shape individual casualty sensitivities in particular missions. As Larson has argued, individuals who perceive elite support for a mission are more likely themselves to support the mission; this, in turn, does shape casualty tolerance. As Kull has argued, an individual's support for the mission is influenced by whether that individual believes that other states are also supporting it. And, as many people have argued, having a personal connection to the people at risk in a military operation does shape one's willingness to pay the human costs of war. But our analyses here show that regardless of how the issue is approached, expectations of success matters the most.

Chapter Two

AMERICA'S TOLERANCE FOR CASUALTIES, 1950–2006

THE CONSTRAINT imposed upon governments by citizens' willingness to bear the costs of war is neither a new nor trivial concern. The Magna Carta of 1215 was spurred in large part by English barons' refusal to pay for King John's expensive wars abroad. Immanuel Kant, in his theory of perpetual peace, argued that popular aversion to both the human and material costs of war would prompt republican governments to avoid conflict and seek peace instead (Doyle 1986). Yet these historical examples and theoretical treatments inform only our speculations of how the public responds to the cost of war. The ability to measure the public's tolerance for war costs—and thus our ability to evaluate competing causal arguments as to whether and when citizens are willing to accept such costs—is a much more recent development. Systematic data are limited to the post–World War II era, when social science research adopted widespread use of surveys from probability samples. Using systematic public opinion data from the Korean War to the current Iraq War, we explore American attitudes toward warfare.

America's military experiences from 1950 to the present span a variety of international contexts, but a consistent domestic context. On the international side, the Cold War era presented the public with a rival of comparable military power and concomitant threats to American security. The end of the Cold War and the demise of the Soviet Union led to unparalleled American military superiority, and threats to American security seemed to diminish as a result. The terrorist attacks of 11 September 2001 demonstrate, however, that serious threat can coexist with American preeminence. Despite these significant differences in the international context, the domestic political context surrounding military engagement is constant across them—remaining uninvolved or withdrawing once involved are plausible policy stances in all the conflicts we examine.[1] This common domestic political context is especially important

[1] We do not, however examine any "nonconflicts." Thus our analysis in this chapter examines only the response of the public to military conflicts in which American leaders chose to become involved. We do not investigate the possible public response to military conflicts in which American leaders chose not to engage. We do, however, address hypothetical conflicts in chapters 3 and 4.

here because of the emphasis that we place on perceptions of success as a determinant of public support.

The United States has used military intervention (or the threat of intervention) as a tool of foreign policy. As long as military force remains a tool of foreign policy, the willingness of Americans to support the use of this tool is an important question. In this chapter, we evaluate public support for some of the most significant American military conflicts since Word War II. We will not evaluate support for every American military operation—doing so would merely replicate a number of prominent studies already in the literature (Mueller 1973; Jentleson 1992; Jentleson and Britton 1998; Larson 1996; Eichenberg 2005). Instead, we will focus on several of the key conflicts that were critical in shaping both academic and popular arguments about public tolerance for war. Our focus is on examining the causal mechanisms that drive the public's attitudes rather than just reporting levels of support in different missions.

While American forces have been deployed in a variety of conflicts since World War II, the operations in Korea, Vietnam, Lebanon, Somalia, Kosovo, and Iraq have been most important in shaping our understanding of American attitudes toward war. The conflicts in Korea, Vietnam, and Iraq stand out as the most costly American operations in both financial and human terms, making them critical cases for understanding public tolerance for costs. Lebanon, Somalia, and Kosovo, on the other hand, are important because they represent the central pieces of evidence supporting the oft-repeated claim that the public is casualty phobic—that even small numbers of casualties (in historical terms) will cause support for a mission to collapse. Abrupt American withdrawals from Lebanon and Somalia in the wake of gruesome and unexpected casualties are the primary events that scholars and pundits (and enemies like Bin Laden and Zarqawi) cite as evidence of a popular "casualty phobia" (Klarevas 2000, 2002). Kosovo, on the other hand, is an American intervention that was so profoundly shaped by the belief in the public's casualty phobia that the Clinton Administration reportedly insisted that the military develop a strategy in which no ground forces would be used and in which no pilots would be shot down. In this chapter we will review each of these engagements in chronological order and evaluate the various arguments about public attitudes toward tolerating the human costs of these conflicts.

Korea and Vietnam[2]

Perhaps the most influential work on public attitudes toward the costs of military conflict is John Mueller's analysis of public support for the Ko-

[2]The sections on Korea, Vietnam, Somalia, and Kosovo draw upon material first published in Feaver and Gelpi (2004).

rean and Vietnam Wars (1971, 1973). Mueller asserts that public support for American wars in Korea and Vietnam can all be explained with a "simple association: as casualties mount, support decreases" (Mueller 2005). A careful look at the data, however, indicates that the simple association is not so simple. Figure 2.1 depicts the poll results that Mueller relies upon for his analyses of support for Korea (1971, 1973, 2005) along with the cumulative number of American battle deaths suffered at the time of each poll. Public support remained high (66 percent) in August 1950, even though the United States suffered more than 4,600 battle deaths just a few weeks into the conflict. This remarkably high level of support is more easily understood once one recalls that by August 1950, U.S. forces had achieved some important battlefield success. The United States had (1) slowed the North Korean advance and (2) set up a perimeter around Pusan, from which they planned to retake the peninsula. While the initiation of the war took the United States by surprise, the rally-'round-the-flag phenomenon and the ability of the U.S. military to stabilize the situation on the battlefield seemed to stiffen the public's tolerance of casualties.

A substantial drop in public support for the war in Korea occurred between August and December 1950. During this period the United States suffered nearly 10,000 battle deaths. The conventional view, which was established by Mueller's analysis, attributes the collapse of public support to the infliction of these casualties. Closer investigation, however, reveals that the casualties alone may not be the principal causal force in eroding support. Just as battlefield successes were evident in the early period, battlefield setbacks characterized this second period of the war. Chinese forces unexpectedly intervened in the conflict in November 1950, which inflicted a series of devastating defeats—including the loss of Seoul—on the badly overextended American forces. The casualties were suffered in battlefield defeats, not in battlefield victories. Casualties in conjunction with battlefield defeat raise the possibility that the drop in public support was prompted not by an unwillingness to take casualties per se, but rather by a reluctance to support an apparently losing cause. Figure 2.1 shows that as the United States overcame these difficulties in Korea—by stabilizing the front, stopping the Chinese advance, and recapturing Seoul—support for the war increased even as casualties continued to mount. Specifically, while the United States suffered more than 8,000 battle deaths between January and August 1951, support for the war increased by 8 percentage points. Finally, support began to wane with mounting casualties once again as the stalemate set in around the 38th parallel, although support declined much more slowly than during the December 1950 period when the United States was suffering more substantial defeats.

This more variable relationship between casualties and war support is also borne out by statistical analyses of these data. Table 2.1 presents

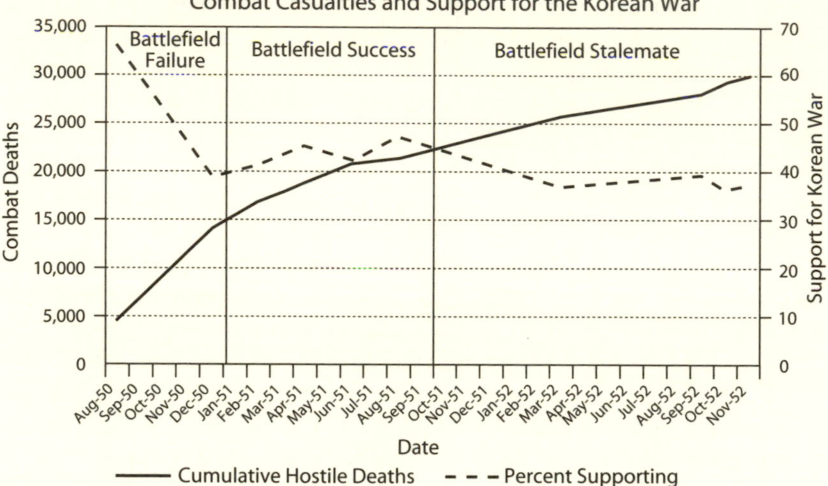

FIGURE 2.1. Combat Casualties and Support for the Korean War

regression analyses of the relationship between U.S. casualties and support for the war in Korea.[3] Consistent with Mueller (1971, 1973, 2005), we regressed the log of cumulative casualties on support for the war. As the conventional wisdom would expect, the coefficient for the relationship between casualties and public support for the war in Korea is statistically significant coefficient ($b = -14.06$, $p < .01$). But if we drop the first phase of the war and analyze the relationship between casualties and support for the war from December 1950 onward, the relationship between casualties and support becomes insignificant ($b = -6.89$, n.s.). In other words, the famous finding that casualties eroded public support for the war in Korea is *entirely a function of events during the first seven months of the conflict, precisely the period when the United States looked to be losing the Korean War.*

The inadequacy of Mueller's "simple association" becomes even clearer if one separates the impact that casualties had on support for the war during two critical periods. From January 1951 to August 1951, U.S. and UN forces were achieving significant battlefield success while rallying from their setback and retaking South Korean territory. At the end of this

[3] Mueller's initial analyses did not account for the possibility of temporal dependence in these data. The analyses in table 2.1 rely on the Prais-Winsten method to account for first-order serial autocorrelation. This correction is not ideal in this instance, since the observations are unevenly spaced. However, the small number of observations makes more advanced methods for estimating temporal dependence in irregular time-series impractical. Although some of the models did indicate temporal dependence, accounting for this fact did not significantly alter the results.

TABLE 2.1.
Combat Casualties and Support for the Korean War

	Oct. 1950–Nov. 1952	*Jan. 1951–Nov. 1952*	*Contingent on success*
Ln of casualties	–14.006 (6.15)**	–6.781 (1.50)	–1.831 (0.40)
Casualties × success		14.197 (2.69)*	
U.S. successful in Korea		–134.405 (–2.56)	
Constant	180.673 (8.01)**	108.210 (2.40)*	56.156 (2.76)*
Observations	11	10	10
Rho	–0.07	0.07	–0.69
R-squared	0.77	0.21	0.99

Absolute value of *t* statistics in parentheses
* significant at 5% ** significant at 1%

period of success, a long stalemate in war began that lasted from mid-1951 through the end of the Truman presidency. Casualties have very different effects on war support during these two periods. We describe the difference in effect in the third column table 2.1. This regression illustrates this distinction by interacting casualties with the progress of combat on the ground. The coefficient for the log of casualties captures the impact of casualties on support during the stalemate period. The coefficient here remains negative ($b = -1.83$), but its size is drastically reduced from the initial analysis—so much so that the effect of casualties during the stalemate period is no longer distinguishable from zero. The interaction term tests whether there is a difference in the effect between the two periods. This coefficient is positive and strongly statistically significant. To calculate the impact of casualties during the rallying period, we add the coefficient for casualties with the coefficient for the interaction term. The net impact of casualties on support during this period is strongly *positive* ($b = 12.37$) and statistically significant ($p < .05$). We are not, of course, implying that the public increased its approval of the Korean War because of the number of soldiers being killed. Rather, we believe that these data suggest the public's willingness to rally to support the mission—despite the casualties—because of the demonstrable success on the ground. Of course, the result from any regression model with ten cases and five parameters must be taken with a grain of salt.[4] We present these analyses only as a preliminary corroboration of our more informal examination of the data in figure 2.1. Consistent with that interpretation, Mueller's data suggest that the public's response to casualties varies substantially depending upon the context in which they occur. Greater confidence in the robustness of this variation must await additional data.

Fortunately, our contention that public support depends on progress on the ground (or visible success) is further supported by several other poll results from this period. American forces enjoyed a striking success in September 1950 with MacArthur's landing at Inchon, and American forces began pressing into North Korea. U.S. advances prompted Chinese intervention into the war in late October, but the initial PRC engagements were limited and did not inflict significant defeats on U.S. forces. Thus in a Gallup poll taken during 12–15 November showed that only 25 percent of the public supported a withdrawal from Korea even if it meant "a world war."[5] In late November, however, Chinese forces intervened in earnest and swept U.S. forces back down the peninsula, leaving significant numbers of soldiers and Marines trapped behind enemy lines. Then in January 1951—as Chinese and North Korean forces were in the midst of retaking Seoul from U.S. forces—one poll found that 66 percent of the public supported withdrawal entirely from Korea "as quickly as possible."[6] By March of 1951 the United States had suffered more than 3,000 additional combat deaths, but had succeeded in recapturing the South Korean capital of Seoul. By that time only 18 percent of the public supported a withdrawal from Korea, while 54 percent stated that they thought the United States should continue fighting until the whole Korean peninsula was free of communist control.[7]

Mueller's "simple association" between casualties and support for the war fails to explain not just Korea, but Vietnam as well. Public support

[4] The fact that this model achieves an *r*-squared of 0.99, for example, raises concerns that it may be over-fitted. An ordinary least squares analysis of these data—which drops the rho parameter estimating temporal dependence—has a lower *r*-squared (0.84) but yields the same substantive results regarding the varying effect of casualties on war support. Nonetheless, an analysis of a single time-series with only ten observations can yield only preliminary results.

[5] Survey by Gallup Organization, November 1950. Retrieved 7 August 2006 from the iPoll Databank, The Roper Center for Public Opinion Research, University of Connecticut, at http://www.ropercenter.uconn.edu/ipoll.html.

[6] Survey by Gallup Organization, January 1951. Retrieved 7 August 2006 from the iPoll Databank, The Roper Center for Public Opinion Research, University of Connecticut, at http://www.ropercenter.uconn.edu/ipoll.html. The authors would like to thank Edwin Redman for bringing these poll results to our attention.

[7] Survey by National Opinion Research Center, March, 1951. Retrieved 12 April 2006 from the iPoll Databank, The Roper Center for Public Opinion Research, University of Connecticut, at http://www.ropercenter.uconn.edu/ipoll.html.

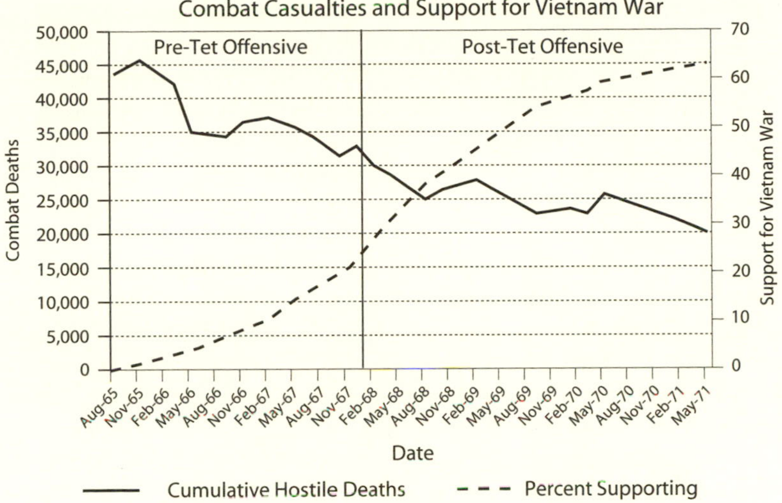

FIGURE 2.2. Combat Casualties and Support for the Vietnam War

for the war in Vietnam is displayed in figure 2.2 along with the cumulative number of U.S. battle deaths.[8] A cursory glance at the data supports Mueller's claim of a general decline in support for the war as casualties mounted. A more careful examination of the data, however, shows that the severity of this decline is not constant over time. Consistent with much of the literature on the Vietnam War, the Tet offensive of 1968 marked a turning point in the relationship between public opinion and casualties.[9] After Tet, casualties appear to have had a much greater corrosive effect on presidential approval.

The Tet offensive was a coordinated effort by North Vietnamese and Viet Cong forces to attack American and South Vietnamese strongholds across South Vietnam, which began on the night of 30–31 January1968. Tet represented one of the most intense periods of combat during the war and for a brief period of time the U.S. Embassy in Saigon was under siege by enemy forces. Eventually, however, U.S. and South Vietnamese forces repelled all of the attacks and inflicted substantial casualties on the North Vietnamese and Viet Cong forces. The implications of the Tet offensive became a topic of heated debate among American elites. U.S. military leaders claimed that Tet was a tactical success for American armed forces that severely weakened the enemy. Media elites such as Walter Cronkite, on the other hand, contended that Tet was a massive (and surprise) setback,

[8]These data are taken from Mueller (1971, 1973, 2005).

[9]See Arnold (1990), Gibert and Head (1996), and Oberdorfer (2001) on the military and political significance of the Tet Offensive.

all the more shocking because the U.S. military had been claiming that the South was largely pacified (Arnold 1990). Over the next several months, Cronkite's interpretation clearly came to dominate the public's interpretation of the event, leading to a growing perception that American pacification efforts were not likely to succeed. Consistent with the defeat-phobic hypothesis, the public was substantially more sensitive to casualties after the war effort was deemed a failure. For example, nearly 46 percent of the public still supported the war in Vietnam in December of 1967, despite the United States having suffered more than 15,000 hostile deaths. After Tet, however, as U.S. casualties mounted, public support declined until barely 30 percent of the public supported the war by September 1969.

Statistical analyses confirm that the relationship between casualties and support for the war varies substantially. We begin by regressing support for the Vietnam War on the log of the number of U.S. casualties. This analysis confirms Mueller's conclusion that overall support for the Vietnam War declined as a function of the log of cumulative casualties ($b = -3.67$, $p < .01$).[10] When we distinguish between the period before and after the Tet offensive, however, the results change markedly. The second analysis in table 2.2 includes a control dummy variable for the Tet offensive interacting with the log of casualties. In this model, the coefficient for the log of casualties captures the impact of casualties on support for the war in Vietnam *prior* to the Tet offensive. The coefficient for the interaction term represents the *change* in impact of casualties on support after Tet. The total impact of casualties after the Tet offensive, therefore, is the sum of the two coefficients. Viewed this way, it is evident that the public's aversion to casualties changed significantly over the course of the war. Prior to the Tet offensive, the log of cumulative casualties did have a significant impact on public support for the war ($b = -3.96, p < .01$). After Tet, the impact of casualties on support *tripled* in size. The coefficient for the interaction term is -8.27 ($p < .01$), indicating that the overall coefficient after the Tet offensive was -12.24 ($p < .01$). This change in magnitude of the effect is exactly opposite what Mueller's theory predicts—casualties should not become more corrosive after the public has already endured lots of deaths. It is, however, consistent with a view of war support that gives pride of place to assessments of success and failure.

Furthermore, if we look again at figure 2.2, we can see that most of the drop in public support prior to the Tet Offensive occurred during a very few months in 1966. During this period, however, the United States suf-

[10] As with the analyses in table 2.1, these results account for first-order temporal dependence with the Prais-Winsten Method. Once again, this method is not ideal because of the irregularly spaced observations., but the small number of observations make more sophisticated methods impractical.

TABLE 2.2.
Combat Casualties and Support for the Vietnam War

	Constant impact	*Pre & post Tet*	*Tet & Fulbright*
Ln combat casualties	−3.667 (−2.79)*	−3.956 (−5.74)**	−1.065 (−1.12)
Tet × ln casualties		−8.270 (2.85)**	−11.520 (−4.41)**
Post-Tet offensive		77.486 (2.59)*	108.130 (4.05)**
Fulbright hearings			−10.158 (3.36)**
Constant	77.541 (12.41)**	84.969 (15.00)**	68.217 (10.56)**
Observations	24	24	24
Rho	0.82	0.04	0.14
R-squared	0.78	0.92	0.95

Absolute value of *t* statistics in parentheses
* significant at 5%   ** significant at 1%

fered a relatively small number of casualties. The drop does coincide with Senator J. William Fulbright's hearings on the Vietnam War and his summer speaking tour against the war. If we add a dummy variable to control for those hearings, then the impact of casualties prior to the Tet offensive disappears entirely. As the third column of results in table 2.2 indicates, the impact of casualties prior to Tet, drops to −1.05 (n.s.), while the impact of casualties after Tet remains statistically significant and substantively large at −12.59 ($p < .01$).

One final piece of evidence suggesting that support for the Vietnam War was not simply a function of American casualties is that many opponents of the war objected to the constraints being placed on U.S. military strategy rather than to the human cost of the war. In the midst of the Tet Offensive, for example, Gallup fielded a public opinion poll. The survey—fielded between 2 and 6 February 1968—asked respondents whether they approved of Johnson's handling of the Vietnam War, and whether they would describe themselves as "hawks" who want to escalate our military effort in Vietnam or "doves" who want to decrease our military effort. Not surprisingly, only 35 percent of Americans approved of Johnson's handling of Vietnam, while 53 percent disapproved (12 percent had no

TABLE 2.3.
Approval of President Johnson's Handling of Vietnam and Attitudes toward Escalation, February 1968

Attitude toward escalation	Approval of Johnson's handling of Vietnam: Disapprove	Not sure	Approve	Total
Dovish	232 29%	33 19%	74 14%	339
Not sure	93 12%	80 45%	69 13%	242
Hawkish	476 59%	64 36%	379 73%	919
Total	801	177	522	1,500

Pearson $r = 0.66$ ($p < .01$) Pearson chi-squared (9 d.f.) = 631.88 ($p < .01$)

opinion). Moreover, we also find—consistent with Verba et al. (1967)—that Johnson opponents tend to be more dovish than Johnson supporters. Nonetheless, as table 2.3 indicates, 59 percent of those who disapproved of Johnson's handling of Vietnam (about 31 percent overall) supported escalating U.S. military efforts. That is, a majority of the respondents who stated that they disapproved of Johnson's handling of Vietnam believed that the solution to the problem was to escalate rather than withdraw military effort. Hawkish sentiment for escalation was even stronger among those who approved of Johnson's handling of the war, but these results still suggest that the public's frustration with Vietnam was not simply a function of the number of U.S. forces killed. Casualty aversion would lead us to expect that most of those who disapproved of Johnson's handling of Vietnam would have preferred military withdrawal. Instead, even as late as February 1968, there appeared to be greater pressure to escalate the war—perhaps in the hopes of achieving a more successful outcome.

Mueller observed that casualties mounted in Korea and Vietnam and that support for the war dwindled. At one level, this is a perfectly accurate depiction—in both Korea and Vietnam the wars concluded with substantially more casualties than they began with, and support for both wars was significantly less than at the outset. An inexorable, logarithmic causal relationship between casualties and support, however, is greatly overstated. The associations that Mueller uncovered were themselves a function of a deeper dynamic that he missed: whether the casualties were sustained in what appeared at the time to be a winning or a losing effort. Since both the wars in Korea and Vietnam culminated in stalemate and defeat respectively—at the very least, not victory—it is difficult to separate the decline in support due to casualties from decline in support that comes from an absence of victory. By breaking up the conflicts into different periods of success, failure, and stalemate, we were able to find that the relationship between casualties and war support is far more varied. When Mueller extrapolates from Korea and Vietnam to other wars like the current one in Iraq and argues that support will decline inexorably with mounting casualties (Mueller 2005), he is necessarily making an unstated auxiliary claim: that the Iraq war will end in failure (see Gelpi 2005).

Lebanon

The American intervention in Lebanon represented the first American experience with a significant number of military casualties after the end of the Vietnam War. As a result, the public's response to the deaths of the 241 soldiers, sailors, and Marines was important in shaping academic and popular perceptions of public attitudes toward the costs of combat. Mueller's "simple association" requires that public support for the placement of troops in Lebanon erode in the wake of the bombing attack.

Burk (1999:55), however, claims that "public support for military deployments [in Lebanon and Somalia] was neither as unsteady nor as uncritically contingent on the absence of casualties as many have claimed." More specifically, Burk finds that the support of the American public appears to have been quite divided about this mission before any casualties were incurred. Specifically, support for the mission ranges between 40 and 50 percent depending on the phrasing of the question. More importantly, however, Burk shows that—contrary to Mueller's expectations—support for the Lebanon mission jumps sharply in the wake of the 23 October bombing attack. Specific comparisons are somewhat difficult because of the differences in question wording. Burk's data show, however, that the same question regarding approval of using U.S. troops for a peacekeeping mission in Lebanon on 24–28 September and 26–27 October generated more than a ten-percentage point increase in support for the mission. Levels of approval move even higher for this question when it is asked again in November. While this same question was not asked in December 1983 or the early months of 1984, public perceptions that the deployment of troops was not a "mistake" appears to have fallen off over this period. Benjamin Schwarz (1994) likewise noted the contrary movement and described it as an escalation dynamic, where casualties lead to an increase in support.

What can explain this rise and fall in approval for the Lebanon mission? Casualties alone cannot be the answer. Burk speculates that the

TABLE 2.4.
Support for Mission in Lebanon, November 1983

Approve of decision to deploy troops		*Preferred response to bombing attack*		*Reagan timetable for withdrawal*	
Strongly approve	668 33%	Take the offensive	292 15%	Stay longer	155 8%
Somewhat approve	621 31%	Better defend themselves	799 42%	Timetable about right	894 46%
Not sure	104 5%	Keep things the same	189 10%	Not sure	272 14%
Somewhat disapprove	247 12%	Bring troops home	636 33%	Shorter timetable	633 32%
Strongly disapprove	360 18%				

public may have "rallied 'round the flag" in the wake of the bombing attack, but that support eroded as hopes for a resolution evaporated. We find this interpretation plausible, but one must consider the impact that elite rhetoric was having on public opinion as well (Zaller 1992; Larson 1996). While the pattern of aggregate public responses to the 23 October bombings clearly contradict the claim that public support always erodes with casualties, the data cannot adjudicate among the various competing explanations for the rise-and-fall pattern.

We address this question by looking more closely at some of the polling data on Lebanon to determine what factors correlate with individual-level support for the mission. While many commercial polls asked a few questions about support for U.S. operations in Lebanon, few surveys asked a wide enough range of questions to allow for a comparison of differing explanations of public support. On 12–17 November 1983, however, the *Los Angeles Times* conducted a more extended survey that asked a variety of questions about Lebanon and the U.S. mission there. Table 2.4 summarizes two measures of support from that survey and shows that the results—as was true with polling about Vietnam—are very sensitive to whether the question asks about approval of U.S. policy or if the question asks about U.S. response to an attack. Reagan's approval ratings on Lebanon were quite low at about 30 percent, but there was little support for an abrupt withdrawal. About two-thirds of the public (67 percent) stated that the United States ought to "take the offensive," "defend ourselves better," or "keep things the way they are." Only about one in three respondents (33 percent) thought that we should "bring the troops home," even though Reagan had just announced that U.S. troops would leave Lebanon within the next 18 months.

The mission in Lebanon gives us an opportunity to adjudicate further between different causal claims about the sources of casualty tolerance. In this analysis, we use the question about potential withdrawal as a dependent variable. We have three independent variables of interest that allow us to compare prominent arguments about casualty tolerance. First, the survey asked respondents whether the United States had "vital national interests" at stake in Lebanon. This question resembles Jentleson's (1992) arguments about the importance of the primary policy objective (PPO) and the tendency for the public to tolerate casualties in missions which national interests are engaged. Second, the survey asked respondents whether they believed that the U.S. mission would succeed. This measure clearly taps the attitudes highlighted by Feaver and Gelpi (2004). Finally, the survey also asked whether the U.S. intervention in Lebanon was "morally justified." This question does not directly capture Jentleson's PPO argument, but it does reflect the extent to which respondents think that the mission was the right thing to do—an attitude to which we will return in subsequent chapters. In addition, we included a number of demographic control variables, including partisan identification.

The results of this analysis are displayed in table 2.5. The results support the claim that public backing for continuing a military mission in the face of mounting human costs is a function both of the importance of the policy objective and the likelihood that the mission will succeed. Specifically, those who believed that U.S. "vital interests" are at stake were significantly more "hawkish" in their determination to keep troops in Lebanon ($b = 0.29$, $p < .01$). Those who believed that the United States was likely to prevail were also more hawkish ($b = 0.17$, $p < .01$). Finally, those who believed that the mission was "morally justified" were significantly more willing to escalate or maintain the U.S. military presence in Lebanon ($b = 0.75$, $p < .01$).

A number of the control variables are significant as well. For example, women are less supportive of military escalation, as are older respondents and minorities. Interestingly, partisan identification is neither statistically nor substantively significant. Not surprisingly, party identification does correlate with questions about approval of Reagan's handling of Lebanon. When it comes to expressing preferences about future policy options, however, party does not seem to have a significant impact—despite Reagan having spoken to the nation just prior to this polling about a strategy for gradual withdrawal.

The American experience in Lebanon is often viewed as evidence in support of the claim that the public will not tolerate casualties, because the United States withdrew from the mission in the wake of the barracks

TABLE 2.5.
Public Support for Escalation or Withdrawal from Lebanon, November 1983

Independent variables	*Coefficients and standard errors*
Lebanon mission a just cause	0.747 (11.61)**
U.S. has vital interest in Lebanon	0.288 (5.44)**
Lebanon mission will succeed	0.157 (3.10)**
Respondent's age	–0.104 (3.21)**
Gender	–0.438 (4.90)**
Level of education	–0.001 (0.02)
Minority	–0.326 (2.43)*
Republican	0.039 (0.36)
Democrat	–0.034 (0.32)
Observations	1860

Absolute value of z statistics in parentheses
* significant at 5% ** significant at 1%

bombing of 23 October. The polling done at the time, however, indicates that public support for military operations does not inexorably decline with casualties. Indeed, in both Vietnam and Lebanon, suffering casualties spurs a portion of the public to press for an escalation of military operations. Respondents' willingness to support escalation appears to be a function both of their support for the goal of the mission and its likelihood of success, but what might have caused support to wane once again during January and February 1984? The answer here is less clear. Attitudes toward the importance of the mission seem unlikely to have changed much during this period, indicating that perceptions of the (lack of) success may be the more important factor in this case. One must also account, however, for the fact that withdrawal became the clear policy of the Reagan administration. Thus elite rhetoric may also have contributed to the perception that the mission would not succeed.[11]

Somalia

The precipitous American withdrawal from Somalia in the wake of the "Black Hawk Down" incident in October of 1993 is considered the iconic example of "casualty phobia." The accepted understanding of this conflict is that the American public eagerly supported the use of U.S. military forces to alleviate critical starvation problems that were garnering substantial media attention in Somalia. But, the conventional wisdom continues, while the public was eager to support a cost-free act of military good will, the public immediately turned its back on the mission and demanded a withdrawal the instant it learned that eighteen U.S. Army Rangers were killed and CNN showed their desecrated bodies being dragged through the streets of Mogadishu.

It is a bit odd that Somalia looms so large in the conventional wisdom. Consider that other public opinion data from recent U.S. military operations contradict the view that the American public will immediately abandon military interventions in the face of casualties. For example, public support for the U.S. intervention in Panama remained almost unwavering at 80 percent or higher despite the twenty-three casualties suffered (Larson, 1996:113). Of course, this is a small number of casualties, but it is nearly identical to the number of casualties that allegedly caused the public to call for a U.S. withdrawal from Somalia.

Nonetheless, Somalia weighs heavily on popular understandings of how the American public responds to casualties. In their interviews with political and media elites, Kull and Destler (1999:91) found that all media respondents and nearly 75 percent of elites overall believed unequivocally that the Somalia case illustrated the public's reflexive opposition to taking any casualties. Louis Klarevas's (2000) analysis of polls on Somalia offers a ringing endorsement of this conventional view, concluding that there is now a "Somalia syndrome," in which "the American public will be supportive (or at least tolerant) of a post–Cold War peace operation—even when the overall policy objective involves more expansive peace-enforcement goals—so long as American soldiers are not losing their lives in the pursuit of interests not considered vital."

[11] Another possible explanation is the collapse of a "rally 'round the flag" effect after the attack on the U.S. soldiers and the invasion of Grenada. As is often the case, aggregate data have difficulty in distinguishing among competing explanations on this point.

But the Somalia case does not conform to the casualty-phobia hypothesis. Data analyzed by both Klarevas (2000) and Burk (1999) show that public support for the presence of U.S. troops in Somalia dropped from 74 percent in December 1992, at the start of the humanitarian relief operation, to 43 percent in mid-September, *before* the Black Hawk was downed in October. Support dropped to 36 percent *after* the October fatalities, but even Klarevas, who otherwise buys into the casualty-phobia conventional wisdom, is obliged to recognize this as modest: "Because support had diminished by September, support did not drastically drop following the October 3 battle in Mogadishu." (Klarevas 2000:526). On the contrary, in the immediate aftermath of the raid, majorities wanted to capture or punish Aideed—the very mission that the public did *not* support prior to the raid (Kull and Destler 1999:106; Burk 1999). Specifically, when asked whether the United States should continue trying to hunt Aideed, 51 percent of the respondents to a 5 October 5 ABC poll stated that the United States should continue this mission. Despite this evidence, some analysts question the public's commitment to escalation. Larson (1996:67), for instance, claims that this support "evaporated" if the survey questions linked such a mission to a delay in the withdrawal from Somalia. It is striking, however, that the public held these views even though virtually no major opinion leaders were talking about capturing and punishing Aideed in the aftermath of the raid. Republicans in Congress called for abandonment of the Aideed hunt and immediate withdrawal. Democrats and the White House called for abandonment of the Aideed hunt and slow withdrawal. Both sets of political elites, in other words, were offering the cut-and-run strategy whereas a sizable portion of the public was supporting the win-and-leave strategy. Since Larson elsewhere argues that a lack of consensus at the leadership level should erode support for military operations at the mass level, the potential public support of military escalation to punish Aideed in the absence of any political leadership in that direction is all the more striking. Had the White House sought to mobilize support for the punishment option, Larson's own data suggest that this effort would have likely succeeded (Larson 1996:67–71, 94–95). Contrary to Larson's interpretation of Somalia but consistent with his overall model, the data show that public support for the mission was available, despite casualties, but merely never mobilized by the Clinton administration.

If anything, the Somalia case illustrates the importance of elite rhetoric, mission success, and policy objective as more important than the number of dead troops in shaping the public's opinion about military operations. First, Somalia confirms that if the president (and by extension the rest of the political elite) does not attempt to mobilize public support in the midst of a costly military operation, then the public support will not be sustained for very long. There was one important audience that was deeply casualty phobic, reacting immediately and reflexively to the sight of bodies being dragged through the streets of Mogadishu: the president, his closest advisors, and members of Congress. They all lost whatever political will they had remaining for the Somalia mission after the Ranger raid and they made no attempt to frame the casualties as the necessary price for victory and thereby tap into the reservoir of public support that might otherwise have been available (Dauber 2001).

Second, the public supports missions that are successful, not necessarily those that are cost-free. Klarevas (2000) claims that public support for Somalia eroded over the summer of 1993 "in large part" because of the gradual mounting fatalities: twenty-four Pakistani peacekeepers killed in June; four Italian soldiers and four journalists killed in July; four American soldiers killed in August, followed by six more wounded in August; and three American soldiers killed in September. It is more likely, however, that these deaths eroded support *indirectly*, by signaling that the operation was a mess. As headlines from that period attest, the hunt for Aideed looked like a failure, not really because soldiers were dying, but because Aideed kept slipping away—because the missions *repeatedly failed to capture him*. Throughout September 1993, the public was reading such stories as, "Rangers Net 17 but Miss Aideed Again; Mogadishu Warlord Frustrates Elite GIs," "Aideed Hunt's Still On, Peacekeepers Insist" (Richburg 1993; Watson 1993) and the obvious implications were that American forces were engaged in an exercise in futility. Somalia affirms the argument that the public is defeat phobic rather than casualty phobic (Feaver and Gelpi 2004)

Finally, the available data from Somalia support Jentleson's (1992) contention that the public distinguishes strongly among differing types of military interventions and is more willing to support some kinds of missions than others. Figure 2.3 summarizes data from Klarevas (2000) on aggregate public responses to questions emphasizing three aspects of the Somalia mission from December 1992 through December 1993: questions involving approval of the president's handling of the issue, approval of the deployment of U.S. troops, and approval for the mission of delivering food to hungry Somalis. These data cover three distinct periods in the Somalia conflict. December 1992 through May 1993 reflect the "Operation Restore Hope" period of the intervention. This mission was an American-led operation focused specifically on delivering food to starving Somalis. In May of 1993, control of the operation was handed over to the United Nations under the name of UNOSOM II, and 1,800 U.S. forces remained as part of the U.N. mission as part of "Operation Continue Hope." Unlike the earlier mission, UNOSOM II was explicitly a "nation-building" mission that sought to disarm the factions in Somalia's

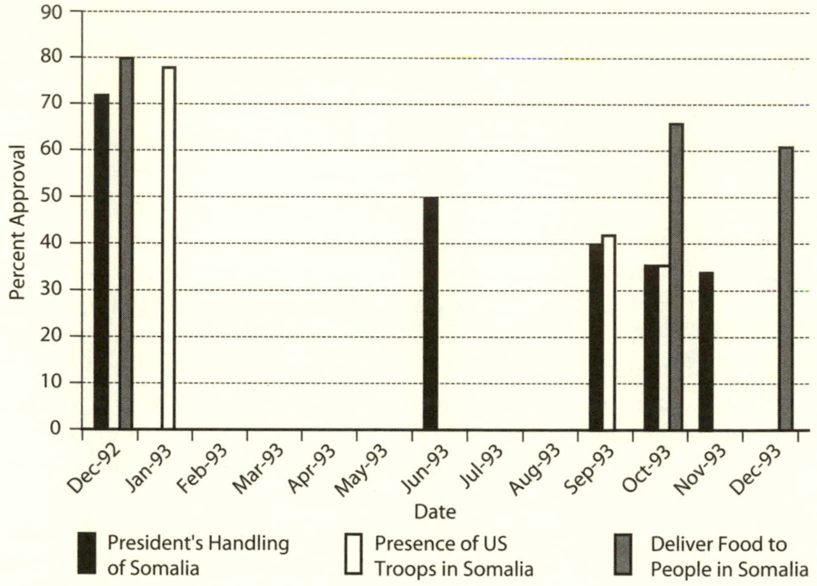

FIGURE 2.3. Approval of Somalia Mission

civil war and restore civil order. Finally, the data cover the post–Battle of Mogadishu period. On 3-4 October1993, U.S. forces engaged in a pitched battle with militia forces loyal to Mohammed Farrah Aideed, and eighteen U.S. Rangers were killed and some of their bodies were mutilated and dragged through the streets of Mogadishu. This battle sparked a quick promise of withdrawal by the Clinton administration.

In December 1992 support for all three aspects of the mission was over 70 percent, indicating that the public was initially quite broadly supportive. By June 1993, however, in the midst of a domestic debate over U.S. participation in the UNOSOM II peacekeeping force and its nation-building mission, approval for Clinton's handling dropped to about 50 percent. By September 1993 support for Clinton's handling of Somalia and for the deployment of U.S. troops there had dropped to about 40 percent. Casualty sensitivity and the "CNN effect" cannot explain this decline, since it occurs prior to the Black Hawk Down incident. The deaths of the eighteen Rangers in October 1993 does depress support for Clinton's handling of Somalia and for the deployment of U.S. forces by about another eight percentage points, but this rather modest decrease pales in comparison to the thirty-point drop in support that occurred prior to the attack. Even more interestingly, while the 7 October poll shows that the public clearly disapproved of Clinton's handling of the issue and of the use of U.S. forces in their current mission, more than 60 percent of Americans still supported using U.S. troops to deliver food to hungry Somalis. This sentiment remained strong through December of 1993 and beyond.

The key distinction here is between the popular "Operation Restore Hope" during the winter of 1992–93 and U.S. participation in UNOSOM II in the summer and fall of 1993, which was never very popular with the American public. When asked in January 1993 whether the United States should limit its involvement to delivering food or should engage in hunting warlords, 52 percent responded that the United States should limit its involvement to food delivery. By September 1993 (prior to the killing of the U.S. Rangers), that number had risen to 69 percent (Klarevas 2000:536).

The measures that we have of aggregate public opinion in response to casualties in Somalia are consistent with a variety of interpretations. One interpretation that does *not* fit the available data from Somalia, however, is that the public abandoned the mission because of U.S. casualties. To investigate the mixed pattern of public responses to Somalia, we turn now to a closer examination of one public opinion survey taken in the immediate aftermath of the Black Hawk Down incident. As noted earlier, commercial polls vary significantly in their question wording, and polls often don't ask the range of questions necessary to compare differing explanations of public support at the individual level. However, one particular poll—taken by CNN, Gallup, and *USA Today* on 5 October 1993—included a number of questions that allow us to evaluate various explanations of public willingness to stay in Somalia in the wake of U.S. casualties. Table 2.6 includes two measures of the public's willingness to support using military force. First, the survey asked respondents what they believed the United States "should do now" in Somalia. Consistent with the data from Vietnam and Lebanon, nearly one in five (19 percent) actually thought that the United States should increase its military commitment. Another one in ten (9 percent) thought that we should keep our involvement the same. In total, just about a quarter of respondents supported a policy more aggressive than the one enacted by Clinton. Another quarter of the public (27 percent) supported Clinton's announced strategy of gradual withdrawal. So, about one half of the population supported plans at least as aggressive as Clinton's (55 percent). However, the other half of the population (45 percent) supported an immediate withdrawal from Somalia. When asked about using the military for humanitarian missions, nearly half (48 percent) of the respondents stated that they had become less willing to support humanitarian missions, while nearly 40 percent stated that America's experience in Somalia had no effect. Less than 13 percent of respondents stated that the Somalia experience had made them more willing to support humanitarian missions.

These data confirm the unpopularity of the Somali mission in the wake of the Ranger's vivid deaths. Did the casualties—and their broadcast on

TABLE 2.6.
Support for Mission in Somalia, October 1993

What should the U.S. do now?		*Somalia & future humanitarian missions*	
Increase commitment	94 19%	More likely to support	63 13%
Keep involvement the same	46 9%	No change in likely support	198 40%
Gradually withdraw	133 27%	Less likely to support	236 47%
Withdraw right away	223 45%		

CNN—cause support to drop? The Gallup/CNN/*USA Today* survey also asked respondents whether they believed that the U.S. should or should not use American troops in order to (1) provide humanitarian relief, (2) stabilize the political situation, and (3) capture and punish Aideed—the Somali warlord fighting U.S. troops. These questions match nicely with the various policy objectives of the changing Somalia mission throughout 1992 and 1993 that Jentleson (1992) would say should influence tolerance for casualties. Moreover, the survey asked respondents whether they regarded the U.S. mission to provide humanitarian relief as successful or unsuccessful. This variable does not correspond perfectly to Feaver and Gelpi's (2004) focus on expected success of the mission, since the question directs respondents to think back to Operation Restore Hope rather than look forward to the success of UNOSOM II, but given the available data, this question will serve as a first cut in testing the "success" argument in Somalia. Finally the survey also asked respondents, "Have you, yourself, happened to see the actual new photos of either a U.S. soldier's corpse being dragged through the streets of Somalia, or the television footage of a captured U.S. pilot being interviewed?" This variable cannot, of course, measure the impact of casualties per se, since respondents may have been aware of the casualties even if they did not see the pictures or video. This variable does, however, serve as a plausible measure of the "CNN effect" on public opinion.[12] That is, a number of scholars and pundits speculated that the vivid portrayal of U.S. casualties on television would have a substantial impact on how the public would respond to these costs.

[12] Approximately 80 percent of respondents said that they had seen the CNN footage. Self-reports of specific media usage can be quite inaccurate, of course, but this question is the best opportunity we have to examine the CNN effect on public opinion with the available polling data. Still, our results should be regarded as preliminary rather than conclusive.

TABLE 2.7.
Support for Troop Deployment in Somalia and Future Humanitarian Missions, October 1993

	What should U.S. do in Somalia?	*Support for future missions*
"Restore Hope" success	–0.419	–1.243
	(2.09)*	(5.77)**
Support mission goals	–0.734	–0.436
	(7.50)**	(4.56)**
Seen body on CNN	0.155	0.271
	(0.85)	(1.42)
Gender	–0.537	–0.215
	(2.83)**	(1.09)
Age	–0.117	–0.204
	(1.74)	(2.89)**
Level of education	0.133	–0.011
	(2.15)*	(0.17)
Minority	0.691	1.072
	(2.12)*	(3.23)**
Democrat	0.035	–0.102
	(0.15)	(0.42)
Republican	–0.129	0.064
	(0.55)	(0.27)
Observations	447	446

Absolute value of *z* statistics in parentheses
* significant at 5% ** significant at 1%

We combine the three main survey questions measuring support for the various policy objectives in Somalia into a single index of support for the goals of the Somalia mission. We then used this index—along with the question about success, the viewing of the gruesome images, and various demographic controls—to predict the public's willingness to remain in Somalia and to engage in future humanitarian missions. The results of these analyses are displayed in table 2.7.

These results suggest that both perceptions of the legitimacy of the Somalia mission and the perceived success of Operation Restore Hope had a substantial impact on the public's willingness to stay in Iraq and its willingness to engage in future humanitarian missions. Respondents who stated that they had viewed the gruesome images of U.S. soldiers, on the other hand, were not significantly different with regard to these attitudes. Specifically, the analysis indicates that those who viewed Operation Restore Hope as successful were 10 percent less likely to support an immediate withdrawal of U.S. troops from Somalia, while those who supported at least one of the Somalia policy objectives were 26 percent less likely to support withdrawal. Similarly, those who believed that Restore Hope succeeded were 30 percent less likely to state that the Somalia experience had made them less likely to support future humanitarian missions, and those who supported at least one of the policy goals were 15 percent less likely to be wary of future missions.

The results regarding the CNN effect, on the other hand are more mixed. As the results in table 2.7 indicate, whether or not respondents had seen the pictures of U.S. soldiers or watched the video of captured soldiers had no significant impact on whether they supported an immediate withdrawal of U.S. troop or whether they were more reticent to deploy troops for humanitarian missions in the future—once we control for respondents' attitudes toward the legitimacy of the mission and the perceived success of Operation Restore Hope. It seems plausible, however, that viewing images from Mogadishu affected support for withdrawal and future humanitarian missions indirectly by altering respondents' views about the legitimacy and success of such missions. To test for this possibility, we regressed the viewing of the CNN images on our measure of support for the Somalia mission goals and on perceptions of the success of Restore Hope. The viewing of the images was not related to perceptions of success, but it was modestly related to support for the goals of the Somalia mission. That is, respondents who had seen the images on CNN were slightly less likely to state that U.S. troops should be used to deliver food and restore civil order. We cannot say with certainty, of course, that this effect is due to the viewing of the images per se as opposed to some broader variable such as media consumption.

To check whether perceptions of the legitimacy of the mission were intervening in between the CNN images and pressure for withdrawal, we reanalyzed the model in table 2.7, but we dropped the perceptions of the mission goals. In this case, the viewing of the CNN images did become statistically significant at the .10 level for attitudes toward withdrawal and at the .05 level for attitudes toward future missions. The substantive size of the effect remained modest in comparison to the influence of success. Those who had seen the images, for example, were 7 percent more likely to support immediate withdrawal and 9 percent more likely to oppose future humanitarian missions. Nonetheless, a Barron and Kenney (1986) test for mediation indicates that support for the Somalia mission goals does mediate the CNN effect on support for withdrawal. That is, the viewing of the CNN images is a significant predictor of support for withdrawal in a bivariate model ($b = 0.35, p < .05$), and it is a significant predictor of support for the Somalia mission goals ($b = -0.53, p < .01$). When the two variables are included together as predictors of withdrawal, however, support for mission goals remains significant, but the impact of the CNN images is reduced in size and is no longer statistically significant ($b = 0.16, p < .31$). These results suggest that the viewing of the gruesome images on CNN may have had some indirect impact on the public pressure for withdrawal through its impact on perceptions of the legitimacy of the Somalia mission.[13]

In sum, the available evidence does not support the claim that U.S. casualties in the Black Hawk Down incident led to strong and precipitous public pressure to withdraw from Somalia. The Somalia mission had already become unpopular before the U.S. Rangers were killed. The erosion of support is better explained by the shift in mission from Operation Restore Hope to American participation in UNOSOM II. The lack of support for that mission, in turn, appears linked to a lack of support for its primary objective (restoring political order and hunting warlords), and mounting frustration with its perceived lack of success.

Kosovo

In one sense, Kosovo is an unusual conflict for studying the American public's response to casualties in warfare. After all, the U.S. military did not suffer any deaths due to hostile fire during this conflict. Kosovo is, however, an essential case in understanding how domestic politics (or at least perceptions of domestic politics) can severely affect military missions. The Kosovo conflict was profoundly shaped by the belief that the public would not tolerate casualties. In the wake of the failed Somalia operation, both pundits and policymakers in the Clinton administration became thoroughly convinced that the public would not tolerate combat deaths (Kull and Destler 1999). As a result, the Clinton administration became so focused on conducting military operations without casualties that it actually forced military planners at the Pentagon to keep reshaping the military strategy and tactics until their war-gaming scenarios predicted no U.S. military deaths (Kitfield 1999).

Public attitudes toward Kosovo provide something of a critical case for the casualty-phobia hypothesis. If ever the public was focused on the avoidance of any casualties as a condition for supporting military action,

[13] Baron and Kenney (1986) tests for mediation were not as strong regarding support for future missions, but they did indicate that the impact of viewing the CNN images may have been partially mediated by support for the mission goals.

then we would expect Kosovo to be that conflict. Policymakers at the time certainly thought so. Indeed, the Clinton administration succeeded in providing the public with a nearly casualty-free use of military force (at least insofar as U.S. deaths go), and the public responded by supporting Clinton's policies throughout the war. In a series of polls from April through June of 1999, ABC News, for example, found that a majority of the public believed that the Clinton administration did the right thing by using force against Serbia.

Planning a mission to avoid U.S. casualties is not without consequences—principally an increase in noncombatant deaths (Kitfield 1999; Record 2000; Boyer 2002). Restrictions on the American military rules of engagement forced U.S. aircraft to bomb from high altitudes to avoid any exposure to Serbian air defenses. Such high-altitude bombing shifted the United States' focus on to fixed military targets and allowed Serbian forces on the ground to operate with relative impunity as they escalated their campaign of ethnic cleansing in the wake of NATO's intervention in the conflict. The Clinton administration's explicit statement that it would not place U.S. ground forces into combat in Kosovo also emboldened the Serb government to believe that it could resist NATO's pressure, extending the conflict until it became clear that the Kosovo Liberation Army (KLA) was capable of providing the ground presence to complement NATO's air assault. Finally, the lack of any presence on the ground left NATO no alternative but to coerce the Serbian government by inflicting suffering on the Serbian civilian population (Downes 2006). The U.S. military certainly sought to strike targets that met the standards of the laws of war and made significant efforts to avoid killing noncombatants. The inevitable consequence, however, of any strategic bombing campaign that focuses on urban targets will be noncombatant deaths.

Thus while the Kosovo campaign was ultimately a success, we would like to know whether the lack of U.S. military casualties was really the linchpin of public support. In some sense, of course, we cannot know, since the United States did not suffer any battle deaths. Nonetheless, we can examine what the public said about its expectations of casualties in Kosovo and whether or not they supported military action. From 19–21 February, Gallup fielded a survey that asked respondents a variety of questions about the Kosovo conflict that can allow us to make some preliminary judgments about the factors that led the public to support the deployment of U.S. troops in this case. Table 2.8 summarizes the responses to three questions that measure the extent of public support for deploying troops to Kosovo and the willingness to stay there in the wake of the conflict. Interestingly, the public was divided almost exactly 50-50 over whether to support air attacks if peace negotiations failed between Serbia and ethnic Albanians in Kosovo. While this result may be some-

TABLE 2.8.
Support for Using Force in Kosovo, February 1999

Approve of U.S. participation in NATO air attack		*Approve of U.S. participation in NATO peacekeeping*		*Approve of fixed timetable for withdrawal*	
Favor	459 50%	Favor	564 59%	Favor	446 47%
Oppose	456 50%	Oppose	396 41%	Oppose	501 53%

what surprising in light of the subsequent support that Clinton's policy received, the public's reticence in February may reflect some concern that all other avenues be explored before resorting to force. Also somewhat surprising is the relatively stronger support that the public expressed for deploying U.S. troops as part of a NATO peacekeeping force in the event that an agreement was reached in Kosovo. Here we see that nearly 60 percent of the public supported such a peacekeeping deployment despite the prominent failure of the UNOSOM II operation. Finally, a more modest majority of the public was willing to make U.S. peacekeeping efforts in Kosovo an open-ended commitment, with 53 percent stating that U.S. withdrawal should be timed "as events warrant" rather than as part of a preset timetable.

But what determined the public's willingness to support air strikes and longer-term participation in peacekeeping operations? Was the public focused on U.S. casualties, the objectives of the Kosovo mission, or its likely success? Unfortunately, the question wordings used in the Gallup poll do not allow us to disentangle these concepts entirely. The available evidence suggests, however, that all three of these factors weighed on the public's calculations. Moreover, the evidence suggests that expectations regarding casualties—while important—were not the central factor in shaping public consideration of the Kosovo mission.

Gallup asked the respondents two questions about their evaluations of what might be viewed as two key policy objectives for the Kosovo mission. First, the survey asked respondents if they believed that the United States needed to be involved in Kosovo "to protect its own interests." This question would roughly correspond to asking whether the United States had national security interests at stake, which Jentleson would label as a foreign policy restraint (FPR) mission. Second, the survey asked respondents whether they believed that the United States had a moral obligation to keep the peace in Kosovo. This question would seem to correspond to support for Jentleson's humanitarian intervention (HI) mission.

TABLE 2.9.
Expectations of Casualties and Success in Kosovo Mission, February 1999

U.S. and NATO effort to establish peace will succeed		*U.S. will be able to accomplish its goals with very few or no American casualties*	
Very confident	112 12%	Very confident	174 18%
Somewhat confident	368 39%	Somewhat confident	358 38%
Not too confident	333 35%	Not too confident	273 29%
Not at all confident	133 14%	Not at all confident	145 15%

The available measures of expectations of success of the mission and the likelihood of casualties, unfortunately, are not as clear-cut. First, Gallup asked respondents how confident they were that "the U.S. will be able to accomplish its goals with very few or no American casualties." This is a classic double-barreled question. How should a respondent who is confident in victory but expects casualties reply? How about a respondent who expects no casualties but believes that the mission will fail? At best we can say that responses to this question reflect some combination of the respondent's expectations regarding success and casualties. Second, the survey also asked respondents how confident they were that "U.S. and NATO efforts to establish peace in Kosovo will succeed." This question does not tap respondents' expectation regarding casualties, and its phrasing is somewhat unclear about whether the interviewer is asking about NATO establishing peace without using military force to coerce a settlement, or whether the question simply asks whether NATO and the United States can establish peace by any means.

The responses to these two questions about success are displayed in table 2.9. Interestingly, the two questions generated relatively similar aggregate responses, but the public was slightly more circumspect about the possibility of the United States and NATO achieving peace than it was about the U.S. accomplishing its goals with few casualties. These responses suggest that the public was not highly concerned about casualties as it approached the Kosovo mission. However, it also seems quite possible that this relative lack of concern was due to public confidence that casualties would be low—either because the United States would succeed or because they knew that the president put a very high priority on limiting casualties.

At any rate, both of these responses would seem to measure public expectations of success to some extent. This suspicion is further substantiated by the fact that responses to the two questions correlate at 0.52 ($p < .01$). Thus we are loath to place both variables in an analysis together as if they were separate concepts. At the same time, one question wording taps public concerns about casualties, while the other does not. Thus we are similarly loath to combine the two variables in an index of success—since we would lose the information on public responses to the mention of casualties. As a result, we present separate analyses of support for intervention in Kosovo using "the U.S. will be able to accomplish its goals with very few or no American casualties" and "U.S. and NATO efforts to establish peace will succeed" as measures of success. By comparing the performance of these measures in the analyses, we hope to get a rough estimate of how much mentioning casualties mattered in the public's willingness to support intervention. The results of these analyses are displayed in table 2.10.

The first thing that stands out about support for the Kosovo conflict is that respondents' attitudes about the engagement of U.S. interests in the conflict and their beliefs about whether the United States had a moral obligation to intervene weighed heavily on their calculations about whether to support a military intervention. For example, respondents who believed that U.S. interests were at stake in Kosovo were 34 percent more likely to support air strikes, 20 percent more likely to support participation in peacekeeping, and 8 percent more likely to make that commitment open-ended. Similarly, those who believed that the United States had a moral obligation to intervene were, respectively, 31, 38, and 14 percent likely to support those missions.

Second, it is clear from these analyses that expectations of success are also an important factor in determining ex ante support for the operation. As noted earlier, we have two separate measures of success—one that also taps expectations of low casualties and another that does not. Both measures are significant predictors of all three measures of support for intervention. For example, respondents who expected the United States NATO to succeed in achieving peace in Kosovo were 21 percent more likely to support air strikes, 31 percent more likely to support U.S. peacekeepers, and 16 percent more likely to support making the mission open-ended.

Third, the analyses in Table 2.11 indicate that adding respondents' expectations of low casualties did little to increase the impact of our measure of success. Specifically, the coefficient for the "U.S. will achieve its goals with few or no casualties" variable is only slightly larger than the "success in achieving a peaceful solution" in the analyses of support for

TABLE 2.10.
Support for Kosovo and Success of U.S. & NATO, February 1999

	Air attack	*Peacekeeping*	*Timetable*
U.S. interests	1.591	1.344	–0.344
	(8.39)**	(6.93)**	(2.14)*
Moral obligation	1.536	1.638	–0.599
	(8.38)**	(9.23)**	(3.72)**
Mission succeed	0.297	0.458	–0.215
	(2.72)**	(4.27)**	(2.39)*
Follow Kosovo	0.331	0.094	–0.028
	(2.99)**	(0.85)	(0.30)
Locate Kosovo	–0.149	–0.125	–0.124
	(0.77)	(0.66)	(0.77)
Gender	0.535	0.131	–0.160
	(3.02)**	(0.76)	(1.09)
Age	0.004	–0.001	0.000
	(0.81)	(0.13)	(0.06)
Education level	–0.193	–0.266	0.054
	(2.47)*	(3.37)**	(0.83)
Minority	0.593	0.394	–0.330
	(2.40)*	(1.61)	(1.60)
Party ID	–0.063	–0.026	0.097
	(1.13)	(0.47)	(2.11)*
Observations	815	849	830

Absolute value of *z* statistics in parentheses
* significant at 5% ** significant at 1%

an air attack. Respondents who expect success and low casualties are 37 percent more likely to support an air attack—a marginal impact that is sixteen percentage points higher than our other measure of success. But the impact of the two measures of success is virtually identical in predicting support for peacekeeping and an open-ended time commitment.

Thus while we can never know with certainty how the public would have reacted to American casualties during the Kosovo operation, the available data suggest that the anticipation of casualties certainly was not the dominant factor in determining public attitudes toward military intervention in the winter of 1999. Instead, the public appeared to be weigh-

TABLE 2.11.
Support for Kosovo and U.S. Success with Few Casualties, February 1999

	Air attack	*Peacekeeping*	*Timetable*
U.S. interest	1.600	1.366	–0.423
	(8.38)**	(7.07)**	(2.67)**
Moral obligation	1.473	1.638	–0.559
	(8.06)**	(9.32)**	(3.52)**
Few casualties	0.548	0.551	–0.142
	(5.45)**	(5.64)**	(1.77)
Follow Kosovo	0.411	0.158	–0.048
	(3.65)**	(1.43)	(0.52)
Locate Kosovo	–0.145	–0.124	–0.168
	(0.74)	(0.65)	(1.05)
Gender	0.565	0.145	–0.190
	(3.15)**	(0.84)	(1.30)
Age	0.002	–0.002	–0.001
	(0.38)	(0.41)	(0.14)
Education level	–0.197	–0.252	0.052
	(2.48)*	(3.18)**	(0.80)
Minority	0.650	0.285	–0.312
	(2.60)**	(1.16)	(1.52)
Party ID	–0.058	0.001	0.100
	(1.04)	(0.01)	(2.20)*
Observations	825	858	838

Absolute value of z statistics in parentheses
* significant at 5% ** significant at 1%

ing concerns about the substantive importance of the mission and its likely success in their calculations.

IRAQ (1990–2006)

The conflict with Iraq has come to dominate American security policy in the wake of the Cold War. The United States has been involved in a military conflict in Iraq at some level since less than ten months after the Berlin Wall fell. Throughout most of this conflict, however, the cost to the

United States in terms of casualties was very low. Even during the Gulf War of 1990–91 America suffered only 383 casualties. Thus in terms of human costs, the Gulf War was roughly analogous to the Lebanon intervention. As war loomed, the public stated that it was willing to bear significantly more casualties in order to liberate Kuwait. For example, one poll taken by the *Los Angeles Times* in November 1990 indicated that 56 percent of respondents would be willing to accept 1,000 casualties or more in order to defeat Iraq. Feaver and Gelpi (2004) report a remarkably similar result in their analysis of public tolerance for casualties later in the 1990s. In the 1990 case, the hypothetical poll results were borne out by the war itself. Public support for the Gulf War remained high despite the 383 casualties. George H. W. Bush's approval ratings shot up to more than 80 percent and did not begin to fall for many weeks after the fighting was over and U.S. troops began to come home.

Thus the first Iraq war indicates once again that American public support for military operations does not uniformly drop with casualties. The public indicated prior to the conflict that it was willing to bear significant costs in order to expel Saddam Hussein from Kuwait, and public support for the operation did not waver in the face of the relatively modest number of casualties that the United States suffered in the conflict. What is less clear, however, is what factors were most important in creating the public's tolerance for casualties in this case. The first Gulf war represents the "perfect storm" of public approval for a military operation according to the literature discussed in chapter 1. The American expulsion of Iraq from Kuwait was a highly successful military operation undertaken in response to a clear military threat, and the president enjoyed comparatively high levels of bipartisan support from Congress and uniquely high levels of support from international institutions and countries around the world in meeting this threat.

The second Iraq war, on the other hand, provides a more substantial test of the public's tolerance for casualties. At the time of this writing in the spring of 2008, the United States had suffered more than 3,400 combat deaths in Iraq since the war began more than four years prior. A combination of circumstances made the public response to the ongoing war in Iraq an important opportunity to evaluate this hypothesis. First, it is the first military conflict since Vietnam to span a presidential election. Second, the war in Iraq is both the most controversial and most deadly U.S. military operation since the Vietnam War. By Election Day in November 2004, nearly 1,200 U.S. soldiers had been killed in action. At the same time, Americans seemed increasingly divided over President George W. Bush's reasons for going to war; the Kay Report, the Duelfer Report, and the 9/11 Commission Report all raised questions about the strength of the ties between Saddam Hussein, weapons of mass destruction (WMD), and the Al-Qaeda terrorist network.[14] Moreover, the public was deluged with information about the war and its cost in terms of American lives. Combat in Iraq was the most covered story on the major network television news broadcasts in 2004, with nearly twice as many minutes of airtime as the second most-covered story: postwar reconstruction of Iraq.[15] Coverage of Iraq has continued to dominate the news with substantial pluralities of the American public repeatedly naming Iraq as the "most important problem" facing the United States.

Our evaluation of responses to casualties during the Iraq War suggests that the public will tolerate significant numbers of U.S. combat casualties under certain circumstances, but will be much less willing to tolerate them in others. As in the examples of Korea, Vietnam, Somalia, and Kosovo, casualties have not by themselves driven public attitudes toward the Iraq War, and mounting casualties have not always produced a reduction in public support. Like the Korean and Vietnam wars, the Iraq case suggests that under the right conditions, the public will continue to support military operations even when they come with a relatively high human cost. But also like Korea and Vietnam, the data from Iraq suggest that the public's tolerance for casualties will drop when events on the ground do not suggest progress toward victory.

Like Korea and Vietnam, the Iraq War allows for an examination of public attitudes toward casualties over time—because of the length of the conflict and the extended period over which the United States is suffering casualties. Thus we began our analysis of the public response to Iraq by collecting weekly data on American combat deaths from 1 January 2003 through 7 August 2006.[16] For the same period, we collected opinion data

[14] See *The 9/11 Commission Report* (New York: W. W. Norton, 2004). The "Kay Report" is not officially published in any single document. David Kay submitted an interim report from the Iraq Survey Group (ISG) to the House Permanent Select Committee on Intelligence, the House Committee on Appropriations, Subcommittee on Defense, and the Senate Select Committee on Intelligence, on 2 October 2003, but Kay resigned prior to submitting a final report. Kay's most influential public statement on the ISG's findings was his testimony to the Senate Armed Services committee on 28 January 2004, following his decision to resign from the ISG. A transcript of Kay's 2 October 2003 testimony can be found on the Central Intelligence Agency website at http://cia.gov/cia/public_affairs/speeches/2003/david_kay_10022003.html. A transcript of Kay's 28 January 2004 testimony can be found on the Carnegie Foundation website at http://www.ceip.org/files/projects/npp/pdf/Iraq/kaytestimony.pdf. For a complete review of the controversy over Iraqi WMD programs leading up to the Iraq War, see The National Security Archive at George Washington University at http://www.gwu.edu/~nsarchiv/index.html.

[15] See The Tyndall Report summary of 2004 campaign coverage at http://www.tyndallreport.com.

[16] Data were drawn from the following official military news sources: the *Army Times*, *Navy Times*, *Air Force Times*, and *Marine Times*. The data are available at http://www.militarycity.com/valor/honormarch.html.

on three crucial issues: approval of the president in general, approval of the president's handling of the situation in Iraq, and whether the Iraq War has been "worth it."[17] Presidential approval is asked frequently with standardized language, giving us a consistent measure of this attitude. The Iraq approval and "worth it" questions are asked less frequently, and their wording varies. One of the significant weaknesses of Mueller's data on Korea and Vietnam is that the observations are not evenly spaced over time. This uneven spacing creates significant statistical problems that raise questions about the robustness of the inferences drawn from those data. Thus we base our analysis of aggregate public responses to casualties during the Iraq War on weekly presidential approval ratings. Presidential approval correlates very strongly with both the "worth it" and "handling of Iraq" questions, but approval is measured on a regular basis with identical question wording.[18]

Figure 2.4 displays average weekly approval ratings for President Bush from January 2003 through August 2006. The data clearly indicate the substantial increase in approval that President Bush received after launching the war in Iraq. This bounce is consistent with the extensive literature on the "rally 'round the flag" effect.[19] The president also appeared to receive at least two other significant "bounces" during this period. The first occurs in December 2003 and ends abruptly in late January 2004, and the second occurs in December 2005 and continues until late February 2006. The first rally would seem to coincide with the capture of Saddam Hussein and appears to end with the release of the Kay Report. The second rally coincides with the first parliamentary elections in Iraq. The president drew attention to these elections with a series of speeches that emphasized the progress he thought America was making in Iraq. This rally appears to have ended, however, around the time that the al-Askari Mosque was bombed. This attack dramatically escalated sectarian violence and strengthened the public's perception that Iraq had descended into civil war. In between these two relatively brief rallies, however, we see a more prolonged period—from May of 2004 through February of 2005—when presidential approval seemed to be drifting slightly upward rather than downward.

[17] Data are available at http://www.pollingreport.com. We included only polls with identical wording of the presidential approval question: "Do you approve or disapprove of the way George W. Bush is handling his job as president?" Thus polls like Zogby, which introduce the category of "mixed feelings" toward the president, were not included in our measure of presidential approval. For weeks in which there were multiple national polls we took the average of these presidential approval ratings. We interpolated the one missing data point to get a continuous 189-observation weekly time-series.

[18] The correlation between overall presidential approval and approval of the president's handling of Iraq was 0.95. The correlation of both of those variables with aggregate opinion of whether the war in Iraq has been "worth it" is 0.91.

[19] Bruce Russett, *Controlling the Sword: The Democratic Governance of National Security*, (Cambridge, Mass.: Harvard University Press, 1990).

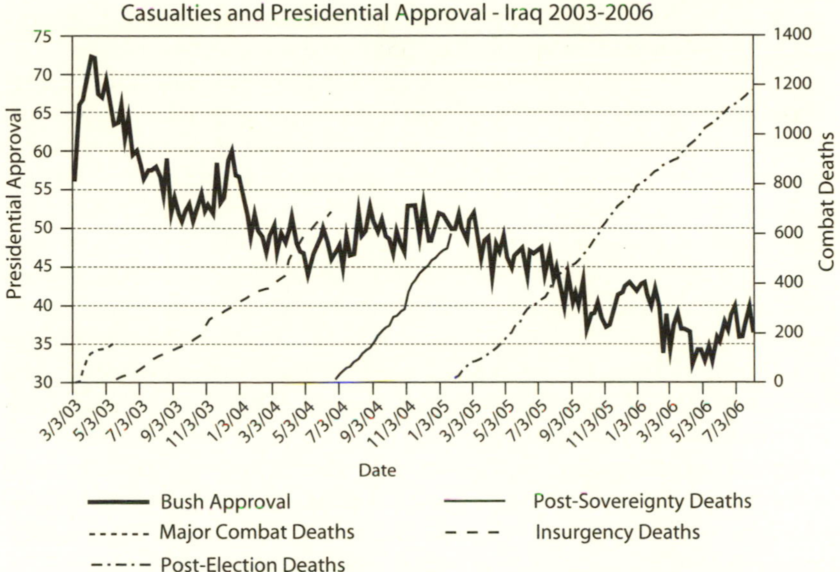

FIGURE 2.4. Casualties and Presidential Approval, Iraq 2003–2006

In terms of casualties, figure 2.4 divides the number of U.S. military deaths in Iraq into four distinct time periods. The dotted line shows fatalities during the "major combat" phase of the war, which covers the initial invasion of Iraq, the toppling of the Ba'ath regime, and the movement of coalition forces into a position of occupation in Iraq. The medium gray line represents military deaths that occurred after the media began to report a coordinated resistance against the U.S.-led occupation in May 2003, but before the coalition transferred sovereignty to an Iraqi authority in June of 2004. We refer to this as the "occupation" period.[20] Third, the dark grey line represents U.S. military deaths that occurred between the transfer of sovereignty to an Iraqi authority and the first elections to occur in Iraq. These constitutional elections at the end of January occurred with great fanfare and became famous for the depiction of Iraqis holding up ink-stained fingers indicating that they had voted. We refer to this as the "sovereign Iraq" period of the war. Finally, the light grey line depicts U.S. combat deaths that occurred in the wake of the Iraqi elections, which—much to the disappointment of the public—did little to quell the mounting violence in Iraq. Instead, Iraq descended into political stalemate and increasing levels of sectarian violence. While the monthly

[20]Media reports for this coding were drawn from The Tyndall Report, and we identified this "occupation" period as beginning in late May 2003. The data are available at http://www.tyndallreport.com.

casualty rate for American forces remained relatively constant, attacks against American forces began to mount in the wake of the elections. Perhaps even more ominously, attacks against Iraqi civilians and security forces began to increase.[21] These trends—which began with the political stalemate following the constitutional elections—were exacerbated in the wake of the bombing of the al-Askari Mosque, which set off a further escalation in bombings and killings among sectarian factions in Iraq. We refer to this as the "post-election" period of the conflict.

A quick review of figure 2.4 shows that U.S. military deaths did not appear to have the same impact on presidential approval in the "major combat," "occupation," "sovereign Iraq," and "post-election" phases of the war. During the major combat phase, approval was increasing despite the fact that the United States was suffering casualties. We are not arguing that the public was increasing its approval of the president because American soldiers were being killed. Rather, we infer that the public was rallying to support the president despite the casualties because of their confidence in American success. After the onset of the insurgency against U.S. occupation, however, presidential approval drops steadily as the death toll increases. After the United States transfers sovereignty to Iraq, on the other hand, the pattern seems to change once again. During this period U.S. casualties continue to mount at the same rate as during the occupation, but presidential approval oscillates at about 50 percent despite the mounting death toll. Then, in the wake of the failure of the constitutional elections to produce stability or security in Iraq, approval appears to decline in response to casualties once again, beginning in February or March 2005.

Thus at first glance the data in figure 2.4 call into question the notion that casualties have a consistent or inexorable effect on presidential approval. Even if one dismisses the shift from major combat to occupation as the fading of a "rally 'round the flag" effect, the second shift after the transfer of sovereignty remains a puzzle. Table 2.12 provides a more systematic analysis of the relationship between American military deaths in Iraq and presidential approval. In addition to the number of U.S. military deaths, we also accounted for the impact of growth in the Dow Jones Industrial Average (DJIA),[22] and we also included measures of the volume of

[21] See Michael O'Hanlon and Joseph Campbell, "The Iraq Index: Tracking Variables of Reconstructions and Security in the Post-Saddam Iraq." (Washington, D.C.: Brookings Institution, 2007). Also available at http://www.brookings.edu/iraqindex.

[22] Since our dependent variable is overall presidential approval, it is important that we control for the public perceptions of the overall performance of the U.S. economy. The Dow Jones Industrial Average (DJIA) represents an excellent summary measure of public perceptions of the economy for two central reasons. First, fluctuations in prices across a broad index such as the DJIA reflect changes across a number of economic indicators; traders incorporate a very wide range of information about economic performance into the trades

media coverage, as measured by the content of the weeknight news broadcasts of ABC, CBS, and NBC news.[23] We divided media coverage into five periods: prewar, major combat, occupation, sovereign Iraq, and post-election. The prewar media coverage variable counts the number of minutes that the crisis with Iraq was covered; during the remaining phases of the war we recorded the number of minutes per week that the network news broadcasts covered combat between the U.S. military and Iraqi or insurgent forces. Since the 2004 presidential campaign seems likely to have influenced presidential approval, we also collected data on the number of minutes that the Bush-Cheney campaign and all of Democratic challenger campaigns were covered on the weeknight network news broadcasts.[24] Finally, we included dummy variables to mark several important events in the flow of the war in Iraq. In addition to dummy variables for the onset of the occupation, sovereignty, and post-election periods, we included dummy variables to account for the brief rally periods noted earlier. Specifically these variables mark the period between the capture of Saddam Hussein and the release of the Kay Report and the period between President Bush's speech at the Naval Academy in anticipation of the Iraqi Parliamentary elections and the bombing of the al-Askari Mosque in Samarra. We include these variables to ensure that our estimate of the impact of casualties on presidential approval is not biased by these brief rally events. We also include a dummy variable for the onset of Hurricane

---

that generate shifts in the DJIA. The DJIA thus serves as something of a composite index of economic factors of political interest. Second, while the members of the public are probably not aware of much of the information that goes into these trades, many of them will be aware of changes in the DJIA because these are so widely published in newspapers and reported on daily radio and TV news broadcasts. Finally, our time-series of presidential approval is made up of weekly aggregation, while most aggregate economic indicators are available only on a monthly or quarterly basis. The DJIA, however, is easily aggregated on a weekly basis and is often reported to the public in terms of weekly changes. Growth was measured as a three-week moving average of the weekly percentage change in the value of the DJIA. As an additional indicator of public perceptions of the performance of the economy, we also collected data on the weekly average price for a gallon of regular gasoline. Data were obtained from the Environmental Protection Agency. Perhaps surprisingly, we found that gas prices had no impact on presidential approval once we accounted for events relating to the Iraq war and the performance of the DJIA.

[23] This measure records only the volume of coverage. It makes no attempt to capture any positive or negative content of the stories. By dividing the coverage into different periods, however, we hope to separate the impact of the largely positive coverage of the major combat phase from the mixed coverage prior to the outbreak of war and the largely negative coverage as the insurgency began to develop. Minutes were aggregated on a weekly basis and data were drawn from The Tyndall Report.

[24] Coverage of Democratic challengers did have an impact on approval and is discussed in our results. Coverage of the Bush-Cheney campaign had no significant impact on approval ratings and was dropped from the model.

TABLE 2.12.
Casualties and Presidential Approval, January 2003–August 2006

	1: *Constant impact*	2: *Contingent impact*
Log of total casualties	–0.823 (1.21)	2.090 (4.23)**
Ln of casualties × U.S. occupation		–10.784 (10.44)**
Ln of casualties × Iraq sovereign		0.459 (0.13)
Ln of total casualties × post–Iraq election		–18.047 (4.70)**
U.S. occupation	–1.344 (0.53)	50.975 (8.80)**
Iraq is sovereign again	–3.332 (0.95)	–21.071 (0.84)
Post–Iraq constitutional elections	–5.666 (1.61)	110.897 (3.92)**
Saddam capture to Kay Report	–0.536 (0.29)	3.059 (2.40)*
Post–Hurricane Katrina	–6.989 (3.52)**	–3.814 (2.59)*
"Victory" speech to mosque attack	1.984 (1.13)	2.214 (2.40)*
Weekly media coverage of Iraq before war	0.026 (0.87)	0.057 (2.19)*
Weekly media coverage of major combat	0.028 (2.19)*	0.030 (3.65)**
Weekly media coverage of U.S. occupation	0.015 (1.41)	0.008 (0.78)
Weekly media coverage post-sovereignty	0.004 (0.26)	–0.008 (0.60)
Weekly media coverage post-elections	0.010 (0.80)	0.015 (1.30)

TABLE 2.12. *(cont.)*

	1: Constant impact	*2: Contingent impact*
Coverage of Democratic primaries	–0.034 (2.62)**	–0.033 (2.62)**
DJI growth 3-week average	8.058 (0.31)	40.125 (1.76)
Constant	58.537 (16.28)**	53.731 (22.79)**
Rho	0.80	0.29
R-squared	0.48	0.89

N = 189; absolute value of *t* statistics in parentheses
* significant at 5% ** significant at 1%

Katrina, because widespread dissatisfaction with the Bush administration's handling of this catastrophe might have caused a reduction in presidential approval that would be spuriously correlated with U.S. casualties from this period overall.[25] All independent variables were lagged one-week.[26]

Model 1 in table 2.12 examines Mueller's hypothesis that support for a war effort will erode with the log of military deaths. Contrary to Mueller's finding on the Korea and Vietnam cases, the log of casualties does not fit the Iraqi War data and, in fact, the overall fit of this model seems to be quite poor. The only variable associated with the war that achieves statistical significance is the volume of media coverage during the major combat phase. Not surprisingly, its effect was to increase presidential approval. On

[25] These dummy variables set a new intercept value for the presidential approval time-series during each event. The dummy variables are coded 0 prior to the occurrence of the event and 1 afterward. Controlling for the initiation of the war as a "rally event" had no impact on the coefficients in table 2.12, and the variable was not statistically significant. This is likely due to the fact that the casualties suffered during the major combat phase capture the rally effect.

[26] Both Dickey-Fuller and Phillips-Perron unit root tests indicated that the presidential approval time-series is trend stationary ($p < .01$). Inclusion of a variable to control for any temporal trend in the mean did not alter the results. The trend variable was not statistically significant and was dropped from the analysis. The coefficients in table 2.12 use the Prais-Winsten correction for serial correlation in a time-series. The initial Durbin-Watson statistics were 1.18 and 1.61, indicating a statistically significant autocorrelation problem for both models. The transformed Durbin-Watson statistics were 2.35 and 2.03, indicating that the Prais-Winsten correction addressed the problem.

the other hand, the volume of media coverage of Democratic presidential candidates and Hurricane Katrina had a significant negative impact on Bush's approval. The coefficient for the log of casualties is very small and does not approach significance indicating that casualties—*on average*—had no impact at all on presidential approval from March 2003 through November 2004.

In model 2, however, we account for the fact that casualties may have had very different effects on presidential approval during the major combat, occupation, and sovereign Iraq phases of the war because of the substantial differences in public expectations of American success. We do so by interacting the log of total U.S. military deaths with dummy variables designating the different phases of the Iraq conflict. These interaction terms will determine if the relationship between casualties and approval changed across the different phases of the war.[27]

First, note that the overall fit of the model is dramatically improved. While model 1 yielded an r-squared of 0.48, making the impact of casualties contingent on the phase of the war increases the r-squared to 0.89. Because of the interactive nature of the relationship between casualties and approval in model 2, calculating the overall effect of casualties for each phase of the war—and the proper standard errors for hypothesis testing—is somewhat more complex. Thus we calculate the overall impact of casualties on presidential approval for each of the four phases of the Iraq war in table 2.13. Clearly the shift from major combat to insurgency against a U.S. occupation had a significant effect on the relationship between casualties and presidential approval. The coefficient flips from 2.26 to −8.69. Both of these effects are statistically significant. Notice, however, that after the U.S. transferred sovereignty to an Iraqi authority, the impact of casualties shifted again. Consistent with our impressionistic evaluation of figure 2.4, the model indicates that between May 2004 and February 2005 casualties had no significant impact whatsoever on presidential approval. The coefficient is actually positive at 2.55, but its standard error is quite large and it does not approach statistical significance. It is particularly striking to see such an attenuation in

[27] We estimate the varying impact of casualties by interacting the log of total casualties with the war-phase dummy variables both because this allows us a more direct test of whether the variation in this relationship is statistically significant and because we believe that the members of the public are likely to be aware of the total number of US casualties but are unlikely to know how many combat deaths occurred in a particular phase. Nor are prior deaths likely to stop having an impact just because the war has entered a new phase. Modeling the relationships in this way, however, does generate relatively high levels of colinearity among the variables. None of the statistically insignificant variables suffered from high levels of colinearity. Nonetheless, as a robustness check we analyzed the model using the log of the number of casualties within each period as our estimate of the impact of casualties. The substantive results remain unchanged.

TABLE 2.13.
Contingent Impact of Casualties on Presidential Approval in the Iraq War

Phase of Iraq War	*Coefficient for impact of casualties*	*Standard error*	*Level of statistical significance*
Major combat	2.26	0.536	< .001
U.S. occupation	–8.69	0.911	< .001
Iraqi sovereignty	2.55	3.55	< .474
Post–Iraq election	–15.96	3.81	< .001

the impact of casualties at that time, since the U.S. death toll was the subject of tremendous media coverage through the late summer and early fall of 2004 as the United States approached the threshold of having 1,000 soldiers killed in action. Finally, as the glow of success from the first Iraqi elections faded into the stubborn reality of a growing civil war, casualties once again began to drive presidential approval downward. During the post-election period, the coefficient for the impact of casualties flips to −15.96 and is highly statistically significant.

Importantly, the shifts between the occupation, sovereign Iraq, and post-election phases of the war clearly indicate that the relationship between casualties and presidential approval is not constant. The data cannot be explained as a brief rally effect followed by a consistent decline in approval due to casualties. Nor can the lack of impact of casualties during the sovereign Iraq period be attributed to the other brief rallies that we observed in the data. Instead, it appears that for some relatively extended periods of the Iraq conflict, the public did not respond to casualties by reducing their support for the president or the war.

The magnitude of this shift in public sensitivity to casualties can be seen by returning to figure 2.4. Here we see that between the onset of the insurgency in June 2003 and the transfer of sovereignty back to an Iraqi government in June 2004, the United States suffered approximately 600 combat deaths. These losses corresponded to a striking twenty-point drop in presidential approval from 65 to about 45 percent. From the Bush administration's surprising success in transferring sovereignty through the much-hailed and surprisingly successful first Iraqi election in January 2005, the United States suffered approximately another 600 combat deaths. In this case, however, the loss of American lives in combat corresponded to a five-point increase in presidential approval from 45 to 50 percent. This result does not imply that the public did not care about U.S. casualties between the transfer of sovereignty and the first constitutional elections, but it does suggest that the public's tolerance for casualties increased between June 2004 and February 2005. Then as political stalemate and continued violence followed the Iraqi election, the United States suffered another 600 combat deaths between February and October of 2005. Under these circumstances, American losses resulted in about a twelve-point drop in presidential approval from 50 to 38 percent.

Accounting for the varying impact of casualties improves the fit of the model so much that it allows us to detect the impact of other variables as well. Returning to table 2.12, we see that the volume of media coverage can have varying influences on presidential approval. For example, media coverage of Iraq evoked a rally effect during both the major combat phase of the war and prior to the outbreak of the war; but coverage of combat since the onset of the insurgency has had no impact one way or the other. Not surprisingly, we find that media coverage of Democratic presidential candidates during the 2004 election reduced presidential approval. Other incidents on the ground in Iraq influenced approval as well. The capture of Saddam Hussein boosted approval by an average of three percentage points until the release of the Kay Report. The president's series of speeches in December 2005 drawing attention to the Parliamentary elections in Iraq also increased the his approval rating by an average of just over two percentage points until the bombing of the al-Askari Mosque.

Despite the prominence of the Iraq War in the public mind, some domestic issues also influenced presidential approval. Public dissatisfaction with the response to Hurricane Katrina lowered the president's approval rating by an average of nearly four percentage points. On the other hand, the coefficient for changes in the Dow Jones Industrial Average is positive and the size of the coefficient indicates that its impact can be substantial. Specifically the model indicates that the change from a three-week period in which the Dow lost a weekly average of 2 percent of its value to a three-week period in which the Dow gained a weekly average of 2 percent of its value will increase presidential approval by an average of 1.6 percent. This coefficient, however, just misses conventional levels of statistical significance ($p < .08$).

Our data on casualties and presidential approval closely correspond with those of Eichenberg and Stoll, who analyzed similar data with a slightly different statistical model and concluded that with every additional one hundred casualties and controlling for the rally effect, approval of the president's handling of Iraq dropped three percentage points and approval of the president overall dropped by about one percentage point.[28] We depart from Eichenberg and Stoll's interpretation by distinguishing

[28] Richard C. Eichenberg and Richard J. Stoll, "The Political Fortunes of War: Iraq and the Domestic Standing of President George W. Bush," paper published by The Foreign Policy Centre; The European Think Tank with a Global Outlook, July 2004.

among the differing effects of casualties during the major combat, occupation, and sovereign Iraq phases of the war. This pattern of varying levels of public casualty sensitivity also fit the pattern noted earlier in this chapter in our reanalysis of Mueller's data on public opinion during the Korean and Vietnam wars. When the public appears to be confident in an American victory, then casualties have little effect on popular support. If the public's confidence in victory is shaken, however, then casualties erode support. When mounting casualties start eroding support, the relationship does appear to be logarithmic. That is, small numbers of casualties will matter early on in a conflict, but as the combat deaths escalate it takes increasingly large increments of military deaths to reduce support. But this relationship is conditional on low expectations of success.

Anecdotal evidence from available polls suggests that these shifts in casualty tolerance may relate to the public expectations of success. During the major combat phase, the public was quite confident, and rightly so, that the United States could successfully invade Iraq and remove Saddam Hussein from power. As early as 27 March 2003—prior to the fall of Baghdad—a Time/CNN/Harris poll reported that 52 percent of the public was already willing to label the war a success.[29] But the onset of the insurgency against the occupation in May shook the public's confidence in a successful outcome. In mid-July Time/CNN asked the same question and found that only 39 of respondents felt that the U.S. effort was a success—even though the United States had toppled Hussein and occupied Iraq.[30] By November 2003 only 25 percent of the public stated that the war had been successful.[31] The granting of sovereignty and creation of an Iraqi government also seems to have caused a similar—though less dramatic—shift in public optimism. By May of 2004 public confidence reached its nadir with only 37 percent of the public stating that the war was going "very well" or "somewhat well." But by the eve of the election in October 2004, that number had risen to 57 percent,[32] and in the wake of the first Iraqi elections at the end of January 2005, 53 percent of respondents indicated that the success of the elections was evidence that President Bush's "policy in dealing with Iraq is working."[33] The public mood turned downward again in the spring of 2005 as the promise of those elections remained unfulfilled. Two ABC News polls, for example, indicated that the percentage of Americans who felt that the United States

[29] 27 March 2003, Time/CNN/Harris Poll.

[30] 16 July 2003, Time/CNN/Harris Poll.

[31] 18 November 2003, Time/CNN/Harris Poll.

[32] 23 May 2004, CBS News Poll. October data from our survey from 15 October through 1 November . Our question labels the second category "fairly well" instead of "somewhat well."

[33] 14 February 2005 NBC/WSJ Poll.

had become "bogged down" in Iraq increased from 54 to 65 percent between March and June of 2005.[34]

The attitude tapped by these polls, however, is different from the "expectations of success" concept emphasized by Feaver and Gelpi. These polls were asking respondents to make a judgment about accomplished fact—was the war a success now—rather than a judgment about an eventual fact—was the war likely to be successful. Feaver and Gelpi suggest that expectations of future success are the key determinants of public casualty tolerance. That is, the public can accept that the war is not *yet* won and will involve continued and even mounting costs, provided that the events thus far are not convincing the public that eventual success is impossible. Other factors, however, may also have been shifting at this time. For example, the shift from the major combat phase to the insurgency phase may also have caused a change in the perceived primary policy objective (PPO) of the mission from what Jentleson would call a foreign policy restraint (based on the goal of eliminating Iraqi WMD) to a state-building intervention in Iraqi domestic politics.

More generally, we cannot base inferences about individual attitudes solely on shifts in aggregate opinion. In fact, one of the principal weaknesses of the other prominent analyses of public opinion and casualty tolerance is the almost exclusive reliance on aggregate data. Thus Mueller, Jentleson, Larson, and often Feaver and Gelpi are left in the difficult position of observing shifts in aggregate support for military operations in published polls and then inferring the cause of fluctuations in support from external events.[35] Such inferences are made even more problematic by the obvious ecological inference problem involved in reaching such conclusions. To reach firm conclusions about the process by which individual members of the public form attitudes about tolerating the costs of war we must collect and analyze data on individuals' opinions. We will turn to this task in chapter 3.

Conclusion

In this chapter we have reviewed the responses of the American public to each of the military operations in which the United States suffered a significant number of casualties. A careful look at the public response to the casualties in these conflicts suggests that a number of widely held

[34] 13 March 2005 and 26 June 2005 ABC/Washington Post Polls.

[35] Mueller, *War, Presidents, and Public Opinion*; Jentleson, *The Pretty Prudent Public*; Reberra L. Britton and Bruce Jentleson, "Still Pretty Prudent," *Journal of Conflict Resolution* 42, no. 4, (August 1998): 395; Larson, *Casualties and Consensus*; Feaver and Gelpi, *Choosing Your Battles.*

views about public attitudes toward war are not well founded in the available data. First, contrary to the first major wave of scholarship on casualties and public opinion, combat deaths do not appear to have a consistent impact on public support for military operations. Mueller (1971, 1973, 2005) has famously argued for a "simple association" between casualties and public support: as casualties increase, public support decreases. His original claim was based on an analysis of the Korea and Vietnam wars (1971, 1973), and more recently he has argued that the 2003 Iraq War fits this same pattern (2005). A more careful look at each of these conflicts, however, suggests that public responses to casualties varied substantially within the context of each of these wars. During some periods, casualties were concurrent with declining support for military operations, while in others they were not.

The evidence reviewed in this chapter also appears to contradict the second wave of scholarship on public casualty tolerance. Much of this work—done in the wake of the U.S. experiences in Lebanon and Somalia—claims that the public is so strongly averse to suffering casualties in military operations that are tangential to American security interests that almost any incidence of casualties will cause the public to demand withdrawal. The aggregate data both from Lebanon and Somalia do not support this view. While public support for Somalia did drop somewhat after the killing of the Army Rangers in October 1993, the data indicate that the vast majority of the erosion in public support for the Somalia mission occurred before the United States suffered any casualties. In Lebanon, moreover, the consequence of the bombing of the barracks that killed 283 marines was to increase public support for an intervention about which the public previously had very mixed feelings. Only after the Reagan administration abandoned the Lebanon mission did the public turn against it.

The pattern is clear and consistent across all the conflicts we examined: In some contexts casualties erode public support and in others they do not. But what aspects of the context are most important? This question is the central issue in the third wave of scholarship discussed in chapter 1. Unfortunately, we cannot answer this question definitively with the aggregate survey data that most of the literature relies upon. Changes in the perceptions of the likelihood of success appear to have an important influence on the public's sensitivity to casualties. It is also possible, however, that changes in the aggregate perception of success happen to coincide with other changes—such as a change in the PPO. We began trying to sort this out by looking at the individual-level data available from commercial polls that asked about success, as well as the appropriateness of the mission under consideration. These data suggest that both perceptions of success and perceptions of the legitimacy of the mission combine to determine public willingness to bear human costs and continue to support a military operation. In the next chapter we isolate these different causal mechanisms with a series of experiments so as to determine which factors can have a causal impact on casualty tolerance. Then in the following chapter we turn to a more detailed analysis of individual-level attitudes toward the 2003 Iraq War—which provides us with an unparalleled opportunity to understand and measure public tolerance for casualties in war.

Chapter Three

MEASURING INDIVIDUAL ATTITUDES TOWARD MILITARY CONFLICT

IN CHAPTER 2, we used aggregate data to investigate whether the public's ability to tolerate the casualties that inevitably come from military operations has varied substantially at different points in time and with different missions. The historical data discussed in that chapter clearly indicate that the public does not respond to combat deaths in anything like a simple monotonic fashion. Instead, our analyses suggested that the public response to casualties depends upon the flow of events on the ground in the conflict and the way those events influence the domestic political discourse. While these aggregate data allow us to draw some important inferences concerning the use of force and the public's sensitivity to casualties, at least two separate problems are inherent in relying on this aggregate level data alone: (1) it is difficult to draw inferences about the nature of individual opinion from aggregate level data, and (2) conclusions must be reached by extrapolating from a fairly small number of conflicts.

Concerning the first problem, inferences from aggregate-level data are subject to the "ecological inference fallacy." Patterns seen at the aggregate level do not necessarily translate to accurate depictions of the dynamics of individual-level opinions. For instance, when aggregate expectations of success drop, aggregate support for the war drops. But it is at least theoretically possible that the linkage is not happening individual by individual—that is, it is at least possible that individuals who have low expectations of success nevertheless tend to support the war. The second problem is more serious in terms of our ability to understand how the public thinks and feels about the use of military force. The United States does not go to war often. Therefore, our inferences concerning the public's support of the use of force are based on a small number of observations. From these few observations have sprung many different competing claims of the causal logic that underlie support for or opposition to military action.

Individual-level survey data affords the opportunity to observe the structure of attitudes at the individual level and increases substantially the number of observations on which we can base our inferences. We took advantage of this opportunity when possible in chapter 2 by examining the individual responses to a number of polls conducted by news organizations that were covering these conflicts. Nonetheless, the analyses of such polls can often only be suggestive and illustrative because the questions asked on the surveys do not necessarily measure attitudes in terms that we find theoretically satisfying nor do they generally ask a wide enough range of questions to measure the kinds of attitudes and demographic factors that we would like to include in a multivariate analysis of public opinion.

We sought to address these problems by developing our own survey on American public attitudes toward the use of military force. Implementing our own survey allows us to develop measures of attitudes toward the use of military force that we think are theoretically appropriate. In addition, constructing our own survey allows us to embed experiments in a nationally representative sample and directly test different causal logics of support for using force and for tolerance of the resultant casualties that were discussed in chapters 1 and 2. This survey was conducted via telephone by the Parker Group, between 22 September and 12 October 2003. A complete text of the survey instrument is available from the authors.

We asked respondents about their support for the use of military force in two general ways. First, we asked a number of questions about real-world issues and the extent to which respondents would support using force regarding those issues. We used real-world issues, but we did not tie them to a specific military mission. We asked these kinds of abstract questions in order to investigate whether ordinary Americans organize their attitudes toward military force in a coherent way. When military force is actually used, of course, it is never in the abstract. Citizens are asked to make a decision about whether to support a specific military mission. Thus we also asked a series of questions that presented respondents with hypothetical—but plausible—missions that the United States might undertake. We use these questions to assess the manner in which general attitudes relate to support for specific missions.

Some might worry that the hypothetical scenarios are unreliable guides to how individuals might respond in a concrete case. It is one thing to express support for some abstract case. It is another thing altogether to support a war when real people are dying. These concerns are valid, but previous studies show they are almost always exaggerated. Hypothetical questions more likely *overstate* the public's sensitivity to casualties (Feaver and Gelpi 2004). The rally-'round-the-flag phenomenon shows that many people who previously did not support the use of force nevertheless rally to the cause once the war starts. Likewise, support does not drop as quickly with real-world casualties as it does with hypothetical scenarios. Hypothetical questions, therefore, can be a useful part of a comprehensive analysis. We rely on data from this survey for all of the remaining analyses in this chapter.

The remainder of this chapter uses the data from our survey to examine the structure, coherence, and organization of individual level-attitudes concerning the use of force and tolerance for casualties. Our central concern in this chapter is to examine the extent to which members of the public organize their attitudes toward military conflict in coherent ways. More specifically, we investigate whether public support for the use of military force may be organized along more than one dimension. For example, we explore whether support for realpolitik "security"-related missions is distinct from support for missions with less-realpolitik goals, such as protecting human rights and stopping ethnic cleansing. Next, we seek to measure the extent to which respondents are willing to tolerate the loss of American soldiers in order to accomplish such goals. Casualty tolerance, we argue is central to the operational concept of "supporting" a war. That is, from both an opinion-formation perspective and a political perspective, the critical public attitude toward military force is whether citizens will demand withdrawal rather than allowing the human costs to mount. Thus we both define and measure the concept of "casualty tolerance" and demonstrate that it is related to other attitudes about the use of military force in sensible ways.

The Structure of Individual Attitudes toward the Use of Force

Deciding whether or not to support the use of military force by one's government is among the most important tasks facing citizens of a democratic country. To what extent are citizens up to the task? Much of the early research on public opinion and American foreign policy took a very dim view of this question. Walter Lippmann, for example, famously concluded, "The unhappy truth is that the prevailing public opinion has been destructively wrong at critical junctures. [The people] have compelled governments . . . to be too late with too little, too long with too much, too pacifist in peace or bellicose in war." (1955:20). And Almond (1950) described an American public whose foreign policy views were closer to erratic mood swings than coherent foreign policy attitudes.

Since that early research, however, much of the scholarship has suggested that we may have been too quick to despair regarding public understanding of foreign policy. No one disputes that the public has a relatively weak grasp on the specific facts about international politics. Indeed, the public seems to know relatively few specifics regarding domestic policies as well. An increasingly large body of scholarship suggests, however, that individual members of the public do have stable and coherent preferences regarding foreign policy. Caspary (1970) and Achen (1975), for example, demonstrate that earlier conclusions about the volatility of public opinion may have been based on faulty survey design and methodology. Page and Shapiro (1982; Shapiro and Page 1988), demonstrate that aggregate public opinion on a variety of international issues has been both relatively stable and responsive to international events. Holsti (1979) and Wittkopf (1986) demonstrate that individual Americans do organize their attitudes toward foreign policy along reasonable substantive dimensions. In particular, this literature suggests that individuals organize their attitudes toward foreign affairs in terms of the extent to which they believe that the United States should be engaged in international affairs (isolationism versus internationalism) and the extent to which America should rely on military or diplomatic tools when it engages the outside world (militant versus cooperative internationalism).

Our work seeks to build on this kind of understanding of the structure of public attitudes, but for at least two reasons we believe that the Holsti and Wittkopf kinds of typologies are not sufficient for our purposes. First of all, our interest in public opinion is more narrowly focused on attitudes toward the use of military force, making the "isolationist versus internationalist" dimension that underlies much of the existing scholarship on public opinion and foreign policy not entirely appropriate for our analysis. For example, a respondent who opposes the use of military force to intervene in any conflict might do so either because he or she is isolationist or because this person is what Holsti would call a "cooperative internationalist"—but for the purposes of describing his or her attitudes toward the use of military force, this distinction would be irrelevant.

Second, the distinction between cooperative and militant internationalists does not capture what has become one of the important dimensions of post–Cold War American foreign policy: the use of military force for humanitarian missions versus more traditional security missions. Thinking back to the American military actions discussed in chapter 2, it is clear that one of the central debates regarding the operations in Lebanon, Somalia, and Kosovo was whether the United States military ought to be in the business of intervening in other countries to address humanitarian problems. At the same time, one of the central axes of debate regarding both of America's wars against Iraq has been the extent to which American national security interests are at stake in Iraq.

The prominence of this humanitarianism versus traditional security cleavage has led the most recent literature on attitudes toward American foreign policy to focus on this cleavage in understanding both public and elite support for military intervention. As we discussed in chapter 1, Jentleson (1992; Jentleson and Britton 1998) and Eichenberg (2005) focus on this distinction in their analyses of the primary policy objective (PPO) and its impact on support for military interventions. Similarly, Feaver and Gelpi (2004) focus on this cleavage in their analysis of elite civil-military attitudes toward the use of military force. Building on these previous works, we seek to determine whether American public attitudes toward the use of force can be usefully described as ranging along two related but distinct dimensions: (1) the extent to which they support using military force in support of traditional national security goals, and (2) the extent to which they support the use of military force for humanitarian goals.

As a first step to understanding public opinion and the use of force, we seek to measure these dimensions at an abstract level—as opposed to support for specific military operations, which we will examine in subsequent chapters. Thus the questions we asked concerned using the military to achieve foreign policy goals, without including any mission specifics. Tapping into a generalized attitude establishes a baseline of support for using military force. We avoided any mention of costs that the United States might endure, prospects of the mission's success, or any other potentially confounding factor. While we cannot say with certainty that respondents kept these considerations at bay while answering the questions, we believe this wording keeps any possible "contamination" to an absolute minimum.

As noted earlier, these support-for-force questions distinguished among different types of foreign policy goals. We asked about foreign policy goals consistent with realpolitik security concerns, such as defending American allies against an invasion, and also other less-realpolitik missions that the military might be expected to perform, such as deploying troops to protect human rights or to stop ethnic cleansing. Specifically, respondents were asked whether they agree or disagree that the United States "must be willing to use military force" to achieve each foreign policy goal.

We would argue that the questions concerning the defense of U.S. allies, containing Chinese military power, the prevention of the rise of a hostile superpower, and the prevention of the development of weapons of mass destruction (WMD) clearly fall into the "realpolitik" category of missions because they involve defending the United States against traditional kinds of interstate threats. These missions continue to view American security through the traditional lens of state sovereignty. The questions regarding the defense of human rights, spreading democracy, the support of international organizations, and the prevention of ethnic cleansing, on the other hand, clearly fall into the "humanitarian" category, since they generally involve the intervention inside the domestic politics of other states or seek goals other than the prevention of traditional interstate threats to the United States. Combating terrorism shares some characteristics with each of these types of missions because it will often involves intervention inside other states, but it also seeks to counter a direct military threat to the U.S. homeland. On balance, however, we view this mission as closer to a "security" mission because terrorism goals seem likely to be viewed as connected directly to American security in the wake of the 9/11 attacks.

Table 3.1 shows the level of support for various kinds of U.S. military missions. Overall, the responses indicate a fairly high level of support for

TABLE 3.1.
Approval of Using Military Force to Accomplish Foreign Policy Goals

	Foreign policy goal								
U.S. must be ready to use military force	*Promote democracy in other nations*	*Combat global terrorist orgs.*	*Defend human rights in other nations*	*Prevent hostile superpower*	*Prevent spread of WMD*	*Increase interntl. cooperation through U.N.*	*Contain Chinese military power*	*Defend American allies*	*Stop ethnic cleansing*
Strongly disagree	240 21%	60 5%	103 9%	97 8%	107 9%	180 15%	171 16%	27 2%	79 8%
Somewhat disagree	276 24%	100 8%	175 15%	159 14%	100 8%	163 14%	257 23%	57 5%	96 9%
Somewhat agree	450 39%	293 25%	470 40%	357 31%	282 24%	362 31%	415 38%	372 32%	274 25%
Strongly agree	196 17%	726 62%	432 37%	535 47%	691 59%	460 39%	253 23%	720 61%	626 58%
Total	1,162	1,179	1,180	1,165	1,096	1,175	1,096	1,176	1,075

all of these military missions. The three foreign policy goals that receive the highest levels of support, with the understanding that military force must be used to achieve these goals, are as follows: defend American allies (93 percent agree), combat global terrorist organizations (87 percent agree), and prevent spread of weapons of mass destruction (83 percent agree). The three that exhibited the lowest levels of support are promote democracy in other nations (56 percent agree), contain Chinese military power (61 percent agree), and "increase international cooperation through (institutions such as) the U. N." (68 percent agree). Thus even the least popular mission had a majority of the public agreeing that using military force was appropriate.

Greater variation becomes apparent, however, if we look at the proportion of the public that "strongly agrees" that military force is appropriate for each mission. Here we see that the public tends to have stronger support for realpolitik missions than humanitarian ones. More than 60 percent of the respondents strongly agreed that force is appropriate to defend our allies and to counter international terrorism, and nearly 60 percent strongly agreed that the use of force to prevent the spread of WMD is appropriate. One traditional mission—confronting China—did generate much less support with only 23 percent of respondents "strongly agreeing" that the United States must be ready to use force. Conversely, only one "humanitarian" mission—preventing ethnic cleansing—attracted more than 40 percent of respondents "strongly agreeing" to the use of force in its attainment. Moreover, the least popular humanitarian mission—spreading democracy—attracted only 16 percent "strong" support. Thus, with a few exceptions, these results seem generally consistent with Jentleson's (1992) hierarchy of PPOs. Foreign policy restraint (FPR) missions seem to generate the greatest support—with the proviso that combating terrorism should be identified as a new FPR mission. The public, however, does not appear to view China as a strong military threat. Humanitarian intervention generates somewhat less support, but the public is willing to respond to a humanitarian crisis. Finally, the public is most reticent to support internal political change (IPC).

These aggregate responses seem consistent with previous research, but our task here is to determine whether these responses reflect separate dimensions of support for military force at the individual level. That is, we want to know whether individual respondents structure their support for different military missions along these two dimensions: traditional security and humanitarian intervention. Using factor analysis—a statistical technique that looks for shared variance among multiple variables—allows us to tease out more precisely the underlying structure of opinion reflected in these data. Factor analysis essentially tells us whether people are answering different survey questions in very similar ways. The more similar the pattern across various items, the stronger the evidence that the answers to these questions are best explained by an underlying attitude or latent variable. Our hypothesis is that two related but distinct attitudes will underlie these responses: security and humanitarianism.

The Security *Dimension*

When applied to the nine items from our battery of questions about using force, factor analysis strongly identifies an underlying variable that loads highly on questions pertaining to traditional security-related goals, which we hereby name *Security*.[1] Table 3.2 reports the factor loadings (or the correlation between the variables and the underlying factor). The two questions that load most strongly on the *Security* factor are "prevent spread of WMD," followed by "prevent hostile superpower." The specific questions that reflect humanitarian goals correlate fairly lowly with the underlying *Security* dimension, with "increase international cooperation" and "stop ethnic cleansing" as the questions least well explained by *Security*.

We interpret the results as evidence for an individual-level attitude that explains support (or opposition) to the use of force for security-related foreign policy goals. Perhaps one of the most interesting results is how well newer security concerns, like the threat of global terrorist organizations, merge with more traditional security concerns, like the containment of superpowers. While we do not have pre–9/11 data that could let us know for certain, we speculate that the strong correlations between "new" concerns and the underlying *Security* dimension may be a consequence of 9/11. As a result of the terrorist attacks on the World Trade Center, the American public has been able to update its beliefs about the potential threats to U.S. domestic security. Even given the visceral effect of the terrorist attacks, however, "prevent hostile superpower" still loads more strongly than "combating global terrorist organizations" on the *Security* dimension. Despite how quickly terrorism has come to be part of an attitude about security, it has not surpassed the most central elements of a worldview based on more conventional views of defense and security. Exactly how long this concern will last is a much more difficult question.

The Humanitarian Dimension

We expected the data to exhibit strong evidence that support for using the military toward humanitarian (or nonsecurity) foreign policy goals would reveal an attitude that is clearly distinct from the motivations for supporting

[1] The *Security* factor was identified without rotation and has an eigenvalue of approximately 2.9.

Table 3.2
Dimensions of Support for Using Force—Factor Loadings

	Unrotated			*Rotated*		
Foreign policy goal	*Security*	*Humanitarian*	*Metternich*	*Security*	*Humanitarian*	*Metternich*
Promote democracy in other nations	0.56	–0.03	–0.10	0.48	0.37	–0.03
Combat global terrorist orgs.	0.64	–0.14	–0.17	0.58	0.25	–0.08
Defend human rights in other countries	0.52	0.27	–0.14	0.34	0.53	0.12
Prevent hostile superpower	0.73	–0.16	0.05	0.73	0.20	0.06
Preventing spread of WMD	0.73	–0.20	0.07	0.75	0.13	0.08
Increase interntl. cooperation through U.N.	0.22	0.29	0.20	0.10	0.21	0.34
Contain Chinese military power	0.58	0.01	0.21	0.57	0.18	0.26
Defend American allies	0.52	0.12	0.06	0.41	0.25	0.20
Stop ethnic cleansing	0.41	0.25	–0.13	0.28	0.38	0.15

use of the military toward traditional security-related foreign policy goals. While the evidence in support of a humanitarian dimension to foreign policy attitudes is not as clear-cut as the evidence for a security dimension, taken as a whole it is consistent and convincing. The interpretation of this evidence turns on two key issues. The first key is thinking about how one should interpret factor analysis results. The second key is considering whether all nonsecurity goals should load into a single humanitarian dimension or whether there are potentially multiple nonsecurity dimensions that structure attitudes concerning the use of force.

Interpreting factor analysis results can sometimes be as much art as science. As a data reduction technique, factor analysis is an invaluable tool. As a mathematical problem, however, factor analysis does not have a "unique" solution, as would many other data analysis tools, like regression. As a result, there are a considerable number of ways to examine the results. None of these answers is any more correct than others—each simply allows one to view the data from a different angle. We exploit these various analysis techniques to build a case that nonsecurity goals stand apart from security goals.

One the many "rules of thumb" concerning factor analysis is retaining "factors" with an eigenvalue greater than 1, and discarding the others.[2] Using this heuristic, one would keep only a *Security* factor and dismiss a *Humanitarian* dimension. While the eigenvalue is small on this second dimension, the factor loadings are highest with the two questions we consider most representative of support for humanitarian foreign policy and with a third question assessing feelings toward international cooperation. The factor loadings for the *Humanitarian* dimension are lowest with those questions that are least related to humanitarian concerns. Thus, the structure clearly indicates that questions "load" in a manner consistent with a *Humanitarian* dimension.

After the first-cut at the data, a common analytic technique is to "rotate" the factors. Rotating factors aids in interpretation by making the

[2] This is the most commonly used rule of thumb (Guttman 1954), but there is no logical basis for this criterion. Eigenvalues represent the proportion of the total variance of the variables explained by each factor. By definition eigenvalues decline for each new factor that is retained because new "explained" variance is calculated after accounting for the variance explained by previous factors. Since the variables are normalized to a 0–1 continuum, the total amount of variance is equal to the number of items in the factor analysis. Thus the rule of selecting factors with eigenvalues greater than 1 comes from the intuitive notion that one should retain only factors that "explain" more than a single item in the scale. But using an arbitrary cutoff threshold does not speak to the question of whether the additional common variation in responses to a set of items is substantively meaningful or empirically important. We suggest that a better criterion for selecting factors is one of substantive comprehensibility and empirical import. That is, if the pattern of factor loadings makes the factor interpretable and the factor has important substantive effects, then it should be retained. The obvious limit on this criterion is that factors with negative eigenvalues cannot be retained, since this would imply that the factor can be entirely explained by prior factors.

factor loadings move toward 0 and 1. That is, this procedure rotates the predicted underlying factors so as to maximize the distinction between questions that do and do not load on each factor. After using Varimax orthogonal rotation (where the identified factors remain perpendicular to one another), a *Humanitarian* dimension is more easily identified. Both of the questions that a priori we believe represent humanitarian concerns ("defend human rights" and "stop ethnic cleansing") have much stronger loadings after rotating the factors. Additionally, "increase international cooperation through (institutions such as) the U.N." loads less strongly with this second factor—making the two *Humanitarian* goals stand out distinctly from other nonsecurity goals. In fact, the third highest loading item on the second dimension (using rotated factors) is supporting the use of force for helping to "promote democracy in other nations." This question is not as centrally about humanitarian intervention as are questions about "human rights" or "ethnic cleansing," but intervention on behalf of democracy has a normative component to it and is related to the defense of individual rights. Thus we expect it to load on a *Humanitarian* dimension more strongly than a question about international organizations and certaintly more strongly than questions about defeating superpowers and so on. The pattern of factor loadings therefore comports with our expectations.

Overall, there is no "right answer" as to whether rotated or unrotated factors are better. We opt for the rotated factors in subsequent analyses for two reasons. First, the pattern of factor loadings with the rotated factors is more clearly consistent with our a priori expectations of what the data would reveal. Second, the two factors are uncorrelated before rotation (−.05), but show a modest positive correlation (.35) after rotation. While we believe that the two are distinct attitudes, we do not expect them to be completely uncorrelated. We believe that there is likely to be a general goal-neutral support for using force that should be part of both. While we want to distinguish the *Security* and *Humanitarian* attitudes as much as possible, we do not want to exaggerate the differences. Here we are primarily interested in how the goals of the missions matter when individuals make judgments about the use of force. By allowing some overlap between the attitudes, we are attempting to separate more clearly support that is contingent on goals from a general attitude of outright opposition to the use of force.

An International or Neo-Metternich Dimension?

Rotating the factors also yields an interesting result concerning the question asking about using force to "Increase international cooperation through (institutions such as) the U.N." Before rotation, this was the highest-loading question on the second factor. After rotation, it is the fourth lowest. (The "U.N." question is the lowest-loading question on the first dimension both before and after rotation.) To answer this question, we turn to the third identified factor with the rotated loadings. This factor groups three related missions: "increase international cooperation through (institutions such as) the U.N.," "contain Chinese military power," and "defend American allies." While the loadings are fairly modest and the eigenvalue for the third factor is small, all three questions do have the common element of dealing with important elements of the international system—either directly with states, as in containing Chinese military power and defending American allies, or with the most visible international organization, the U.N. We are not exactly sure how to interpret this result. Our best guess is that it captures some facet of "respect" for an international status quo—what might be considered a "Metternich" position after the famous Austrian diplomat who strove to preserve elements of a familiar international system at the Congress of Vienna. With the limited evidence, it is difficult to do much more than speculate. Nonetheless, we consider this a fruitful topic for future research. We are intrigued that attitudes toward the international system might somehow stand apart from attitudes about *Security* and *Humanitarianism*.

A Typology of Public Attitudes toward the Use of Force

We used the two central dimensions of attitudes toward the use of force—*Security* and *Humanitarianism*—to create an aggregate-level typology of public attitudes on this issue. Specifically, for each respondent we coded whether he or she scored above or below the mean level of support for both security and humanitarian missions. This procedure yields a 2x2 typology that places respondents in one of four categories. The distribution of responses is displayed in table 3.3.

Here we can see that approximately 26 percent of the public scores below the mean in their support for both humanitarian and security missions. These respondents could reasonably be coded either as "doves" or as "isolationists" depending on their reasons for opposing the use of force. Nearly 18 percent of our respondents scored above the mean in terms of their support for security missions but below the mean in their support for humanitarian missions. These "security hawks" are balanced by an almost identical number of "humanitarian hawks" who scored above the mean in their support of humanitarian missions but below the mean in their support for security missions. Finally, the modal respondents in our typology are the 38 percent who scored as "overall hawks," who are above mean on both underlying attitudes. This result indicates

TABLE 3.3.
A Typology of Public Attitudes toward the Use of Military Force

Support for humanitarian use of force	*Support for security-oriented use of force*		
	Below mean	*Above mean*	*Total*
Below mean	315 26%	211 18%	526 44%
Above mean	214 18%	460 38%	674 56%
Total	529 44%	671 56%	

once again that the public is—in the abstract—quite supportive of the use of military force.

War Support, Casualty Tolerance, and Paying the Human Costs of War

The questions previously analyzed tap general attitudes toward "support" for the use of military force, and they are analogous to the understanding of "support" for specific military missions that are used in many analyses. Mueller (1971, 1973, 2005), for example, focuses on various questions asking whether the public views military conflicts as a "mistake." Burk (1999) and Hermann, Tetlock, and Visser (1999) follow with a similar strategy, while Gartner and Segura (1998, 2000) focus on approval for the president's handling of a conflict. Such generalized measures may be appropriate for addressing a variety of questions, but our analysis is focused on a more specific aspect of war support. Questions about whether a military conflict was a "mistake" have a retrospective quality to them that essentially ask the public, "If you could do it all over again, would you stay out of this war?" As we will discuss in chapter 6, such attitudes seem important when individuals make judgments about the competence of their leaders and make voting choices based on those judgments. Questions about the president's handling of a conflict have a similarly retrospective quality. Attitudes about whether force would be a mistake may also be important in forming public ex ante judgments about whether to support a military mission. But these attitudes do not directly measure the dimension that is most critical in the debate over public constraints on the use of force. A widely held consensus view among scholars in this area holds that American presidents are relatively unconstrained in their initial decisions to use force, and the extensive "rally 'round the flag" literature demonstrates that the public will initially tend to support the president immediately after the use of force (Russett 1990; Parker 1995; Baker and Oneal 2001; Baum 2002). The central question in the debate over public constraints on the use of force is: under what conditions will the public withdraw its support for an ongoing military mission? That is, we want to understand to what extent the American public will place pressure on its leaders to withdraw U.S. forces from a military conflict.

Public pressure to withdraw is the central issue in the debate over public impact on foreign policy, and the desire to withdraw is distinct from—though related to—other aspects of war support. At the time of this writing, for example, disapproval of President Bush's handling of the Iraq War is nearly 70 percent, but only about 30 percent of the public wants a complete withdrawal of U.S. forces from Iraq. If one wants to understand the dynamics of how respondents construct their attitudes toward the Iraq War, therefore, one would not want to conflate disapproval of Bush with support for withdrawing U.S. forces. Instead, one should seek to disaggregate these attitudes and examine the way in which they relate to one another.

So, in addition to general questions about using force for specific foreign policy goals, we also asked questions designed to capture "support" in the context of ongoing missions with a mounting human cost. We believe that asking questions in this context most usefully measures the aspects of public attitudes that are central to this debate. Using these questions, we identify a latent variable for individual-level casualty tolerance. Using similar factor analysis techniques as before, we find an underlying structure to the data that explains a significant portion of the variance on our casualty tolerance questions. Before we proceed to the analysis, however, it is necessary to take a brief detour into some of the problems associated with asking respondents about their tolerance for casualties.

Casualty-tolerance questions are notoriously difficult to ask. Survey results tend to exaggerate casualty sensitivity generally, and can be sensitive to even small wording changes. Questions asking respondents about whether the level of casualties in a conflict has been "worth it," for example, consistently elicits higher levels of support than questions asking whether the level of casualties has been "acceptable" (Feaver and Gelpi 2004). Our survey uses a novel approach to measuring casualty sensitivity that we believe avoids many of the problems associated with asking this type of question. Rather than asking respondents directly how many casualties they would tolerate—the question format used in Feaver and Gelpi (2004) —we asked if they would support a mission if it resulted in no U.S. military deaths. If a respondent said no, the interviewer skipped to the next item on the survey. However, if a respondent said she would support the mission if it resulted in no U.S. military deaths, she received a follow-up question asking if she would support the mission if it resulted in fifty U.S. military deaths. If she said no, she was skipped ahead to the next item in the survey. Because she was willing to support the mission if it resulted in no deaths, but was unwilling to support the mission if it resulted in fifty deaths, then we infer that the threshold of where her support turns to opposition is somewhere between one and fifty casualties.

If our respondent said she was willing to support the mission if it resulted in fifty deaths, she was asked whether she would support the same mission, but with a higher number of casualties. We asked about support for the mission at the following casualty levels: 0 deaths, 50 deaths, 500 deaths, 5000 deaths, 50,000 deaths, or more than 50,000 deaths. This branching format gives us an ordinal scale of casualty tolerance. Our question does not yield a specific "threshold" number—or the point at which someone flips from support to opposition of a mission. Until the research community discovers which questions produce specific and reliable estimates of the number of deaths one will tolerate before opposing the use of force, we believe that this ordinal measure strongly surpasses any open-ended questions that directly ask, "How many deaths would be acceptable" or anything similar.[3] In our example in the previous paragraph, we said we inferred that the threshold for support turning to opposition for continued military operations is between one and forty-nine. Taken away from a hypothetical, it is at least plausible that her support for a mission would endure even after forty-nine battle deaths. But, we suspect that, on average, someone who reports his or her threshold as between one and forty-nine will be less willing to continue supporting a war in the face of casualties over the fifty threshold than someone whose self-reported threshold is between fifty and five hundred.

Questions asking for a specific casualty tolerance number simply may not be possible. As we and many others argue, support for a specific mission depends on more than simply the number who have died to date. Therefore, the very idea that there could be a specific threshold, even at the individual level, of some "magic number" that turns support to

[3] Note further that asking about whether casualties are "acceptable" also exaggerates the public's sensitivity to casualties. Feaver and Gelpi (2004) found that using the word "acceptable" in asking about casualties biased reported casualty tolerance downward. Similarly, an experiment done in a series of ABC polls during the Iraq conflict show that asking whether casualties were "acceptable" generated lower estimates of tolerance than questions asking whether the benefits were worth the costs. Questions that specified a particular benefit in the question—e.g., mentioning removing Hussein from power—generated still higher estimates of casualty tolerance. See ABC polls conducted from March through October 2003, available at http://abcnews.go.com/sections/politics/PollVault/PollVault.html.

TABLE 3.4.
Public Tolerance for Casualties in Various Military Conflicts

	Eliminate Iranian WMD programs	*Defend South Korea from North Korean invasion*	*Stop starvation in the Congo*	*Continue military action in Iraq*
Opposed regardless of U.S. deaths	351 30%	319 28%	281 24%	179 15%
Will not tolerate 50 U.S. deaths*	184 16%	175 15%	279 24%	290 24%
Tolerate at least 50 U.S. deaths	184 16%	156 13%	274 24%	—
Tolerate at least 500 U.S. deaths	188 16%	195 17%	193 17%	390 33%
Tolerate at least 5,000 U.S. deaths	130 11%	138 12%	65 6%	194 16%
Tolerate at least 50,000 U.S. deaths	123 11%	174 15%	66 6%	136 11%

**Note:* For Iraq scenario the United States had already suffered 300 deaths at the time of the survey. Thus respondents did not receive the "50 deaths" question, but went directly from "opposed regardless of U.S. deaths" to being asked about tolerating 500 deaths. This category reflects the number of respondents who stated that they did not oppose force if there were no additional casualties but did not support continuing to fight if the United States suffered 500 deaths.

opposition should be called into question. In this section we show that casualty tolerance is fundamentally an ordinal variable, where some people possess more than others and that questions asking for more specific casualty thresholds do not yield measures any more reliable than our branching format.

We used this branching format to ask about the war in Iraq as well as three hypothetical missions that the United States might plausibly undertake—eliminating an Iranian WMD program, defending South Korea from a North Korean invasion, and intervening to stop a government-caused starvation in the Congo. When we applied the branching format of our casualty-tolerance question to Iraq, the initial question had to be rephrased from "zero deaths" total to "no more additional deaths" because the war had already started and the United States had already suffered casualties. Table 3.4 shows the frequency of responses to the full branching series for the four questions.

The marginals show that there is a fair amount of similarity in the overall pattern of the responses across the different mission scenarios. Similar-looking marginals, however, may understate the variation in the population and this may blunt our ability to determine the causal significance of the different scenarios. Looking more closely at the individual-level results yields new insights.

How similar are individuals' responses to the four different casualty tolerance questions? For the most part, the correlations across scenarios are about .5. The lowest correlation is between eliminating Iranian WMD and humanitarian intervention in the Congo (.39), while the highest correlation is between defending South Korea and Congo intervention (.51). Clearly, there is some underlying structure to the data—the answer to how many casualties one will support in a given mission depends, inter alia, on one's general tolerance for casualties. Some people show generally high tolerance for casualties and others show generally low tolerance, regardless of the mission. The pattern may be evident even when individual responses vary across the type of mission. For instance, a casualty-tolerant and security-oriented individual would report a willingness to support security-oriented missions despite high levels of casualties, and report a willingness to support only lower levels of casualties in humanitarian missions. Even so, however, that same individual might support higher levels of casualties on humanitarian missions than a casualty-intolerant and humanitarian-oriented individual. This humanitarian-oriented individual might show greater support for humanitarian missions than for other types of missions, but his general casualty sensitivity has him registering lower levels of casualty tolerance overall, even for his "favored" scenario. By asking these casualty-tolerance questions across a number of scenarios, we are much better able to "control" for differences in individual-level casualty tolerance when examining the causal impact of other factors.

If we use factor analysis, as we did with the general willingness to support force questions, then we are able to reduce the data to a clear "casualty tolerance" factor. All four of the ordinal casualty-tolerance variables load very strongly on this latent variable. Results are consistent with what one would expect going in—the highest casualty tolerance is defending South Korea, a long-standing treaty ally, and the lowest is the humanitarian mission in the Congo, a mission that has had essentially no discussion in the public debate and so the public has not been primed to view this as a realpolitik security interest of the United States. Table 3.5 shows factor loadings (because only one factor is identified, rotation is unnecessary).

The clarity of the structure underlying the casualty responses increases our confidence that these questions are measuring a real underlying attitude despite the difficulty that respondents might have in assessing their own willingness to tolerate the human costs of war. Moreover, while there

TABLE 3.5.
A Model of Casualty Tolerance—Factor Loadings

	Loadings	*Uniqueness*
Eliminate Iranian WMD	0.6549	0.5711
Defend South Korea from North Korea invasion	0.7271	0.4713
Stop starvation in Congo	0.6038	0.6354
Continue military action in Iraq	0.7039	0.5046

is some variance in the responses to individual items—which may be due to differing levels of support for security and humanitarian missions—there is clearly one attitude that underpins the responses to all of these casualty scenarios. We identify that attitude as a respondent's overall casualty tolerance. The negative eigenvalues for all other factors clearly indicate that no other common dimensions underlie these responses.

Support for Security Missions, Humanitarian Missions, and Casualty Tolerance

The descriptive statistics discussed thus far are suggestive of underlying patterns in the data. To better establish and probe those patterns, we construct several statistical models that examine various predictors of one's willingness to support force for security and humanitarian missions and one's willingness to tolerate casualties. These models treat the *Security*, *Humanitarian*, and *Casualty* variables developed in the previous section as the dependent variables—the attitudes to be explained.[4] The first set of models look only at demographic variables as possible predictors, and exclude other attitudinal measures, with the important exception of partisan identification. For some variables, like education, there are relatively intuitive causal theories supporting the relationship. We think that people with more education will think differently about the world and the role of the United States and its military as a result of having that education. For some other variables like race or sex, it is more difficult to say with precision what is causing the observed differences. The results to these initial "control variable only" models are in table 3.6.

Party Identification is negatively signed, indicating that Democrats are less supportive of using force than Republicans. This finding could be a result of at least three distinct causal processes. On the one hand, Demo-

[4] Question wording and coding for all questions are available from us, the authors.

TABLE 3.6.
Demographic Sources of Support for the Use of Force and Tolerance for Casualties

	Security	*Humanitarian*	*Casualty tolerance*
Sex	–0.078	–0.030	–0.325
	(1.61)	(0.79)	(6.42)**
Age in decades	–0.098	–0.047	–0.037
	(7.06)**	(4.34)**	(2.48)*
Education	–0.083	0.012	0.019
	(4.15)**	(0.76)	(0.91)
Party ID	–0.176	–0.056	–0.193
	(10.68)**	(4.38)**	(11.24)**
Black	–0.054	–0.080	–0.246
	(0.62)	(1.17)	(2.67)**
Hispanic	–0.032	0.060	–0.092
	(0.33)	(0.78)	(0.87)
Catholic	0.028	–0.006	–0.125
	(0.48)	(0.12)	(2.03)*
Non-religious	–0.336	–0.141	–0.219
	(5.93)**	(3.20)**	(3.69)**
Military service	–0.080	0.041	–0.090
	(1.07)	(0.70)	(1.16)
Constant	1.088	0.275	1.126
	(7.23)**	(2.35)*	(7.20)**
Observations	1110	1110	1020
R-squared	0.18	0.05	0.21

Absolute value of *t* statistics in parentheses
* significant at 5% ** significant at 1%

crats may generally be more dovish and/or more isolationist than Republicans. Alternatively, we may observe Republicans as being more supportive of military force because the president at the time of our survey was a Republican, George W. Bush, and they may have been more supportive of "their" leader using force. This effect may have been accentuated by the fact that our survey took place in the midst of an ongoing military conflict. Thus while none of our questions about general support for the use of force asked about Iraq, respondents may have relied upon their feelings about Iraq and the president's decision to use force there in responding to our items. Finally, it may be the case that the Iraq War stands out as unusually partisan in nature, and this division may have shaped the responses to our questions about military missions.

While we cannot definitively adjudicate between these explanations, we are skeptical of the first and third arguments. Democrats did not historically appear to be more reticent about supporting the use of military force in places like Korea and Vietnam. And while it is true that Vietnam caused something of a partisan realignment regarding foreign policy, Democrats have not been reticent about supporting military operations in Kosovo and Somalia when a Democrat sat as president. It is possible, on the other hand, that the Iraq War represents a new level of partisan difference over the use of force (Jacobson 2007), but any change appears to be one of degree rather than kind. Republicans tended to be more supportive of the mission in Lebanon than Democrats, while Democrats were more supportive of the conflict in Kosovo. Discussion of the current war with Iraq may be more bitter in its partisan rhetoric than any conflict since Vietnam, but the pattern of public support appears to remain similar.

Age, Education, and *Non-Religious* all have a significant impact on support for security goals. An increase in *Age* is associated with a decrease in *Security*. The more educated are also less likely to report supporting the use of force for traditional security goals. Those who are *Non-Religious* are less supportive of using force.[5] We can only speculate as to the reasons for these demographic effects. For example, we suspect that those who are *Non-Religious* are simply more likely to hold liberal political views—that this is part of a bundle of attitudes that reflect liberalism in a broad sense.[6] Older and more educated respondents may be less supportive of using force because they may be skeptical of the efficacy of the military force for achieving the stated objectives. Fleshing out these causal mechanisms, however, would be an interesting topic for future work.

When we examine the *Humanitarian* dimension, *Party Identification* is again negatively signed, showing that as one's political leanings become less Republican and more Democratic, one becomes less likely to support

[5] The term *nonreligious* may be slightly misleading here. Rather than measuring religiosity per se, it more appropriately captures people who do not report participating in mainstream organized churches. The category lumps together both who say "other" or "none" when asked about their religious preference. There are few attitudinal differences between the two groups, whereas both are significantly different from Protestants and Catholic on many attitudinal measures. For this reason, they are combined here. In self-reported worhip attendance, Jews fall about halfway between "other" and "none."

[6] We doubt that there is something inherent in being religious that causes one to support force. However, research into "right-wing authoritarianism" (Altemeyer 1996) finds support for an attitude bundle of aggression and conventionalism that is an analog to what we are proposing for the *Non-Religious* and liberal political beliefs.

a *Humanitarian* mission. While still negatively signed, the coefficient is much closer to zero in the *Humanitarian* model than in the *Security* model. Nonetheless, Democrats appear to be less likely to support using military force across the board. The same result holds true for older respondents and for those who are not religious. The coefficients for each of these variables are significant and negative—but their effects are substantively smaller than their impact on *Security*. Education does not have a significant impact on support for humanitarian missions. Thus overall, we can see that the same set of predictors does a poorer job explaining variation in *Humanitarian* than it does *Security.*

The basic demographic model does a relatively good job, on the other hand, explaining individual-level casualty tolerance. Six out of the nine explanatory variables reach statistical significance. As expected, *Party Identification* is significant and negatively signed, meaning that Democrats are less apt to tolerate casualties than are Republicans. We suspect that the same causal mechanism of being willing to pay greater costs in support of "our" leader's mission is the most likely explanation of this pattern. The *Non-Religious* indicator variable is significant, just as it was with *Security* and *Humanitarian*. Three different dummy variables—*Sex*, *Black*, and *Catholic*—are significant for casualty tolerance even though none was significant as a predictor for either *Security* or *Humanitarian.*

Interestingly, women have lower casualty tolerance, on average, than men, even though there is no effect from sex in predicting attitudes about using force. This is consistent with previous work in this area and suggests a greater sensitivity to the specific human costs of war per se—perhaps because of traditional gender roles—rather than a broader skepticism about the military or the efficacy of force. We find that *Blacks* tolerate fewer casualties than non-blacks. The specific causal mechanism here is not entirely clear, however, it seems plausible that fears among African American respondents that their community will be asked to bear a disproportionate burden in terms of combat deaths may be the reason for this difference. Since the advent of the all-volunteer force in 1973, African Americans have been disproportionately likely to volunteer for military service. The available data suggest that Aftrican American soldiers are not at disproportionate risk of death in combat (Gifford 2005), but their substantial presence in the military may suggest a greater bearing of the overall burden.[7] We continue to find that the *Non-Religious* have

[7]Interestingly, Gifford (2005) finds that Hispanics are at greater risk of suffering combat deaths due to their high rates of volunteering for the military, and high rates of volunteering for the Marines and for special operations forces. We do not find any evidence that this has influenced Hispanic attitudes toward the use of force. There are, however, only sixty-eight Hispanic respondents in our October 2003 survey.

lower casualty tolerance. This may be due both to their overall "liberal" predisposition and to the fact that they are less likely to support the use of force regardless of costs. Interestingly, *Catholics* have lower levels of casualty tolerance than other Christians. We suspect that this result for *Catholics* may be less about general political attitudes and more related to beliefs associated with Catholic teachings on the sanctity of life and the strong, near-pacificist strain in U.S. Catholic teachings. Questions that specifically tap into attitudes about tolerance for death may call these teachings to mind among Catholics more strongly than do general questions about the use of force.

Age is also a significant predictor of casualty tolerance; older respondents are less willing to tolerate casualties than younger ones. This result is interesting because older respondents have lived through at least one (and often multiple) conflicts where the United States experienced very high levels of casualties (e.g., World War II, Korea, and Vietnam). Younger respondents, however, have been exposed only to conflicts and military operations with very low numbers of U.S. casualties. With this in mind, one might expect that age would be a significant, but positively signed, predictor—meaning that older respondents are more apt to accept a high number of casualties. However, it may be that older respondents, having lived through the amazing technological advances in warfare over the past sixty years, now simply expect those advances to keep American soldiers from harm. Or, it could even be that the more distant and bloodier wars, World War II especially, were perceived to be of much greater importance. Whatever one's opinion of the war in Iraq, it was hard to equate it in importance with stopping the Nazis and striking back at Japan.

Matching Casualty Tolerance to War Support

We believe the data analysis clearly shows that there is an important underlying structure to two related yet distinct attitudes: support for the use of force and willingness to tolerate the human costs that attend the use of force. These attitudes are obviously related. The measures for the scenarios correlate with one another at about 0.45. At some level, those more willing to support force are, on average, also willing to tolerate a greater number of casualties. In theory, at least, the attitudes are also distinct. Person A could support nearly all possible uses of force as long as there are few to no casualties, and quickly come to oppose missions that suffer even moderate human costs. Person B, however, may generally oppose the use of the force. Opposition to using force is not sensitive to casualties, in that this person either opposes force regardless of cost or supports it regardless of cost. So, when Person B is willing to support a mission, that support

TABLE 3.7.
(Mis)Matching Casualty Tolerance and Support for Using Force

	Support for military force quartile			
Casualty tolerance quartile	*1st quartile (lowest support)*	*2nd quartile*	*3rd quartile*	*4th quartile (highest support)*
1st quartile (lowest casualty tolerance)	127 12%	67 6%	35 3%	23 2%
2nd quartile	67 6%	91 8%	61 6%	75 7%
3rd quartile	40 7%	58 5%	81 7%	94 9%
4th quartile (highest casualty tolerance)	24 2%	51 5%	75 7%	125 11%

comes with a blank check in terms of the human cost. The analytical challenge is to assess how related and how distinct these two attitudes are.

In comparing support for force and casualty tolerance, we see that there are more than a few "mismatched" respondents—those who support force but do not express a willingness to tolerate casualties, and those who say they oppose force but then are willing to accept significant casualties in the hypothetical missions. To examine these groups more closely, we divide the sample into quartiles for *Security* and *Casualty Tolerance.* Table 3.7 shows how many people are in each of the possible sixteen categories.[8]

The cells that are bolded represent the categories that we consider "mismatched." Those in the upper-right corner support force, but do not indicate a willingness to tolerate casualties in specific missions. We shall label these respondents "timid hawks" since they express a willingness to use force in the abstract but a reluctance to pay the costs of force in specific scenarios. In the lower-left corner are the respondents who do not

[8]Instead of the factor analysis estimates from table 3.2, we use a single scale from all questions answered about general goals for the use of force so that we can minimize the missing data that results from using case-wise deletion for the factor analysis. Breaking the sample into quartiles from the factor analysis correlates with breaking the scale into quartiles at .89. In the multivariate work that follows, we use the factor scores because we want to use the additional information that comes from identifying multiple dimensions of support for force. Retaining the extra cases as we do in table 3.7 comes at the cost of retaining measures for multiple dimensions of support for force. For the purposes of this table, however, we are not interested in distinguishing among dimensions of support for using force, and so retaining the extra cases seems worth it.

indicate that they are willing to support the use of force generally, but do indicate that they are willing to accept casualties in specific missions. We shall label these respondents as "reluctant hawks" since they express little support for using force in the abstract but are express a willingness to pay the costs of war when presented with a concrete scenario. After taking account of respondents who are excluded from the analysis because of missing data, approximately 20 percent of the sample falls into one of these mismatched categories (roughly 10 percent in each type of mismatch). Some subtle but important differences emerge when we look at a demographic analysis of the non-mismatched and the mismatched.

We would not necessarily expect the same factors to influence the tendency to be a casualty-phobic hawk as would influence the tendency to be a reluctant hawk. Thus we analyze these "mismatched" respondents through the use of multinomial logit analysis. This model simultaneously analyzes the impact that the same set of variables has on the likelihood of falling into each of the mismatched categories. Thus in this instance, our multinomial logit analysis yields two sets of coefficients. The first set of coefficients describes the likelihood of falling into the "timid" hawk category as compared to the non-mismatched category, and the second set describes the likelihood of falling into the "reluctant hawk" category as compared to the non-mismatched category.

The results in table 3.8 yield relatively few strong and consistent patterns, but the model appears to describe the "timid hawk" phenomenon more clearly than the "reluctant hawks." Women, African Americans, and Hispanics tend to be more likely to fall into the "timid hawk" category, as do younger respondents and less-educated respondents. Few of those variables, however, have much impact on determining which respondents are "reluctant hawks." Only age appears to have a consistent impact: older respondents are more likely to be "reluctant hawks." None of the other variables from the "timid hawk" analyses is significant here. Instead, we find that Catholics are less likely to be reluctant hawks—perhaps because of their overall aversion to casualties. The only other variables that approach statistical significance are party identification and military service. Specifically, we find that Republicans are more likely to be "reluctant hawks" than Democrats and veterans are more likely to be "reluctant hawks" than non-veterans, but both of these tendencies are of marginal statistical significance.

War Support as a Cause of Casualty Tolerance

Thus far, we have discussed the general levels of public support for security humanitarian military missions as well as the demographic antecedents of those attitudes. We have also identified the attitude of "casu-

Table 3.8.
Multinomial Logit Analysis of the Mismatch between War Support and Casualty Tolerance

	Timid hawks	*Reluctant hawks*
Sex	0.723	–0.181
	(3.29)**	(0.81)
Age in decades	–0.105	0.150
	(1.67)	(2.40)*
Education	–0.308	0.127
	(3.41)**	(1.37)
Party ID	0.049	–0.087
	(0.67)	(1.18)
Black	0.784	–0.880
	(2.57)*	(1.44)
Hispanic	0.859	0.027
	(2.54)*	(0.05)
Catholic	0.280	–0.630
	(1.14)	(2.07)*
Non-religious	–0.294	–0.030
	(1.13)	(0.12)
Military service	–0.291	–0.456
	(0.83)	(1.59)
Constant	–1.784	–1.085
	(2.57)*	(1.87)
Observations	1019	1019

Absolute value of z statistics in parentheses
* significant at 5% ** significant at 1%
Note: Excluded category for multinomial logit is no mismatch.

alty tolerance" as a critical attitude in determining the public's willingness to continue to support an ongoing military mission, and we have described the demographic antecedents of that attitude. Finally, we have demonstrated that instances of abstract support for military missions and casualty tolerance in more concrete scenarios appear to be related to one another, but do not involve identical concepts. Thus we now turn our attention to the extent to which abstract "war support" may be a cause of casualty tolerance even after accounting for these demographic effects. Establishing causal relationships among attitudes is inevitably a difficult and inexact task—especially when coping with cross-sectional survey data.

Nonetheless, we believe that it is reasonable to posit that our *Security* and *Humanitarian* dimensions of "war support" may cause casualty tolerance in the more specific scenarios with which we present respondents. Drawing upon Hurwitz and Peffley (1987), we expect that more specific attitudes about foreign policy questions—such as the casualty scenarios that we posit—will be determined by broader attitudes about the use of military force. Thus in the analyses that follow, we examine the extent to which our measures of support for security and humanitarian missions influence our overall measure of casualty tolerance and influence casualty tolerance in particular scenarios. Once again, in our measures of support for security and humanitarian missions we use the rotated factor scores.[9]

The first column of table 3.9 displays the impact of *Security* and *Humanitarian* on respondents' overall level of casualty tolerance—along with the demographic factors discussed earlier. Clearly, the two general attitudes about the use of force have a significant impact on overall casualty tolerance. Interestingly, these attitudes about force appear to have a very similar substantive impact on casualty tolerance. This result makes sense since the overall casualty tolerance measure is made up of responses to casualty scenarios that are both security oriented and humanitarian in nature. It is an important result, however, because the factor scores for our *Humanitarian* dimension were determined after identifying respondents' scores on the first dimension: *Security*. The eigenvalue for our *Humanitarian* factor was much lower than for *Security*, raising some concerns about whether two underlying dimensions of attitudes toward the use of force really exist. The fact that the *Humanitarian* dimension seems to influence more policy-specific attitudes about casualty tolerance, however, suggests that the second dimension that we identified in table 3.2 has some substantive impact.

The demographic effects from table 3.6 also remain almost entirely unchanged in this analysis. Only the impact of age disappears once we account for the two general dimensions of war support. Women, Democrats,

[9] Recall that when we were choosing which set of factor analysis results to use, we made the argument that rotated factors were a better choice because (1) they more clearly exhibited the structure we expected to see a priori, and (2) estimates for *Security* and *Humanitarian* showed a modest correlation suggesting that there is some overlap in attitudes about using force for security and humanitarian missions. When we include *Security* as a predictor for *Humanitarian* to account for this overlapping variance, *Security* is significant and all variables except *Education*, including *Party ID*, wash out and are nonsignificant. We bring up the topic of whether we use the rotated or unrotated factors because our results are sensitive to these modeling choices. The magnitude and direction of the coefficient for *Party ID* is sensitive to which set of scores we use for *Humanitarian*. With the unrotated factors, *Party ID* is significant, but it is positive rather than negative (the more Democratic one's identification, the greater the support for humanitarian-type missions). We are more confident in the results of the rotated factors.

TABLE 3.9.
Attitudes toward Security and Humanitarian Missions as a Cause of Casualty Tolerance

	Casualty tolerance	*Iran*	*South Korea*	*Congo*
Sex	–0.304 (6.38)**	–0.045 (0.38)	–1.038 (8.74)**	–0.333 (2.87)**
Age (decades)	–0.001 (0.08)	–0.084 (2.32)*	0.031 (0.90)	–0.036 (1.02)
Education	0.037 (1.84)	–0.049 (0.97)	0.177 (3.64)**	0.143 (2.92)**
Party ID	–0.136 (7.96)**	–0.374 (8.56)**	–0.206 (4.97)**	–0.032 (0.77)
Black	–0.231 (2.66)**	–0.211 (0.98)	–0.595 (2.76)**	–0.174 (0.81)
Hispanic	–0.092 (0.93)	0.135 (0.56)	–0.534 (2.20)*	0.146 (0.64)
Catholic	–0.122 (2.08)*	–0.256 (1.79)	–0.229 (1.64)	–0.256 (1.80)
Non-religious	–0.104 (1.84)	–0.136 (0.95)	–0.154 (1.11)	–0.093 (0.68)
Military Service	–0.065 (0.89)	–0.152 (0.84)	–0.337 (1.87)	–0.058 (0.32)
Security	0.254 (8.03)**	1.232 (13.01)**	0.368 (4.65)**	0.238 (3.05)**
Humanitarian	0.222 (5.58)**	0.076 (0.74)	0.536 (5.29)**	0.947 (9.21)**
Constant	0.760 (5.02)**	—	—	—
Observations	1019	1075	1074	1074
R-squared	0.30	—	—	—

Absolute value of *t* statistics in parentheses
* significant at 5% ** significant at 1%
Note: Analysis of overall casualty tolerance is a regression analysis. Analyses of specific scenarios are ordinal logit analyses because of the ordinal nature of those variables.

African Americans, Catholics, and the non-religious remain less tolerant of casualties. Education continues to have a positive impact on casualty tolerance. The stability of these demographic effects suggest that the attitudes measured by *Security* and *Humanitarian* appear to be capturing aspects of casualty tolerance that are not well described by demographic categories. The insignificance of age in this model, on the other hand, does not indicate that age has no impact on casualty tolerance. Instead, it suggests that the relationship we observed between age and casualty tolerance in table 3.6 is probably due to older respondents being generally more supportive of using force for security or humanitarian missions.

In columns 2 to 4 of table 3.9 we break down our analysis of casualty tolerance by separating the three hypothetical scenarios with which we presented respondents: South Korea, Iran, and the Congo. Our South Korea scenario asked respondents about how many casualties they would tolerate to defend South Korea against an invasion by North Korea, while our Iran question asked about tolerance for casualties to eliminate Iran's nuclear weapons program. The question about the Congo, on the other hand, asked respondents about their tolerance for casualties to take military action to stop government-created starvation in Congo. Both common sense and the factor analyses described in table 3.2 suggest that the South Korea and Iran missions qualify as "security" oriented, while the Congo mission is most aptly described as a "humanitarian" use of force. We would like to investigate whether the distinctions that we drew regarding *Security* and *Humanitarian* dimensions of support for the use of force have any empirical weight when it comes to determining attitudes toward specific military operations.

As we noted earlier, our *Humanitarian* factor does appear to correlate with overall casualty tolerance. But is this dimension really measuring support for humanitarian missions? If the distinction we draw between security and humanitarian uses of military force has empirical weight, then we would expect that respondents' attitudes toward the hypothetical military operations in Korea and Iran would be more heavily influenced by their support for military action toward security-oriented goals, while their support for using force in Congo would be more strongly influenced by their willingness to support force for humanitarian purposes. In particular, given the factor loadings in table 3.2, we would expect the Iran scenario to be most heavily influenced by security attitudes because our question about WMD loaded so strongly on the *Security* dimension. We would expect the South Korea scenario to be influenced by both attitudes, but primarily security. Our "defense of allies" and "promotion of democracy" items both loaded more strongly on the *Security* dimension, but the gap between the two dimensions was not as large. Finally, casualty tolerance for the Congo mission should be more heavily influenced by humanitarian attitudes, because our questions about human rights and ethnic cleansing clearly loaded more strongly on the *Humanitarian* dimension. If on the other hand, our distinction between the *Security* and *Humanitarian* dimensions of the use of force is a false one, and if there is only one dimension of attitudes toward the use of force, then we should see our *Security* factor dominate these analyses. Finally, if both measures are capturing some generalized support for using force, then we should see relatively similar coefficients for the two dimensions across all three scenarios.

Our results are strongly consistent with our expectations both regarding the linkage between general attitudes toward force and casualty tolerance for specific operations and regarding the substantive distinction between security and humanitarian missions. With regard to Iran, we find that respondents' attitudes toward security-oriented missions have a significant impact on their tolerance for casualties in eliminating Iranian WMD. Attitudes toward humanitarian missions, on the other hand, have no significant impact. Casualty tolerance in the defense of South Korea is driven both by attitudes toward security missions and humanitarian ones. While we expected a somewhat mixed result for this scenario, the strength of the humanitarian attitudes here is somewhat surprising. Finally, with regard to the Congo, we find that humanitarian attitudes have a much more substantial impact on casualty tolerance. While both the *Security* and *Humanitarian* dimensions are statistically significant in this analysis, the coefficient for humanitarianism is more than three times as large as the security coefficient.

To judge the substantive size of the effects described in table 3.9, we estimated the impact of changes in support for security and humanitarian missions on casualty tolerance for the South Korea, Iran, and Congo missions. As noted previously, casualty tolerance regarding the Iran mission is dominated by attitudes toward security-oriented missions. Specifically, increasing a respondent's support for security-oriented missions from the 10th to the 90th percentile decreases the probability that he or she will oppose the mission entirely by 42 percent and decreases the likelihood of tolerating less than fifty casualties by 13 percent. The probability that such a respondent would tolerate at least between fifty and five hundred casualties remains virtually unchanged, while the likelihood that he or she would tolerate at least five hundred casualties would increase by a striking 55 percent. A similar increase in such a respondent's support for humanitarian missions from the 10th to the 90th percentile, on the other hand, only decreases the probability of opposing force to eliminate Iranian WMD by 2 percent. Their likelihood of tolerating less than fifty for such a mission decreases by 1 percent and their probability of tolerating fifty to five hundred casualties remains unchanged. The likelihood that they will tolerate at least five hundred casualties does increase, but only by 3 percent.

Casualty tolerance for a hypothetical American intervention in the Congo to prevent starvation in that country, on the other hand, is more substantially influenced by general attitudes toward humanitarian missions. In this case an increase in a respondent's support for humanitarian uses of force from the 10th to the 90th percentile decreases the probability that he or she will oppose the Congo mission regardless of casualties by 21 percent. The probability that such a respondent will tolerate less than fifty casualties for this mission decreases by 12 percent, while the probability that he or she will tolerate at least fifty to five hundred casualties increases slightly by 3 percent. The probability that such a respondent will tolerate at least five hundred casualties, however, increases by nearly 31 percent. That is, the probability that a respondent whose support for using force in humanitarian missions is in the 10th percentile will tolerate at least five hundred casualties to prevent starvation in the Congo is approximately 18 percent. The probability that a respondent who scores similarly on the other variables in our model but whose support for humanitarian military missions is in the 90th percentile will tolerate at least five hundred casualties is just over 48 percent.

Attitudes toward security-oriented missions, on the other hand, have a much less substantial impact on casualty tolerance for the Congo mission. In this case, a shift from the 10th to the 90th percentile decreases the probability of opposing the mission entirely by a modest 7 percent, and reduces the probability of tolerating less than fifty casualties by 4 percent. The probability of tolerating at least fifty to five hundred casualties edges up by 1 percent and the probability of tolerating at least five hundred casualties increases by about 10 percent. The predominance of humanitarian attitudes in this analysis supports our earlier contention that public attitudes toward the use of force are arrayed along at least two distinct substantive dimensions. Not only do the factor analyses suggest the presence of a *Humanitarian* dimension to public attitudes, but also our estimates of this underlying dimension have a significant impact on policy-related questions about humanitarian intervention.

As we noted earlier, casualty tolerance regarding the defense of South Korea is related to both security and humanitarian attitudes toward using force. This mission generated the highest level of casualty tolerance of the three scenarios—perhaps because it involved a response to the most blatant disturbance of the international status quo or because South Korea is such a long-standing American ally. Thus the effects of changing general attitudes toward the use of force were observed at higher levels of casualty tolerance for this scenario. Specifically, a change in a respondent's support for security-oriented missions from the 10th to the 90th percentile increased the probability that a respondent would tolerate as many as five thousand U.S. casualties by approximately 19 percent, while a similar increase in support for humanitarian uses of force increases the probability of tolerating five thousand casualties in Korea by about 20 percent.

Summarizing Attitudes about Casualty Tolerance and the Use of Force

In this chapter, we have identified three key variables: a general propensity to support the use of force for security-related goals, a general propensity to support force for humanitarian missions, and a measurement of casualty tolerance at the individual level. Through a number of statistical models, we have shown that the public has constructed these attitudes in sensible ways, suggesting that our respondents have relatively coherent foreign policy belief systems. Moreover, we have been able to show that general orientations toward foreign policy and the use of force are important in shaping the public's thinking about specific foreign policy events and their willingness to pay costs in order to achieve various foreign policy goals. Our demonstration that these dimensions of public attitudes operate in expected ways improves our confidence in the validity of the measures and their utility in understanding the determinants of public responses to specific military conflicts. In the next chapter, we use these attitudes as additional predictors in a series experiments designed to test a number of the theories presented in chapter 1 regarding the sources of support for American military operations.

Chapter Four

EXPERIMENTAL EVIDENCE ON ATTITUDES TOWARD MILITARY CONFLICT

IN THIS CHAPTER, we use a series of experiments embedded into our survey to test various causal claims about support for military action and the tolerance of casualties. The experiments examine the most prominent causal mechanisms posited by the scholarly literature summarized in chapter 1. Previous research has largely sought to test those competing arguments through the analysis of the available aggregate survey data on U.S. military operations—an approach that we used in chapter 2. In chapter 3, however, we argued that such a research design is limited both by a lack of data and by difficult problems of inference. We went on to demonstrate that such questions can be evaluated effectively at the individual level because Americans can and do organize their attitudes toward the use of military force in sensible ways that are amenable to measurement and testing. In this chapter, we begin testing these arguments through a set of survey experiments asking respondents about their approval of hypothetical military missions. In each of these experiments, respondents are randomly assigned to different information conditions, such as different combinations of support from political elites or different goals for the military missions. We can then compare the responses among subjects in the various conditions to infer the causal significance of different aspects of support for the use of military force. One must, of course, be careful in extrapolating the results of such hypothetical experiments to real-world behavior, and we begin to undertake that task in chapter 5. Nonetheless, these experiments are ideal for demonstrating causal influences that can only be suggestively observed from the aggregate data presented in chapter 2.

EXPERIMENTAL EVIDENCE ON SUPPORT FOR MILITARY MISSIONS

Our first experiment tests the claim of the "pretty prudent public" and the principal policy objective (PPO) (Jentleson 1992; Jentleson and Britton 1998, Eichenberg 2005). The second experiment tests claims made about the importance of domestic and international elite messages (Larson 1996, 2000; Kull and Destler 1999) for the public to support the use of force. Finally, we use a unique survey experiment to test claims made by Feaver and Gelpi (2004) and Eichenberg (2005) that confidence in victory is an important variable explaining public support for military missions. This experiment compares the impact of expectations of success to the impact of casualties that is emphasized by other scholars (Mueller 1971, 1973, 2005; Luttwak 1995; Klarevas 2000).

Because these explanations are not mutually exclusive, it is theoretically possible that all are correct (or incorrect). In fact, these survey experiments do show that all of these causal mechanisms matter: mission objective, elite consensus, confidence in victory, as well as death toll. Thus the next step to advance the debate will be to assess which of these mechanisms explains the most about support in the context of a real-world mission. Although our sample size is relatively large for a national sample of adults (n = 1203), the sample is not large enough for a factorial experiment design that could directly evaluate the relative contribution of each construct while controlling for the others. As a consequence, we were not able to use factor analysis to compare directly the effects of these different explanations on these hypothetical questions. Using other forms of multivariate analyses, however,we are able to make direct comparisons.

In chapter 3 we argued that the concept of "casualty tolerance" was the most theoretically and politically useful measure of "war support" because it most directly relates to the trade-off facing most Americans as they decide whether to support an ongoing conflict. We continue to believe that casualty tolerance is critical to understanding public pressure to withdraw from ongoing conflicts, and so we will return to this concept as our dependent variable in chapter 5 as we analyze public support for the Iraq War. In this chapter, however, we focus on hypothetical missions that have not yet occurred, and so measures of ex ante "approval" or "disapproval" of the use of force are more appropriate than they would be in the context of an ongoing conflict. While we could measure casualty tolerance for each of these hypothetical missions, constructing the ordinal casualty-tolerance measure developed in chapter 3 would add a large number of questions to the battery required for each experiment. Thus in these experiments we focus on ex ante approval or disapproval as a way of maximizing the number of substantive questions and experiments that we could fit into a telephone survey without drastically reducing our response rate.

The data for these experiments was gathered during the same survey that was used in chapter 3 to construct our measures of casualty tolerance and to measure the security and humanitarian dimensions of support for the use of force. This survey was conducted via telephone by the Parker

Group, between 22 September and 12 October 2004 and yielded a total of 1,203 respondents. The complete text of the survey instrument is available from the authors.

Changing the Primary Policy Objective

Bruce Jentleson has argued that when it comes to supporting the use of force, citizens base their decision, at least in part, on the mission objective, or what he calls the primary policy objective (PPO) (Jentleson 1992; Jentleson and Britton 1998; Eichenberg 2005). While Jentleson has observed this pattern at the aggregate level, the likely individual-level causal mechanism creating this variation in casualty tolerance is that individuals may vary in the extent to which they think accomplishing different kinds of missions are "worth it" in terms of the likely human cost. That is, underlying Jentleson's aggregate data is an assumption about how individuals assess the benefits of accomplishing various kinds of missions.

To test Jentleson's claims about a "pretty prudent public" that rationally responds to mission objectives, we employed a survey experiment with three different treatments. These three treatments are designed to test two of Jentleson's original PPOs, foreign policy restraint (*FPR*) and humanitarian intervention (*HI*) and an important new policy objective for the post–9/11 world—support for the war on terror (*WT*). These three experimental conditions were embedded in a hypothetical question about supporting the use of force against the government of Yemen. We chose Yemen as the target of intervention because it is a country that is sufficiently obscure that most respondents would have had few predetermined attitudes about it. At the same time, respondents who were more politically aware would have recognized it as a real country and thus may have been less likely to dismiss the scenario as unrealistic. Moreover, Yemen provided a variety of plausible reasons for intervention, which lends itself to our PPO experiment. The *FPR* condition asked respondents if they would support a mission against the government of Yemen if that country were threatening the shipping of oil through the Persian Gulf. The *HI* condition was tested by asking support for a mission against the government of Yemen to stop ethnic cleansing and forced slavery. Finally, we tested the *WT* condition by asking support for a mission if Yemen provided safe haven to Al-Qaeda terrorist bases.

We display the levels of support for using force against Yemen for these various reasons in table 4.1. We code support on the basis of a four-point Likert scale ranging from "strongly approve" (4) to "strongly disapprove" (1). These responses strongly indicate that the military mission's objective influences levels of support, but our results do not strictly conform to

TABLE 4.1.
Support for Military Intervention in Yemen Depending on Policy Objective

	FPR mission: Protect oil	*HI mission: Ethnic cleansing*	*WT mission: Terrorist bases*
Strongly approve	83 21%	134 36%	166 45%
Somewhat approve	101 26%	92 25%	93 25%
Somewhat disapprove	75 19%	66 18%	48 13%
Strongly disapprove	129 33%	80 22%	60 16%
Total	388	372	367

Jentleson's ranking of support by objective. We had no formal a priori hypothesis about the effect of *WT* relative to the other objectives, since Jentleson does not address these kinds of missions. Given the prominent concern over terrorism in America since the attacks of 11 September 2001, however, we did expect to see high support. This expectation was confirmed—the *WT* condition had the highest levels of support of the three experimental treatments with 70 percent of our respondents either approving or strongly approving the use of force. With regard to the other two missions, Jentleson argues that the *FPR* mission would engender more support than the *HI* mission. Our experiment, however, shows significantly higher support for an *HI* mission (stopping the government of Yemen from engaging in ethnic cleansing and forced slavery) than for the *FPR* condition (threatening the shipping of oil). Specifically, we found that 60 percent of our respondents supported using force to stop ethnic cleansing in Yemen, but only 47 percent approved of using force to protect access to Persian Gulf oil.

Next, in an effort to investigate what causes these experimental conditions to generate such varying levels of support, we performed a statistical analysis of these responses using ordered logit; the results are shown in table 4.2. We begin, of course, by specifying dummy variables that identify each of the experimental conditions. In addition, we sought to examine whether our measures of general support for security-oriented and humanitarian military missions (developed in chapter 3) influenced support for these specific scenarios. In particular, if respondents are arranging their attitudes in the relatively nuanced manner that we suggest, then the relative importance of these different dimensions should shift across the differing experimental scenarios. Finally, along with a set of demographic controls, we included two more variables that were specific to the Yemen scenario. First, we asked respondents how many casualties they expected U.S. forces to suffer during such a mission in order to see whether expectations of casualties might influence support. Second, we asked respondents about their perceptions of the likelihood that the United States would be successful in such a mission. This measure draws upon Feaver and Gelpi's (2004; see also Eichenberg 2005) argument that expectations of success are the most significant determinant of support for military operations. Jentleson's causal mechanism focuses on whether respondents think the benefits from accomplishing a mission are important, while Feaver and Gelpi emphasize the extent to which individuals believe that the potential benefits of the mission—whatever they might be—will actually be achieved. The inclusion of this variable will allow us to compare the influence of PPO and expectations of success. That is, we can begin to compare the influence of the benefits of success to the probability of achieving those benefits.

Table 4.2 presents one set of results in two separate ways. The first column presents the results for the full sample, while columns 2 to 4 present the results separately for each experimental condition. The analysis of the overall sample shows us the net impact of the treatment conditions, while analyzing the treatment categories separately assesses Jentleson's causal mechanism, which is essentially a framing argument about how respondents construct their attitudes toward a mission.

Somewhat surprisingly, demographic variables, including *Party ID,* are not significant as a whole or in any of the three conditions. This result is especially surprising in light of the partisan effects that we observe in our next experiment and in light of the highly partisan divide over the current Iraq War. It suggests—consistent with many of the results in chapter 2—that military conflict is still not necessarily a partisan issue unless citizens are cued to think of the conflict in those terms.

At any rate, after accounting for other factors, the first column of results indicates that all three of the experimental conditions are statistically significant. The coefficients for the *HI* and *FPR* dummy variables are negative and statistically significant, demonstrating that each of these conditions generates less support than the *WT* mission. Moreover, a chi-squared test reveals that the *HI* and *FPR* conditions are significantly different (38.78, 1 d.f., $p < .00$). Both the *Security* and *Humanitarian* dimensions of support for using force are significant and appear to have similar substantive effects, although we expect these coefficients to vary by treatment category.

Consistent with Feaver and Gelpi (2004) and Eichenberg (2005), expectations of the likely success of the mission also have a statistically

TABLE 4.2.
Logit Analyses of Support for Intervention in Yemen

	PPO treatments	*FPR PPO*	*HI PPO*	*WT PPO*	*Interactions*
HI dummy	–0.230 (2.52)*				–0.235 (2.58)**
FPR dummy	–0.787 (8.60)**				–0.818 (8.82)**
Sex	–0.027 (0.36)	–0.091 (0.71)	0.104 (0.80)	–0.054 (0.39)	–0.025 (0.34)
Age	–0.022 (0.97)	0.025 (0.62)	–0.050 (1.24)	–0.038 (0.95)	–0.024 (1.07)
Party ID	–0.009 (0.32)	–0.023 (0.50)	0.011 (0.23)	–0.015 (0.31)	–0.010 (0.36)
Education	0.026 (0.81)	0.018 (0.32)	0.041 (0.75)	0.001 (0.02)	0.021 (0.64)
Security	0.406 (7.63)**	0.619 (6.36)**	0.193 (2.13)*	0.495 (5.25)**	0.502 (5.66)**
Humanitarian	0.343 (5.14)**	0.121 (1.00)	0.568 (5.02)**	0.337 (2.88)**	0.337 (2.91)**
Exp. deaths	0.084 (2.43)*	0.010 (0.18)	0.129 (2.14)*	0.098 (1.47)	0.082 (2.38)*
Exp. success	0.411 (8.12)**	0.536 (6.10)**	0.335 (3.76)**	0.375 (4.02)**	0.415 (8.15)**
FPR * *Security*					0.116 (0.93)
HI * *Security*					–0.351 (2.98)**
FPR * *Human*					–0.240 (1.44)
HI * *Human*					0.224 (1.40)
Observations	965	329	322	314	965

Absolute value of *z* statistics in parentheses
* significant at 5% ** significant at 1%

significant impact on support for intervention. In fact, the impact of expectations of success is greater than the impact of *Security*, *Humanitarian*, and even the experimental treatments. For example, changing a respondent's expectation success from "not at all likely" to "very likely" increases his or her probability of approval by more than 40 percent. Changing the respondent's support for security-oriented missions from the 10th to the 90th percentile, on the other hand, increases approval only by about 30 percent, and the same shift in support for humanitarian missions increases support by 20 percent. The 40 percent shift in approval caused by perceptions of success is even larger than the experimental treatment effects displayed in table 4.1.

The respondent's expectations regarding the number of casualties that would result from the conflict have a statistically significant but substantively modest impact on support for intervention. Unfortunately, the coefficient for this variable seems to be in the wrong direction! Contrary to our expectations, the positive coefficient indicated that respondents who stated that they expected a larger number of casualties tended to be more supportive of intervention. The mention of casualties within a survey question generally decreases support for the use of military force (Mueller 1994; Larson 1996; Feaver and Gelpi 2004). In this instance, however, our question about expected casualties was asked *after* the question about support for intervention. By asking the questions in this order we sought to measure respondents' support for the mission without cuing casualties. Then we asked about their expectations of casualties to see if those expectations matched up with their policy preference regarding intervention. We had some concern that those having expressed a preference for intervention might feel pressure to state that they did not expect casualties—creating a potential endogeneity problem. This concern, however, turned out to be unfounded. Those who supported the mission expected more casualties.

Another possible explanation of this result might be that the expected casualties variable is essentially noise. Respondents may have very little sense of how to form expectations about casualties and may guess wildly. In the aggregate, however, this did not seem to be true. Respondents could state that they expected 0 casualties, 1-50 casualties, 50-500 casualties, 500-5,000 casualties, 5,000 to 50,000 casualties or more than 50,000 casualties. The modal response was fifty to five hundred casualties (42 percent of respondents), with 20 percent choosing the categories both above and below that level. Approximately 13 percent stated that they expected zero casualties, while only about 5 percent stated that they expected more than five thousand casualties. Thus the responses showed some variation but generally appeared to be reasonable estimates of what the United States might experience in such a mission.

Finally, a closer look at the data suggests that the positive relationship between expected casualties and support is driven almost entirely by respondents who stated that they expected zero casualties. More than 40 percent of those who stated that they expected zero casualties had previously stated that they strongly opposed U.S. intervention in East Timor. This is much higher than the 15 percent of those who expected one to fifty or 18 percent of those who expected fifty to five hundred casualties. Moreover if we drop the zero-casualties respondents from the analysis, we find that the coefficient for expected casualties drops near zero and does not approach statistical significance. Thus we believe that the best interpretation of this coefficient is that expectations of casualties did not influence support for undertaking the mission.

It is important to note that this result does not imply that respondents will not respond to casualties once they occur. Wide-ranging sources of data from previous research indicates that—at least under some circumstances—the public does respond to the occurrence of U.S. casualties (see, for example, Mueller 1971, 1973; Larson 1996; Gartner and Segura 1998; Klarevas 2000; Feaver and Gelpi 2004; Eichenberg 2005; Gelpi, Feaver, and Reifler 2005/2006). Moreover, our result does not indicate that the public will not respond to the anticipation of casualties when the possibility is brought to their attention. Once again, extensive research suggests that cuing respondents about the possibility of casualties reduces their support for using force (Mueller 1994; Herrmann, Tetlock, and Visser 1999; Feaver and Gelpi 2004; Eichenberg 2005). Instead, our result here suggests that the anticipation of casualties does not influence public support for a military mission when the prospect of casualties is not specifically brought to the attention of respondents.

Next, we turn our attention to columns 2 through 4 to see how the sources of support vary depending on the goal of the mission. For the *FPR* condition, there are two significant predictors: *Security* and *Success*. These results strongly match our expectations. First, support for security-related missions remains statistically significant and the coefficient increases in substantive size. Support for humanitarian missions, on the other hand, is no longer significant and is drastically reduced in substantive importance. In addition to testing against the null hypothesis of no effect, we want to test the null hypothesis that *Humanitarian* and *Security* are not significantly different from one other. We find that the two are significantly different, chi-square (1) = 7.93 ($p < .01$), indicating that using a security-related justification for the mission causes respondents to draw on their general attitudes toward security missions in formulating their approval of this specific mission. Expectations of success remain statistically significant and substantively large. Expectations of casualties is no longer statistically significant, and its substantive impact remains modest.

For the *HI* condition, *Humanitarian* and expectations of success and expectations of casualties are significant while *Security* is not. Given the nature of this mission (intervention against ethnic cleansing and forced slavery), we are not surprised that *Humanitarian* has a stronger effect than *Security* variable. We are confident that the observed difference in effect between *Humanitarian* and *Security* is measuring a real difference and is not due to chance error (chi-square (1) = 7.87, $p < .01$). The impact of *Humanitarian* and expectations of success are roughly equal within this treatment. Changing expectations of success from "not very likely" to "very likely" and changing support for humanitarian missions from the 10th to 90th percentiles each increases approval by 30 to 35 percent. The impact of expected casualties, on the other hand, is much more modest. An increase in expected casualties from zero to five thousand reduces approval of the mission by 11 percent.

In the *WT* condition, both *Security* and *Humanitarian* are significant. *Security* has the larger coefficient, which is to be expected, given the nature of the mission in this condition. One should not, however, read too much into the difference, because it is not significant, (chi-square = 0.41, $p < .53$). Once again, expectations of success have an impact that is roughly equal to the larger of the *Security* and *Humanitarian* variables. In this case, shifts in *Security* and expectations of success each produces about a 40 percent shift in approval for the use of force. Expectations of casualties are significant once again in this treatment category, but their impact remains modest. An increase in expected casualties from zero to five thousand deaths still reduces approval of this *WT* mission by about 10 percent.

The substantial variation that we observed in support for intervention across experimental conditions is consistent with Jentleson's expectations that the perceived PPO has a significant impact on mission support. Moreover, the varying impact of support for humanitarian and security-oriented missions across experimental treatments may also shed light on causal mechanisms lying behind this effect. Specifically, respondents appear to rely upon the primary policy objective provided in the experimental treatment as a kind of frame for forming their attitudes toward the mission (Kinder and Iyengar 1987; Iyengar and Simon 1993; Berinsky and Kinder 2006). These frames alert respondents as to which kinds of attitudes they should draw upon in forming their support for this hypothetical mission. If the frame indicates humanitarian goals, then the respondents will refer to their attitudes toward humanitarianism in forming a response. Frames that referenced security objectives, on the other hand, would cue respondents to draw upon their attitudes toward security missions in formulating a response. The varying coefficients for security and humanitarian missions in columns 2 to 4 of table 4.2 suggest that the stated PPO acts as a frame, but we test this hypothesis directly by interacting the experimental treatment conditions with the humanitarian and security attitudes. This method provides a more direct test of the framing hypothesis by testing for difference in specific coefficients across treatments while holding other coefficients constant. Results of this analysis are displayed in column 5 of table 4.2.

We find strong interaction effects between the experimental conditions and the humanitarian and security attitudes. As with the previous analyses, we include dummy variables for the *HI* and *FPR* treatments and leave the *WT* treatment as the excluded category. Thus the coefficients for security and humanitarian in column 5 reflect the impact of these attitudes for the terrorism frame, and the interaction of these attitudes with the *HI* and *FPR* frames represents the difference in the coefficient for that variable between that frame and the *WT* frame. The interaction terms are generally of substantial size. The one exception is the interaction of the humanitarian with the *FPR* frame, indicating that the impact of humanitarian attitudes changes little across the *WT* and *FPR* frames. Although the interaction terms are all substantively large, they are not all statistically significant. This often occurs due to problems of colinearity with so many interaction terms. However, a likelihood ratio test reveals that the overall fit of the model with interaction effects is significantly better (20.28, 4 d.f., $p < .01$).

Table 4.3 displays the impact of the security and humanitarian attitudes across the three experimental treatments. Here we can see that the coefficient for *Security* changes from 0.49 ($p < .01$) in the *WT* scenario to 0.59 in the *FPR* scenario ($p < .01$) and then drops to 0.07 ($p < .40$) in the *HI* scenario. The impact of our *Humanitarian* measure, on the other hand, shifts from 0.32 ($p < 01$) in the *WT* scenario to 0.03 ($p < .83$) in the *FPR* scenario, and then up to 0.55 ($p < .01$) with the *HI* frame.

Overall, we find that Jentleson is correct that the public is sensitive to the "primary policy objective" of a mission. Our findings also suggest, however, the need for refining Jentleson's argument. First, our results are not consistent with Jentleson's ordinal ranking of which missions will engender the most support. In fact, while Jentleson's conclusion that the PPO influences public support for military missions appears robust, we see little reason to expect a particular rank ordering of missions among the public to remain robust over time. New types of missions and threats—such as the renewed prominence of terrorism since the 11 September attacks—make it likely that the public will periodically reevaluate the nature of American national interests. Moreover, policymakers may try to persuade the public that different kinds of missions are important, and their efforts may raise or lower the salience of certain issues in the public mind.

Second, our analyses suggest that PPO has an impact on public support through its influence as a frame for interpreting mission. That is, the stated mission PPO tells the public what attitudes to draw upon when

TABLE 4.3.
Impact of Security and Humanitarian Attitudes on Support for Military Intervention in Yemen Depending on Policy Objective

	Coefficient	*Standard error*	*Significance lvl.*
Support for security-oriented missions			
FPR treatment: Protect oil	0.62	0.09	0.00
HI treatment: Ethnic cleansing	0.15	0.08	0.08
WT treatment: Terrorist bases	0.50	0.09	0.00
Support for humanitarian missions			
FPR treatment: Protect oil	0.10	0.12	0.42
HI treatment: Ethnic cleansing	0.56	0.11	0.00
WT treatment: Terrorist bases	0.33	0.12	0.01

deciding whether to approve of a particular conflict. As a result, the effect of the PPO treatment is contingent on the preexisting attitudes within the public about different goals for the use of force. That is, different segments of the population will be moved to support different missions based on the mission objectives. This is an important inference, and one that simply could not have been made with aggregate-level data. The impact of PPOs as frames implies that changes in policy objectives may or may not shift aggregate levels of public support, depending upon the distribution of public support for various missions, and this distribution seems likely to shift over time.

Importantly, while we find strong framing effects with regard to the influence of a mission's PPO, we cannot say to what extent these frames are "objective" realities of the mission or are subject to influence by elite rhetoric. Our questions simply provide respondents with a frame, and they have no other information with which to construct an alternate frame. We cannot define what "objective" aspects of a mission would define its PPO, nor can we determine what flexibility elites have to redefine these realities. In our next experiment, we begin to investigate the impact of elite statements on support for military missions, but the flexibility of foreign policy frames remains an important and poorly understood question.

Finally, the impact of respondent's expectations regarding the likely number of casualties was surprisingly modest and of sometimes tenuous statistical significance. This held true even within the humanitarian intervention mission – where scholars such as Klarevas (2000) have argued that casualties should have their greatest impact on support. The perceived likelihood of success, on the other hand, has a substantial and significant impact on support across all of our experimental conditions. In fact, its impact is as large or larger than the experimental effects and the impact of *Security* and *Humanitarian* across all of our treatment conditions. We find the differing effects of the variables of interest across experimental conditions to be strong additional evidence of a "rational public" that is able to use available information to make judgments about foreign policy (that is, they make decisions that seem consistent with their preferences/attitudes). Whether those preferences lead to "prudent" choices is another matter, as such judgments will depend upon the wisdom of those preferences and the manipulability of the policy frames.

Elite Rhetoric and Casualty Tolerance

As we discussed in chapter 1, a number of prominent arguments about tolerance for casualties in warfare emphasize the role of elite rhetoric in shaping public opinion. Eric Larson (1996, 2000), for example, argues that opinion among the general public is driven by cues about whether domestic political leaders of both parties—especially those in Congress—support involvement in the conflict. When elites share a consensus in favor of a military mission, he argues, this translates into robust support among the general public, regardless of mounting costs. When elites sharply disagree among themselves, on the other hand, he expects that the general public will also be wary and that support will drop quickly with mounting costs. Kull and Destler (1999) share Larson's focus on elites, but they argue that cues from the international community—especially the United Nations, and other multilateral international organizations—are decisive. Both of these arguments are generally consistent with Zaller's (1992) perspective on the formation of public opinion, which places greatest emphasis on elite cues.

In addition to their differing domestic and international focus, Larson and Kull and Destler also specify different causal mechanisms for their theories. For Larson, elite consensus could affect public doubts. When consensus exists, the public may become more confident that the government will maintain its resolve to follow through with the mission, or they may generally feel reassured. When it doesn't exist, this causal mechanism results in confusion or wariness among the public, which would make them unwilling to tolerate costs. Viewed this way, Larson seems to argue that elite consensus affects perceptions of success. Kull and Destler, on the other hand, argue that international institutions such as the U.N.

and NATO provide a measure of legitimacy to American uses of military force. Much like Jentleson's argument about mission PPO, Kull and Destler seem to suggest that the public will view missions as more worthwhile if they have the stamp of multilateral approval.

Bringing Zaller's (1992) perspective more directly to bear on these arguments also raises the question of whether elite cues influence all members of the public equally or whether different individuals in the public cue off of different members of the elite. For example, suppose there are two movie-goers, whom we'll call Walker and Percy. Suppose further that there are two movie critics, whom we'll call Gene and Roger. We may observe that Walker and Percy attend (or "support") a movie if Gene and Roger both agree that it is worth it. Suppose still further, however, that Walker only listens to Gene's opinion and the Percy only listens to Roger's. If someone who didn't have this extra information saw the two at the movies, they might conclude that they went to see it because Gene and Roger *agreed* that the movie was good (that is, the existence of consensus was how Walker and Percy had formed their opinion), when it was simply that Walker received a signal that the movie was good from Gene and Percy received a similar signal from Roger.

Given its prominence as a cleavage for interpreting political communication, the most likely division for attending to elite cues would be party identification. If this were happening, then the presence of dissensus among the domestic elites would cause a partisan division within the general public as each member of the public follows the (now diverging) cues from the specific elite whom those members of the public most trust. Larson and Kull and Destler do not distinguish among these causal pathways because of their focus on aggregate data, but our use of elite cues within the context of an experiment provides us with an excellent opportunity both to test for the influence of elite cues and to test for whether these cues affect all respondents similarly, or whether their influence is mediated by political cleavages.

We test these questions on individual level-data using a survey experiment where our experimental treatments expose subjects to different levels of consensus among various foreign policy elites. These conditions are embedded within a hypothetical scenario of sending troops to East Timor in response to an Indonesian attack against the newly independent state. Because we are measuring the effect of elite consensus we wanted to choose a mission that would not overpower the elite cues in the experimental conditions. As with Yemen, we chose East Timor because it is obscure enough that respondents probably have few well-entrenched predispositions regarding that county, yet the plausibility of an actual incident of this type would prevent respondents with greater political information from dismissing the scenario as impossible.

TABLE 4.4.
Support for Intervention in East Timor Depending on Elite Cues

	All elites approve	*Domestic elites approve*	*International elites approve*	*Only the president approves*
Strongly approve	98 35%	47 19%	50 18%	30 11%
Somewhat approve	112 40%	56 22%	85 30%	35 13%
Somewhat disapprove	29 10%	58 23%	71 25%	63 24%
Strongly disapprove	43 15%	88 35%	76 27%	139 52%
Total	282	249	282	267

Our experimental treatment provided respondents with information about the views of three major elite groups regarding a potential intervention in East Timor: the views of the president, those of the U.N. Security Council and our NATO allies, and those of Democratic and Republican leaders of Congress. The baseline condition for analysis is one in which only the president supports a mission, while Congressional leadership of both parties, the U.N. Security Council, and NATO allies all oppose sending force (we refer to this condition as *President*). The president's views are constant across all the categories, since U.S. intervention is essentially a moot issue without presidential support. Other conditions include: all parties agree on the of force (*All*); president, U.N. Security Council, and NATO allies support while Congress opposes (*International*); and the president and Congress support, but the U.N. security council and NATO allies oppose (*Domestic*). Condition names can be used as a heuristic to see who supports a mission.

We expect that *All* will have the strongest support (imagine every critic liking the same movie). At the other end of the spectrum, we would expect *President* to have the lowest support. We are agnostic as to whether *International* or *Domestic* should have more support—Larson makes the case that domestic consensus should hold sway, while Kull and Destler argue that international consensus matters more.

Table 4.4 presents the level of support for intervention by treatment category, and these results strongly indicate that elite messages can influence support for intervention. As expected, the public has the most support for an East Timor mission when there is a unified message from elites (*All*) and shows the least support when the president supports a mission, but all other elites are opposed (*President*). The effects, however, are strikingly large. Nearly 75 percent of respondents support intervention in East Timor if the U.N. and NATO and Congress join in support, while only 25 percent support intervention if the president stands alone against the views of these other elites. Interestingly, the net impact of disapproval by Congress or by the U.N. and NATO appears to be about equal, with about 48 percent approving when the U.N. and NATO endorses and about 42 percent when Democrats and Republicans in Congress do so.

These results provide solid support for the arguments made both by Larson and Kull and Destler, but aggregate differences cannot address the causal mechanisms that may be generating these effects. To take a closer look at the correlates of support within each treatment category, we turn to a statistical analysis of the responses. The results of this analysis are presented in table 4.5.

As before, we present our analysis in three related but distinct ways. The first column pools the data for all four treatment categories and includes dummy variables for each treatment with *President* as the excluded category. As with the Yemen experiment, we also include a series of explanatory variables, including attitudes toward security and humanitarian military missions, casualty tolerance, expected casualties for the East Timor mission, expectations of success, party identification, and several demographic controls. Columns 2 to 5 present our statistical model for each condition separately, which will help us discern which explanatory variables may interact with the experimental conditions, and column 6 provides a formal test of these interaction effects. Consistent with table 4.4, this analysis shows that even after accounting for the impact of other explanatory variables, the public has the most support for an East Timor mission when there is a unified message from elites (*All*); it shows the least support when the president supports a mission but all other elites are opposed (*President*); and there is little substantive difference between the influence of *Domestic* and *International* elites. These results are indicated by the positive and statistically significant coefficients for the *All*, *Domestic,* and *International* treatment categories. The substantive size of these coefficients also indicates that the impact of the *Domestic* and *International* treatments is approximately equal, since their coefficients are not significantly different (.05, 1 d.f., $p < .82$). The *All* treatment, however, generates significantly more support even after controlling for other causes of support (44.57, 1 d.f., $p < .00$). Consistent with our expectations—and with our analysis of the Congo questions discussed in chapter 3, we find that attitudes toward security-oriented missions have no impact on support for intervention in East Timor. Attitudes toward the humanitarian use of force, however, have a significant effect.

TABLE 4.5.
Logit Analysis of Support for Intervention in East Timor

	Cue effects	*All*	*Domestic*	*International*	*President*	*Interactions*
International	–0.639 (6.58)**					–0.833 (3.66)**
Domestic	–0.721 (7.20)**					–0.034 (0.15)
President	–1.234 (11.88)**					–0.753 (3.16)**
Sex	–0.163 (2.29)*	–0.283 (2.01)*	–0.158 (1.07)	–0.226 (1.63)	0.004 (0.03)	–0.165 (2.31)*
Age	0.016 (0.77)	0.071 (1.68)	0.001 (0.03)	0.004 (0.10)	–0.025 (0.55)	0.013 (0.63)
Education	–0.034 (1.11)	0.051 (0.84)	–0.090 (1.38)	0.022 (0.37)	–0.140 (2.14)*	–0.040 (1.28)
Party ID	–0.022 (0.85)	0.050 (0.99)	–0.162 (2.77)**	0.096 (2.01)*	–0.145 (2.45)*	0.042 (0.89)
Security	0.134 (2.66)**	0.128 (1.34)	0.291 (2.46)*	0.088 (0.93)	0.088 (0.79)	0.129 (2.55)*
Humanitarian	0.324 (5.02)**	0.309 (2.50)*	0.333 (2.42)*	0.324 (2.57)*	0.398 (2.82)**	0.331 (5.11)**
Exp. deaths	0.075 (2.37)*	0.144 (2.20)*	0.005 (0.06)	0.071 (1.22)	0.075 (1.18)	0.073 (2.32)*
Exp. success	0.387 (8.14)**	0.395 (4.42)**	0.422 (4.24)**	0.326 (3.46)**	0.364 (3.40)**	0.372 (7.79)**
Intl.* PID						0.061 (0.94)
Dom * PID						–0.232 (3.31)**
Pres * PID						–0.163 (2.27)*
Observations	1016	263	243	263	247	1016

Absolute value of *z* statistics in parentheses
* significant at 5% ** significant at 1%

The same is true of the respondent's expectations regarding the number of casualties that would result from the conflict. Consistent with our results in the Yemen experiment, expectations of the likely success of the mission also have a statistically significant impact on support for intervention, and its impact is substantively large. For example, changing a respondent's expectations of success from "not very likely" to "very likely" increases the probability that he or she will approve of the intervention in East Timor by approximately 45 percent. In fact, the impact of success is larger than the impact of the signals from either domestic or international elites—though not larger than the impact of those two treatments combined. Also consistent with the Yemen scenario, the coefficient for expected casualties is in the wrong direction. A very similar pattern appeared to hold for these data as in the Yemen scenario. This coefficient seemed to be driven by a large number of respondents who opposed the mission strongly and stated that they expected zero casualties. Absent those respondents, expected casualties had no effect. Thus as we discussed earlier, we believe that the best interpretation of this result is that expectations of casualties do not influence support for military missions when respondents are not cued to think about casualties.

Finally, none of the demographic controls has any impact—including party identification. Before concluding definitively that party does not influence support for the use of force, however, we turn to the interaction of partisan cleavages and the source of elite cues.

Columns 2 to 5 display the impact of the explanatory variables within each of the treatment categories. In general, the coefficients for the explanatory variables remain remarkably constant across all four treatments. The two exceptions to this consistency are *Party identification* (*Party ID*) and *Education*. The varying impact of *Party ID* is important because it demonstrates that respondents seem to differentiate between the sources of elite cues. When all elites support the use of force (*All*), we see that *Party ID* has no impact on support for the mission. But in the frame where the international community supports the East Timor mission but Congress does not (*International*), *Party ID* is significant and positive. That is, the more one identifies with the Democratic Party, the stronger the support for the mission in these conditions. However, in the two frames where the international community opposes the East Timor mission (*Domestic* and *President*), *Party ID* is significant (at the .1 level) and negative. That is, when the international community opposes the use of force, the more one identifies with the Democratic Party, the stronger the opposition to the mission. In addition to being consistent with Kull and Destler's claim about the influence of international elite, this result is strongly supportive of the kind of partisan cuing by elites that is expected by Zaller (1992) as well as Berinksy and Druckman (2006).

Interestingly, this dynamic is also consistent with the partisan polarization that we have observed regarding the Iraq War. As we noted in chapter 2, most American uses of military force have not evoked highly partisan differences in support. The Iraq War, on the other hand, has been more partisan than any other American military conflict for which we have polling data. To place this gap in context, consider that during the Kosovo mission discussed in chapter 2, the gap between Democratic and Republican approval of U.S. air strikes in Kosovo and U.S. participation in peacekeeping there was only about 10 percent—even after Clinton was impeached by the House of Representatives in an extremely partisan fight. Similarly, after the "Black Hawk Down" incident in Somalia, the polls discussed in chapter 2 revealed only a 2 percent partisan gap in expressing the view that Somalia was a "mistake." And even in the midst of the Tet offensive, the polling from chapter 2 indicated that the partisan gap on whether the Vietnam War was a "mistake" was only 10 percent.

By November 2005, on the other hand, the Pew Center for People and the Press found that more than 70 percent of Democrats and less than 20 percent of Republicans believed that the Iraq War was a mistake. The party divide on Iraq is growing, but it was large before the war ever began. By October 2002, according to a *New York Times* poll, the gap between Republican and Democratic support for using force against Iraq ranged between 25 and 40 percent, depending upon the specific question asked. Even in the wake of the U.S. invasion—which generally sparks a rally 'round the flag response—the partisan gap continued to grow. In March of 2003, a Harris poll found a 40 percent partisan gap in approval of the president's decision to attack.

What caused the partisan polarization of the Iraq War compared to other U.S. military conflicts? Undoubtedly a variety of factors contributed, but the results from our experiment suggest that the Bush administration's decision to attack Iraq despite its failure to gain the approval of the U.N. Security Council may have had a substantial impact on the extent to which Democrats believed that military force was unjustified. Can our experimental treatment really explain such a large partisan gap? We found that if the president, Congressional leaders, and the U.N. and NATO had supported this intervention, then 75 percent of strong Republicans and 77 percent of strong Democrats would have supported the mission. If the president and Congress had recommended force but the U.N. and NATO had not, on the other hand, then 72 percent of strong Republicans but only 20 percent of strong Democrats would have supported the mission. Other polling is also consistent with the argument that partisan cuing of messages from international elites contributed to the polarized response to Iraq before the war even began. In October 2002, almost no Democrats expressed opposition for using force against Iraq in principle.

Instead, more than 80 percent of Democrats stated that the United States should wait to give the U.N. time before using force, but only 54 percent of Republicans expressed a desire to wait, even though the president himself was approaching the U.N. at that time. Thus our experiment supports Kull and Destler's claim that messages from international elites influence opinion through the partisan cuing expected by Zaller. These messages seem to have had a powerful influence on the perception that the use of military force was justified.

Consistent with Larson, we do find that messages regarding domestic elite consensus have an impact on support for military force, but they do not appear to work through the same partisan cuing mechanism suggested by Zaller. Returning to table 4.4, we can see that the overall level of support for intervening in East Timor shifts substantially between the *President* and *Domestic* treatments, and between the *All* and *International* treatments. In the former case, the withdrawal of support by Republican and Democratic Congressional leaders lowers support by about 25 percent, and in the latter case it reduces support by more than 15 percent. In table 4.5, however, we can see that the coefficients for party identification do not change significantly across these treatment categories. Thus the bipartisan endorsement of military force by Congressional leaders affects the level of support, but it does so across the board rather than by cuing Democratic respondents differently than Republican ones. This result suggests that while Kull and Destler's international elites influence opinion through partisan changes in attitudes toward the justification of the war, Larson's domestic elites appear to influence opinion through the bipartisan "confidence" mechanism that raises respondents' expectations regarding the success of the mission. Of course, our survey was conducted at a time when the same party controlled both the presidency and the Congress. A different dynamic might operate when control over the branches is divided between the parties.

Finally, in column 6 of table 4.5 we formally test the hypothesis that the impact of party identification varies across experimental treatment categories. Two of the three interaction terms are statistically significant and a log-likelihood ratio test clearly indicates that the model, including the interaction terms, is a significantly better fit (chi-squared 23.46, 3 d.f., $p < .01$). More specifically, table 4.6 presents the coefficients for party identification across experimental conditions when holding other coefficients constant. These results echo those of columns 2 to 5, and they indicate that the greatest partisan divide occurs when Congress and the president approve of the use of force, but the international community does not. In this case, strong Republicans are approximately 30 percent more likely to approve of intervention than strong Democrats. The impact of partisanship in this case is larger than the substantive impact of support for humanitarian missions. Increasing *Humanitarian* from the 10th per-

TABLE 4.6.
Impact of Party ID on Support for Military Intervention in East Timor Depending on Elite Cues

	Coefficient	*Standard error*	*Significance lvl.*
All elites endorse mission	0.04	0.05	0.38
Domestic elites endorse mission	–0.19	0.05	0.00
International elites endorse mission	0.10	0.05	0.05
Only the president endorses mission	–0.12	0.06	0.05

centile to the 90th increases support for intervention by about 20 percent. Expectations of success, however, remain the largest substantive variable in the model. A change in expectations of success from "not very likely" to "very likely" increases approval of intervention in East Timor by approximately 40 percent.

In sum, we find that elite signals do matter when it comes to supporting military missions. Both domestic consensus and international consensus matter, but they do so through different causal mechanisms—one linked to views of the justification of the use of force and the other to confidence in American leadership. These effects hold even after we account for the other major factors influencing mission support. As we expected, attitudes toward humanitarian uses of force had a consistent impact on support for intervention in Timor, as did expectations regarding the success of the mission. In fact, success is the only explanatory variable that is significant at least at the $p < .01$ level for all four experimental conditions, and it has the largest substantive impact of any of the variables—including partisanship and elite cues. Moreover, the effect of going from believing that success is very unlikely to very likely rivals the effect of the changing experimental condition, and this impact is consistent across all four conditions.

Expectations of Casualties and Success

Our final survey experiments give us more insight into the effect of casualties on mission support—especially as compared to the effect of the likelihood of success. Feaver and Gelpi (2004) and Eichenberg (2005) argue that the likelihood of success in a mission matters at least as much as the expected death toll. In other words, a mission unlikely to succeed even with relatively low human costs will have less support than missions that come with a much higher human cost but that are seen as likely to succeed. On the other hand, Mueller (1971, 1973, 2005), Klarevas (2000), Luttwak (1995) and others suggest that the primary factor shaping public responses to military operations is the number of casualties suffered by the United States.

To investigate these claims, we utilize an innovative survey experiment. Each respondent is asked three questions about support for a nonspecific military mission that gives a level of confidence of victory expressed by the Joint Chiefs of Staff (JCS) and an expected number of soldier deaths for that mission. In this instance, we did not provide respondents with a specific mission because we wanted to focus their attention on the messages about confidence and casualties.[1] We chose to present respondents with a message from the JCS rather than the president because of the potentially partisan cuing that a presidential message might send—as indicated in our previous experiment. The JCS are "experts" on the use of military force who are likely to be viewed as less biased than other potential message-senders (King 2003), making them more likely to influence respondents' attitudes. Across the experimental conditions, we vary both the confidence in victory of the JCS and the expected number of deaths. On the confidence dimension, respondents are told that the JCS are either "extremely confident," "somewhat confident," or "not very confident." On the deaths dimension, respondents are told that the expected number of casualties is "50," "500," or "5,000." We chose these three levels of expected casualties because they move up in orders of magnitude. This increase matches Mueller's expectation that support will decrease linearly according to the log of casualties. These two dimensions (and the three questions each respondent receives) create a design with nine different conditions. Each respondent is asked to answer three questions by holding one dimension constant (for example, "extremely confident") and asking about the three options on the other dimension. This novel design allows us to have a sufficient number of responses in each cell of the 3x3 treatment matrix despite our survey having only 1,203 total respondents. Treating responses rather than respondents as observations raises the obvious problem that the responses from the same respondent are likely to be correlated with one another. Our analysis allows for this fact by the

[1] Not providing respondents with any specific mission might raise concerns that respondents would have difficulty answering the question or would reject using force outright in the absence of some mission to justify the use of force. However, refusal rates for this scenario remained low and were not significantly different than other questions. The overall level of support was lower than for the Yemen experiment but was comparable to the average support for intervening in East Timor.

clustering of standard errors across each of the respondents rather than assuming the cases are independent.

We represent the different experimental treatments with a series of dummy variables. Specifically, we include dummy variables identifying responses in which the respondent was told that the JCS was "somewhat confident" in success and "very confident" in success, as well as dummy variables for responses in which the respondent was told that the JCS expected five hundred casualties and five thousand casualties. Thus "not very confident" was the excluded category for the confidence treatment and fifty casualties was the excluded category for the casualty treatment.[2] We also include respondents' overall attitudes toward humanitarian and security-oriented missions and a set of demographic control variables.

The results, displayed in table 4.7, clearly indicate that both JCS expressions of confidence in the likely success of the mission and their estimates of the likely number of casualties have a significant impact on support for the mission. Both confidence dummies are positive and significant, indicating that expressions of high or medium levels of confidence by the JCS improve support significantly over low levels of confidence. Interestingly, while both the medium and high levels of confidence generate more support than low confidence, and high confidence generates the most support, the distinction between medium and high levels of confidence is not statistically significant (chi 1.73, 1 d.f., $p < .19$). Each increase in the expectation of casualties has a statistically significant—and negative—impact on support for the mission. The coefficients, however, suggest that, contrary to the "log of casualties logic," the increase from 50 to 500 casualties does not have as much of an impact as the increase from 500 to 5,000. The coefficients also indicate that the impact of these two variables appears to be roughly comparable. While the absolute value of the coefficient for high confidence is larger than the coefficient for high casualties, the difference is not statistically significant (chi 0.73, 1 d.f., $p < .39$). The distinction between medium levels of confidence and 500 casualties, on the other hand, is significant, with medium levels of confidence having a greater impact (chi 19.9, 1 d.f., $p < .00$).

To get a clearer sense of the substantive effects described by the model, table 4.8 displays predicted probabilities of respondents approving of a mission (either strongly or somewhat). Overall, moving from the highest to the lowest level of confidence has about the same impact as mov-

[2] Analyses using a single, ordinally ranked variable for confidence and casualties yielded similar results, but obviously could not detect the moderately nonlinear effects across categories of success and casualties. We also examined possible interactions between JCS expectations of success and casualties, but did not find significant interactions with either the dummy variable or ordinal variable specifications.

TABLE 4.7.
Logit Analysis of Expectations of Success and Casualties Regarding Support for Military Force

	Support for military mission
JCS "very confident"	0.909 (8.65)**
JCS "somewhat confident"	0.784 (7.97)**
JCS expects 5,000 casualties	–0.793 (8.84)**
JCS expects 500 casualties	–0.183 (2.12)*
Security	0.596 (7.98)**
Humanitarian	0.513 (5.47)**
Party ID	–0.324 (8.96)**
Age in decades	–0.012 (0.43)
Education	0.030 (0.69)
Sex	–0.194 (2.02)*
Observations	3002

Robust z statistics in parentheses
* significant at 5%   ** significant at 1%

ing from the lowest to the highest level of casualties. In either case, the probability of supporting the mission drops by about 20 percent. It is worth noting, however, that these variables seem to have their greatest impact at different times. Casualties do not have much substantive impact on support until they get to very high levels—at least compared to American conflicts since Vietnam. Changing casualties one order of magnitude from 50 to 500 reduces the probability of supporting a mission only by about 5 percent. Increasing casualties by another order of magnitude to five thousand, on the other hand, reduces support by about 15 percent.

TABLE 4.8.
Probability of Approving of Military Force Depending on JCS Expectations of Success and Casualties

	JCS expects 50 deaths	*JCS expects 500 deaths*	*JCS expects 5000 deaths*
JCS is extremely confident	.57	.52	.37
JCS is somewhat confident	.54	.49	.35
JCS is not very confident	.34	.31	.19

While casualties have their impact at very high levels, confidence in success appears to have a larger impact at relatively low levels. That is, even modest confidence about success seems to be enough to boost approval of a military operation. Specifically, shifting from a message stating that the JCS are "not very confident" to one in which they are "somewhat confident" increased support for using force by about 20 percent. But an additional increase in the confidence of the JCS to "extremely confident" increased support only by another 2 to 3 percent. Thus the public appears to be willing to support military missions even if there is only a moderate chance of success, and they will not be deterred by casualties unless the expectations of casualties become quite high.

It is also interesting to note that JCS statements about expected casualties have a substantial impact on mission support when the respondent's own judgments of expected casualties in the Yemen and East Timor experiments had more limited effects. We can only speculate, of course, as to why we see this change in the impact of expected casualties, but it seems plausible that respondents may give greater weight to JCS statements because of their status as "experts." Alternatively, the JCS experiment presented respondents with casualty estimates prior to asking about support, while the Yemen and East Timor scenarios asked about support and then asked about expected success and casualties afterward. Thus the JCS experiment may have "primed" respondents to think about casualties in formulating their response, increasing the impact of casualties relative to what it might have been if respondents had not been cued to think about them (Kinder and Iyengar 1987; Krosnik and Kinder 1990; Iyengar and Simon 1993). Cuing respondents to think about casualties is the nature of the experimental treatment in this case, so we would not want to avoid this kind of priming. The changing impact of expected casualties does indicate, however, that casualties may influence public opinion substantially when they are drawn to the public's attention, but casualties may not be the most salient factor that respondents consider if they are not specifically cued to do so.

Regardless of one's interpretation of the contingent impact of expectations of casualties, the JCS experiment provides strong individual-level evidence that confidence in success is a crucial variable in explaining public support for military missions. These results strongly bolster the contention that likelihood of success is at least as important as the number of deaths that come from sending American forces into harm's way.

Conclusion

As a whole, the results of these three separate experiments confirm many of the expectations about the causes of support that were based on inferences from aggregate data. Our experiments, however, have pushed beyond this aggregate work by documenting the casual mechanisms in place at the individual level, increasing our confidence that the correlations observed at the aggregate level reflect real patterns in the way that Americans form their opinions about the use of force. Moreover, in some cases we have been able to distinguish between the kinds of causal mechanisms at work behind aggregate correlations, and we have been able to compare the relative importance of different mechanisms.

First, our experiment about a hypothetical intervention in Yemen demonstrates that changing the stated principal policy objective of the mission can have a substantial impact on the aggregate level of support. Our findings, however, also suggests that changes in the PPO influence public opinion by acting as a frame through which respondents construct their attitudes. As a result, while changes in frames will cause respondents to draw upon different sets of attitudes in forming their opinion about a mission, such changes in frame may or may not result in a shift in aggregate support. The net shift in support will depend upon the aggregate distributions of the attitudes highlighted by the frames. Thus we agree with Jentleson that the public is "pretty prudent," and makes intelligent calculations about the use of force depending on mission objective. We show, however, that mission objectives may sometimes evoke somewhat different levels of support than suggested by Jentleson (1992; Jentleson and Britton 1998).

Second, our experiment about a hypothetical intervention in East Timor confirmed the arguments by Larson (1996), Kull and Destler (1999), Berinsky and Druckman (2006), and many others that elite messages about military operations provide cues that shape public support. Our data suggest that cues from both domestic and international elites may influence public opinion, though the two appear to do so through different causal mechanisms. Consistent with Kull and Destler (1999), we find that endorsements from international organizations such as the U.N. and NATO influence public support for military intervention. In our experiment, these messages did so through the kind of partisan cuing expected by Zaller (1992). That is, Republicans appear to trust messages from the president and Congress regarding the legitimacy of intervening in East Timor, but Democrats cue strongly from the opinions of international organizations. Thus Democrats appear to be using the U.N. and NATO as a "second opinion" on whether intervention is legitimate (Grieco 2005). Consistent with Larson (1996, 2000) we also find that bipartisan endorsement from Congressional leaders also increases mission support. It does not, however, have partisan cuing effects. That is, Zaller's mechanism would lead us to expect that a bipartisan Congressional endorsement would have a greater impact on Democrats because they would not be moved by a Republican president's endorsement alone. Instead, we see both parties responding equally to this message, suggesting that Congressional unity may work through Larson's "confidence" mechanism as a cause of optimism regarding the success of the mission.

Finally, through both of these experiments we find that expectations of success are a statistically significant and substantively powerful predictor of support for the use of force. In fact, expectations of success consistently had as strong or stronger effects than any other variables in our analyses. These results were echoed in our experiment regarding messages from the JCS about confidence in success and expectations of casualties. Consistent with Feaver and Gelpi (2004) and Eichenberg (2005), we find that expectations of success are at least as important as casualties in determining mission support. Moreover, the results indicate that even moderately high prospects for success may be sufficient to maintain public support, while casualties did not curtail support until they reached fairly high levels.

Collectively, these experimental results suggest that respondents construct their attitudes toward specific military missions in sensible ways by connecting their general attitudes about the importance of different kinds of missions to more specific attitudes about the justification of this particular mission and its likelihood of success. In the next chapter we turn from our evaluation of these theoretical mechanisms in an experimental context to a focused empirical evaluation of how they operate in a specific military conflict: the Iraq War. This conflict provides an excellent opportunity to evaluate the formation of public attitudes toward a real military engagement that involves substantial costs while the conflict is still ongoing. Thus we will be able to evaluate the substantive importance of our experimentally tested mechanisms in a real-world context. In developing our analysis of opinion during the Iraq War, we draw upon these experimental results as well as the aggregate results from chapter 2 and the individual-level results from chapter 3 to argue that respondents will be supportive of the Iraq War to the extent that they believe that the Iraq mission was the right thing to do and to the extent that they remain confident that the effort can succeed.

Chapter Five

INDIVIDUAL ATTITUDES TOWARD THE IRAQ WAR, 2003–2004

In chapter 2 we demonstrated that the American public's tolerance for casualties at the aggregate level actually has varied over time and across differing military operations. In particular, our analysis of President George W. Bush's average weekly approval rating demonstrated that the public's tolerance for casualties has varied across differing periods of the Iraq War. Anecdotal evidence suggests that this aggregate variation in casualty tolerance is consistent with the importance of success as a determinant of casualty tolerance. Nonetheless, the relative paucity of cases created by aggregate analysis, combined with the correlations among various factors that drive casualty tolerance, makes it difficult to rely on aggregate data to distinguish among competing causes of casualty tolerance in these real-world cases. Moreover, such analyses inevitably suffer from problems of ecological inference if one is interested in how individual respondents form their attitudes.[1]

Thus, in chapter 3 we demonstrated that concepts such as casualty tolerance could be reliably measured at the individual level, and we also showed that various demographic factors and basic underlying attitudes about the use of military force influence casualty tolerance. In chapter 4 we presented experimental evidence supporting various arguments about the sources of public tolerance for casualties in war. Variations in the mission's objective, the extent of domestic and international elite consensus in support of the mission, and perceptions of the likely success of the operation all appeared to change the extent to which respondents expressed a willingness to pay the human costs of war. Such experimental results are useful in isolating causal influences on the formation of individual attitudes, but their significance is also limited by the hypothetical and artificial nature of the experimental treatments.

Consequently, in the current chapter we turn our attention to a more detailed evaluation of individual attitudes toward one specific American military conflict: the Iraq War. A combination of circumstances makes the

[1] See King (1997) on ecological inference and a possible statistical solution; for critiques of this solution, see Cho and Gaines (2004) and Herron and Schotts (2004).

public response to the ongoing war in Iraq during the presidential campaign of 2003–04 an important opportunity to understand the conditions that cause the public to tolerate casualties in war. First, the war in Iraq is both the most controversial and most deadly U.S. military operation since the Vietnam War. By Election Day in November 2004, nearly 1,200 American soldiers had been killed in action in Iraq. At the same time, Americans seemed increasingly divided over the president's reasons for going to war—both the Kay Report and the 9/11 Commission raised questions about the strength of the ties between Saddam Hussein, weapons of mass destruction (WMD), and the Al-Qaeda terrorist network. Moreover, the public was deluged with information about the war and its cost in American lives. Combat in Iraq was the most-covered story on the major network TV news broadcasts in 2004, with nearly twice as many minutes of airtime as the second most-covered story: postwar reconstruction of Iraq.[2] Finally, an examination of the war in Iraq allows us to combine the strengths of gathering individual-level data—as we were able to do in the experiments discussed in chapter 4—with an analysis of attitudes toward a real-world ongoing conflict—as we were able to do in our analysis of aggregate data in chapter 2. This combination of individual-level data regarding attitudes toward a costly and controversial war made salient in the context of a presidential election provides an ideal circumstance for comparing the substantive importance of various mechanisms that determine an individual's response to casualties during war.

Prewar Attitudes toward the War in Iraq

The invasion of Iraq has been the subject of widespread discussion and speculation for many years. Throughout the 1990s the scenarios varied but the public generally supported the prospect of military operations against Iraq, with support averaging 62 percent throughout the decade and reaching as high as 79 percent during Operation Desert Fox in December 1998.[3] The debate (and hence the polling) ratcheted up after 9/11, reaching a fever pitch once President Bush took the issue back to the United Nations' Security Council in September 2002. In general, despite a vocal opposition, polls consistently showed majority support for using military force against the Hussein regime, with support climbing as the diplomatic endgame intensified in February and March 2003. Support varied according to the wording of different survey questions, with the

[2] See The Tyndall Report summary of 2004 campaign coverage at http://www.tyndallreport.com.

[3] The overall average is reported in Eichenberg, "Victory has Many Friends," table 2. The 1998 high point is reported in Aggie S. Mulvihillu, "U.S. Strikes Iraq; Americans Rally Around Clinton and Iraq Effort, Polls Indicate," *Boston Herald*, 18 December 1998, p. A18.

public supporting diplomatic efforts aimed at resolving the issue short of war. For instance, the public clearly supported the Bush decision to seek broader authorization from the United Nations and from allies, and in response to some hypothetical questions, respondents identified this as a necessary condition for their own approval.[4]

While the prospect of casualties dampened support for military action somewhat, it did not prevent a majority of Americans from supporting a war against Iraq. When asked if "removing Saddam Hussein from power is worth the potential loss of American life," the public was unequivocal. In nearly every CBS News poll that asked this question, a majority agreed the cost was "worth it."[5] At the same time, other polling showed that a sizable majority of Americans believed there would be "significant numbers" of casualties.[6] Comparable majorities professed to be "a great deal worried" that "U.S. forces might suffer a lot of casualties."[7] While ecological inference problems blunt our ability to make powerful inferences from these data, it seems that the American public was cognizant of the potential human cost of a conflict with Iraq and yet still supported the war.

Just how many casualties the public considered to be "significant" or "a lot" is uncertain. Consistent with surveys from the late 1990s on this question,[8] the median respondent expressed tolerance for approximately five hundred U.S. battle deaths. The upper limit that still engendered broad support for war in Iraq, was probably about one thousand U.S. military deaths. A Gallup poll from October 2002 walked respondents through various hypothetical scenarios of the number of casualties that the United States might suffer in Iraq. Half (51 percent) of the respondents supported war under a scenario of one hundred casualties; just under half (46 percent) supported war with one thousand casualties; yet only one-third (33 percent) supported war if there were five thousand casualties.[9] That support for a hypothetical mission would begin to drop precipitously after one thousand casualties is further supported by CBS polling that regularly asked respondents to estimate whether there would be less than 1000, between 1000 and 5000, or more; well over 60 percent thought "less than 1000."[10] Again, ecological inference problems limit our ability to make bold claims, but it makes sense that support for war in the Gallup poll drops once the hypothetical casualty estimate is beyond what the public is expecting.

[4] Steven Kull et al., "Americans on the Conflict with Iraq." Steven Kull et al., "Americans on Iraq and the U.N. Inspections II."

[5] CBS News Poll, 27–31 October 2002.

[6] ABC News Poll, 30 January–1 February 2003; and 5–9 March 2003.

[7] "February 2003 News Interest Index," Pew Research Center for the People and the Press and Council on Foreign Relations, 12–18 February 2003.

[8] See Feaver and Gelpi, *Choosing Your Battles*.

[9] 3–6 October 2002, Gallup/CNN/*USA Today* Poll.

[10] CBS News Poll, 27–31 October 2002.

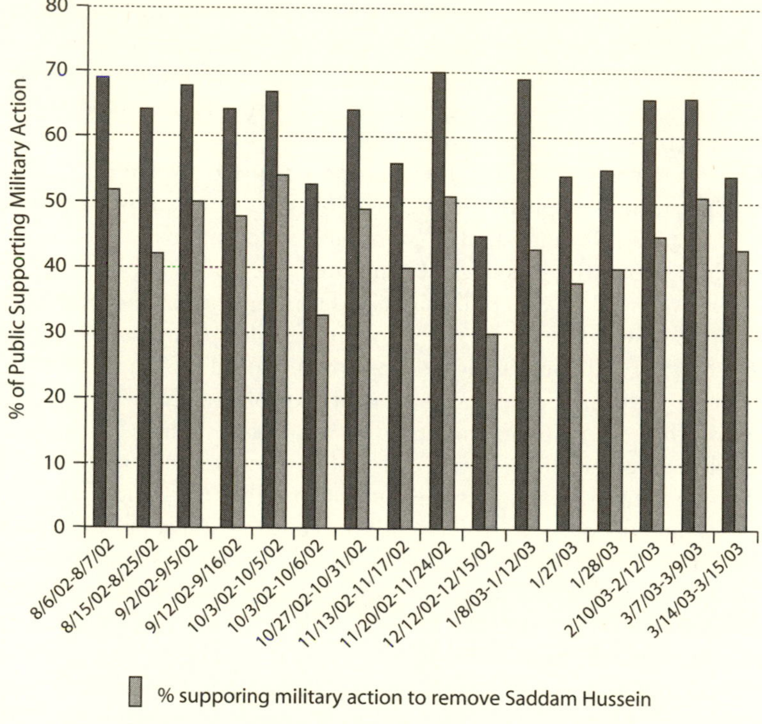

FIGURE 5.1. Decline in Public Support for Hypothetical War in Iraq when Casualties Are Mentioned

Nevertheless, raising the prospects of casualties *did* dampen public support for going to war. Figure 5.1 summarizes data from polls that asked some variant of the two-part question: "Do you support using military force in Iraq," followed up by "What if there are substantial casualties?"[11] The pattern is striking: regardless of whether hypothetical support is relatively high or relatively low, mentioning casualties has the effect of dropping that expressed support by thirteen to twenty-two points. This effect is not merely an artifact of "controversial wars," for remarkably

[11]The polls referenced in figure 5,1 are as follows (dates shown as month/day/year): 8/6–8/7/02, Fox/OD Poll; 8/15–8/25/02: Pew Poll; 9/2–9/5/02: CBS/NYT Poll; 9/12–9/16/02: Princeton Poll; 10/3–10/5/02: CBS/NYT Poll; 10/3–10/6/02: CNN/USA Today/Gallup Poll; 10/27–10/31/02: CBS/NYT Poll; 11/13–11/17/02: ABC Poll; 11/20–11/24/02: CBS/NYT Poll; 12/12–12/15/02: ABC/WP Poll; 1/8/–1/12/03: PEW/Princeton Poll; 1/27/03: ABC Poll; 1/28/03: ABC Poll; 2/10–2/12/03: CBS/NYT Poll; 3/7–3/9/03: CBS/NYT Poll; 3/14–3/15/03: Zogby International Poll. Note: Polls on 11/13/02, 12/12/02, 1/27/03, and 1/28/03 asked questions on casualties only to those who favored military action.

similar results show up in polls in the aftermath of 9/11 asking about military action in Afghanistan.[12]

Thus the prewar polling on Iraq presents a mixture of evidence both contradicting and in some ways supporting the view that the American public is casualty phobic. Most polls showed majority support for the war even though substantial casualties were widely anticipated. Yet specific changes in question wording that highlighted the issue of casualties did significantly—and sometimes dramatically—reduce support. At the same time, as we discussed in chapter 3, the available evidence suggests that respondents tend to exaggerate their aversion to casualties in hypothetical questions.[13] Consequently, as the war in Iraq approached, it remained quite unclear to what extent the American public would tolerate casualties.

The pundits, on the other hand, had already made up their minds. They were once more invoking the "lessons of Vietnam" as the war with Iraq loomed, arguing that the public simply did not have the stomach for the kind of bloody fighting required in Iraq.[14] Based on reports of interviews with former Iraqi commanders, Saddam Hussein himself evidently thought as much, specifically invoking the Somalia incident as proof that the American public was casualty phobic.[15] The war was barely a week old when observers began to worry that news of combat fatalities would cause public support to collapse.[16]

America's swift and successful removal of Saddam Hussein from power—and the resulting rally of presidential support—temporarily submerged the issue of public casualty tolerance. But soon after Hussein's statue fell in Baghdad, the mission seemed to become more difficult rather than less so. Widespread looting of Iraq's infrastructure, the failure to locate any stockpiles of weapons of mass destruction, the murder and desecration of American contractors in Fallujah, gruesome videotapes of the beheading of American citizens, the Abu Ghraib prisoner abuse scandal, and the continuously mounting toll of U.S. casualties raised the costs of the war in Iraq much higher than Bush administration officials may have expected before the war began. By October of 2004, as presidential elections loomed

[12] Feaver and Gelpi (2004:189).

[13] Ibid., chap. 4.

[14] Eric Schmitt and Thom Shanker, "U.S. Refines Plan for War in Cities," *New York Times*, 21 October 2002, p. A1; Thomas E. Ricks, "Duration of War Key to U.S. Victory," *Washington Post,* 19 March 2003.

[15] David Zucchino, "Iraq's Swift Defeat Blamed on Leaders," *Los Angeles Times*, 11 Aug 2003; and Thom Shanker, "Regime Thought War Unlikely, Iraqis Tell U.S.," *New York Times*, 12 Feb 2004, p. A1.

[16] Thomas E. Ricks, "U.S. Casualties Expose Risks, Raise Doubts about Strategy," *Washington Post*, 24 March 2003, p. 1; Todd S. Purdum, "A Nation at War: The Casualties; Delicate Calculus of Casualties and Public Opinion," *New York Times*, 27 March 2003, p. B1. Janet Elder and Adam Nagourney, "A Nation at War; POLL; Opinions Begin to Shift as Public Weighs Cost of War," *New York Times*, 26 March 2003, p. B1.

in the United States, nearly 1,200 U.S. military personnel had been killed in Iraq fighting against an insurgency that continued unabated.

Had most of the pundits foreseen this turn of events, they would have predicted a complete collapse of public support for the Bush administration and for the war in Iraq. Moreover, they would have predicted a lopsided electoral defeat for the president in November. As the aggregate data in chapter 2 suggest, however, neither collapse occurred in 2004. While the president's approval ratings returned to pre-9/11 levels, he was undeniably successful in his campaign for reelection—even capturing the victory in the popular vote that eluded him in 2000. And while support for the war had receded somewhat, the available evidence indicates that the majority of Americans still supported the war in Iraq and—as we demonstrate below—stated that they would continue to do so even if the United States suffered as many as 1500 military deaths. Moreover, in the wake of the U.S. election, public support for the war did not wane despite heavy casualties taken during November and December of 2004 as the United States conducted a major assault on the insurgent stronghold of Fallujah. The apparent success of this operation combined with the relatively successful Iraqi elections in January 2005 temporarily lifted support for the president and the military effort. Persistent violence and political stalemate in the wake of the elections, however, sent support declining again through the summer and fall of that year.

Support for the war rallied once again in December 2005 in response to another successful election and a series of presidential speeches designed to draw attention to the progress made in Iraq—only to have support wane once again in response to continued violence. While casualty rates for U.S. troops remained fairly constant, the public increasingly perceived the escalating sectarian violence as an intractable civil war. This growing perception helped drive public support for the war—and the president—downward through the summer and fall of 2006 culminating in an eventual Democratic electoral victory in November as Republicans lost control of both the House of Representatives and the Senate.[17] In January 2007, the president's response to the widespread dissatisfaction with the war that led to Democratic success was to replace the Secretary of Defense and the senior military command in Iraq, and to shift to a different strategy that involved an increase in the number of U.S. force in Iraq.

This shift in strategy and the accompanying increase in military forces was controversial and was received skeptically by the American public.

[17]For instance in, a 10–12 March 2006 Gallup Poll asked a national sample of adults, "Which do you think is more likely to happen in Iraq? The situation will turn into chaos and civil war OR the Iraqi people will be able to establish a stable government." 55 percent answered "chaos and civil war." By the end of 2006, fully 65 percent of American adults assessed Iraq to be in a civil war, according to a 8–11 December *Los Angeles Times*/Bloomberg Poll.

Thus by the spring and summer of 2007, support for the president and his handling of the Iraq War had ebbed into the mid-to-high 20s, and the public debate between Congress and the president regarding funding of U.S. forces began to focus on the conditions under which Congress should continue to fund the presence of U.S. troops in Iraq. The president's preferred position remained unconditional funding of the war effort, while others seemed arrayed along a spectrum of "pressure for withdrawal." Some members of Congress—especially moderate Republicans and some conservative Democrats—supported setting "benchmarks" of progress and making some funding of the war effort, such as aid to the Iraqi government, contingent on meeting those benchmarks. The Democratic leadership in Congress, including Nancy Pelosi and Harry Reid, supported setting a specific timeline for withdrawal of U.S. forces in 2008. And some of the most militant war antiwar activists supported an immediate end to the funding of U.S. participation in the war, but this remained a marginal position in the public discourse.

Public attitudes toward the war echoed these various sentiments, with relatively few Americans at either end of the spectrum and most expressing some ambivalence about the conditions for U.S. withdrawal. One year prior to this writing (spring 2008) surveys demonstrated substantial shifts in opinion depending upon the wording of the specific question and the response options provided. For example, CBS surveys done in both April and May 2007 asked respondents a simple "yes or no" question regarding whether they supported a timetable for withdrawal and found that nearly 65 percent of the public favored setting a timetable. At the same time, other questions that allowed respondents to express support for a specific withdrawal timetable or the more flexible "benchmarks" option indicated that "benchmarks" was the median position. Specifically, a Fox News poll indicated that 39 percent supported setting a timetable, 32 percent supported "benchmarks" and 24 percent supported "giving the surge time to work." Thus while the public had become increasingly dissatisfied with the Bush administration's handling of this conflict, the public pressure to end U.S. participation in the war has been remarkably slow to materialize.

Key Attitudes toward the Iraq War: Success and Doing the "Right Thing"

While support for the war has both waxed and waned, the public has shown remarkable staying power in Iraq, far exceeding what almost any pundit would have predicted before the outbreak of the war. But what has been the most important factor in shaping the ebb and flow of public resolve over this period? To address this question, beginning in October 2003 and extending through October 2004 we conducted a series of surveys of public attitudes toward American decisions to use force and toward the current war in Iraq in particular. The data from October 2003 were collected in the same telephone survey discussed in chapters 3 and 4, while the subsequent data were collected via the Internet by Knowledge Networks through their nationally representative internet panel. As discussed in chapter 1, Knowledge Networks' sampling methodology provides probability sampling that is highly robust and has been shown to be at least as efficient as other methods of recruiting respondents. Both the implementation of the survey via the Internet and the use of the Knowledge Networks panel do not threaten the validity or comparability of the results.[18] Thus—with the exception of a few minor formatting changes required by the change in survey mode that we next discuss—we are confident in the comparability of the October 2003 data with the subsequent surveys.

As discussed in chapter 1, we suggest that respondents' tolerance for casualties in the war in Iraq will be a function of two central explanatory variables: (1) the extent to which they believe that president Bush did the *Right thing* in attacking Iraq, and (2) the extent to which they believe that the United States will achieve *Success* in its mission. This argument is supported both by the aggregate data presented in chapter 2 and by the experimental results presented in chapter 4. In those experiments we found that expectations of success were a powerful determinant of support for all of our hypothetical missions. Changes in the perceived principal policy objective (PPO), on the other hand, appeared to shape support for the Yemen mission by providing a frame through which respondents could judge the benefits of *Success*. This attitude seems very close to one's judgment about whether using force is the right thing to do. Similarly, international elite cues about support for the war appeared to influence support for intervention in East Timor by shaping attitudes toward the justification of the mission. That is, the cues seem to influence perceptions that force is the right thing to do.

Those who feel strongly that the president did the right thing in attacking are expressing a belief that the Bush administration had good cause for using military force in this case. Specifically, we asked respondents, "I would like to know whether you think President Bush did the right thing by using military force against Iraq. Would you say that you strongly approve, somewhat approve, somewhat disapprove, or strongly disapprove of his decision?" The perceived reasons for approval or disapproval could be many—including the desire to enforce U.N. resolutions, the desire to

[18] See Dennis (2005) for an evaluation of interview mode effects, sampling, and panel effects that compares the Knowledge Networks panel to RDD telephone interviewing.

keep America secure from suspected Iraqi weapons of mass destruction (WMD), the desire to prevent Iraq from sharing suspected WMD with terrorists, the desire to promote human rights and punish a vicious dictator, or the desire to instill democratic governance in the Middle East. Whatever policy goal individuals may emphasize in their own thinking about why the president did the "right thing," we are arguing that it is something for which they would be willing to pay a cost if the goal were successfully achieved.

As noted before, we gathered data on public attitudes toward this question in a series of surveys from October 2003 through October 2004. The aggregate summary of those responses is displayed in table 5.1. Interestingly, public attitudes toward whether using force was—in retrospect—the right thing to do at the time, remained remarkably stable over the twelve months of surveys. The only substantial shift comes between October 2003 and February 2004. During that time we see the proportion of those who "strongly approve" of the president's decision drop from 42 percent to 30 percent. What can account for such an erosion of support? One prominent explanation could be the release of the Kay Report in January 2004, which cast serious doubt on the president's claim that the United States needed to use force in order to prevent Iraq from obtaining weapons of mass destruction. Such a shift would be broadly consistent with the contention that the public is both "rational" and "prudent" in its support of military force.[19]

Before being too confident in such conclusions, however, it is important to recall that the format of the response options shifted between the October and February survey waves. The October data were collected through a telephone survey and relied on the usual "branching" method for offering responses over the phone. That is, respondents were first asked whether they approved or disapproved of the decision to attack Iraq. Interviewers then followed up with a question about whether they strongly approved or somewhat approved of the decision (or strongly or somewhat disapproved, depending on the respondent's initial answer). The subsequent waves of the survey—from February through October 2004—all collected responses via the Internet, and, as if completing a typical mail survey, respondents made a single response to each of the full set of four responses. The available evidence on survey formats and survey responses suggest that the branching format tends to generate more extreme responses than presenting respondents with the entire response set at once.[20]

Returning to table 5.1, we can see that while the percentage of respondents that "strongly approve" of Bush's decision dropped twelve points

[19] Jentleson (1992); Jentleson and Britton (1998); Larson (2000).

[20] See Aldrich et al. (1982) and Bowers and Ensley (2003) on the impact of question formats.

Table 5.1.
Public Attitudes about Whether President Bush Did the Right Thing by Attacking Iraq, October 2003–October 2004

	22 Sept.–12 Oct. (n = 1,203)	*6–20 Feb. (n = 891)*	*25 Feb.–4 Mar. (n = 870)*	*5–18 Mar. (n = 930)*	*19 Mar.–2 Apr. (n = 889)*	*2–16 Apr. (n = 881)*	*17–29 Apr. (n = 899)*	*18–28 June (n = 900)*	*15 Oct.–1 Nov. (n = 1,125)*
Strongly approve	42%	30%	31%	32%	30%	31%	29%	30%	30%
Somewhat approve	19%	31%	32%	29%	29%	30%	31%	29%	26%
Somewhat disapprove	11%	18%	15%	19%	19%	16%	17%	15%	17%
Strongly disapprove	27%	21%	22%	19%	22%	23%	23%	27%	27%

between October 2003 and February 2004, the percentage that strongly *disapproved* of Bush's decision also decreased by six points. This would suggest that about half of the shift away from the "strongly approve" responses is due to question formatting rather than to a real shift in opinion. Moreover, if we pool the responses across the "approve" and "disapprove" categories to make the format of the responses comparable between October and February, we can see that the proportion of respondents who approved of the president's decision to attack Iraq remained unchanged at 61 percent. Thus the available evidence suggests that the Kay Report reduced some enthusiasm for the president's decision to attack Iraq by several points, but that attitudes toward whether the president did the right thing in attacking Iraq remained quite stable throughout our survey period.

The second key variable in our explanation captures a respondent's judgment about the likelihood that the United States will be able to achieve whatever goals he or she believes are at stake in Iraq (*Success*). Our measure makes an effort to separate beliefs about likely victory from any expectations of benefits. Specifically, we asked respondents, "regardless of whether you think that the president did the right thing, would you say that the United States is very likely to succeed in Iraq, somewhat likely to succeed, not very likely to succeed, or not at all likely to succeed?" We did not specify for respondents what "success" might mean; as we discuss later, we probed precisely that question in follow-up surveys.

The aggregate responses to this question are summarized in table 5.2. As with attitudes toward whether Bush did the right thing, perceptions of success remained relatively stable over this period. We do see, however, more erosion in public confidence about success than we do a public reevaluation of whether Bush's initial decision was the right thing. For example, the proportion of respondents who stated that the United States was either "very likely" or "somewhat likely" to succeed eroded from over 76 percent in October 2003 to just under 62 percent in June of 2004.[21] Between June and October 2004 this erosion appears to have stopped, and public confidence even edged up slightly, though in October 2004 it was not nearly as high as it had been a year earlier.

Interestingly, public expectations of success also appear to have shifted sensibly in response to real-world events. The period from October 2003 to June 2004 was marked largely by bad news for U.S. forces in Iraq who faced an increasingly active and coordinated insurgency. As we noted in chapter 2, however, June 2004 brought the transfer of sovereignty back

[21] Note that this shift cannot be attributed to the branching question format in the October 2003 survey, because we are comparing across the initial categories offered in the branching format.

TABLE 5.2.
Public Attitudes about Whether the United States Will Succeed in Iraq, October 2003–October 2004

	22 Sept.– 12 Oct. (n = 1,203)	*6–20 Feb. (n = 891)*	*25 Feb.– 4 Mar. (n = 870)*	*5–18 Mar. (n = 930)*	*19 Mar.– 2 Apr. (n = 889)*	*2–16 Apr. (n = 881)*	*17–29 Apr. (n = 899)*	*18–28 June (n = 900)*	*15 Oct.– 1 Nov. (n = 1,125)*
Very likely	34%	30%	26%	27%	27%	25%	26%	25%	27%
Somewhat likely	42%	40%	42%	41%	40%	40%	40%	37%	37%
Not very likely	17%	24%	24%	24%	24%	27%	24%	28%	27%
Not at all likely	7%	6%	9%	8%	8%	8%	10%	11%	9%

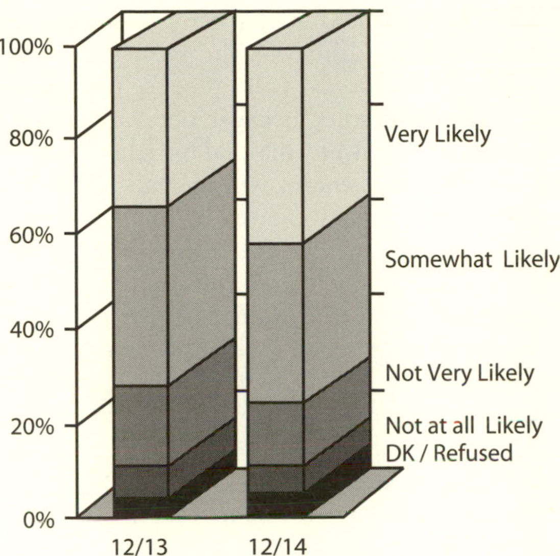

FIGURE 5.2. A "Natural Experiment": The Capture of Hussein and Expectations of Success, an MSNBC/Wall Street Journal Poll

to Iraq and this progress appears to have stemmed the erosion of public confidence.

A more dramatic example of how public attitudes shift in response to real-world events can be found in the public's response to the one major piece of good news for U.S. forces during this period: the capture of Saddam Hussein. We had the surprisingly good fortune of having MSNBC agree to field our question regarding public expectations of success at exactly the time that U.S. forces captured Hussein. Specifically, MSNBC and the *Wall Street Journal* began fielding a poll on 13 December 2003 that included our question about expected success. That very night U.S. forces captured Saddam in his spider hole and Americans awoke to a flood of news regarding his capture. MSNBC continued to field its survey—giving us a very nice "natural experiment" to measure the impact of the capture of Hussein on expectations of success in Iraq. The results of this natural experiment are displayed in figure 5.2. The capture of Hussein created an overnight "bounce" of 8 percent in the proportion responding that the United States is "very likely" to succeed in Iraq, indicating that the public quickly absorbed this information and incorporated it into their judgments about the likely success of the mission. Moreover, this experiment probably gives us a conservative estimate of the impact of Hussein's capture, because some respondents may not have heard about the capture or may have taken more time to make judgments about the likely impact of his capture.

Consistent with our argument in chapter 1, we expect that these two attitudes—whether invading Iraq was the right thing and whether the United States is likely to succeed—will influence tolerance for casualties in combination with one another, because one variable taps the benefits that a respondent hopes might be obtained by using force while the other taps the probability that the benefits will be realized. Tolerance for costs should be a function of benefits weighted by the probability of achieving them. These two attitudes can combine in four basic combinations. Respondents in the first category, which in this case might be considered the "Bush Base," believe the war was right and that the United States will win. Those in the opposite category, which we would call "the Vietnam Syndrome" believe the war was wrong and the United States will lose. Obviously, we would expect the former group to have much greater casualty tolerance than the latter group. But respondents with intermediate attitudes—the "Noble Failure" view that the war was right but we will lose, and the "Pottery Barn—we broke it, we'll fix it" view that the war was wrong but we will win—pose more interesting theoretical questions that allow us to compare the relative importance of the two attitudes in shaping casualty tolerance.

Based on the anecdotal evidence from chapter 2 and the experimental evidence from chapter 4, we contend that expectations of success will matter more and thus the "Pottery Barn" respondent will express a greater tolerance than the "Noble Failure" respondent for the human costs of war. While our expectation is based partly on our previous empirical results, there is also an intuitive logic to the proposition that prospective expectations of success will matter most in determining citizens' willingness to continue paying the costs of an ongoing conflict. Even if one believes that the United States was unjustified in attacking Iraq, an American failure in Iraq could damage its reputation or leave Iraq vulnerable to the infiltration of terrorist groups. All of which would mean that American lives were lost in vain. Indeed, some could argue that once a conflict has begun, America has an intrinsic national interest in winning regardless of the original rationale. In chapter 4 we found that expectations of success mattered most in determining ex ante support for military operations. Once an operation is already underway and respondents are faced with whether or not to support its continuation, we expect success to carry an even greater weight in their calculations.

As noted earlier, our theory calls for a statistical model in which the impact of each of our key variables depends upon the value of the other variable. We test this interactive theory against a simpler model, which simply holds that both perceptions of whether invading Iraq was the *Right thing* to do and perceptions of the likely *Success* of the mission have independent influences on casualty tolerance.

Measuring Casualty Tolerance in the Iraq War

As in chapter 3, our dependent variable is the respondents' willingness to continue to support military operations in Iraq as the human cost continues to mount. As we argued in that chapter, "casualty tolerance" measures support for the Iraq War in the most theoretically and politically meaningful way because it focuses on the crucial issue of whether increases in casualties will cause the public to place pressure on their leaders to withdraw from an ongoing military conflict. Perhaps the most commonly used measures of "war support" are questions that ask respondents whether a particular military operation was a "mistake." The "mistake" question, however, does not lend itself well to studying policy preferences or costs in cross-sectional studies. Mueller (1973) adopts the mistake question because it is the only one that "tapped a sort of generalized support for the war and that was asked repeatedly in both wars" and "seems to be a sound measure of a sort of general support for the war" (Mueller 1973:43). Thus this question became the standard question not because it ties to a specific theoretical or empirical concern, but because pollsters asked about it during both the Korean and Vietnam Wars. Among the very notable weaknesses of the mistake question is that it "says little about policy preferences at any given moment" (Mueller 1973:43). We question the utility of a dependent measure of war support that cannot be tied to policy choices or the central question of costs. While the question of whether the war was a "mistake" may be relevant to other important questions—such as the impact of the war on electoral behavior—the relationship between casualties and pressure for withdrawal is central to the theoretical debates outlined in chapter 1. Moreover, casualty tolerance focuses our attention directly on the dilemma facing policymakers: At what point do the costs of war necessitate American withdrawal?

We also believe that our measure of casualty tolerance does a better job of gauging the policy relevant issue of continued support of an ongoing military operation than do other more commonly used measures of casualty sensitivity—such as questions about whether the war has been "worth it." For example, after asking whether the Iraq war has been "worth it," we probed respondents about why the war has or has not been "worth it." Approximately 45 percent of respondents who felt that the Iraq war has not been "worth it" indicated that the primary reason they felt that way was "the United States should not have gone to war over this issue in the first place." Less than one-third of those who stated the war has not been "worth it" stated that their most important reason for their response was the number of U.S. soldiers killed. Moreover, in October 2004 more than 25 percent of the respondents who stated that the Iraq war had not been "worth it" still stated that they would support the war if there were as many as 1,500 U.S. combat deaths. Thus "worth it" questions appear to tap some mixture of respondents' views about casualty tolerance, their evaluation of the reasons for fighting, and their evaluation of the prospects of success, making those data less useful for evaluating relationships among those various attitudes. We believe that our measure more effectively isolates attitudes about the willingness to pay costs and frames the question in a way most relevant to policymakers: Will the respondent be willing to continue to support an ongoing military operation in the face of rising costs? This distinction may explain why public opposition to the war—measured in terms of public demonstration and demand for abandoning the conflict—has not grown as swiftly as the number of respondents saying the war has not been "worth it."

Our measure of casualty tolerance in Iraq relies on the same ordinal measurement scale that we constructed in chapter 3. Specifically, we asked, "Regardless of whether you think the president made the right decision in attacking Iraq, as you know the United States is engaged in an ongoing military operation there and has suffered about ______ military deaths in combat.[22] Would you support continued U.S. military action in Iraq until a new Iraqi government can take over if it resulted in no additional U.S. military deaths?" If a respondent answered affirmatively, we asked again, raising the number of deaths. (Those who answered negatively were skipped to the next question.) In the October 2003 survey each respondent had a chance to answer if he or she would support the war if there were up to 500 deaths, then to 5,000, finally to 50,000, jumping to the next level if the respondent stated that he or she would continue to support the operation. The lowest casualty threshold—five hundred deaths was updated in subsequent survey as the number of U.S. combat deaths increased.[23] We continued to ask about tolerance for a number of casualties that was about 200 to 400 deaths higher than the number of U.S. casualties at the time of the survey. Since the rate of U.S. military deaths has remained quite consistent since the end of major combat operations, our question essentially asks respondents if the are willing to continue supporting the war in Iraq for at least the next three to six months.

This series of questions produces a five category ordinal variable. The first category represents those who said they would not support the war even if there were no more U.S. deaths; one might think of this as a "stop now" sort of response. The second category represents those who stated

[22] For each wave of the survey we inserted the appropriate death toll at the beginning of the wave.

[23] Note that any potential bias from changes in question wording would tend to *exaggerate* the apparent casualty sensitivity in the new surveys. As we are arguing that the public is more casualty tolerant than commonly believed, this poses no problems for our analysis.

that they would support the war if no more U.S. soldiers were killed, but would not support the war if there were a total of five hundred U.S. military deaths. We would label these respondents as "casualty phobic" because they are willing to support the operation, but only if the human costs are minimally higher than they were at that point (around 300 combat deaths). The third category of respondents essentially offers policymakers a "window of opportunity" to prosecute the war. They stated that they would support the war despite an additional 200 deaths, but would not support the war if 5,000 Americans were killed. The remaining categories of respondents were varying levels of "Iraqi hawks," promising continued support for the war even if casualties mounted to levels far in excess of anything military experts expected given the situation in October 2003. The fourth category promised continued support if five thousand U.S. soldiers were killed but would withdraw their support if the U.S. suffered fifty thousand military deaths. The fifth category of respondents stated that they would support the war even if the United States suffered 50,000 deaths.

We followed up the October 2003 survey with a series of shorter polls from February through June 2004, asking a similar casualty question updated to reflect the new casualty tally. In the surveys from February through April we set the "window of opportunity" threshold for casualty tolerance at one thousand U.S. military deaths. In June 2004, we increased the "window of opportunity" to 1,500 because of the increasing U.S. death toll. Finally in the last two weeks of October 2004 we conducted a larger survey in the context of the impending presidential election. In this survey the "window of opportunity" was also set at 1,500.

Table 5.3 presents the summary statistics for the questions used to construct our ordinal dependent variable. These are separate samples, not panel data, limiting our ability to draw inferences about changes over time. The results, however, suggest four important points. First, our survey question appears to be tapping into real attitudes because the numbers are stable yet move in sensible ways; as the casualty toll mounts, the proportions in the various groups shift accordingly, except for the "Iraqi hawks," whose professed casualty tolerance vastly exceeds the actual mounting death toll.

Second, like most questions about tolerance for casualties, our surveys tend to exaggerate public casualty sensitivity.[24] While mounting casualties did shift the aggregate response to our casualty tolerance question, they did not do so by as much as the earlier survey responses suggested they would.[25] Moreover, the response options capture only crude jumps. Someone who

[24] See Feaver and Gelpi, *Choosing Your Battles*, for an account of question wording effects and the use of hypothetical scenarios to measure casualty tolerance

[25] One possible explanation for this phenomenon is "sunk costs" thinking on the part of the respondents. That is, as the United States pays higher costs in Iraq, the public may become more determined to ensure that those losses are not in vain.

Table 5.3.
Public Tolerance for U.S. Military Deaths in Iraq, October 2003–October 2004

	22 Sept.– 12 Oct. (n = 1,203)	*6–20 Feb. (n = 891)*	*25 Feb.– 4 Mar. (n = 870)*	*5–18 Mar. (n = 930)*	*19 Mar.– 2 Apr. (n = 889)*	*2–16 Apr. (n = 881)*	*17–29 Apr. (n = 899)*	*18–28 June (n = 900)*	*15 Oct.– 1 Nov. (n = 1,125)*
Opposed regardless of U.S. deaths	15%	23%	21%	23%	23%	24%	24%	25%	23%
Will not tolerate 500/1000/1500 U.S. deaths	24%	32%	32%	33%	33%	30%	28%	31%	24%
Tolerate at least 500/1000/1500 U.S. deaths	32%	19%	22%	20%	21%	18%	18%	16%	20%
Tolerate at least 5,000 U.S. deaths	16%	15%	14%	13%	11%	15%	17%	13%	17%
Tolerate at least 50,000 U.S. deaths	11%	11%	11%	11%	12%	12%	14%	15%	16%
Approximate U.S. deaths as survey begins	300	520	535	540	565	600	685	800	1,100

might tolerate up to 2000 or even 4000 casualties but not 5000 is coded as accepting "at least 1000" in our data. Third, even with this biased estimator, the public shows more casualty tolerance than the conventional wisdom expects. Finally, consistent with our expectations from the analysis of presidential approval in chapter 2, our individual-level data suggest that public casualty tolerance actually increased between June and October 2004. Specifically, in October 50 percent of the respondents stated that they would be willing to tolerate 1,500 U.S. military deaths, while only 44 percent expressed that view in June. This increase occurred despite the massive media coverage given to passing the threshold of one thousand U.S. combat deaths in Iraq.[26]

While these results—along with those presented in chapter 3—indicate that our measure of casualty tolerance is relatively reliable and robust as a measure of casualty tolerance in the abstract, some questions might be raised about how adequately such a measure can capture public attitudes in a specific and concrete historical context such as the war in Iraq. For example, our question asks respondents about the number of battle deaths in Iraq, but many opponents of the war raised questions about whether the public was actually aware of the human cost of the war. This controversy was most prominently visible in the debate over whether the media should be allowed to take pictures of the arrival of caskets bearing fallen soldiers at Dover Air Force Base.[27] Moreover, opponents also questioned the extent to which knowledge of the number of soldiers wounded in Iraq might turn the public against the war.[28]

We took several steps to ensure that our measure is not biased by such issues. First, with regard to public knowledge of the number of U.S. military deaths, the available polling data suggests that the public was quite accurate in its perception of the number of U.S. soldiers killed in Iraq.[29] Nonetheless, to ensure that we were capturing public attitudes that accurately reflected the current context of the Iraq conflict, we provided

[26] See, for example, James Dao, "How Many Deaths Are Too Many?" *New York Times*, 12 September 2004; or Monica Davey, "For 1,000 Troops, There Is No Going Home, *New York Times*, 9 September 2004.

[27] See, for example, Bill Carter, "Pentagon Ban on Pictures of Dead Troops Is Broken," *New York Times*, 23vApril 2004; Sheryl Gay Stolberg, "Senate Backs Ban on Photos of G.I. Coffins," *New York Times*, 22 June 2004.

[28] Much of this kind of argument was made by bloggers and other non-mainstream new sources, but mainstream media did raise the question of public knowledge about casualties. In asking about the likely impact of casualties on public support for the Iraq War, for example, Jim Lehrer asked, "Now, on the casualties issue, well, first of all, do the polls in any way reflect a lack of knowledge on the part of the public? I mean, do people want more information, are do they feel they have enough information to answer these polls?" *The Jim Lehrer News Hour*, 7 October 2002.

[29] See Kull et al. 2003a, 2003b).

TABLE 5.4.
Experimental Impact of Number Wounded on Casualty Tolerance in Iraq

Opposed regardless of U.S. deaths	207 23%	Opposed regardless of U.S. deaths & wounded	50 25%
Will not tolerate 1,500 U.S. deaths	220 24%	Will not tolerate 1,500 U.S. deaths & 10,000 wounded	44 22%
Tolerate at least 1,500 U.S. deaths	189 21%	Tolerate at least 1,500 U.S. deaths & 10,000 wounded	37 19%
Tolerate at least 5,000 U.S. deaths	156 17%	Tolerate at least 5,000 U.S. deaths & 30,000 wounded	36 19%
Tolerate at least 50,000 U.S. deaths	145 16%	Tolerate at least 50,000 U.S. deaths & 300,000 wounded	32 16%
Cases in treatment category	917		199

Pearson chi-squared: (4 d.f.) = 1.15, $p < .886$

respondents with information about the number of U.S. soldiers that had been killed at that time.

Second, in order to determine whether information about the number of wounded would alter public attitudes, we conducted a question wording experiment to evaluate sensitivity of our measure of casualty tolerance to the inclusion of information about those wounded in combat as well as those killed. Specifically, while most of the respondents received the series of questions about casualty tolerance that reminded them of the number of U.S. soldiers who had been killed, we randomly selected 20 percent of the respondents to receive information both about the number of U.S. soldiers killed and the number of U.S. soldiers wounded. Then those respondents were asked if they would support a continuation of the war effort at increasingly levels of military dead and wounded. Thus while 80 percent of the respondents in the October 2004 survey were told that approximately 1,000 US soldiers had been killed, 20 percent were told that the United States had suffered about 1,000 killed and nearly 7,000 wounded. Then instead of being asked whether they would tolerate 1,500 U.S. deaths, they were asked whether they would tolerate 1,500 deaths and over 10,000 wounded. Those who were willing to tolerate that level of casualties were then asked about 5,000 U.S. deaths and over 30,000 wounded, and eventually 50,000 U.S. military deaths and 300,000 wounded.

The results of this experiment are displayed in table 5.4. Clearly our measure of casualty tolerance is quite robust to the inclusion of informa-

position on the war did not change during the time we were surveying. We can observe the impact of the U.N.'s failure to endorse the U.S. invasion, however, by examining individual attitudes toward multilateralism influence casualty tolerance in Iraq.

Numerous polls indicate that the American public looks favorably on gaining allied support for U.S. military operations and on gaining U.N. Security Council authority for using force. This minimal level of multilateralism, however, does not adequately measure the impact that multilateralism should have on casualty tolerance and the war in Iraq. After all, even many policymakers who are widely viewed as "unilateralist" would agree that ceteris paribus it is better to have multilateral international support. The critical question is what should the United States do if it is *unable* to obtain international legitimization for a particular mission? With regard to U.N. authorization, for example, should the president proceed with a mission alone if he deems it necessary and cannot persuade the U.N. to sanction force? Or should the president postpone the mission until he is able to obtain support from the Security Council? To the extent that multilateralism has a substantive constraining effect on U.S. policy, we contend that it implies the latter attitude.[33] Thus Kull's argument about the impact of multilateralism on public support implies that respondents who hold the latter belief should be substantially less willing to tolerate casualties in Iraq, since the president chose to launch the attack without explicit U.N. approval.[34]

Analyzing Individual Attitudes toward Casualty Tolerance

The results of our individual-level analysis of public tolerance for casualties in Iraq in October 2004 are displayed in table 5.5. We use ordered logit, which is analogous to linear regression but is the most appropriate

[33] This is the same attitude that we believe we were tapping with our experimental treatment in chapter 4 when we observed that a withdrawal of U.N. support lead to a reduction in approval for using force.

[34] Specifically, we asked, "Before deciding to take military action, the president often seeks the approval of international organizations like the United Nations. What should the president do if he is not able to gain that approval?" The response options were (1) "He should not take military action period, regardless of whether he can get international approval": (2) "He should delay military action until he receives international approval"; (3) "He should take military action even without international approval if he thinks it is necessary": and (4) "He should not seek international approval before deciding to take military action."

TABLE 5.5.
Individual Sources of Public Tolerance for Casualties in Iraq, October 2004

	Additive Model	*Interactive Model*
President Bush did right thing	0.451	0.038
	(5.23)**	(0.27)
U.S. will succeed	0.957	0.582
	(9.84)**	(4.18)**
Right thing × *Success*		0.241
		(3.64)**
Perceived elite consensus	0.657	0.645
	(5.27)**	(5.19)**
Oppose force without U.N. approval	–0.348	–0.333
	(–3.60)**	(3.45)**
Terrorism is PPO in Iraq War	0.127	0.158
	(1.60)	(1.99)*
Female respondent	–0.242	–0.242
	(–2.01)*	(2.01)*
Non-white respondent	–0.698	–0.666
	(–4.06)**	(3.91)**
Age	0.130	0.122
	(2.20)*	(2.07)*
Education level	0.281	0.273
	(4.37)	(4.24)**
Party ID	–0.93	–0.084
	(–2.49)*	(2.25)*
Observations	995	995
Log likelihood	–1262.088	–1255.489

Likelihood ratio test: Interactive Model > Additive Model = 13.2 (1 d.f.). $p < .01$
Absolute value of z statistics in parentheses
* significant at 5%   ** significant at 1%

statistical method for analyzing our ordinal measure of casualty tolerance. The results provide strong support for each of our expectations regarding the nature of the public's tolerance for casualties. To begin with, the results clearly indicate that our theory about the interactive impact of *Right thing* and *Success* fits the data better than a simpler model in which each of the variables has an independent impact. The coefficient for the interaction between these two attitudes is strongly statistically significant, and a likelihood ratio test clearly indicates that our data are more likely to have been generated by the interactive model.[35]

Interpretation of the specific coefficients requires some care because of the interactive nature of the relationship among the perceived rightness or wrongness of the war, expected success, and tolerance for costs; but a careful review of the coefficients in the model indicates that our interactive model of the rightness (*Right thing*) of the war and expectations of *Success* has a very significant impact on tolerance for casualties.[36]

The coefficient for respondents' attitudes about whether President Bush did the *Right thing* represents the impact of respondents' views regarding the rightness of the war on their tolerance for casualties *when respondents believe that the United States is not very likely to succeed*. Similarly, the coefficient for respondents' attitudes about whether the United States is likely to achieve *Success* in Iraq represents the impact that expectations of success have on respondents' tolerance for casualties *when they strongly disapprove of the president's decision to go to war*. As expected, the coefficient for expectations of success is larger than the coefficient for the justification of the war. A chi-squared test reveals that this difference is statistically significant (chi = 13.04, 1 d.f., $p < .001$). This result indicates

[35] As with any interactive model, the levels of colinearity for the interaction term and its constituent components are relatively high. Specifically, the auxiliary r-squared values for *Right thing*, expectations of *Success*, and their interaction are 0.86, 0.75, and 0.91 respectively. Colinearity levels for *Right thing* and *Success* are somewhat lower in the additive specification at 0.64 and 0.49 respectively. The colinearity present in the interactive specification is not a problem for our model, however, since the consequence of colinearity is to increase the standard errors of the coefficients, and both rightness and success have a statistically significant impact. The one possible exception would be the fact that "*Right thing* does not have a statistically significant impact when *Success* is at its minimum value (0). However, this result appears to be driven by a very small coefficient rather than an inflated standard error. Comparing the additive and interactive specification, for example, indicates that the shift to the interactive specification reduces the coefficient for *Right thing* from 0.451 to 0.038, while the standard error for this coefficient increases only from 0.09 to 0.14. Thus the impact of *Right thing* would have remained statistically insignificant in the interactive model even if its standard error had not increased at all due to higher levels of colinearity. Auxiliary r-squared values for all other variables were below 0.5 and most were below 0.1.

[36] There is no simple "goodness of fit" measure for ordinal logit models. Pseudo r-squared measures vary widely and other intuitive measures like the percentage of correct predictions are also arbitrary. See Demarchi, Gelpi, and Grynaviski, "Untangling Neural Nets," *American Political Science Review* (June 2004). The best available measure of fit for dichotomous logit or probit models is the Receiver Operating Characteristic curve (see Demarchi, Gelpi, and Grynaviski, "Untangling Neural Nets." But this measure is not appropriate for polytomous dependent variables. If one uses the model in table 5.3 to make dichotomous predictions about whether respondents will fall in the "window of opportunity" category (tolerate at least 1,500 U.S. deaths), the area under the ROC curve in this model is a respectable 0.78 (95 percent confidence interval 0.76 to 0.81).

that expectations about victory have a greater impact on casualty tolerance when respondents are skeptical about the justification of the war than their views about the rightness of the war have when they are skeptical about victory.

Those who are skeptical of the rightness of the war yet expect to win may be willing to pay higher costs than those who believe in the cause yet expect to lose, but the results in table 5.5 also clearly indicate that these attitudes interact and work together in determining an individual's tolerance for casualties. The coefficient for the interaction term "*Right thing* × *Success* is positive and statistically significant, indicating that each of our key variables—views of the rightness of the war, and expectations of success—has a greater impact on casualty tolerance as the *other* variable increases. That is, one's expectations regarding success have a greater impact on casualty tolerance if one believes that Bush was right to attack Iraq than if one believes that Bush was wrong to do so. Similarly, one's views regarding the rightness of the war have a greater impact on casualty tolerance if one expects the United States to win the war than if one is skeptical of success.

While the impact of both *Right thing* and *Success* on casualty tolerance increases as the other attitude increases, the rate of increase for both variables is determined by the interaction term. Thus *Success* continues to have a larger impact on casualty tolerance than belief in the rightness of the war (*Right thing)* at the corresponding level of the other attitude. More specifically, the coefficients for *Right thing* and *Success* in the interactive model in table 5.5 indicate that *Success* has a larger impact on casualty tolerance when *Right thing* takes on a value of 0 than does *Right thing* when *Success* is 0. The same holds true as each variable increases. Thus success has a greater impact on casualty tolerance when *Right thing* is 1 than does *Right thing* when *Success* takes on a value of 1, and so on. Since both variables are four-point scales ranging from 0 to 3, this result supports our expectation that prospective judgments about success will matter more than retrospective judgments about the "rightness" of the conflict (*Right thing*) when deciding whether to continue to support an ongoing military conflict. We describe the substantive size of this difference in greater detail later.

While the data indicate that our interactive specification is a better description of respondents' casualty tolerance than the additive model, we would note that this conclusion about the primacy of success as a cause of casualty tolerance is not an artifact of this specification. The coefficients for *Right thing* and *Success* in the additive model in table 5.5 also indicate that success has the greater impact. Specifically the coefficient for expectations that "U.S. will achieve success" is more than twice as large as the coefficient for whether the "president did the right thing."

The difference between these coefficients is strongly statistically significant ($p < .01$).

While our argument concerning the sources of casualty tolerance receives strong statistical support, so too do the arguments made by Jentleson, Larson, and Kull. Each of the control variables measuring perceptions of the links between Iraq and the war on terror, perceptions of an elite consensus, and support for international constraints on the U.S. use of force are statistically significant in the expected direction. Specifically, both the belief that Iraq is a part of the war on terror, and the belief that Democratic and Republican leaders all support a continued U.S. presence in Iraq, significantly increase a respondent's casualty tolerance. On the other hand, the multilateralist belief that the United States should delay using force in order to obtain U.N. approval reduces casualty tolerance in this case.

Thus, just as was the case in the experimental results in chapter 4, we find statistical support for all of the four central arguments about the sources of casualty tolerance—but how important are these various attitudes relative to one another? The substantive effects of the rightness of the war (*Right thing*) and expectations of *Success* are displayed in figure 5.3. The vertical axis displays the probability that respondents would tolerate at least 1,500 casualties.

The axis running from left to right depicts changes in a respondent's attitude about the likelihood that the United States will succeed in Iraq, while the axis running from the front of the figure to the back depicts changes in a respondent's attitude toward whether President Bush did the right thing in choosing to use force against Iraq. The columns depicting predicted casualty tolerance clearly demonstrate the interactive nature of the relationship between these variables. Not surprisingly, casualty tolerance is at its lowest point in the left-front "Vietnam Syndrome" corner of figure 5.3 when a respondent strongly disapproves of the decision to attack in the first place and thinks we are not at all likely to succeed, and casualty tolerance is at its highest in the right-rear "Bush Base" corner when a respondent strongly approves of the decision to attack and thinks that the United States is very likely to succeed. What the figure also clearly demonstrates is that the impact of each of these variables on an individual's willingness to pay costs and support the war varies dramatically. For example, if we examine each row of columns moving from front to back, we can see the impact that changes in a respondent's attitude toward the rightness of the war has on his or her tolerance for casualties at each level different level of expectations regarding American success. Similarly, if we examine each row of columns moving from left to right we can see the impact that expectations of success depending on the respondent's level of approval for the initial attack.

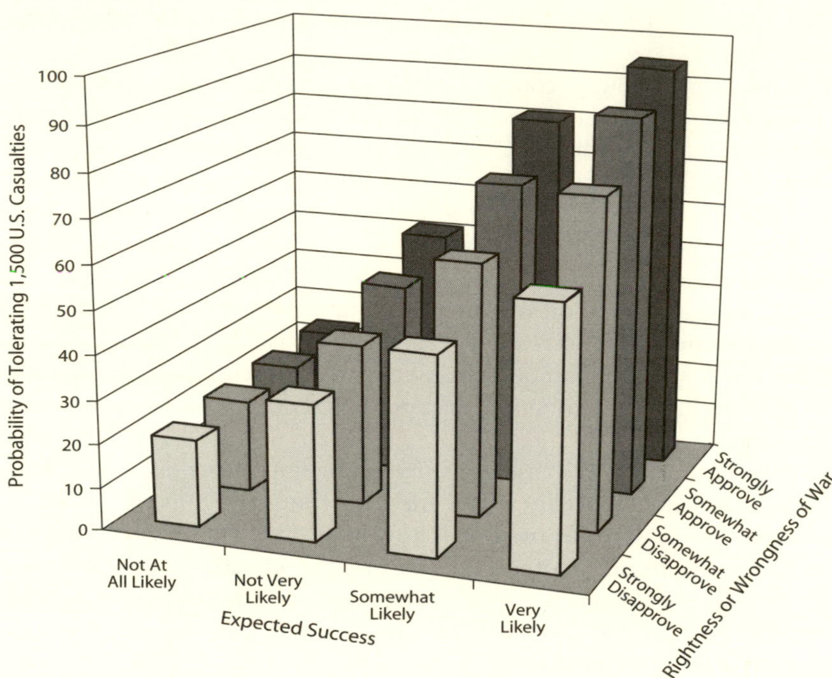

FIGURE 5.3. Impact of Belief in Success and Rightness of War on Tolerance for Casualties, October 2004

Turning to the far left-hand column we can see that there is virtually no change in a respondent's casualty tolerance as we move from the front to the back of the figure. This row captures the effect of changes in a respondent's attitude toward the rightness of the war when he or she believes that victory is "not at all likely." Under these circumstances, changes in one's attitude about whether President Bush did the right thing in attacking Iraq has no impact on tolerance for casualties. Specifically, increasing a respondent's attitude toward the justification for the attack from "strongly disapprove" to "strongly approve" increases only from 20 to 23 percent the probability that a respondent will provide the Bush administration with a "window of opportunity" to prosecute the war.

Moving to the far right-hand row, we can see that the impact of the respondent's attitudes toward the rightness of the war becomes much more important if the respondent is optimistic about the prospects for success. Our model predicts a 50 percent chance that a respondent who "strongly disapproves" of the president's decision but still believes that the United States is "very likely" to succeed will tolerate at least 1,500 casualties. In this case, however, increasing the respondent's view of Bush's justification for the war to "strongly approve" increases to over 90 percent the likelihood that he or she would tolerate at least 1,500 casualties.

The same type of interactive relationship holds for the impact of expectations of success, but the relationship is stronger in this case. As the front row indicates, for a respondent who "strongly disapproves" of the decision to use force, increasing his or her optimism from "not at all likely" to succeed to "very likely" to succeed increases from 20 to 50 percent the probability that he or she will tolerate at least 1,500 casualties. But if a respondent already "strongly approves" of Bush's decision to attack, then increasing his or her level of optimism from "not at all likely" to succeed to "very likely" to succeed increases from 23 to 90 percent the probability that he or she will support a "window of opportunity" for the president.

The predicted probabilities in figure 5.3 allow us to say more about which attitude is a more important cause of casualty tolerance: beliefs about the rightness of the attack, or the likelihood of success. Clearly both attitudes are important and they work together in determining a respondent's threshold for the tolerable human costs of war. The results, however, also indicate that—at the margin—attitudes toward expectations of success are more influential than attitudes toward the rightness or wrongness of the conflict. The greater influence of expectations for success can be seen in several places in figure 5.3. First, it is illustrated through a comparison of the right-front and left-rear corners of the figure. By comparing the right-front and left-rear columns, we can see that the "Pottery Barn" respondent (skeptical of the justification, but optimistic regarding success) has a 50 percent chance of tolerating 1,500 casualties, while the "Noble Failure" respondent has only a 23 percent chance.

One can also see the greater impact of expectations for success by examining some of the intermediate columns. For example, our model predicts that no matter what their views on the justification of the war, a majority of respondents will not tolerate at least 500–1000 casualties if they also believe that victory is "not very likely" or "not at all likely." Even among those who "strongly approve" of the decision to attack, slightly less than 50 percent of such respondents will tolerate 1,500 casualties if they think that victory is "not very likely." Expectations of success, however, have a considerably greater impact. Our model predicts that 75 percent of respondents who "somewhat disapprove" of Bush's decision to attack will nonetheless tolerate at least 1,500 U.S. military deaths if they believe that victory is very likely. This implies that the president can garner the support from a majority of those who are moderately skeptical of the war's justification by persuading them that victory is very likely.

Of course, these two attitudes are not the only factors determining a respondent's willingness to tolerate costs in war. As we noted earlier, we also find support for arguments made by Jentleson, Larson, and Kull.

TABLE 5.6.
Impact of Additional Sources of Casualty Tolerance in Iraq, October 2004

Explanatory variable	*Change in explanatory variable*	*Change in probability of tolerating at least 1,500 U.S. military deaths*
Perceived elite consensus	No to yes	+14%
Oppose force without U.N.	No to yes	–6%
Terror is Iraq War PPO	"Distraction" to "central front"	+10%
Age	18–29 to 60+ years old	+8%
Gender	Male to female	–5%
Race	White to non-white	–16%
Level of education	No H.S. to college degree	+18%
Party ID	Strong Rep. to strong Dem.	–11%

Substantive effects of the variables examined in their studies and the demographic controls are displayed in table 5.6. With regard to Jentleson's contention that PPO is the key to public support, we find that those who believe that the war in Iraq is the "central front" in the war on terrorism are 10 percent more likely to tolerate 1,500 casualties than a respondent who believes that Iraq is a distraction from the war on terror. Perceptions of an elite consensus supporting U.S. troops in Iraq raises by 14 percent the likelihood that a respondent will tolerate 1,500 combat deaths. Finally, consistent with Kull's emphasis on multilateralism, we find that those who believe that the U.S. president should refrain from using force until he obtains U.N. sanction are 6 percent less likely to tolerate 1,500 U.S. military deaths.

While the variables identified by Jentleson, Larson, and Kull all influence tolerance for casualties, the substantive impact of these variables does not approach the influence of the interaction of the "rightness" of the war and expectations of success depicted in figure 5.3. While other factors may bump the proportion of respondents who are in the "window of opportunity" up or down by 10 to 20 percent, the interaction of the rightness and success variables can have as much as a 70 percent shift up or down in the proportion of respondents in the "window." Once we account for this interaction, other factors recede in terms of their relative importance.

These results, however, do not necessarily imply that the overall impact of the perceived PPO, elite consensus, and multilateralism are minimal. The effects displayed in table 5.6 are estimated on the assumption that attitudes toward the rightness of the war and expectations of success remain constant. Thus our results could indicate that variables such as elite consensus, perceived PPO, and multilateralism influence casualty tolerance indirectly through their impact on attitudes toward the rightness of the war and its prospects for success. We return to this issue in greater detail in chapter 7.

Finally, we found that a number of demographic factors also had a significant impact on the public's tolerance for casualties.[37] With one exception, these effects were in the direction one would expect from intuition and previous research, but none of these effects approaches the substantive importance of a respondent's expected value calculation regarding the tolerable cost of the war.

One might expect that those closer in age to most of the soldiers risking their lives would identify more closely with the casualties suffered and would be less willing to tolerate these costs, and we find that respondents who are older than 59 are about 13 percent more likely to tolerate at least 1,500 casualties in Iraq than respondents under 30 years old.[38] This effect is quite robust across our nine waves of surveys, but it differs from previous findings on the impact of age.[39] While our data do not allow us to make clear inferences about the reason for this pattern, we suspect that older respondents are more likely to have experienced conflicts—such as Korea, Vietnam, or World War II—in which the United States suffered substantially larger numbers of military deaths than we have yet experienced in Iraq. This greater familiarity with the costs of war may cause them to be more willing—on average—to tolerate the human costs of war.

Second, we find that women are about 6 percent less likely than men to support a "window of opportunity" for continuing the war. Unlike our findings regarding the impact of age, however, this result is consistent with previous research on casualty tolerance.[40]

[37] Feaver and Gelpi, *Choosing Your Battles.*

[38] Our measure divides respondents into four age categories: 18–29, 30–44, 45–59, and over 59

[39] Feaver and Gelpi (2004).

[40] Wilcox et al. (1993); Bendyna and Finucane (1996); Gartner, Segura, and Wilkening (1997); Nincic and Nincic (2002); Eichenberg (2003); Feaver and Gelpi (2004).

Third, we find that non-white respondents are about 15 percent less likely than white respondents to tolerate at least 1,500 casualties. Once again, there are a variety of possible explanations for this pattern. It is possible, for example, that minority respondents are less willing to tolerate casualties because they believe that the risks of military service are not borne equally by whites and non-whites. Alternatively, minority respondents may resent the diversion of fiscal resources toward the war away from domestic programs that benefit minority communities. It is worth noting, however, that while demographic patterns regarding casualty tolerance such as the gender gap are consistent across a variety of conflicts, minority respondents appear to be less supportive of some wars and more supportive of others.[41]

Education also has a significant impact on the public's tolerance for casualties in Iraq. The likely reason for this effect is that while the costs of military conflict are both vivid and concrete, the benefits are often diffuse and difficult to measure—especially in a conflict like the current war in Iraq, where American soil and American citizens were not directly at risk. More educated respondents are more likely to have a broader and more abstract view of American "national security interests." As a result, they would tend to see more at stake for the United States in conflicts such as the war in Iraq and are willing to tolerate greater costs in order to prosecute such a war. Specifically, we find that a college-educated respondent is about 20 percent more likely than a respondent who has not completed high school to tolerate at least 1,500 casualties in Iraq.[42]

Finally, and perhaps not surprisingly, party identification has a significant impact on casualty tolerance—especially in the midst of an election year. Debates over the war in Iraq have often been depicted as highly—if not predominantly—partisan contests. It is true that if one makes a simple comparison of partisanship and casualty tolerance, one finds very strong effects. For example, our data indicate that more than 83 percent of our respondents who identify as Republican or leaning Republican stated in October 2004 that they would be willing to tolerate at least 1,500 casualties.[43] Less than 35 percent of those who identified as Democratic or leaning Democratic stated that they would be willing to tolerate that many casualties.

Describing such partisan differences, however, is not the same thing as explaining them. Our analysis indicates that much of the reason for the

[41] Ibid.

[42] Education level is coded into four categories: less than a high school diploma, completed high school, some college, and B.A. or higher degree.

[43] We code party identification as a seven-category variable with the following labels: strong Republican, not strong Republican, leans Republican, undecided/independent, leans Democrat, not strong Democrat, strong Democrat.

deep partisan divide over the war in Iraq is not due to party loyalty per se. Instead, these differences in tolerance for war costs are largely due to differing estimations among Democrats and Republicans about the rightness/wrongness of the war and expectations of success. Once we account for a respondent's views regarding the rightness of the war and their expectations for success, however, partisanship has only a modest impact on casualty tolerance. Specifically, table 5.6 indicates that a respondent who identified him or herself as "strongly Democratic" is only about 10 percent less likely to tolerate at least 1,500 U.S. casualties than if he or she had identified as "strongly Republican"—holding constant the respondent's views on the "rightness" and likely success of the war.[44]

Of course, like the perceived PPO, elite consensus, and multilateralism, partisanship may be a key factor in determining those underlying values. Consistent with our experiment regarding East Timor in chapter 4, partisanship seems to be especially important in shaping respondent's attitudes regarding whether President Bush did the right thing in choosing to attack Iraq. Nearly 60 percent of our respondents who identified as Republican or leaning Republican stated that they "strongly approved" of the president's decision to attack. Just over 90 percent stated that they either "strongly" or "somewhat approved." Only about 40 percent of Democrats "strongly" or "somewhat approved." The pattern is similar but not quite as strong with regard to expectations of success. Once again, we return to this issue in greater detail in chapter 7.

A Robust Pattern of Casualty Tolerance?

The October 2004 results that are presented in table 5.5 describe a coherent structure of public attitudes toward casualties. But how robust is this structure? We sought to address the robustness of our results both across space and over time. First, to ensure that the process that we are observing is robust over time, we analyzed casualty tolerance across our other eight waves of surveys from October 2003 through June 2004. Unfortunately, we were not able to collect data on the control variables regarding attitudes toward elite consensus, the PPO, or the multilateral use of force across these earlier waves of the survey. Nevertheless, we were able to collect data on our key attitudes of casualty tolerance, whether Bush did the right thing (*Right thing*) and whether the United States will succeed (*Success*). Thus we can test the robustness of the causal process that we hypothesize over time. Analyses of the other survey waves are displayed in

[44]This result suggests that support for the war and the president may be related but distinct attitudes. See Gelpi, Reifler, and Feaver, "Iraq the Vote."

table 5.7.[45] The coefficients for all the key variables of interest remain very stable across this period, indicating that our results are quite robust. Specifically, the coefficient for the interaction between *Right thing* and *Success* is statistically significant across seven of the nine survey waves, and it is substantively large across all nine waves. Moreover, the impact of the likelihood of success is larger than the impact of perceptions of whether Bush did the "right thing" across eight of the nine survey waves. The size of the substantive effects varies slightly across the various waves, but the effects depicted in figure 5.3 appear to be generally reflective of public attitudes across the entire period that we surveyed.

In terms of testing the robustness of our results across space, we first sought to determine whether our findings are more reflective of certain sub-populations of respondents. For example, the Iraq war has been closely identified with President Bush—sometimes to the point of suggesting that it was driven by personal animosity between the president and Saddam Hussein. Such a personal linkage between the president and "his" war might have several different kinds of effects on our results. For example, support for the war might really be a function of whether one supports the president rather than any of the more specific attitudes that we emphasize. We sought to control for this effect by controlling for party identification, but the results in table 5.5 remain robust if we include overall presidential approval as a control variable. This fact should not be too surprising, since the two variables are so closely related. Nearly 91 percent of Republicans in our October 2004 survey approved of the job that the president was doing while only 19 percent of Democrats approved.

Perhaps a greater concern might be that the war's close personal linkage to the president might also mean that some respondents are not able to make the kind of "cost-benefit" calculation that we observe in the overall analysis. For example, one might hypothesize that those who approve of the president's overall performance are open to considering more specific information regarding the specific decision to use force in Iraq or the likely success of the war. According to this logic, those who disapprove of the president will refuse to tolerate costs in the war and will not make more specific calculations about success or whether using force was the right thing. Conversely, one might imagine that those who support the president could be willing to tolerate casualties as long as the president wants to continue to fight, regardless of their individual attitudes about the likelihood of success and so on. According to this logic, only those

[45] As noted previously, the October 2003 survey used a branching format in asking the "right thing" and "success" questions that shifted the distribution of responses to those questions. To make the data more comparable to the subsequent waves, we categorized the responses from the October 2003 wave as "approve" or "disapprove" of the decision to use force and "likely" or "not likely" to succeed.

TABLE 5.7.
Robustness of Impact of *Right thing* and *Success* on Casualty Tolerance, 2003–2004

	22 Sept.– 12 Oct.	*6–20 Feb.*	*25 Feb.– 4 Mar.*	*5–18 Mar.*	*19 Mar.– 2 Apr.*	*2–16 Apr.*	*17–29 Apr.*	*18–28 June*
Right thing	0.555	0.259	0.127	0.152	0.462	0.277	0.216	0.378
	(1.65)	(1.67)	(0.86)	(1.08)	(3.07)**	(1.87)	(1.49)	(2.82)**
Success	0.918	0.345	0.506	0.443	0.668	0.245	0.562	0.677
	(4.85)**	(2.35)*	(3.45)**	(3.13)**	(4.68)**	(1.66)	(3.88)**	(4.94)**
Right thing × *Success*	0.457	0.250	0.226	0.244	0.102	0.304	0.232	0.129
	(1.23)	(3.45)**	(3.13)**	(3.62)**	(1.46)	(4.22)**	(3.26)**	(1.95)*
Female	–0.643	–0.345	–0.358	–0.401	–0.722	–0.624	–0.521	–0.425
	(5.64)**	(2.72)**	(2.82)**	(3.20)**	(5.63)**	(4.84)**	(4.06)**	(3.35)**
Minority	–0.634	–0.412	–0.341	–0.434	–0.028	–0.400	–0.585	–0.581
	(4.21)**	(2.58)**	(2.06)*	(2.78)**	(0.17)	(2.34)*	(3.56)**	(3.56)**
Age	0.063	0.125	0.073	0.111	0.240	0.203	0.265	0.136
	(1.13)	(1.99)*	(1.25)	(1.79)	(3.82)**	(3.19)**	(4.15)**	(2.21)*
Education	0.160	0.297	0.366	0.375	0.227	0.213	0.387	0.163
	(2.58)**	(4.61)**	(5.52)**	(6.20)**	(3.47)**	(3.33)**	(5.99)**	(2.59)**
Party ID	–0.136	0.010	–0.069	–0.069	–0.084	–0.058	–0.171	–0.105
	(4.74)**	(0.28)	(1.91)	(1.88)	(2.25)*	(1.59)	(4.71)**	(2.98)**
Observations	1074	865	856	906	870	855	870	881

Absolute value of z statistics in parentheses
* significant at 5%   ** significant at 1%

who disapprove of the president will consider their more specific attitudes in deciding whether to tolerate the human costs of the Iraq war.

In order to test for these possibilities, we reestimated our model of casualty tolerance on two separate populations: those who approved of the president's overall job performance and those who disapproved. The separation of the sample in this manner obviously reduced the number of cases substantially, while also reducing the variance and increasing colinearity of the variables. As a result, the coefficient for the interaction term is not significant within either sub-sample. Perception of the likelihood of success, however, remains statistically significant in both sub-samples, and it continues to have a substantively larger impact on casualty tolerance than any other variable in the model. Furthermore, we reestimated the analyses in table 5.7 separately for Republican, Democratic, and Independent respondents.[46] Because of the robustness of the causal process described in the table 5.7, we pooled the respondents across the survey waves in order to increase the number of cases and alleviate the problems of colinearity discussed earlier. In this case the interactive impact of the perceptions that using force was the right thing and perceptions that the United States will succeed nearly mirrors the results in table 5.7 within each of the separate Republican, Democratic, and Independent sub-samples. Specifically, the interactive impact of rightness and expected success remains statistically significant, and perceptions of success remain the most influential single variable.

Finally, we examined the robustness of our results across space by examining whether the structure of public attitudes toward Iraq varied geographically. Much has been made of the polarization of American politics over the past several decades, and politics under the Bush administration has often been viewed as especially divisive and geographically fragmented.[47] America has often been viewed as deeply divided between "red" and "blue" states that are politically and culturally polar opposites. Do opinions about the Iraq war form in the same manner in both red and blue states? We once again divided our analysis of the October 2004 survey into two sub-samples—respondents from "red" states that voted for George W. Bush in 2000 and "blue" states that voted for Al Gore.[48] The results for respondents from both red and blue states mirror the results displayed in table 5.5. That is, while the voters in "red" and "blue" states

[46] These surveys gathered information on party identification but did not specifically ask respondents about their approval of the president. However, as we noted earlier, the relationship between these two variables is very strong.

[47] See Rohde (1991) and Aldrich (1995) on the conditions conducive to partisan polarization. Regarding partisan divides and the Iraq War, see Toner and Rutenberg, "Partisan Divide on Iraq Exceeds Split on Vietnam," *New York Times*, 30 June 2006, p. 1.

[48] We categorized the "red" and "blue" states according to the results of the 2000 election.

may have reached different conclusions about their willingness to pay the costs of the Iraq War, they appeared to reach these conclusions through a similar process of attitude formation. Voters in red states tended to be more likely to accept the president's decision to use force as the right thing to do and tended to be optimistic about the likely success of the mission, while those in blue states appeared to be more skeptical on both counts. Nonetheless, voters in both places appear to be making similar kinds of cost-benefit calculations when they try to determine whether they can bear the human costs of this war.

As a result, we remain confident that the rational "cost-benefit" calculation regarding tolerance for casualties is broadly representative of the respondents in our various samples and not overly influenced by a subset of respondents. The results remain consistent both over time and across respondents who support the president and those who do not. Moreover, our tests clearly continue to indicate that the most important single factor determining casualty tolerance is a respondent's perception of the likelihood that the mission will be successful.

Casualty Tolerance and Catastrophic Events

Finally, one of the common beliefs about the American public's response to casualties is that public revulsion over the vivid depiction of American casualties by the news media will cause the public to reflexively reject the military mission and demand withdrawal. This is the so-called "CNN effect" that is often viewed as the critical factor in generating the public's demand for a withdrawal from Somalia, as we discussed in chapter 2. There is no doubt that the vivid depiction of soldiers dying is an extremely disturbing experience for anyone with even a modest measure of empathy. But does this disturbing and upsetting experience cause the public to demand military withdrawal in order to avoid such upsetting events? The data on Somalia suggests that the public was initially divided over how to respond to the "Black Hawk Down" incident, but the tepid and timid response by the Clinton administration and by some members of Congress led the public to reject the mission.

Unfortunately, the war in Iraq provided another opportunity to examine the public's response to the vivid depiction of casualties, this time through the events surrounding the ambush, murder, and mutilation of four U.S. military contractors working in Fallujah on 31 March 2004. One of our survey waves began two days after the attacks, on 2 April 2004, and a second wave began on 17 April. In both of these surveys we asked questions about how members of the public felt we should respond to the atrocities. Like the Black Hawk Down incident, it is clear that the attacks on the U.S. military contractors received massive attention from the U.S. media. In the 2 April survey we found that already more than 81 percent of the respondents stated that they had seen or heard something about the attacks in Fallujah. Media coverage of the event was persistent, and two weeks later we also found that about 80 percent of respondents still said they had heard about the attacks. We then asked the respondents how they felt the United States should respond to this attack. We were primarily interested in whether respondents felt that we should escalate or reduce our involvement in Fallujah, but because the "escalation" could take on different forms, we asked the question two different ways. Half of the sample was asked whether the United States should increase or decrease the number of U.S. *troops* in Fallujah, while the other half was asked whether the United States should increase or decrease its military *pressure* on the insurgents. The responses to these questions—both for the 2 and 17 April surveys—are displayed in table 5.8.

Regardless of how the question was phrased, the public's response to Fallujah was clear: the United States should escalate its military commitment. Across both phrasings of the question and across both waves of the survey, only about 15 percent of the public stated that we should respond to the attacks in Fallujah by reducing our presence. The proportion of respondents who stated that the United States should escalate its commitment varied slightly depending on how that escalation was phrased. Approximately 75 percent of the respondents stated that the United States should escalate military pressure on insurgents in Fallujah, while a slightly lower 69 percent of respondents stated that our nation should escalate the number of troops committed to Falljuah. Moreover, we found that respondents who stated that they had seen or heard news about the Fallujah attacks were 10 to 20 percent *more* likely to say that we should escalate (either troops or pressure) than those who stated that they had not seen or heard of the attacks. Thus if the vivid media coverage had any effect on public opinion, it caused a rally in support for the mission rather than a desire to withdraw.

Finally, as a followup to the questions about whether to escalate U.S. military efforts in Fallujah, we also asked respondents whether they believed that the attack carried out on U.S. military contractors in Fallujah "was conducted by a small group of extremists and do not reflect the feelings of most Iraqis toward the United States," or whether the attack "reflects the anger of most Iraqis toward the United States." In the 2 April survey nearly 57 percent of respondents stated that they thought the attacks were conducted by a "small group of extremists" and by the 17 April survey that number had edged up to 60 percent. Not surprisingly, those who felt that the attack was conducted by extremists were more likely to want to escalate U.S. efforts than those who felt that the attacks

TABLE 5.8.
Public Response to Insurgent Atrocities at Fallujah

Troop levels	*2–16 Apr.*	*17–29Apr.*	*Military pressure*	*2–16 Apr.*	*17–29Apr.*
Decrease the number of U.S. forces in Fallujah	59 14%	64 15%	Dramatically cut back military pressure on the insurgents in Iraq	62 15%	62 14%
Keep the number of U.S. forces in Fallujah the same	74 17%	67 16%	Keep the deployment of U.S. forces as they are now	44 10%	45 10%
Increase the number of U.S. forces in Fallujah	295 69%	295 69%	Step up the military pressure on the insurgents in Iraq	320 75%	328 76%
Total	428	426	Total	426	435

reflected a broader anger of the Iraqi people. It is, however, worth noting that a solid majority—between 57 and 66 percent, depending on the survey wave and question wording—of those respondents who felt that the Fallujah attacks reflected a general anger of the Iraqi people *still* thought that the United States should escalate its military efforts. Thus it is clear that while they may have been shocked by the brutal treatment of the U.S. contractors, the overwhelming majority of respondents were not intimidated.

What can account for this relatively resilient response? We would suggest that political leadership by the Bush administration, combined with the relatively strong overall optimism of the public regarding the mission at the time, generated a rallying response as opposed to a desire to "cut and run." President Clinton's initial response to the attacks on U.S. forces was ambivalent at best, emphasizing his desire to ask others how America should respond. "I want to emphasize that tomorrow I will be consulting with Congressional leaders in both parties and with others, and then I will report to you and to the American people," the President stated.[49] The following day, Clinton set a deadline of 31 March 1994 for

[49] Remarks by the president upon signing of the Hatch Act of 1993, 6 October 1993. William J. Clinton Library and Museum.

withdrawing troops from Somalia—a tacit admission of failure. This admission was made more explicit when in a response to a question regarding what would happen if Somalia was not stabilized by the deadline, Secretary of State Warren Christopher quipped, "The president said there was no assurance of success."[50] Contrast Christopher's pessimism with Scott McClellan's expression of confidence in the ultimate success of the Iraq mission in response to the grisly murder of the American contractors in Fallujah. "The president is saddened by the loss of life, and our nation is forever grateful for their service and sacrifice," said McClellan. "The president believes the best way to honor those who have made the ultimate sacrifice is to show resolve and make sure we finish the job."[51]

Nonetheless, it seems unlikely that presidential leadership alone can always be sufficient to sustain public morale in the long term—absent some corroborating evidence of progress on the ground. Looking back to chapter 2, we can see that salient attacks such as the Tet offensive can turn the public against a war regardless of how emphatically the military claims victory. What made the difference between the public response to Fallujah on the one hand and Somalia and Tet on the other? It would appear to be a complex admixture of presidential rhetoric, media interpretation of the events, and the public's residual level of patience and resolve. Untangling this complex knot remains an important task for future research.

Conclusions

The political campaign season of 2003–04 provides an unusually good opportunity to examine the American public's tolerance for paying the human costs of the Iraq war. Our ability to gather individual-level data regarding a costly and controversial war made salient in the context of a presidential election provides an ideal circumstance for comparing the substantive importance of various mechanisms that determine the public's response to casualties in war.

Consistent with much of the recent work on public opinion in wartime, we find that members of the public appear to be engaging in simple but clear calculations about the expected value of continuing to engage in armed conflict. That is, individuals make judgments about the potential benefits of the conflict and weigh those potential gains by the probability that their government will be able to achieve them.

[50] Press briefing by Secretary of State Warren Christopher, Secretary of Defense Les Aspin, and Admiral David Jeremiah., 7 October 1993. William J. Clinton Library and Museum.

[51] David Sanger, "Grisly Deaths Don't Dent an Upbeat Bush Message Stressing Iraq Successes," *New York Times*, 2 April 2004,p. A5-8.

Much of the existing literature focuses on the reasons for the war as the determinant of public support.[52] Others have focused on the likelihood of success as the key.[53] Larson acknowledges the role of both potential benefits and likely success in the determination of the public's tolerance for casualties, but he emphasizes the importance of social cues from domestic elites regarding the legitimacy of the conflict as opposed to a rational expected value calculation by individual members of the public.[54] Moreover, Larson's aggregate analysis lacks the individual-level data necessary to investigate the formation of public attitudes.

Our findings suggest that believing in the "rightness" of a war combines with expectations of success to determine an individual's tolerance for the human costs of war. Once one takes account of the interaction of these two attitudes, other prominent variables in the literature have only a modest direct impact on casualty tolerance. This interaction effect even outweighs the independent impact of partisanship. Rather than implying that those other factors are not important, however, it seems likely that many of the variables identified in the literature—such as the partisan cues, primary policy objective, elite consensus, and multilateral support—may be most important through their impact on respondent's views about the "rightness" of the war and the prospects for success. We return to this issue in chapter 7.

While both the rightness of the war and expectations of success are important, our data and analyses indicate that success appears to be the more important factor in this case. Not only do expectations of success have a larger marginal impact on casualty tolerance, but the public also has remained optimistic about success even as it has remained divided regarding the justification for the war.

During the first several years of the war, the public did not turn on the mission reflexively as casualties mounted, but neither did it give the Bush administration a blank check for the war on Iraq. Public support for the war was surprisingly robust throughout 2003 and 2004, surviving numerous shocks that one might have expected to be fatal : the emergence of an insurgency that evidently caught the war-planners off-guard; numerous psychological thresholds such as the death of more than 1,000 U.S. soldiers in combat; the emergence of a vigorous terrorist threat in Iraq; and the failure to find large stockpiles of weapons of mass destruction, one of three key rationales offered for the war beforehand. To be sure, public support for the war *did* erode, and these adverse developments

[52] Jentleson, *The Pretty Prudent Public*; Britton and Jentleson, *Still Pretty Prudent*; Larson, *Casualties and Consensus*; Destler and Kull, *Misreading the Public*.

[53] Feaver and Gelpi, *Choosing Your Battles*.

[54] Larson, "Putting Theory to Work."

doubtless had a negative effect. Moreover, by late 2006 a majority of the public seemed to have turned decidedly if not decisively against the war. Yet we have shown that the best way to understand these and other factors is through a model that links public tolerance for casualties and public expectations of success. The latter proved surprisingly resilient (though not limitless) and this helped shore up the former.

Chapter Six

IRAQ THE VOTE: WAR AND THE PRESIDENTIAL ELECTION OF 2004

At first glance, the parallels between the 1992 and 2004 presidential elections appear striking. Both elections featured an incumbent named George Bush who had enjoyed tremendous public support after launching a war in Iraq. Despite the high levels of support, both President Bushes soon found themselves deadlocked in the polls against surprisingly robust Democratic challengers, who were buoyed by widespread perceptions of a weak economy and skyrocketing healthcare costs. Yet Bush "43" eventually won reelection, while Bush "41" met defeat. What can explain this change in electoral fortunes? There are many possible and complementary explanations for why Bush 43 won despite facing a daunting electoral environment. In this chapter, we focus on one explanation that has been the subject of extensive public comment: the role of the ongoing Iraq War.

Pundits reconcile the different fates by stating that "Commanders-in-Chief do not lose elections in wartime." For this law-like aphorism to hold, incumbents must actually be able to obtain their party's nomination. Harry Truman and Lyndon Johnson were so unpopular—due in large part to public disenchantment with American participation in the Korean and Vietnam wars—that they abandoned their efforts to run for reelection.[1] Moreover, the belief that Americans will not oust incumbent presidents during wartime flies in the face of the even more well-entrenched view that Americans will not tolerate casualties in war. The war in Iraq was barely a week old when observers began to worry that news of combat fatalities would cause public support to collapse (Elder and Nagourney 2003; Purdam 2003; Ricks 2003a, 2003b). By October of 2004, as presidential elections loomed, more than 1,100 U.S. military personnel had been killed in Iraq fighting against an insurgency that continued more or less unabated. Had most pundits foreseen this turn of events, they surely would have predicted a complete collapse of public support for the Bush administration and for the war in Iraq. Moreover, they would have

[1] Truman was eligible to run but withdrew after losing in the New Hampshire primary to Estes Kefauver. Johnson announced his decision not to run for reelection after the Tet offensive in Vietnam prompted challenges from Eugene McCarthy and Robert Kennedy.

predicted a lopsided electoral defeat for the president in November. With these competing views of how the war in Iraq would play out politically, pundits and political observers had inadvertently pitted the irresistible force (the effect of casualties on public opinion) against the immovable object (an incumbent president during war).

The relationship between the war in Iraq, American casualties, and the presidential election is—to say the least—a matter of widespread debate. In this chapter we seek to make sense of these contradictory expectations by extending our argument about casualty tolerance to the issue of presidential vote choice in 2004. In doing so, we unite two distinct public opinion literatures, electoral behavior and foreign policy, within a single theoretical framework derived from Fiorina's (1981) theory of retrospective voting. The economic voting literature has long examined the relative weight of retrospective versus prospective evaluations in explaining things like presidential approval and vote choice. The literature on support for the use of force and casualty tolerance literature—including chapter 5 of this book—is also keenly interested in comparing the weight of retrospective and prospective evaluations. Few works, however, have tried to integrate these two literatures. This chapter is an effort to examine the contribution of retrospective and prospective foreign policy evaluations to both voting and casualty tolerance. Moreover, our analysis balances the importance of normative judgments (retrospective evaluations of the "rightness" of the war in the first place) against empirical judgments (prospective judgments of the war's eventual success).

Once again, we argue that the willingness of the public to pay the costs of war and to reelect incumbent presidents during wartime are dependent on these two attitudes and the interaction between them. In contrast to our analyses of casualty tolerance in chapter 5, we show that the retrospective normative judgments serve as the more powerful predictor for vote choice. These claims are consistent with the broader literature on how foreign policy influences voting behavior, and the literature that examines the public's response to war and casualties. We also show that these retrospective and prospective judgments are interactive—a person's attitude toward one of them conditions its effect on the other. This interaction operates on "political" support (vote choice) as well as "mission" support (casualty tolerance).

To our knowledge, no other work integrates political support for the president and support for American war efforts into a single theoretical model and uses the same predictor variables to explain the separate dependent variable measures of vote choice and casualty tolerance. This chapter bridges important gaps in the literature by using one theoretical framework to connect two separate research questions: (1) whether and how foreign policy affects political evaluation and choice, and (2) the conditions under which American citizens will bear the financial and human cost of military missions. We view these two questions as inherently linked—support for missions should connect to the Commander-in-Chief responsible for executing such missions. We find that these judgments are in fact connected, yet with important differences. We find that the normative judgments are more important for vote choice, while chapter 5 shows that the empirical judgments better explain casualty tolerance.

Foreign Policy Attitudes and Vote Choice

As we discussed in chapter 1, scholars have long been troubled by Americans' inability to answer survey questions "correctly." Poor performance on surveys has led observers to view the American public as an ill-informed lot with little ability to think coherently about the substance of politics (Campbell et al. 1960; Converse 1964), with issues playing a small to nonexistent role in shaping citizens' voting decisions. Foreign policy evaluations were viewed as among the least likely to affect political choices. When forming attitudes about the performance of the economy, citizens have their personal experience to fall back on. But foreign policy is so removed from the everyday lives of most citizens, it was argued, that it is simply unreasonable to think that what happened beyond U.S. borders would have a large impact on Americans' political behavior. In support of this claim many studies showed, at best, weak evidence that foreign affairs affected the voting decision (for example, Almond 1950; Stokes 1966). As Almond writes, "Foreign policy attitudes among most Americans lack intellectual structure and factual content."

This traditional view has been challenged by two reinforcing lines of research illuminating the importance of foreign policy judgments. The first line of research shows that foreign policy attitudes are well structured and that the public responds rationally and intelligently to developments in the international arena. The second line of research shows that these foreign policy judgments affect vote choice and presidential approval.

Jon Hurwitz and Mark Peffley (1987a, 1987b; Peffley and Hurwitz 1993) demonstrate that citizens have reasonably structured attitudes concerning foreign policy. Attitudes of foreign policy affect political evaluations, and citizens respond in understandable ways to changing world events.

Such evidence of a "rational public" regarding foreign affairs is widespread (Holsti 1997; Page and Shaprio 1988; Wittkopf 1990). Aggregate opinion on foreign and defense policy is often considered remarkably stable, and changes "have seldom, if ever, occurred . . . without reasonable causes, such as the actions of foreign friends or enemies or changes in the United States' position in the world" (Page and Shaprio 1988: 220–21). In research on public attitudes toward the Cold War, Christopher Wlezien (1995, 1996) shows that the public's preferences for defense spending responded to spending levels as well as feelings toward the Soviet Union.[2]

Not only does the public have well-structured attitudes about foreign policy, but mounting evidence suggests that these attitudes have an impact on political behavior. It has long been known that economic evaluations have an effect on presidential approval and vote choice (for example, Kiewiet 1983; Kinder and Kiewiet 1979; Kinder and Kiewiet 1981). An increasing amount of evidence has emerged showing that foreign policy judgments matter as well as, and in roughly equal magnitude to, economic evaluations. In an analysis of the 1980 and 1984 presidential elections, Aldrich, Sullivan, and Borgida (1989) find that foreign policy issues were just as powerful a vote determinant as domestic issues.

In a times-series analysis of aggregate quarterly presidential approval data, Nickelsburg and Norpath (2000) show that the president is as much "Commander-in-Chief" as "Chief Economist." Adding major foreign policy events as predictor variables to their model, these international events matter at least as much as economic evaluations. Using individual-level data from several national random sample surveys conducted from 1983 to 1987, Wilcox and Allsop (1991) find that approval of Reagan's foreign policy was consistently a good predictor of his overall approval, though its strength relative to domestic issues did depend on the salience of economic or foreign policy issues. However, the impact of foreign policy on electoral choice does appear to wax and wane with the flow of current events. This pattern is hardly surprising. As we note later, survey responses regarding the nation's "most important problem" suggest that the economy is nearly always salient in the minds of voters, while concern about foreign affairs varies substantially.

While analysts generally agree that public opinion is stable and responds to events, substantial differences of opinion exist concerning whether citizens respond to the international events themselves, or if foreign policy attitudes are mostly mediated by elite rhetoric and framing. Of course, American citizens are (mostly) incapable of witnessing inter-

[2]Witko (2003) offers a less sanguine explanation of the rational public by showing the changes in defense spending preferences to be a function of the way U.S. policy leaders talked about the Soviet Union, rather than specific actions taken by the former Soviet Union. In other words, citizens respond to what political leaders are saying and not the events themselves. This account is substantially in accord with Zaller's (1992) account of mass opinion and attitude change being driven primarily by elites. Unanswered is how well policy leaders represent what is happening in the world. The fidelity of the link between elite statements about the world and the "true" state of the world is an important topic for future research.

national events without them first being mediated by the press. Thus, the press certainly has the potential to shape opinion uniformly—as long as the reporting from different bureaus is substantially similar—regardless of how well the reporting reflects the reality on the ground. If the press systematically reports international events differently than they occur, then we should expect citizen opinions to reflect media coverage more than the "events themselves." The Tet Offensive during the Vietnam War may be a classic example of where the media were unified in their reporting, but where the reporting arguably differed sufficiently from the actual events. Thus the resulting changes in opinion were moved by the reporting, rather than the event. More specifically, while Tet was a tactical failure for the attacking Communist forces, it was reported to the American public as a disaster for the United States and evidence of a stalemate (Johnson and Tierney 2006).

Even if the press accurately reports international events, political elites may be able to control how the public understands the issues. Looking again to the public's preferences for changes in spending for defense, Witko (2003) found exactly this—the public did not respond to what the Soviet Union was doing but rather to how policy elites were talking about the Soviet Union. This account is substantially in accord with Zaller's (1992) account of mass opinion and attitude change being driven primarily by elites and in many ways. Berinsky (2007) goes one step further to argue that responses to international affairs are primarily endogenous to political predispositions.

Important questions remain that we hope scholars will address. First, to what extent is press coverage of military conflict "accurate" and how would we measure such accuracy? Second, how much latitude do elites have in reframing press coverage of military conflict and how influential can their framing efforts be? Third, to what extent are perceptions of international affairs endogenous to political predispositions? Fortunately, for our purposes we do not need to resolve these debates in order to proceed with our analysis. Our central focus is the impact of perceptions of the war in Iraq on the willingness to continue fighting in Iraq and the propensity, in 2004, to have voted for Bush. We remain agnostic on the question of whether these perceptions reflect "reality" or elite rhetoric, though as we note in chapters 7 and 8, we think that our research focuses new attention on the importance of addressing this debate. The endogeneity of foreign policy views, on the other hand, is more of a concern, and we return to this question in chapter 7.

Nonetheless, we would point to three well-supported findings concerning foreign affairs and political behavior: (1) Citizen attitudes about foreign policy are well structured, (2) Foreign policy evaluations matter for presidential approval and presidential vote choice, and (3) Citizen attitudes respond to changes in the international arena. The three findings, however, are not quite enough to connect the events of war to presidential elections. For example, if foreign policy judgments are going to matter in voting decisions, then those attitudes need to be accessible for the voter (Aldrich, Sullivan, and Borgida 1989). The salience of foreign affairs in the minds of the American public has varied significantly over the past several decades, but it will not be surprising to many observers that foreign policy was a salient issue during the 2004 election campaign. After all, during the four years that had elapsed since the 2000 presidential election, the United States experienced a startling domestic attack from a foreign enemy and the naiton embarked on high-profile conflicts in Afghanistan and Iraq. Looking at the Gallup poll's most important problem over the past several presidential elections, foreign affairs dramatically stands out as more salient in 2004. The Gallup survey reports that in 2004 roughly the same proportion of voters stated international concerns (22 percent) and economic issues (26 percent) as the "most important problem." While 22 percent for foreign affairs had been the highest percentage for that issue since 1984, the economy still trumped international concerns by a 2-to-1 margin (47 to 23 percent) in Reagan's reelection. In the three presidential elections from 1992 to 2000, mentions of international affairs were 5 percent or less.[3]

The polling that we conducted also shows that respondents report foreign affairs as an important concern in the voting decision. In six of our surveys from March 2004 through October 2004, we used a closed-ended question to ask respondents which issue (economy, foreign policy, social issues) was most important to them personally when choosing which candidate to vote for.[4] Because we polled only in this election, we cannot make inferences about the importance of foreign affairs compared to other years based on this data alone. Table 6.1, however, shows that the

[3] Gallup does not have apples-to-apples data for 1988. In most years, the "most important problem" question allows respondents to mention more than one problem, that is, the same respondent could say both "the economy" and "foreign affairs." Because of the multiple responses, the cumulative total of the marginals exceeds 100 percent, sometimes by a wide margin. In 1988, Gallup used a single-response format. In the single-response format, 9 percent of respondents mention something related to foreign affairs or defense policy as the most important problem. This proportion is still more than double what was reported in the multiple response format during the 1990s.

[4] The surveys were conducted by Knowledge Networks, which maintains a panel of respondents recruited through Random Digit Dialing (RDD), who are equipped with WebTV and complete surveys online. Detailed sampling information is available from the company website, http://www.knowledgenetworks.com. Studies have found that the Knowledge Networks' sampling methodology yields representative samples (Couper 2000; Krosnick and Chang 2001), with results comparable to RDD telephone surveys.

Table 6.1.
Most Important Issue in Voting for a Presidential Candidate, March–November 2004

	5–18 Mar.	*19 Mar.– 2 Apr.*	*3–16 Apr.*	*17–29 Apr.*	*18–28 June*	*21 Oct.– 1 Nov.*
Foreign policy issues like Iraq and the "War on Terrorism"	16%	19%	20%	24%	26%	30%
Economic issues like jobs and taxes	72%	70%	67%	63%	61%	59%
Social issues like abortion and gay marriage	10%	9%	11%	11%	11%	10%
N	930	889	881	899	900	1125

proportion stating foreign policy as the most important issue doubled between the conclusion of the Democratic primary campaigns and the general election in November.

In the 2004 election, then, foreign policy was a salient concern. The war in Iraq was shaping up to be, in the words of Secretary of Defense Donald Rumsfeld, a "long, hard slog"—with a mounting human toll, making the election of 2004 an ideal place to examine the electoral politics of war.

Iraq, Incumbency, and a Model of Vote Choice in 2004

We build on Fiorina's (1981) model of retrospective voting to construct a model that uses the same antecedent attitudes as predictors of vote choice and casualty tolerance. Fiorina's landmark work successfully synthesizes what many saw as the irreconcilable traditions of behavioralism and rational choice by creating a generalized voter's calculus containing three distinct components: (1) political predispositions, (2) retrospective evaluations of the incumbent, and (3) prospective judgments or future expectations.

We likewise argue that two logically distinct attitudes—one's willingness to continue to pay a human cost in the war in Iraq and one's vote choice in the 2004 election—are functions of retrospective and prospective judgments, as well as one's political predispositions (*Party ID*). Retrospectively, voters are judging whether the decision to invade Iraq was the right one. Prospectively, voters are judging whether the war in Iraq will turn out to be successful.

Consistent with our discussions in chapters 1 and 5, the impact of these retrospective and prospective attitudes on vote choice and casualty tolerance is strongly intuitive. If the war is hopeless, why continue to pay a price? Thus we expected prospective attitudes about the likelihood of success to have the greatest impact on casualty tolerance. Our analyses in chapter 5 confirmed this expectation. With regard to the reelection of an incumbent president during wartime, however, the likely voter calculus is somewhat different. If you believe that the decision to invade Iraq was wrong, then it makes sense to cast a vote against the leader most associated with that choice, especially if the opposing candidate is arguing that he would make (or would have made) different choices. Thus when thinking about vote choice in a reelection bid for an incumbent president, we expect that what matters most is the retrospective normative attitudes about whether attacking Iraq was the right thing to do. That is, we argue that both casualty tolerance and vote choice can be understood within the same model of attitude formation that emphasizes the interaction of the retrospective (normative) and prospective (empirical) judgments about American policy in Iraq. The differing kinds of judgments being made with regard to casualty tolerance and vote choice, however, lead us to expect that the relative weight assigned to retrospective or prospective judgments will differ across these two processes. Deciding whether to continue an ongoing military conflict is largely a prospective enterprise. Citizens will be asking themselves "what do we do now?" Building on Fiorina (1981), however, the vote choice literature teaches us that the reelection of incumbent presidents will be dominated by retrospective judgments.

We additionally argue that the effect of these two attitudes both on vote choice and casualty tolerance will be interactive. According to the logic outlined earlier, we would expect attitudes about whether attacking Iraq was the right thing to have little impact on casualty tolerance for respondents who feel that success is unlikely. If victory is unlikely, the initial wisdom of the decision to use force has little impact on the expected benefits (and thus the tolerable costs) of the war. But if victory is likely, then attitudes about whether the war was the right thing should have a substantial impact on the expected benefits from the conflict and influence casualty tolerance.

Similarly, the likely prospects for success should have little impact on one's judgment about the wisdom of using force if one does not believe that using force was the right thing in the first place. If one believes, however, that the initial decision to use force was the right thing to do, then one's attitude about the likelihood of success should have a significant impact on one's judgment of the overall wisdom of U.S. policy, and thus on one's willingness to reelect the president.

Data and Methods

We propose here a latent variable approach in place of an explicitly spatial model. Rather than utility functions of competing candidates, we see "Bush support" as an underlying attitude expressed as a latent variable. Individuals possess an amount of "Bush support" or "casualty tolerance," which we model as follows:

$$y_i^* = x_i \beta + \epsilon_i \tag{1}$$

We keep this compatible with Fiorina (1981) by using independent variables consistent with his generalized voter's calculus. We include separate evaluations for political predispositions (long-term past experience), political past experience (near-term experience under an incumbent), and future expectations, which yield the following equation:

$$y_i^* = PID_i + RJ_i + PJ_i + \epsilon_i \tag{2}$$

In Equation 2, y_i^* is how much "Bush support" one possesses. The variables $x_i\, \beta$ are expressed generally as the long-term political past experience (*Party* ID or *PID*), political past experience under an incumbent (retrospective judgments or *RJ*), and future expectations (prospective judgments or *PJ*).

Like our casualty tolerance measure in Chapter 5, our vote choice measure is a five-point ordinal scale. The data we analyze come from the same survey we analyzed in that chapter, which was conducted from 15 October to 1 November 2004—immediately prior to the presidential election. Table 6.2 reports the responses for our vote choice question in several ways. First, we report the results for our five-point ordinal variable from all of our respondents.[5] Next, we display our dichotomous vote choice results, which pool together strong supporters with "leaners" and drop the undecided voters. Finally, to provide a point of comparison, we display the actual 2004 voting results.

Interestingly, our survey, which was conducted over a two-week period, came closer to predicting the national voting results than many sur-

[5] The distribution on our dependent variable does not change significantly if we restrict our attention to registered voters or "likely voters" or if we identify likely voters as those who state that they are registered and will definitely or probably vote. Voters who stated that they intended to vote for Nader and refused to choose a candidate when asked whether they leaned more toward Bush or Kerry were coded as "missing" on our vote choice variable.

TABLE 6.2.
Voting Intentions and Voting Results 2004

Vote Choice	*With leaners*	*Dichotomous*	*Actual vote*
Kerry	40.5%	48.2%	48.6%
Lean Kerry	6.6%		
Undecided	2.2%		
Lean Bush	4.8%		
Bush	45.9%	51.8%	51.1%

veys that were fielded more closely to the election and that aimed specifically at predicting electoral results. Our poll, for example, did much better than the infamous exit polls that led to early predictions of John Kerry's success. These data suggest that our survey provides a reasonable basis for evaluating national electoral behavior in 2004.

Because we are using an ordinal scale to represent underlying latent propensity to vote for Bush, ordered logit is an ideal estimation technique. Since we found little difference between the "likely voter" responses and those of the whole sample, we conduct our analyses on the full sample of respondents. We estimate four models to evaluate the impact of the Iraq War on vote choice. Consistent with our analyses in chapter 5, we begin by comparing additive and interactive models of the influence of attitudes toward the war on vote choice. The first model posits a simple additive impact of attitudes toward *Right thing* and *Success*, while the second model tests our hypothesis of an interaction between these retrospective and prospective attitudes. Each of these models also accounts for the impact of *Party ID* as well as the respondent's gender, race, age, and level of education. The third model drops the Iraq variables from the model to examine whether adding these variables significantly improves the fit of the model over and above the impact of partisanship and demographic effects. Finally, the fourth model drops the four demographic control variables to examine whether demographic factors jointly make a significant contribution to the explanation of vote choice over and above the influence of partisanship and attitudes toward Iraq.

We want to emphasize that our goal in these analyses is not to provide a complete or fully specified model of vote choice. Such a model would require data regarding self-placement and candidate placement on a variety of domestic issues and so on. We were not able to gather such data on our survey, since space was limited and our primary focus was on attitudes toward the Iraq War. Nonetheless, we were able to control for the most prominent cause of vote choice that is most likely to confound our inferences about the impact of the war in Iraq: *Party ID*.[6] As a result, we remain confident that our model provides a valid description of the impact of attitudes toward Iraq on vote choice. We would readily concede, however, that we cannot present a complete description of vote choice in 2004.

The results of our analyses of vote choice are presented in table 6.3. *Party ID* is a three-category partisan identification question, coded as Democrat (−1), Independent (0), and Republican (1). As in chapter 5, *Right thing* and *Success* are both four-point Likert scales. *Right thing* asks respondents if they approve of the original decision to use military force against Iraq and is coded from "Strongly disapprove" (0) to "Strongly approve" (3). *Success* asks respondents if they think that the United States is likely to succeed in Iraq, and is coded from "Not at all likely" (0) to "Very likely" (3). The independent variables are coded so that we would expect to see positive coefficients in the ordered logistic regressions. In other words, we expect that a one-unit increase in each independent variable should be associated with a respondent possessing a greater quantity of the underlying attitude under investigation—propensity to vote for Bush.

A comparison of the first two models in Table 6.3 demonstrates that our argument about the interaction of retrospective and prospective attitudes about Iraq provides a better description of the impact of Iraq on vote choice than does the simpler additive model. Not only is the interaction term "strongly" statistically significant, but a likelihood ratio test indicates that the vote choice data were significantly more likely to have been generated by the interactive process ($p < .01$). Consistent with our analyses of casualty tolerance in chapter 5, this result provides further evidence that respondents combine retrospective and prospective attitudes about Iraq in using these opinions to make other political judgments—such as deciding whether to support a continuation of the conflict and choosing which candidate will get their vote.

We must, of course, be careful in interpreting the coefficient estimates for expectations of success and whether Bush did the right thing because of the interaction between these variables. Since each of these variables is coded so that its minimum value is 0, the coefficients for *Success* and

[6] We did ask respondents brief questions about whether they believed that President Bush or Senator Kerry would do a better job handling economic issues, social issues, and foreign policy. Including respondent's views on handling the economy and social issues did not alter the impact of the Iraq War described in table 6.3. Controlling for the candidates' expected handling of foreign policy did eliminate the estimated impact of attitudes toward Iraq. This result was not unexpected, however, since expectations about handling foreign policy are the mechanism through which attitudes about Iraq should influence vote choice. Controlling for an intervening variable should eliminate the estimated impact of the antecdent variable. See King, Keohane, and Verba (1994) for a discussion of controlling for intervening variables.

TABLE 6.3.
Impact of Attitudes toward Iraq on Vote Choice in 2004

	Model 1: Additive Iraq & Party ID	*Model 2: Interactive Iraq, Party ID & demographics*	*Model 3: Interactive Iraq & Party ID only*	*Model 4: Party ID & demographics only*
Party ID	1.569 (12.49)**	1.604 (12.50)**	1.603 (13.05)**	2.006 (18.73)**
Iraq *Right thing*	1.292 (12.77)**	0.544 (2.79)**	0.533 (2.75)**	
Expect *Success*	0.644 (5.20)**	–0.031 (0.16)	–0.057 (0.30)	
Right thing × *Success*		0.460 (4.24)**	0.471 (4.36)**	
Female	0.320 (1.84)	0.326 (1.87)	0.030 (0.21)	
Minority	–0.350 (–1.58)	–0.311 (1.38)		–0.541 (2.78)**
Age	0.096 (1.15)	0.070 (0.83)		0.001 (0.01)
Education level	–0.078 (–0.88)	–0.092 (1.03)		–0.227 (3.01)**
Observations	1007	1007	1007	1015
Likelihood ratio vs. interactive model	18.3 (1 d.f.). $p < .01$	—	7.5 (4 d.f.) n.s.	427.7 (3 d.f.) $p < .01$

Absolute value of *z* statistics in parentheses
* significant at 5% ** significant at 1%

Right thing in table 6.3 reflect the impact of these variables when the other variable is at its minimum value. Thus the results indicate, as expected, that *Right thing* is a significant predictor of vote choice even when respondents believe that success is "not very likely." The same cannot be said of *Success*, however, which does not have a significant effect when respondents "strongly disapprove" of the president's initial decision to use force against Iraq. The insignificant coefficient for *Success*, however, does not indicate that success does not matter, because the interaction between *Right thing* and *Success* is statistically significant. This coefficient captures the increase that we observe in the impact of each of these variables for each one-unit increase in the *other* variable. Thus the impact of *Success* on vote choice is −0.06 and does not approach statistical significance. When respondents "somewhat disapprove" of the decision to use force, however, the impact of *Success* is 0.41 ($p < .01$). The impact of *Success* reaches its maximum for respondents who "strongly approve" of the president's decision to go to war, when its coefficient is 1.36 ($p < .01$).

Of course, the impact of *Right thing* also increases as respondents become more confident in America's eventual success. The maximum impact of *Right thing*, for example, occurs for respondents who think success is "very likely," when it has a coefficient of 1.95 ($p < .01$). Thus retrospective judgments about whether the president "did the right thing" consistently have a larger impact on vote choice than do expectations of success at each respective level of the other attitude. As was the case in chapter 5, this result is not an artifact of our interactive specification. For example, examining the additive model in table 6.3 indicates that the coefficient for beliefs about whether President Bush did the right thing is just more than twice as large as the coefficient for expectations of success. The difference between these coefficients is strongly statistically significant ($p < .01$). This reversal in terms of the influence of prospective and retrospective judgments about the war is consistent with Fiorina (1981) and with our own expectations about the impact of war on the reelection of an incumbent president.

Not surprisingly, we also find that party identification has a significant and substantial impact on vote choice even after controlling for attitudes toward Iraq. Indeed, we would be suspicious of any model that did not show that party identification influenced vote choice. The size of this coefficient suggests that its impact is quite large—even relative to the influence of attitudes about the Iraq War—but we will return to a more detailed evaluation of substantive effects later. Interestingly, the first two columns of table 6.3 indicate that none of the demographic control variables is significant. To test whether the demographic variables contribute to the vote-choice model when taken as a group, model 3 in table 6.3 drops all of these variables from the analysis. A likelihood-ratio test indicates no significant difference in the overall performance of the model when all demographics are dropped. Given the many widespread belief that the Republican Party suffers from a "gender gap" and the fact that the GOP is at a massive disadvantage in terms of support from African Americans, this result is quite surprising. The coefficient for gender even approaches statistical significance in the "wrong" direction, since the positive coefficient indicates that women were more likely to vote for Bush after accounting for the impact of the other variables in the model.

What can account for these surprising effects? The answer appears to lie largely in the way in which the support of these demographic groups for Bush operates through their attitudes toward the Iraq War. To illustrate this point, model 4 in table 6.3 analyzes vote choice with only party identification and the demographic controls. Here we can see that there is no "gender gap" in either direction in propensity to vote for Bush; the coefficient for gender is 0.03 and does not approach statistical significance. At the same time, we can see that minority respondents were significantly less likely to vote for Bush with a negative coefficient of -0.54 ($p < .01$). While education was not significant in our initial analysis of vote choice, it too becomes significant and negative once we remove the Iraq variables.

An auxiliary regression of party identification and the demographic controls on our two Iraq variables reveals that women, minorities, and educated respondents were significantly less likely to believe that the president did the right thing by attacking Iraq. More educated respondents were also less likely to believe that the United States would succeed in Iraq. Thus the combination of results in models 1, 2, and 4 indicate that President Bush would have had an advantage among women voters except for their opposition to the Iraq War and that opposition to the war cost the president votes among educated voters and among minorities. What impact this had on the overall electoral outcome, however, is a more complex question that we will address later.

The coefficients in table 6.3 can give us some sense of the direction and significance of the effects of different variables, but judging the substantive impact of variables from their logit coefficients is extremely difficult. As a result, we use predicted probability graphs to show the relationship between variables and the importance of the interaction term. Figures 6.1 and 6.2 show predicted probabilities of voting for George W. Bush (estimated from model 2). Consistent with our expectations (following from Fiorina) respondents' retrospective judgments on whether attacking Iraq was the right thing has the greater impact on vote choice. Figure 6.1 shows how the predicted probability of voting for Bush changes across values of *Right thing*, and the course of this change depends on the values of *Success*. Clearly *Right thing* matters more as one ascends through *Success* from "not likely at all" to "very likely." Moreover, the graph shows that *Right thing* always matters in predicting the probability of voting for Bush. For example, even among respondents who believe that success is "very unlikely" in Iraq, a shift in attitude about whether Bush did the right thing from "strongly disapprove" to "strongly approve" increases the probability that the respondent would vote for Bush from nearly 0 to nearly 30 percent. When respondents are optimistic about the prospects for success in Iraq, the impact of *Right thing* becomes truly striking. In this case a shift from "strongly disapprove" to "strongly ap-

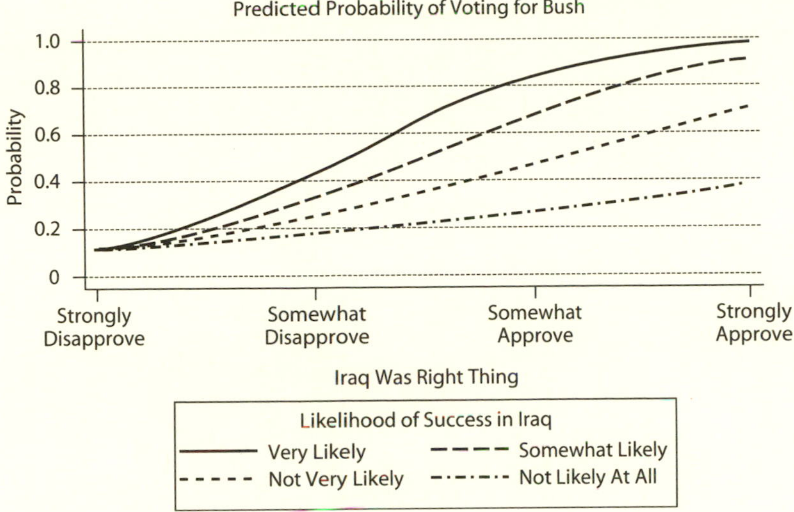

FIGURE 6.1. Vote Choice Predicted Probabilities by *Right thing* (estimated from Model 2)

prove" increases the likelihood of voting for Bush from nearly 0 to nearly 90 percent.

Next, in figure 6.2 we graph the predicted probability of voting for Bush as a function of *Success*. Unlike our results regarding *Right thing*, we find that this *Success* does not always influence vote choice. Nonetheless, as retrospective approval of Bush's decision to go to war increases, expectations of success do begin to have a substantively large impact on vote choice. For example, when respondents "strongly disapprove" of the decision to attack Iraq, the probability that they will vote for Bush remains constant and nearly 0. Respondents who strongly disapproved of the decision to begin the war were very unlikely to vote for Bush regardless of their prospective beliefs about the war. As respondents begin to believe that Bush did the right thing, however, expectations of success begin to have an impact on their propensity to vote for Bush. Thus for respondents who "strongly approve" of the president's initial decision, changing their prospective confidence from "not likely at all" to succeed to "very likely" to succeed increases the probability from about 40 to about 90 percent that they will vote for Bush.

How powerful is the impact of the Iraq War on vote choice in comparison to other variables? As column 2 in table 6.3 indicates, the only significant control variable in our analysis is party identification—which does have a very large impact on vote choice. Even this variable that is so central to electoral behavior does not, however, overwhelm the impact of

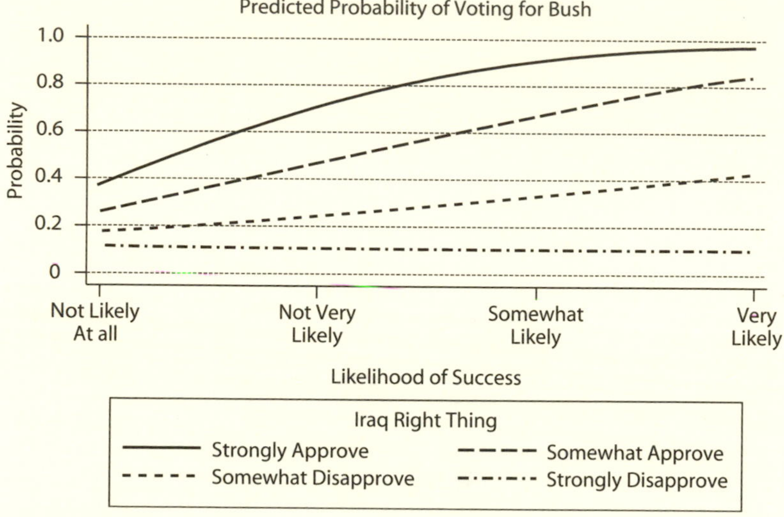

FIGURE 6.2. Vote Choice Predicted Probabilities by *Success* (estimated from Model 2)

retrospective attitudes toward the Iraq War. Shifting a respondent's party identification from Democrat to Republican increases the predicted probability that he or she will vote for Bush by more than 65 percent. This effect is very large, but for respondents who believe that success in Iraq is "somewhat likely" or "very likely," retrospective judgments about Bush's decision to launch the war matter more.[7]

WHO VOTES ON THE WAR?

The results in table 6.3 indicate that attitudes toward Iraq played a very significant role in voter's calculations in 2004, but how broadly does this result generalize across the electorate? Did all voters use roughly the same calculus in making their choices? Given the varying priorities that exist across the American electorate, it seems likely that some voters may have given more weight to their views on Iraq than others. To probe the robustness of our results, we re-ran the analyses across three different sets of voters: (1) those who said that foreign policy is the most important

[7] Adding other more specific control variables does not alter this result. For example, if we place respondents' judgments about which candidate (Bush or Kerry) would handle the economy and social issues better, we do find that these variables have a significant impact. The impact of *Right thing*, however, remains larger than those variables when respondents think success is "somewhat" or "very" likely.

TABLE 6.4.
Impact of Iraq on Vote Choice by "Most Important Issue"

	Foreign policy–oriented voters	*Economic policy–oriented voters*	*Social policy voters*
Party ID	1.617	1.637	1.452
	(4.70)**	(10.69)**	(3.33)**
Iraq *Right thing*	0.196	0.700	0.310
	(0.38)	(2.86)**	(0.46)
Expect *Success*	0.038	0.095	–0.125
	(0.09)	(0.39)	(0.16)
Right thing ×	0.862	0.293	0.672
Success	(2.85)**	(2.20)*	(1.48)
Female	0.233	0.264	0.211
	(0.51)	(1.27)	(0.31)
Minority	–0.764	–0.159	–0.979
	(1.25)	(0.59)	(1.03)
Age	–0.277	0.142	0.397
	(1.33)	(1.36)	(1.24)
Education level	–0.018	–0.090	–0.295
	(0.07)	(0.82)	(1.08)
Observations	305	590	102

Absolute value of *z* statistics in parentheses
* significant at 5% ** significant at 1%

issue in determining their vote, (2) those who say economics is the most important issue in determining their vote, and (3) those who say that social issues are the most important in determining their vote.[8] These results suggest that the Iraq War definitely had a significant impact on the choices made by most voters, but its influence on other voters was less clear.

The first column in table 6.4 analyzes vote choice for the 30 percent of the public who stated that foreign policy issues like Iraq and the war on terror were most important to them in choosing a candidate. As we can see from these results, attitudes toward Iraq remain very important and influential, however, the way in which these attitudes matter shifts somewhat.

[8] The specific question wording stated, "When choosing for whom to vote, which of the following issues are most important to you personally?" The three response options available were (1) "foreign policy issues like Iraq and the War on Terrorism," (2) "economic issues like jobs and taxes," and (3) "social issues like abortion and gay marriage."

The impact of *Right thing* remains larger than *Success*, but the fact that both of these variables are insignificant on their own in the equation indicates that neither variable has a significant impact on vote choice when the other variable is at its minimum value. At the same time, we see that the interaction between these two attitudes is much larger than we observed in the full sample. Thus while the impact of *Right Thing* is not significant when foreign policy–oriented respondents believe that success is "not at all likely," it is highly significant for all the other categories, and by the time respondents believe success is "very likely" the coefficient for *Right thing* is 2.78 ($p < .01$)—a 50 percent larger impact than it had in the full sample. *Success* also has a greater impact on vote choice among foreign policy– oriented voters. While we see that the impact of *Success* when respondents "strongly disapprove" of the president's decision to use force does not differ from its impact in the full sample, by the time respondents "strongly approve" of the initial decision to use force the coefficient for *Success* is 2.63 ($p < .01$). In sum, foreign policy–oriented voters give a great deal of weight to Iraq in making their vote choices. And while they conform to our expectations regarding the importance of retrospective judgments of whether force was the right thing, they consider their prospective judgments about success almost as strongly.

Next we examined the decisions of respondents who cite economic concerns as the most important issue in choosing a candidate. Nearly 60 percent of respondents stated that this was their top concern, so it should not be surprising that the results for this sample closely resemble our findings from the full sample results in table 6.3. In this case, however, retrospective attitudes regarding Bush's initial decision get somewhat more weight than in the full sample, when respondents think success is "not at all likely." The somewhat smaller interaction term, however, indicates that retrospective attitudes do not work as strongly in combination with prospective judgments about success. For example, table 6.4 shows that when respondents think that success is "not at all likely" the coefficient for *Right thing* is 0.70 ($p < .01$), but increasing confidence in success to "very likely" doubles the coefficient only to 1.58 ($p < .01$). In the full sample analysis, this coefficient nearly quadruples with the same shift in confidence. Nonetheless, our central results remain constant: (1) attitudes toward Iraq have a substantial impact on vote choice, (2) retrospective judgments about Iraq matter more for vote choice than prospective ones, and (3) when confidence in success is high, these retrospective judgments have a larger impact on vote choice than party identification.

Finally, we turn to our analysis of voters who stated that social issues such as abortion and gay marriage were most important to them in choosing a candidate. Our conclusions here are somewhat more tentative because only about 10 percent of our sample cited these issues as their top concern, and so we have only a little over 100 respondents in this category. Here we see that the only statistically significant variable that seems to influence vote choice for socially oriented voters is *Party ID*. None of the Iraq variables is significant.

One might want to conclude from these results that socially oriented voters did not consider Iraq when making their vote choices. A quick look at the substantive size of the coefficients for the Iraq variables, however, indicates that our best guess as to the impact of these variables did not change much in comparison to the other two groups of voters. Instead, what we see is that the standard errors for these coefficients are several times larger than those that we observe for the other categories of respondents. Two issues seem likely to be at work here. First, as noted earlier, we have a smaller sample of socially oriented voters, and so we have less information and wider confidence intervals. Second, the voting choices of these socially oriented voters seem badly over-determined. Nearly 75 percent of the voters who identified social issues as their top priority voted for Bush. Nearly half of these socially oriented voters are Republican, and 100 percent of the Republican socially oriented respondents stated that they would vote for Bush. At the same time more than 70 percent of these voters thought that Bush did the right thing and more than 65 percent expected the United States to succeed.

With such a broad consensus among the small number of socially oriented voters, it becomes difficult to distinguish among the various causes of their votes for George W. Bush. Nonetheless, while we cannot test the specific interaction, we can hypothesize with great confidence and test whether the Iraq variables as a whole contribute to the vote-choice equation. A likelihood ratio test revealed that when considered jointly, the Iraq variables are highly significant (chi-squared = 35.86, 3 d.f., $p < .01$). Thus we cannot be highly confident in the relative weights of the retrospective and prospective attitudes for these voters, nor can we be especially confident in the nature of their interaction. We can, however, be confident that attitudes toward Iraq had a significant impact on the choices of socially oriented voters, and our best estimate suggests that our argument about the importance of retrospective attitudes is supported.

Conclusions

So what is the substantive significance of these retrospective and prospective attitudes about Iraq and the interaction between them in light of the results presented both here and in chapter 5? People who held both beliefs—that the war was right and that the United States would win—indicate the strongest support for continuing military action even in the

TABLE 6.5.
Support for President Bush by Attitudes toward Iraq

	Percent of electorate	*Percent vote for Bush*
"Bush Base"	49%	83%
"Noble Failure"	8%	53%
"Pottery Barn"	15%	26%
"Vietnam Syndrome"	29%	13%

face of mounting casualties and for reelecting President Bush. Likewise, people who held the opposite view—that the war was wrong and that the United States would lose—have the strongest opposition both to paying any more human cost and to reelecting Bush. Recall our labeling of the former as the "Bush Base" and the latter group as the "Vietnam Syndrome" crowd. The intermediate attitudes—the "Noble Failure" view (the war was right but we will lose) and the "Pottery Barn" or "you break it, you fix it" view (the war was wrong but we will win)—operated in surprising ways. The "Pottery Barn" crowd was, on average, more likely than the "Noble Failure" crowd to stomach continued military action, but tended to express the intention to vote for John Kerry. In contrast, the Noble Failure subgroup was ready to give up on Iraq, but still planned to vote for President Bush.

What can these results tell us about why Bush 43 was able to win the majority of the 2004 popular vote—which eluded him in 2000—despite a costly and controversial war? First of all, we can see that the war did not help Bush 43 simply because the public reflexively refuses to oust the commander-in-chief during wartime. After all, a significant proportion of the public was strongly opposed to the war and sought vigorously to remove the president as a result. Instead, the war helped the president to win the national vote and maintain support for the war because he was able to persuade a majority of the public of two simple points: (1) attacking Iraq was the right thing to do, and (2) the United States would ultimately succeed in Iraq. Specifically, we found that 49 percent of our respondents fell into the "Bush Base" category, while 15 percent were identified as "Pottery Barn," 8 percent as "Noble Failure," and 29 percent as in the "Vietnam Syndrome" category. Support from "Bush Base" and "Noble Failure" voters kept the president in office, while "Bush Base" and "Pottery Barn" respondents maintained popular support for the war (see table 6.5).

Our results clearly indicate that Iraq weighed heavily on the calculus of voters in 2004. This impact was perhaps most pronounced for the 30 percent of the electorate who felt that foreign affairs was the most important issue in determining their vote. But our results also demonstrate that even those who identified the economy or social issues as most important also gave significant weight to Iraq in making their vote choices. Interpreting the impact of these attitudes on the national vote is relatively straightforward. Because the president is elected on the basis of fifty separate state-level votes, however, determining the impact of Iraq on the actual electoral outcome in 2004 is more difficult. Our data—which is drawn from a national sample—is not well suited to answer this question because the nature of the state-level races implied that small constituencies of voters in certain closely divided states held much more sway over the outcome than other voters. Whether Iraq hurt or helped the president in the Electoral College would depend upon the distribution of attitudes about Iraq in a few key states and constituencies. While we cannot replicate our model within each of these niche constituencies, we are able to reanalyze the models in table 6.3 separately for "blue" and "red" states—defined as states won by Gore and Bush in the 2000 election. We find that the model yielded nearly identical coefficients in Republican and Democratic states, suggesting that even the battleground states were likely shaped by these same dynamics.

Thus our evidence suggests that the presidential election of 2004 was profoundly influenced by judgments about the war in Iraq—but the public did not reelect the Commander-in-Chief simply because there was a war on. Instead, the public appears to have drawn carefully reasoned judgments both about the war and about the election. Our analysis indicates that a single theoretical model can be used to describe both Americans' willingness to support continued fighting and their willingness to reelect the president. Specifically, we build upon the central attitudes from our model of casualty tolerance—one prospective and the other retrospective—as key factors in shaping vote choice. While our analyses in chapter 5 indicate that casualty tolerance was driven primarily by prospective judgments about success, our reading of the electoral behavior literature leads us to expect retrospective attitudes to matter more in a reelection campaign for a sitting president. Consistent with Fiorina (1981), we find that retrospective judgments about the president's decision to use force were most influential in determining vote choice.

Chapter Seven

THE SOURCES AND MEANING OF *SUCCESS* IN IRAQ

CHAPTER 5 demonstrated that an individual's willingness to tolerate the human costs of continuing to prosecute the war in Iraq was a function of the interaction of two separate beliefs: (1) the retrospective belief that President Bush did the right thing in attacking Iraq, and (2) the prospective belief that the United States will ultimately succeed in its mission. Of these, a prospective belief in success appeared to be the more central factor in determining casualty tolerance. This helps explain why public support for the war remained fairly robust well into 2005, despite an unexpectedly bloody and long counterinsurgency, and despite serious doubts being raised about several of the chief justifications for the war. Even as late as spring 2005, Americans remained fairly optimistic about the prospects for success in Iraq.

This optimism did begin to recede markedly in the summer of 2005 despite the achievement of political milestones, such as an initial election of a transitional Iraqi assembly in January 2005, and then the adoption of a constitution negotiated in August and approved by referendum several months later. This decline in public optimism seemed to be linked to the delays in forming the interim government and then in negotiating a constitution, and also to renewed civil violence in Iraq after a brief post-election lull. Public support for the war rallied slightly at the end of 2005 as Iraqis elected their first constitutionally based government, but political deadlock ensued in the actual formation of a government, and the civil violence continued to escalate. By the summer of 2006 more than 100 Iraqis per week were dying in suicide bombing attacks and sectarian violence, leading many—including Iraq's prime minister—to speculate that Iraq was on the brink of outright civil war. The continued violence and fears of civil war undermined whatever confidence may have been instilled by the elections and thus undermined support for the war. Consequently, the proportion of the public endorsing a withdrawal slowly mounted, although the "get out now regardless of the consequences" option was still a decidedly minority position.

Dissatisfaction with the lack of progress in stabilizing Iraq helped sweep the Democratic Party to control of both the House of Representatives and the Senate in the fall of 2006. In response, President Bush announced changes in the personnel responsible for overseeing the conflict, along with a change in political, economic, and diplomatic approaches, as well as new military tactics and an increase in the number of American troops in Iraq. By the summer of 2007, however, authorities in the Pentagon were conceding that little progress had been made at that point, though they continued to claim that it was too early to make a conclusive assessment.[1] As a consequence, support for the war eroded substantially, and a growing percentage began pressing more forcefully for an end to American participation in the conflict.

In short, the public's willingness to stick it out in Iraq seemed to be primarily a function of the public's expectation that some successful outcome could still be achieved there rather than a hindsight judgment on the merits of prewar arguments. Moreover, the erosion of support seemed more clearly linked to prospects for success than American casualties per se, since the escalation in Iraqi civil violence was actually matched by a downward trend in the incidence of U.S. fatalties.[2] This evidence of public opinion tethered to prospective judgments further indicates a "prudent" American public when it comes to the use of force—especially since the public's focus on success seems to reflect a pragmatic concern about "what to do now" after a conflict is underway.

Chapter 6 demonstrated that the interaction of these same two attitudes also sheds important light on voters' decisions in the polling booth in November 2004. Consistent with previous work on electoral choice, however, we find that in vote choice, retrospective attitudes about whether the decision to use force was the right thing take center stage. Once again, these results are consistent with our characterization of a "prudent" public that chooses its leaders on the basis of judgments about their track record. Our findings also provide further evidence that foreign policy issues can have a significant impact on voting behavior. To be sure, the war in Iraq was not the central issue for all voters, but for the nearly one-third of voters in the November election who stated that foreign policy issues were of greatest importance to them, the interaction of attitudes about whether Bush did the right thing and whether the United States will succeed made a powerful contribution to vote choice.

These findings help settle some longstanding questions about the determinants of public casualty tolerance; but they also raise new ones: What do people mean when they say that the president did the "right thing" in attacking Iraq? What do they mean by "success" in Iraq? Moreover, what

[1]David S. Cloud and Damien Cave, "Commanders Say Push in Baghdad Is Short of Goal." *New York Times*, 5 June 2007, p.1.

[2]Iraq Coalition Casualty Count, "Trends in Casualties since the Fall of Baghdad." Accessed on 7 August2006 at http://icasualties.org/oif_a/CasualtyTrends.htm

causes respondents to believe that the president did the right thing and what causes them to believe that the United States will succeed?

In chapter 5 we found that several widely discussed attitudes—such as the perceived primary policy objective (PPO) of the mission, the perceived consensus of American leaders in support of the mission, and opposition to using force without U.N. approval—had a statistically significant but substantively modest impact on casualty tolerance in Iraq. At that time, we noted the possibility that those other factors might have been influential because they may have *caused* respondents to believe that war was the right thing or that the United States would succeed. We explore this possibility in greater detail in this chapter along with the possibility that attitudes toward whether war was the right thing and whether the United States would succeed may also be simultaneously causing one another. Before attempting to model this relatively complex structure of public attitudes toward the war in Iraq, we begin by examining what respondents meant when they stated that the president had done the "right thing" in attacking Iraq or that they believed that the United States would "succeed" in its mission.

How Does the Public Decide Whether Attacking Iraq Was the "Right Thing"?

The public's substantive understanding of whether the president was doing the right thing by attacking Iraq would appear to be relatively straightforward. Whether or not one agrees with the ultimate decision, there is no disputing that the merits of using force to remove Saddam Hussein were widely debated by American politicians and the news media. Between January 2003 and the launching of the attack on 19 March, the three major TV news networks (ABC, NBC, and CBS) devoted an average of more than eight-five minutes per week of coverage on Iraq. Since the network news broadcasts have only a total of about 360 minutes of air-time per week, we can see that the subject received a good deal of exposure. Despite this massive attention by the TV news media, however, the volume of network coverage barely scraped the surface of the massive public debate over the invasion of Iraq throughout the fall of 2002 and the spring of 2003.

In responding to our question about whether President Bush did the right thing by attacking Iraq, we expect respondents to have recalled their attitudes about the justifications for the war that were offered in the weeks and months leading up to the invasion. The central issues in this debate were fairly clear. The administration advanced three main rationales for using force against Saddam Hussein.[3] The first and most-emphasized rationale was the allegation that Saddam Hussein was illegally and surreptitiously building a weapons of mass destruction (WMD) program in defiance of some fifteen U.N. Security Council resolutions. This rationale was emphasized the most because it provided (arguably) a legal predicate for war—enforcement of U.N. resolutions—and (ironically) because it was the one on which there was the greatest global consensus. While there was some debate about the extent of Iraq's WMD programs, there was almost no serious debate among experts about whether Iraq was defying the U.N. sanctions regime; even countries like France and Germany, which strenuously opposed using force against Iraq, believed Hussein to be in violation at least to some extent.[4]

While enforcing U.N. resolutions served as a legal predicate, the logic behind this rationale rested on the "Bush Doctrine" and the notion of preemptive self-defense. One of the central lessons that the president drew from the attacks of 11 September 2001 was that the United States should not and would not wait to be attacked before using force. The matter was summarized in the National Security Strategy issued in fall 2002: "[I]n an age where the enemies of civilization openly and actively seek the world's most destructive technologies, the United States cannot remain idle while dangers gather."[5] While the specifics of the legal issues at stake were clearly important and hotly contested—especially outside the United States—the key substantive issue for the American public was whether or not the president was justified in striking first in these sorts of cases.

The second major rationale was Iraq's support for anti-Israeli terrorist groups and the allegation that this support might one day lead Hussein to provide WMD to the al-Qaeda terrorist network. The Bush administration argued that al-Qaeda was seeking more devastating weapons—indeed, Bin Laden had claimed that it was the moral duty of his followers to secure and use WMD against the United States—and they claimed that one way to get such weapons could be from an actor that shared their antipathy for the Americans and that had WMD capability. The Bush and Clinton administrations believed that the Iraqi regime and al-Qaeda had reached out to each other over the previous decade, and the Bush

[3] See, Eric Schmitt "The Struggle for Iraq: Greenwich Village," *New York Times*, 22 September 2003, p. 8. See also Peter J. Boyer, "Paul Wolfowitz Defends His War," *The New Yorker*, 1 November 2004.

[4] See Peter Slevin, "U.S. Says War Has Legal Basis; Reliance on Gulf War Resolutions Is Questioned by Others," *Washington Post*, 21 March 2003, p. A14. See also John Burns and Thom Shanker, "U.S. Officials Fashion Legal Basis to Keep Forces in Iraq," *New York Times*, 25 March 2004, p. 10.

[5] National Security Strategy of the United States, September 2002.

administration argued that these contacts could blossom into a collaborative relationship.[6]

The third rationale focused on the humanitarian and security benefits of replacing Saddam Hussein with a democracy that respected human rights and could be a beacon of freedom in the Middle East. This third rationale—the so-called "neo-conservative" argument for the war—posited that the way to deal with terrorism in the long run was to nudge the region that was home to the terrorists in the direction of democracy. Proponents of this view argued that establishing a democracy in Iraq could be the catalyst that would accelerate political reform in the region.[7] Moreover, they contended—based partly on the extensive "democratic peace" literature—that democratic regimes in the Middle East would be peaceful toward one another and would not threaten the United States through their support of terrorism.[8] This argument was advanced before the war, but it was raised somewhat later and did not receive nearly as much emphasis as the WMD and terror links rationale.[9]

According to the Bush administration, each of these reasons had some sort of link to 9/11. It asserted that the alleged Iraq WMD threat was intolerable because 9/11 had shown the consequences of delay and ineffective action while threats gathered. The administration contended that Iraq's links to terror might lead Hussein to seek common cause with al-Qaeda, joining two unlikely bedfellows that loathed each other—a quasi-secular dictator and a radical Islamist terror organization. It also claimed that the project of establishing a democracy in Iraq would accelerate the achievement of a long-term solution to terrorism. Thus the Bush administration argued strenuously that the war in Iraq should be viewed as part of the broader war on terror that began on 9/11.[10] While each of these ar-

[6] 9/11 Commission Report, p. 128. See also Mike Allen, "Al-Qaeda at Work in Iraq, Bush Tells BBC; President Suggests Connection Between Terrorist Group and Hussein Government," *Washington Post*, 16 November 2003, p. A22. See also Anne E. Kornblut, "Bush Talks of 'Real Threat' of Al-Qaeda, Voices Confidence in Weapons Hunt and Again Defends Case for War in Iraq," *Boston Globe*, 31 July 2003, p. A2.

[7] See Toby Harnden, "Democracy in Iraq Could 'Reshape the Middle East,'" *Daily Telegraph (London),* 7 February 2003, p. 15. See also Alan Murray, "Political Capital: Bush Officials Scramble to Push Democracy in Iraq," *Wall Street Journal*, 8 April 2003, p. 4.

[8] For a summary of the "democratic peace" literature, see Ray (1995), Oneal and Russett (2001), and Reiter and Stam (2002).

[9] For example, in a 26 February 2003 address to the American Enterprise Institute justifying his confrontation with Iraq, President Bush stated, "The world has a clear interest in the spread of democratic values, because stable and free nations do not breed the ideologies of murder. They encourage the peaceful pursuit of a better life. And there are hopeful signs of a desire for freedom in the Middle East." Remarks archived at http://www.whitehouse.gov/news/releases/2003/02/20030226-11.html.

[10] The president's 2003 State of the Union address heavily emphasized the confrontation with Iraq as part of the war on terror. For example, the president asked listeners to "[i]mag-

guments was offered before the war, the rhetoric gradually shifted away from the first and toward the second and especially the third as the post-war evidence did not support their claims regarding Iraqi WMD programs and as the evidence regarding the likelihood of collaboration between Hussein and al-Qaeda was called into question.[11]

So what does it mean to say that President Bush did the "right thing" when he attacked Iraq in March 2003? We would expect that attitudes toward this question would have been determined primarily by respondents' attitudes toward these underlying rationales. In our analysis, we emphasize the first two pillars, which were also the ones most stressed before the war—WMD and terrorism—and disaggregate them into three distinct debates: (1) Was Saddam Hussein developing WMD, (2) Was the Bush Doctrine a legitimate interpretation of "self-defense," and (3) Was Saddam Hussein cooperating with al-Qaeda? Reasonable people may differ regarding the strength of these claims made by the Bush administration. Indeed, the authors themselves are not entirely in agreement as to the answers to these questions. Nonetheless, we expect that attitudes toward the justification for the war would have been shaped by respondents' views on these three points.

How Does the Public Define and Measure Success in Iraq?

Understanding public conceptions of success in Iraq is somewhat more complex than understanding whether respondents believed that the president did the "right thing." While the extensive debate over justifications for the use of force in Iraq give us a strong foundation for understanding what factors the public was likely to consider in making retrospective judgments about the justification for using force, no such debate occurred about the meaning of a successful mission in Iraq. One might infer the meaning of "success" from the justification for using force, but such measures of success would be retrospective—looking back toward the initial decision—rather than prospective and looking toward the completion of the mission. This distinction becomes especially important in the case of the Iraq War, because some of the initial reasons given for using force—such

ine those 19 hijackers with other weapons and other plans—this time armed by Saddam Hussein. It would take one vial, one canister, one crate slipped into this country to bring a day of horror like none we have ever known." Remarks archived at http://www.whitehouse.gov/news/releases/2003/01/20030128-19.html.

[11] The president began making the argument that Iraq had become "the central front" in the war on terror during the summer of 2003. In particular, a 7 September 2003 prime-time television address to the nation highlighted this phrase. Remarks archived at http://www.whitehouse.gov/news/releases/2003/09/20030907-1.html.

as Iraqi WMD—proved to be based on very faulty intelligence. What, then, can success mean in this context?[12]

One possibility that would be especially damaging to our argument would be if the public focused on the absence of U.S. military casualties as its measure of success. If the number of U.S. soldiers killed became the public's measure of (the lack of) success, then our argument about the perception of success as the key to tolerating casualties becomes circular. Respondents who believed that too many soldiers had been killed (and thus who had a low tolerance for additional casualties) would have tended to say that they did not believe that the United States would succeed in Iraq. Such a pattern would indicate that the public's perceptions of the likelihood of success were a consequence of their tolerance for casualties, not its cause. On the other hand, if the public's attitudes toward success really were prospective judgments about the ability of the U.S. government to create some desirable future outcome in Iraq, then attitudes toward success were not a consequence of casualties and our argument remains valid.

What future outcomes would the American public be looking toward? The most likely candidates appear to be the criteria for success that were being stressed by the Bush administration in public rhetoric during much of 2003 and 2004. Specifically, the Bush administration emphasized that the mission in Iraq would be a success when the following happened: (1) Iraqi security forces were able to protect Iraq's citizen and its borders. (2) The Iraqi people were provided basic services such as power, water, and education. (3) The Iraqi government was democratically elected. These themes came up repeatedly in the Bush administration's discussion of the future of Iraq.[13]

So what were our respondents thinking about when they answered our question about the likelihood of success in Iraq? Were they thinking retrospectively about the elimination of Iraqi WMD and links to terrorism? Were they thinking simply about a "successful" mission being one that minimized U.S. casualties? Or were they thinking prospectively about the likelihood of creating a stable, democratic, and self-sufficient Iraq? To address this question, beginning February 2004, we followed up our "expectations of success" question with several additional questions probing the meaning and measurement of success. We asked respondents what

[12] An interesting counterfactual analysis that we cannot resolve for obvious reasons would be considering what might have happened if the coalition had found the large stockpiles of WMD that the Bush administration argued they would find. In that case, the toppling of the regime would have counted as a more unambiguous retrospective success, and our data might take our argument in very different directions.

[13] For example, President Bush emphasized these goals in a highly publicized joint press conference with Iraqi Prime Minister Allawi on 23 September 2004. Remarks archived at http://www.whitehouse.gov/news/releases/2004/09/20040923-8.html.

success meant to them, based on a range of possible answers that were prominent in public discussions. Table 7.1 presents results to this question.

Several remarkable patterns emerge. First, the responses to the question of the definition of *success* are very stable from February through June of 2004. In fact, they are astonishingly stable when one considers that these results come from seven different national samples polled over five very turbulent months in Iraq. "An Iraqi government that is stable and democratic" was always the number-one choice, followed closely by "Iraqis provide for their own security" and "Iraqis are able to live peaceful, normal, everyday lives." Moreover, the popularity of these definitions were quite consistent across various categories of respondents. For example, we find no substantial shifts between the definitions of success offered by male and female respondents. Minority respondents were slightly less likely to offer "a government that is stable and democratic" as their most important measure of success than were white respondents, but this difference was a fairly modest 8 percent gap. Age also had only a very modest impact on definitions of success. About 7 percent fewer of the respondents under thirty years of age cited democracy as their definition of success than did respondents over sixty years old. Younger respondents were correspondingly more likely to define success as "Iraqis are able to live peaceful, normal everyday lives." Even party identification had little effect on definitions of success. The only substantial difference across party lines was that about 10 percent more of the Republican respondents stated that a stable democratic Iraqi government was their definition of success than did Democratic or Independent respondents. Republicans were correspondingly less likely to offer "peaceful, normal, everyday lives" for Iraqis as their definition. Interestingly, education levels accounted for the largest difference in definitions of success across the various demographic groups. Specifically, 15 percent fewer of the respondents with less than a high school education referred to democracy as their definition of success than did respondents who had completed college. Instead, the less-educated respondents were more likely to refer to an absence of WMD or a lack of links to terrorism as their definition of success. Despite these modest shifts in definitions of success, the general pattern of responses was remarkably stable and robust. Most importantly for all of these groups, the top three definitions of success were the same: a democratic Iraq that provides for its own security and allows its people to live normal lives.

Second, the results in table 7.1 strongly suggest that the public moved on from the WMD and terrorism arguments even as events on the ground moved past those *casus belli* as well. The public did not treat the apparent absence of WMD stockpiles as a sign that it was time to declare victory and go home. Likewise, simply deposing Hussein and thus ending any connection he might have had to terrorists was not "success enough" to warrant stopping the war. On the contrary, the public moved on to

TABLE 7.1.
The Public's Understanding of Success in Iraq

	6–20 Feb. (n = 891)	*25 Feb.– 4 Mar. (n = 870)*	*5 Mar.– 18 Mar. (n = 930)*	*19 Mar.– 2 Apr. (n = 889)*	*2–16 Apr. (n = 881)*	*17–29 Apr. (n = 899)*	*18–28 June (n = 900)*
Iraqis provide for their own security and maintain order	24	24	21	24	25	25	25
The Iraqi economy is rebuilt and oil production is restored	5	4	5	6	5	4	4
An Iraqi government that is stable and democratic is established	29	33	29	29	30	29	28
Iraqis are able to live peaceful, normal, everyday lives	24	24	27	24	23	24	22
The Iraqi government is prevented from producing WMD	5	4	3	4	5	3	4
The Iraqi government is prevented from supporting international terrorist organizations	11	10	12	11	11	12	9
Iraq is not a threat to its neighbors							8
Refused	3	1	2	1	2	2	1

define success in prospective terms that had relevance to the Iraqi situation as it stood in the winter and spring of 2004. Even among the group most likely to refer to terrorism and WMD as its definition of success—those with less than a high school education—only about 20 percent of the respondents offered either one of these definitions (as opposed to about 10 percent of college graduates).

Third, the findings suggest that the public may have taken its cues on defining success from the Bush administration, which was itself shifting its rhetorical emphasis from the WMD argument to the importance of establishing a stable democracy in the Middle East.[14] As noted earlier, this argument was present in Bush rhetoric from the beginning. The importance of spreading democracy was part of the National Security Strategy released in 2002 and was mentioned in the State of the Union address in 2003. Still, it was WMD that dominated the prewar debate, and a retrospective-based definition of success should have given WMD more prominence. We cannot say definitively what impact Bush administration rhetoric had on definitions of success. To answer such a question systematically we would have needed panel data from surveys beginning prior to the initiation of hostilities and continuing through the shifts in administration rhetoric. Unfortunately, we do not have such data, nor are we aware of any other organizations that collected this information. Nonetheless, the very close match between the aggregate public responses about "success" in Iraq during the spring of 2004 and Bush administration language about the subject reinforces the hypothesis that the administration may have been successful in shaping public definitions of success in Iraq.[15]

After having asked respondents how they defined *success* in Iraq, we followed up this question by asking respondents how they believed one could best judge whether the United States was on a path toward success. That is, we asked respondents what measures they used to track and estimate future success, again directing respondents to choose from a list of plausible factors. Table 7.2 presents the results to these questions.

In general, attitudes toward how to judge success in Iraq were also quite stable. Once again, three major responses stood out as by far the most common benchmarks for measuring success: (1) what kinds of essential services are being provided to Iraqis, (2) how soon can democratic elections be held, and (3) whether Iraqis are cooperating with U.S. forces against the insurgents. Moreover, one response was consistently the most frequently offered across all eight survey waves—from February through October 2004. Whether Iraqis were cooperating with the United States

[14] Dana Milbank and Mike Allen, "U.S. Shifts Rhetoric on Its Goals in Iraq," *Washington Post*, 1 August 2003, p. A14.

[15] We return to the question of whether and how the Bush administration shaped public opinion in the Iraq war at the end of this chapter.

Table 7.2.
The Public's Measurement of Success in Iraq

	6–20 Feb. (n = 891)	*25 Feb.– 4 Mar. (n = 870)*	*5–18 Mar. (n = 930)*	*19 Mar.– 2 Apr. (n = 889)*	*2–16 Apr. (n = 881)*	*17–29 Apr. (n = 899)*	*18–28 June (n = 900)*	*15 Oct.– 1 Nov. (n = 1,125)*
How well the Iraqi economy is doing, including how much oil is being produced	8	7	8	7	6	5	7	6
What services, such as education, health care, and utilities, are being provided to Iraqis	25	26	26	27	23	21	25	19
How soon Iraq can hold free elections	18	18	17	17	14	15	13	14
Are Iraqis cooperating with U.S. authorities and not protecting terrorists or insurgents	30	32	29	29	35	38	34	39

How many attacks are made against U.S. soldiers and Iraqis who cooperate with the U.S.	7	7	8	8	8	10	10	8
How many U.S. soldiers are killed or wounded	3	3	2	3	2	3	3	4
How many terrorists and insurgents are killed or arrested	2	2	2	2	3	3	4	4
How much money the U.S. has to spend	4	4	5	4	4	3	3	4
Refused	3	2	3	2	4	3	2	2

against the insurgents was consistently the most popular indicator of success. As with definitions of success, these responses were quite consistent across various groups of respondents. While demographic variables had some impact on the pattern of responses, the effects were quite modest—even for *Party ID*. Thus the public seems to have been relatively united in its measurement of success in Iraq.

Although the same three measures of success dominated the responses throughout the winter and spring of 2004, and the relative rankings never changed, the number-one indicator, "whether Iraqis are cooperating with U.S. authorities and not protecting terrorists and insurgents," increased markedly in prominence as time progressed. This shift is especially noteworthy because it may help to explain both the erosion of confidence in the spring of 2004 and its stabilization during the summer and fall. The Fallujah and Sadr uprisings that began in mid-March 2004 were dramatic signs that the coalition had not won the Sunni hearts and minds, and that it might, indeed, be in danger of losing a key Shiite constituency as well. Moreover, this ominous view was compounded by reports that the Iraqi security forces trained by the coalition to take over the policing function failed spectacularly in that job.[16] Nevertheless, the transfer of sovereignty to Iraq and the creation of an Iraqi government appeared to have stemmed this tide—at least for a time. By the summer of 2005, however, these props under public confidence were weakening. News accounts emphasized the slowness of ISF training, and the persistence of violence, even after successful elections, cast doubt on whether Iraq could ever be stable. The drop in optimism, however, does not undermine our causal argument unless it could be argued that the drop was unrelated to these prospective judgments.

Most importantly, these results show rather convincingly that our model of casualty tolerance is not a circular argument. The public does *not* measure success in terms of whether our soldiers are being killed or wounded nor whether the terrorists/insurgents are being killed or wounded. Specifically, the proportion of respondents who stated that the number of U.S. casualties was their measure of American progress toward success was less than 5 percent across eight separate waves of surveys. In most of the waves the number was more like 2 to 3 percent. Thus while the public clearly cares about U.S. casualties and weighs those costs seriously, it is not fixated on the U.S. body count as its barometer for whether an operation is going well.[17] Instead, the measures adopted by the public are rather

[16] Richard Sisk, "Iraqis Now Fight Alongside U.S.," *New York Daily News*, 15 May 2004, p. 7.

[17] Some might contend that this result is contaminated by the fact that our previous question—asking for a definition of success—does not offer "casualties" as part of the definition. Having forced respondents to define success in other terms, one might argue, we primed them not to judge success in terms of casualties. As table 5.1 indicates, however, our

different, and indeed come closer to the "winning the hearts and minds" idea that most experts (and, indeed, Bush administration rhetoric) would identify as the critical factor.[18]

The Relationship between *Right Thing* and *Success*

Thus far we have demonstrated that the public does have definitions of success in Iraq that are independent of the number of U.S. soldiers that are killed in the war. Moreover, we have shown that these attitudes toward success are prospective judgments about the likelihood of achieving future goals such as a democratic and stable Iraq. In thinking about success, the public is focused neither on the body count of U.S. soldiers nor on Iraqi weapons of mass destruction, Saddam Hussein's links to al-Qaeda, or other issues that have arisen in the extensive debate over whether the president did the right thing in attacking Iraq.

Nonetheless, there are a variety of reasons to expect that attitudes toward whether the president did the right thing by attacking Iraq and whether the United States is likely to "succeed" in Iraq are likely to be related to one another. For example, while chapters 5 and 6 highlighted the importance of the "Pottery Barn" and "Noble Failure" views of the Iraq War, such combinations of attitudes show nuanced views on the part of respondents. Nuanced views require cognitive effort, and numerous studies indicate that individuals tend to want to minimize the cognitive effort necessary to allow them to organize their understanding of the world around them. Moreover, respondents may have had emotional reasons to bring these two attitudes into line with one another. This is especially true since we were asking respondents about their current beliefs (about success) and their past judgments (about whether force was the right thing). In this case, admitting that one's current judgment about success does not comport with one's previous judgment about the rightness of the mission could have created emotional as well as cognitive tension.[19] It seems much easier, for example, to think that President Bush did the right thing by attacking Iraq and that the United States will succeed (the "Bush Base"

October 2004 survey dropped the "success definition" question but kept the "success metric" question. Results for the metric question were unchanged—less than 5 percent of respondents stated that they measured progress toward success in terms of U.S. casualties. Indeed, this holds true despite the fact that our casualty tolerance question—which was asked immediately prior—arguably primed respondents to think about casualties in defining progress.

[18] Public attitudes and elite rhetoric are clearly correlated in this case, but we cannot determine the direction of causal influence.

[19] Richard Ned Lebow, *Between Peace and War* (Baltimore: Johns Hopkins University Press, 1981); Deborah Larson, *The Origins of Containment: A Psychological Explanation* (Princeton: Princeton University Press, 1985).

view), than it would be to believe that the president was right but that the United States is now not likely to succeed (the "Noble Failure" view). To take the latter position requires the respondent to face up to the uncomfortable realization that while he or she supported the president in going to war, one must now oppose the president's desire to continue prosecuting the war.[20] Similarly, it seems easier to hold the view that the president was wrong to attack Iraq and that the United States will fail (the "Vietnam Syndrome" view), than it is to admit that while one opposed the decision to use force, the United States can indeed succeed in this mission (the "Pottery Barn" view). Once again, the latter view leads the respondent to become supportive of continuing a war that he or she claims to have initially opposed.

The hypothesis that attitudes toward the rightness of the war and its prospects for success are related is clearly supported by a simple cross-tabulation of responses to the two items. Table 7.3 displays the responses to these items for our October 2004 survey.

The "Bush Base" and "Vietnam Syndrome" combination of attitudes are by far more common than the "Noble Failure" or "Pottery Barn" sets of responses. For example, more than 70 percent of those who stated that they think the United States would "very likely" succeed also stated that they "strongly approved" of the president's decision to use force. Conversely, more than 80 percent of those who stated that they thought the United States was "not at all likely" to succeed also stated that they "strongly disapproved" of the decision to use force. In between the polar extremes, however, these two attitudes show more independent variation. For example, more than one-third of those who stated that success was "somewhat likely" also stated that they strongly or somewhat disapproved of the use of force (a "Pottery Barn" view), while more than a quarter of those who stated that success was "not very likely" also stated that they somewhat or strongly approved of the initial attack (a "Noble Failure" view). Nonetheless, these two attitudes do appear to correlate strongly. A simple bivariate correlation of these two attitudes reveals a coefficient of 0.66 ($p < .01$). This correlation ranges from 0.62 to 0.65 across the other eight waves of surveys, indicating that this relationship appears to be quite stable and robust. Attitudes toward the "right thing" question and likely success are distinct, but respondents did tend to prefer consistency across these two attitudes for some combination of cognitive and emotional reasons.

Noting a relationship between these two attitudes, however, raises the

[20] Of course, this combination of attitudes also forces respondents to address the uncomfortable question of whether they themselves were mistaken in supporting the initial decision to use force.

TABLE 7.3.
Interdependence of Whether President Bush Did the Right Thing and Whether the United States Will Succeed in Iraq

Bush did the right thing attacking Iraq	*U.S. will succeed In Iraq*				
	Not at all likely	*Not very likely*	*Somewhat likely*	*Very likely*	*Total*
Strongly disapprove	84 81%	155 51%	49 12%	8 3%	296
Somewhat disapprove	12 12%	68 22%	91 22%	15 5%	186
Somewhat approve	3 3%	63 21%	167 41%	60 20%	293
Strongly approve	5 5%	17 6%	105 25%	211 72%	338
Total	104	303	412	294	1,113

Pearson $r = 0.66$ ($p < .01$) Pearson chi-squared (9 d.f.) = 631.88 ($p > .01$)

next important question: What is the relative influence between them? Does one's prospective belief about success influence one's retrospective judgment regarding the rightness of the decision to go to war? Or does the causal influence flow in the opposite direction? More generally, what are the factors that influence a respondent's beliefs about the "rightness" of the war and the likelihood of success?

The answer to this last question has important consequences for our interpretation of the results in chapters 5 and 6. As we discussed, the effects of perceptions of success and whether Bush did the right thing that we presented in those chapters represented the direct effects of those attitudes, controlling for the other variables in the models. Those results did *not* include any indirect effects of the other variables.[21] In chapter 5 we argued that perceptions of success had a substantially larger impact on

[21] Note that this endogeneity between *Right thing* and *Success* does not threaten to bias the coefficients in chapters 4 and 5. Causal relationships between exogenous variables do not threaten to bias coefficients. Thus our analyses in chapters 4 and 5 cannot address the issue of indirect effects, but their estimates of the direct effects of variables are consistent. For endogeneity to threaten the analyses in chapter 4, one would need to hypothesize that casualty tolerance causes respondents to say that the president did the right thing or caused respondents to perceive success as likely. We do not see a persuasive argument in support of the former claim, and our data describing the meaning of success demonstrates that the latter claim is not correct.

casualty tolerance than did beliefs about whether the war was the right thing to do. If beliefs about success are largely a function of beliefs about whether the war was the right thing to do, however, then our focus on *Success* as the critical variable may be misplaced. Conversely, in chapter 6 we emphasized retrospective attitudes about whether force was the right thing as a determinant of vote choice, but if that retrospective judgment is largely a function of whether one thinks the mission is likely to succeed, then we may not have given sufficient weight to attitudes toward success in that regard.

Moreover, in chapter 5 we noted that the impact of attitudes toward success and whether force was the right thing were substantially larger than other causes of casualty tolerance that have been hypothesized in the literature. Consistent with arguments made by Eric Larson, Bruce Jentleson, Steven Kull, and others, we did find that attitudes toward the level of elite consensus in support of the war, the perceived primary policy objective (PPO) of the war, and respondents' level of support for multilateralism in the use of force all had a significant impact on their willingness to tolerate the costs of war. Not surprisingly, party identification also had an impact in what has been portrayed as a highly partisan battle over the war. None of these effects, however, approached the substantive impact of our hypothesized interaction between attitudes toward success and whether force was the right thing. At the time, however, we noted that our analyses were capturing only the direct effect of these variables on casualty tolerance and that these concepts might be quite influential to the extent that they have an indirect relevance through their impact on attitudes about whether the war was the right decision and whether the United States would succeed.

To address these various questions, we constructed a model of public attitudes toward the war in Iraq. This model is displayed in figure 7.1, and we will use data from our October 2004 survey to estimate the relationships in this model. The arrows in the model depict the hypothesized flow of causal influence. The two central variables in this model are a respondent's attitudes toward whether attacking Iraq was the right thing to do (*Right thing*) and whether the United States would succeed in Iraq (*Success*). These two attitudes are endogenous—that is, they are caused by the other variables in the model—and they are allowed to cause one another. As with our analyses in chapters 5 and 6, we also include demographic factors—gender, age, and race—along with education levels and party identification as exogenous causes of the two endogenous variables.

Finally, we need to determine what other attitudes might be significant causes of a respondent's attitude toward whether the Iraq war was the right thing to do and whether the United States would succeed. We begin

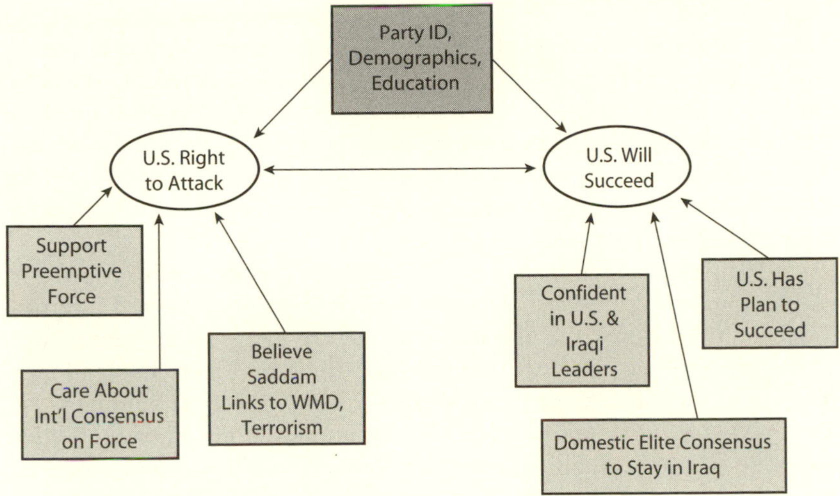

FIGURE 7.1. A Model of Public Attitudes toward the War in Iraq

by thinking about the causes of attitudes toward whether the president did the right thing by attacking Iraq. Bruce Jentleson's work on the impact of the PPO on public support for military operations focuses primarily on justifications for the use of force. That is, Jentleson's essential claim is that members of the public will think that using military force is the right thing to do if the issue at stake in the mission fits certain categories that the public is predisposed to view as important. As we noted in chapter 5, we think that the best measure of this argument is the extent to which respondents viewed the war in Iraq as a part of the broader war on terror. While Jentleson does not talk about terrorism per se as one of the key PPO's in his work, it seems a straightforward extension of his thinking to argue that the war on terror evoked a sense of threat against the U.S. homeland that is likely to elicit a level of support even greater than what he finds for the "foreign policy restraint" missions of the 1980s and 1990s. Indeed, our experimental analyses from chapter 4 indicate that the terrorism PPO evoked a higher level of support than any other mission. Thus one key variable that we include as a cause of attitudes toward whether war was the right thing is the belief that the war in Iraq is part of the war on terror, which we relied on in chapter 5. Although we believe that this one question about the PPO for the Iraq war is the best single measure of Jentleson's claim, we also included two other questions regarding the justification for the war in Iraq as causes of our "right thing" attitude. First, we included respondents' beliefs about the extent of any connection between Saddam Hussein and the terrorist group al-Qaeda.[22] And second, we included respondent's beliefs about the status of Saddam Hussein's WMD programs prior to the U.S. invasion.[23] Both of these beliefs measure the extent to which respondents thought that there was a factual basis for the most prominent arguments that the Bush administration initially used in justifying its decision to invade Iraq. Thus we expect that these factual beliefs about Iraqi WMD and links to al-Qaeda influenced respondents' retrospective judgment on whether the president did the right thing by attacking Iraq.

In addition to respondent's beliefs about the specific justifications for the mission, we also expect that respondents' attitudes toward international multilateralism and the use of force are likely to influence their judgment about whether war was the right thing to do. In chapter 5, we found that respondents' attitudes toward the importance of gaining U.N. approval before using military force had a significant impact on their willingness to tolerate casualties in the Iraq War. As with Jentleson, however, the core of Steven Kull's argument about multilateralism is that gaining multilateral sanction for the use of force—especially through the United Nations—will persuade the public that military action is the right thing to do. Certainly the administrations of President Bush and Prime Minister Tony Blair both seemed to view the debate in the U.N. Security Council this way.[24] Moreover, the interaction of international elite cues with partisanship in our analyses in chapter 5 suggests that these cues operate through their impact on beliefs about whether force is justified. Thus we included the same measure of attitudes toward using force without U.N. approval that we relied upon in chapter 5. In addition, because of the prominence of the "Bush Doctrine" in the public debate leading up to the war, we also included a measure of respondents' attitudes toward the preemptive use of military force.[25] The Bush Doctrine was also presented as a justification for the use of force based on the notion of preemptive self-defense. While international law has generally been construed to justify the use of military force only in response to a direct attack or in anticipation of an imminent threat—or, more recently, in an effort to prevent

[22] See authors for specific question wording.

[23] See authors for specific question wording.

[24] Perhaps the most salient episode of these campaigns to achieve U.N. sanction was Colin Powell's 5 February 2003 address to the U.N. Security Council in which he explicitly and repeatedly argued that the use of force was justified against Iraq because of its violation of previous U.N. Security Council Resolutions. Text of Secretary Powell's remarks are archived at http://www.whitehouse.gov/news/releases/2003/02/20030205-1.html.

[25] The doctrine of preemptive self-defense was articulated in the National Security Strategy of the United States released in September 2002 and became a source of intense public controversy. The strategy document is available at http://www.whitehouse.gov/nsc/nss/2002/index.html. On the prominence of preemption in the public debate, see for example, Bill Keller, "The Year in Ideas; Preemption," *New York Times*, 15 December 2002, p. 114.

genocide—the Bush Doctrine sought to expand the understanding of self-defense to include the preemptive use of force in situations where one perceived a threat that was less than imminent but that would involve such horrific consequences that the country could not afford to "remain idle while dangers gather."[26] Attitudes toward preemptive force are not—strictly speaking—a part of Kull's argument about multilateralism. Many members of multilateral international institutions, however, rejected the Bush administration's expansive redefinition of anticipatory self-defense, and many international legal experts likewise questioned the legitimacy of this new interpretation.[27] Thus we would argue that attitudes toward the Bush Doctrine should—for reasons generally consistent with those presented by Kull—influence attitudes toward whether the president made the "right" decision by attacking Iraq.

The next key issue we needed to address with regard to the causes of beliefs about success in Iraq and whether attacking was the right thing are attitudes toward elite consensus. As we noted in previous chapters, Eric Larson has frequently argued that the critical factor in explaining public tolerance for casualties is the extent of elite consensus in support of the mission. We found strong support for this contention in chapter 4, but in chapter 5 we also found that its influence was substantially smaller than the interaction of the *Right thing*" and *Success* variables. As we noted in chapter 4, however, one could construe Larson's argument as contending that elite consensus may matter either through its influence on public beliefs that using force is justified or through beliefs that the mission will succeed. For example, elite consensus might have persuaded members of the public that using force was the right thing because they might have concluded that if opinion leaders in *both* the Democratic and Republican parties could have agreed that a mission was in the national interest, then it must have been a good idea. Moreover, recent work on source effects in persuading the public to support the use of force indicates that voters tend to look to opinion leaders within their own party for cues as to whether to support the use of force.[28] Thus, if respondents believe that both parties support the mission, then they will follow suit.

[26] See the 2002 National Security Strategy. For a discussion of the Bush Doctrine and international legal standards of self-defense, see Anthony Clark Arend, "International Law and the Preemptive Use of Military Force," *Washington Quarterly* 26, no. 2 (2003):89–103. See also Robert Jervis, "Understanding the Bush Doctrine," *Political Science Quarterly* 118, no. 3 (2003):365–88.

[27] For legal critiques of the Bush Doctrine, see, for example, Tom J. Farer, "Beyond the Charter Fame: Unilateralism or Condominium?" *American Journal of International Law* 96, no. 2 (2002):359–64. And see Richard N. Gardner, "Neither Bush Nor the 'Jurisprudes,'" *American Journal of International Law* 97, no. 3 (2003):585–90).

[28] Berinsky (2004).

At the same time, it seems likely that perceptions of elite consensus could also have influenced perceptions of the likelihood of success in Iraq. One of the key lessons that flows from the experience of Vietnam, Beirut, and Somalia is that the greatest barrier to success in a mission is maintaining the willingness of American leaders to continue the fight.[29] Thus perhaps the greatest obstacle to success—at least in the views of some—may not have been the insurgency on the ground in Iraq, but the resolve of American leaders to see the mission through. Thus we would expect respondents who believed that Republicans and Democrats were united in their determination to continue fighting should also have believed that the United States would succeed.

Our results in chapter 4 suggested that the latter mechanism may be stronger than the former, because domestic elite consensus did not interact with partisan identification. Nonetheless, we tested both of these arguments by allowing the perception of elite consensus to act both as a cause of attitudes toward whether the Bush administration did the right thing by attacking Iraq and as a catalyst for beliefs about whether the United States would succeed in Iraq. Consistent with our expectations from chapter 4, we found that perceived elite consensus had no impact on perceptions about whether force was the right thing, but it did have a significant effect on perceptions of likely success.[30] Thus we allowed this variable to remain in the model as a cause of belief in success, but we excluded it as a cause of the belief that force was the right thing.[31]

Finally, we needed to consider what other factors might lead respondents to believe that the United States was likely to succeed in Iraq. One belief that we hypothesized would be an important cause of optimism about success in Iraq was the belief that American political leaders had a plan for winning the war. Our survey was done in the midst of a closely contested election, and it was not clear at the time of the survey whether President Bush or Senator John Kerry would prevail. Not surprisingly,

[29] See Larson (1996). See also Feaver and Gelpi (2004) for elite attitudes toward casualties and the use of military force.

[30] Elite consensus was not insignificant in this equation due to problems of multicolinearity. Auxiliary regressions revealed an r-squared of only 0.06 for the elite consensus variable. Auxiliary r-squared levels for all the variables in the analysis of whether Bush did the "right thing" were below 0.5.

[31] This may be an artifact of the time period during which we were surveying, that is, after the war had started. It is possible that a similarly constructed model using data from a preinvasion poll might find elite consensus equally important for *Right thing* and *Success*. In that case, however, both attitudes under consideration would be prospective. The deeper point may be that elite consensus matters for prospective judgments more than retrospective judgments. This may be because prospective judgments are especially uncertain—who can predict the future with great confidence?—and the public may be more reliant on experts and elites in such situations.

opinions about which candidate had a "plan to win the war" were divided sharply along party lines. Some respondents, however, indicated that they felt that both candidates had plans to win the war, while others felt that neither one did. We expect that, despite the strongly partisan atmosphere, those respondents who stated that *both* Bush and Kerry had a plan to win the war were expressing an underlying confidence in American leadership, and that this confidence would lead them to be optimistic about success for the mission. Conversely, those who stated that *neither* their own preferred candidate nor his opponent had a plan to win were expressing an underlying pessimism and would not be optimistic about the outcome of the war. We asked respondents whether they "strongly agree," "somewhat agree," "somewhat disagree," or "strongly disagree" that George Bush and John Kerry had "a clear plan for handling the situation" in Iraq. We then added these two responses together, giving us a variable that ranges from 2 (strongly disagree that either candidate had a plan) to 8 (strongly agree that both candidates had a plan).[32]

We hypothesized that a respondent's overall level of confidence in the Bush administration's leadership—including the White House, the U.S. military, and the Department of Defense—would have a significant impact on optimism about success in Iraq. Moreover, we expected that confidence in the leadership of the interim Iraqi government—which took power in June 2004 and was preparing for the Iraqi elections in January 2005—would also influence beliefs about success. We asked respondents to rate their level of confidence in several institutions. "For each one," we asked, "please tell me if you are very confident, somewhat confident, not very confident, or not at all confident in the people running each" of the following: (1) the White House, (2) the Department of Defense, (3) the U.S. military, and (4) the new government in Iraq. Not surprisingly, the responses to these four items scaled together quite closely, and so we created a single aggregate index of confidence in the Bush and Iraqi governments.[33]

Finally, we hypothesized that respondents who believed that the use of force is an efficacious way to seek foreign policy goals will be more likely to believe that the United States would succeed in Iraq. Thus we asked respondents whether they believed that the United States "must be willing to use military force" to achieve various foreign policy goals. Similar to the scale we constructed in chapter 3, we asked them about whether the United States must be ready to use military force to do the following:

[32] We also tried using the two variables separately to capture beliefs toward Bush's and Kerry's plans for handling the war. Modeled in this way, we find that beliefs about Kerry's plans do not—by themselves—have a significant impact on optimism, while beliefs about Bush's plans do. The composite variable, however, shows a more substantial effect than either of the individual responses.

[33] The alpha score for the index was a very high 0.86.

(1) help bring a democratic form of government to other nations, (2) combat global terrorist organizations, (3) promote and defend human rights in other countries; (4) prevent the spread of weapons of mass destruction, and (5) support and defend American allies. In this instance, we created a single index of the respondent's "military hawkishness" rather than using factor analysis to distinguish between security and humanitarian dimensions. We made this simplification because, as we noted earlier, the Bush administration's arguments in favor of the war bridged across the security/humanitarian divide.[34] We expected military hawks to be more optimistic about America's prospects for successfully using military force in Iraq.

Returning our attention to figure 7.1, we estimated the hypothesized effects in this model of public attitudes toward the Iraq War through a two-stage least-squares analysis that allows for attitudes toward the likelihood of success and attitudes toward whether launching the war was the right thing to cause one another.[35] Analyzing simultaneous causation through a structural equations model such as this requires that we include some variables as causes of one of the endogenous variables while excluding them as causes of the other endogenous variable. These exclusion restrictions give us information about the variation in each endogenous variable that is independent of variation in the other endogenous variable, allowing us to isolate the causal relationship between them.[36] Specifically, two-stage least-squares creates consistent coefficient estimates for a simultaneous causal relationship between variables by creating "instruments" for the endogenous variables based on estimates made by all the

[34] The alpha score for this index was 0.82

[35] We chose to rely on two-stage least-squares rather than three-stage least-squares or other "full information" estimators because two-stage least-squares are more robust to problems of misspecification and less prone to allowing bias to diffuse across coefficients in the model. Estimating our model with three-stage least squares had virtually no effect on the coefficient estimates or standard errors. The only exception to this was the coefficient for elite consensus, which was somewhat reduced in substantive size and statistical significance ($p < .06$) in the 3SLS model.

[36] See Griffiths, Hill, and Judge (1993) and Hanushek and Jackson (1977) for a discussion of two-stage least-squares and the requirements for an identified model. This model is "overidentified" in the sense that we have more exclusion restrictions than are required by the order condition. To check the robustness of our exclusion restrictions, we relaxed each assumption one at a time and allowed each excluded factor to become an independent variable in both equations at once. All of these tests supported the exclusion restrictions that we placed on the model. None of the excluded variables was statistically significant when these restrictions were relaxed, and the coefficients were substantively small. The robustness of our exclusion restrictions bolsters our claim that attitudes toward success and whether war was the right thing are indeed separable attitudes. Moreover, the fact that respondents' beliefs about Hussein's WMD and links to al-Qaeda were significantly related to opinions about whether the president did the right thing but were not related to perceptions of success further supports our contention that the former attitude is retrospective and the latter is prospective.

exogenous variables in the model in the "first stage" of the least-squares regression.

Put another way, the statistical analysis proceeds in stages. First we assess how the attitudes at the bottom of figure 7.1 shape (cause) the attitudes in the middle ring. Then we use the equations that this analysis generates (the "if X, then Y" equations) as surrogates for the middle stage (the endogenous) variables. If we have strong predictors in the first stage, then they can be used as surrogate (instrumental) variables for the second stage without much loss of explanatory power.

Our analysis suggests that the relationships outlined in figure 7.1 provide a good set of instruments for this estimation. The r-squared for the first-stage regression on whether "President Bush did the right thing" was a very strong 0.68. The r-squared for the first-stage regression on whether the "U.S. will succeed in Iraq" was almost as high at 0.58.[37] This close fit between the instruments and the endogenous variables provides a solid foundation for proceeding with the estimation of the structural coefficients hypothesized in figure 7.1. The results of our analysis of the second stage or structural equations (that is, examining the structural relationships we hypothesized) are displayed in table 7.4.

These results corroborate the cross-tabulation of *Right thing* and *Success* in table 7.3. There appears to be a strong simultaneous relationship between these attitudes that creates a "feedback loop" driving respondents toward the "Bush Base" or "Vietnam Syndrome" attitudes and away from the more dissonant "Noble Failure" or "Pottery Barn" viewpoints. The first column of coefficients reflects the impact of each variable on a respondent's perception that President Bush did the right thing by attacking Iraq. The second column of coefficients captures the impact of each variable on a respondent's perception that the United States is likely to succeed in Iraq. Blank cells denote the exclusion restrictions discussed earlier.

The coefficients are unstandardized regression coefficients, making it easy to understand and compare the relative impact of the variables in the model. Specifically, each coefficient reflects the expected change in the dependent variable for each one-unit change in the independent variable. Thus table 7.4 indicates that each one-unit increase in a respondent's perception of the likelihood of success produces an average increase of 0.743 units in his or her attitude as to whether attacking Iraq was the right thing. Thus an increase in optimism of three categories (from "not at all likely" to "very likely" to succeed) would increase a respondent's judgment

[37] One rule of thumb for judging the quality of instruments for a two-stage least-squares analysis suggests that the f-statistic obtained when regressing each endogenous variable on its instrument should exceed 10 (Cameron and Trivedi 2005). The f-statistics for each of these instruments exceed 1,000.

TABLE 7.4.
Structure of Attitudes toward Whether President Bush Did the Right Thing and Whether the United States Will Succeed in Iraq

	Bush did right thing	*U.S. will succeed*
U.S. will succeed in Iraq	0.743 (10.34)**	
Terrorism is PPO in Iraq War	0.158 (4.34)**	
Iraq WMD before war	0.114 (3.34)**	
Iraq ties to Al-Qaeda	0.108 (3.60)**	
Oppose force without U.N. approval	–0.111 (3.02)**	
Support "Bush Doctrine"	0.127 (2.87)**	
Bush Did the "right thing"		0.451 (8.34)**
Perceived elite consensus		0.102 (2.44)*
U.S. leaders have plan to win		0.046 (1.99)*
Confidence in Bush & Iraq govts.		0.274 (5.12)**
Military hawk		0.164 (3.64)**

(cont.)

of the rightness of the president's decision by an average of just over two categories (from "strongly disapprove" to "somewhat approve"). The causal flow in the opposite direction—from *Right thing* to *Success*—is also significant but not quite as large. In this case a one-unit increase in support for the president's initial decision increases a respondent's optimism about America's ultimate success by 0.451 units.

Just as in chapters 5 and 6, the coefficients in table 7.4 reflect the direct effects (or structural effects) of each of the variables in the model. The

TABLE 7.4. *(cont.)*

	Bush did right thing	*U.S. will succeed*
Female respondent	–0.111	0.014
	(2.29)*	(0.33)
Non-white respondent	–0.208	0.111
	(3.13)**	(1.93)
Age	0.018	–0.031
	(0.75)	(1.57)
Education level	0.001	–0.003
	(0.04)	(0.16)
Party ID	–0.071	–0.001
	(4.50)**	(0.10)
Constant	–0.325	–0.422
	(1.37)	(2.19)*
Observations	964	964
R-squared	0.61	0.54

Absolute value of *t* statistics in parentheses
* significant at 5% ** significant at 1%

model also clearly indicates, however, that there is a strong positive feedback loop between attitudes toward *Right thing* and *Success*. Thus a one-unit increase in optimism about success will cause an average 0.743-unit increase in support for war being the right thing. That increase in support for Bush's initial decision will—in turn—increase the respondent's optimism about success by 0.743 x 0.451, or by an average of 0.335 units. This feedback loop swings back and forth like a pendulum, with each loop becoming smaller in magnitude until the system stabilizes again at a new equilibrium level. Thus, in addition to the direct effects of *Right thing* and *Success* on one another, we would also like to know what the total effect of each variable is after we account for the impact of the feedback loop. These "total effect" coefficients are displayed—along with the direct effects—in figure 7.2.

The total effect of perceptions of success on the belief that Bush did the right thing is 1.118, while the total effect of approval of the president's initial decision on optimism regarding success is 0.678. Thus, regardless

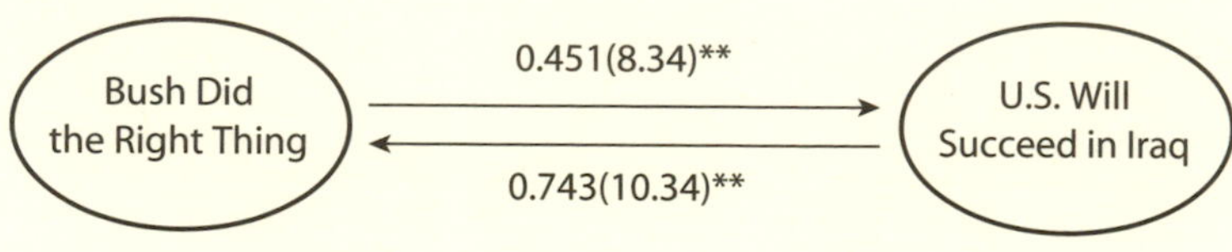

Total Effect of Bush Did Right Thing on U.S. Will Succeed = 0.678
Total Effect of U.S. Will Succeed on Bush Did Right Thing = 1.118

FIGURE 7.2. Direct and Indirect Effects of Beliefs that President Bush Did the Right Thing and that the United States Will Succeed in Iraq

of whether one relies on the direct or the total effect of these variables, the impact of perceived success on attitudes toward whether war was the right thing are about 60 percent larger than the causal impact going in the other direction.

What do these results mean for the formation of attitudes toward the Iraq war? First, as we've already noted, they do suggest that respondents tend to shape their retrospective attitudes about the decision to go to war and their prospective attitudes toward the likelihood of success so that the two conform to one another. We did not adopt a research design that would allow us to test various possible explanations for these results—for instance, whether cognitive or emotional mechanisms are driving this convergence—but it is clear that the more consonant categories of Bush Base and Vietnam Syndrome are more prevalent than the dissonant views found in the categories of Noble Failure or Pottery Barn.

Second, while both these central attitudes do influence one another, the primary engine driving this feedback loop appears to be perceptions of success. That is, prospective judgments about the likely success of the mission appear to be more influential in reshaping retrospective judgments about whether using force was the right thing to do than the other way around. This is good news for our argument in chapter 5, which placed perceptions of success at the crux of public tolerance for casualties, since these results suggest that the effects of perceptions of success are even stronger than depicted in that chapter. With regard to our analysis of vote choice in chapter 6, these results suggest that the *Success* variable may have been more important than we could discern in those analyses.

The results further show that our argument connects well with other prominent ones in the literature. First, consistent with Bruce Jentleson's arguments about the primary policy objective (PPO) of the mission, we find that respondents' beliefs about whether the war in Iraq is linked to the war on terror has a significant impact on whether they believe that the war was the right thing to do. Interestingly, the impact of this variable is larger and more statistically robust as a cause of attitudes toward whether the war was the right thing than it was in chapter 5 as a direct cause of casualty tolerance. The coefficient for this variable indicates that a change in one's attitude from believing that the Iraq War was a distraction from the war on terror to believing that it was the "central front" in that war increases one's approval of the president's attack as the "right thing" by an average of nearly two-thirds of a point. Depending on the respondent's perception of the likelihood of success, the analysis in chapter 5 suggests that such a change in attitudes about the PPO of the Iraq War could have a substantial *indirect* effect on tolerance for casualties. Respondents' factual beliefs about the extent of Iraqi WMD programs prior to the U.S. invasion and beliefs about the extent of links between Saddam Hussein's government and the al-Qaeda terrorist network also have a significant impact, though their effect is slightly smaller than one's attitude toward the Iraq War PPO.

Consistent with the arguments made by Kull and others, we also find that a respondent's attitude toward multilateral military operations and the importance he or she placed on gaining U.N. approval for military action had a significant impact on the belief that President Bush did the right thing by attacking Iraq in March 2003. The coefficient for this variable is negative and statistically significant, indicating that respondents who believe that the president should delay military action in order to obtain U.N. approval were less supportive of the decision to attack Iraq than those who did not think the president should wait. While the impact of this variable is statistically significant, its impact does not appear to be substantively quite as large as the effect of the mission PPO. In particular, while this variable is a four-point scale—just like the PPO question—nearly 85 percent of respondents recorded their views as a 2 or a 3 on this scale.[38] That is, most respondents stated that the president should use force if he felt it necessary even if he could not obtain U.N. approval, or they felt that the president should await U.N. approval. Few expressed the view that the president should not even attempt to seek U.N. approval or that the president should not use force regardless of U.N. approval. Thus, for most respondents, one is likely to observe only a one-unit increase in this variable, resulting in an average of a one-tenth of a unit decrease in approval for the president's decision.

Support for the "Bush Doctrine" also had a significant impact on approval for the president's decision, and attitudes toward this issue seem to have had an impact that is roughly similar to the impact of multilateralism. Our measure of this attitude offered three response options: (1) military

[38]Recoding this as a dummy variable slightly increased the estimated effect, but it remained smaller than the impact of the mission PPO.

force should be used only in response to an attack on America; (2) force may also be used to defend America against the threat of an imminent attack; (3) force may be used whenever the president believes that is the best way to defeat America's enemies. These categories do not capture specific attitudes about the Bush Doctrine. They do, however, roughly parallel differing understandings of what using force in "self-defense" might mean, and we would expect that those who offered the third response would be most likely to support the Bush Doctrine and should therefore be most supportive of the decision to attack Iraq. Those who offered the first response should not be supportive of the Bush Doctrine or the decision to attack Iraq, and those who chose the second response should be in between. Only about 12 percent of our respondents chose the first response, while nearly 60 percent chose the second option, and 28 percent chose the third. The coefficient in table 7.4 indicates that shifting a respondent from the first category to the third will, on average, increase his or her belief that the president did the right thing in attacking Iraq by one-quarter of a point.[39]

As we noted, the perception of an elite consensus in support of remaining in Iraq did not have any impact on respondents' attitudes toward whether the president did the right thing by attacking Iraq. Perceived elite consensus did, however, have a significant impact on respondents' optimism that the mission in Iraq would succeed. The effect of this variable, however, is rather modest. Since we measure this with a dummy variable—respondents perceive a bipartisan consensus in support of remaining in Iraq or they do not—the perception of an elite consensus increases optimism about success only by an average of one-tenth of a point.

The perception that U.S. leaders had a plan to win also had a significant impact on the perception of the likelihood of success. Since the variable ranges from 2 to 8—the coefficient of 0.046 indicates that shifting from strongly disagreeing that either Bush or Kerry had a plan to succeed in Iraq to strongly agreeing that they both did increases optimism about success by an average of nearly one-quarter of a point.

The most important cause of the perception that the United States would succeed in Iraq other than the perception of whether attacking Iraq was the right thing was a respondent's confidence in the Bush administration and the Iraqi transitional government. Levels of confidence varied widely across the full range of this variable—from a lack of confidence in any of the listed institutions to a great deal of confidence in all of them. Overall, an increase in confidence from the minimum value on the scale to the maximum increased a respondent's perception that the United

[39]This effect is somewhat larger than the impact of multilateralism when we rely on the four-category coding of that variable. It is very similar, however, to the impact of multilateralism when we rely on a dummy variable coding.

States would succeed in Iraq by an average of about three-quarters of a point. Interestingly, this index of confidence in the Bush administration does not appear simply to be a proxy variable for presidential approval. In particular, if we disassemble the scale and place its component parts into the regression instead, the variable with the largest impact on optimism is confidence in the Iraqi transitional government. Confidence in the Department of Defense and the U.S. military are also larger than the influence of confidence in the president. Confidence in "the White House" does not approach statistical significance on its own. Moreover, if we introduce a dummy variable for presidential approval as a cause of perceptions of success, its impact also does not approach statistical significance.

A respondent's overall belief that military force can be effective in achieving policy goals also had a statistically significant impact on optimism in Iraq—though its impact was somewhat more modest than the impact of confidence in the Bush administration and the Iraqi government. In this case, an increase in a respondent's hawkishness from the minimum value on the index to the maximum increases his or her optimism about success in Iraq by an average of nearly half a point.

Finally, we turn to the impact of demographic factors on respondents' attitudes toward the chances of U.S. success in Iraq and whether attacking Iraq was the right thing to do. First, with regard to perceptions that the president did the right thing, we can see that gender and race both have statistically significant effects. That is, women and minority respondents were less supportive of the president's decision to attack Iraq. Notably, these effects remain even after we control for party identification—which we later discuss. Thus the president did face a race and gender gap in persuading voters to support the use of force against Iraq. Substantively, the size of the gender gap is about the same size as the effect of a respondent's attitude toward multilateralism. The racial gap on this question was somewhat larger—similar to the impact of attitudes toward Iraqi WMD or links to terrorism.

As we noted in chapters 4 and 5, the debate over the Iraq war has been highly partisan,[40] and we found in chapter 5 that party identification did have a significant direct impact on casualty tolerance. We found, however, that the direct impact of party was relatively modest, especially in comparison to the impact of attitudes toward the rightness and success of the war. At that time, however, we noted that the more substantial impact of party identification might be through its impact on judgments about whether the president did the right thing in attacking Iraq. Thus we should not be surprised to find that *Party ID* has a significant impact in the *Right thing* equation in table 7.4. Nevertheless, the impact of party,

[40] Toner and Rutenberg (2006).

while statistically significant, remained substantively modest. The coefficient for *Party ID* is −0.071, and this variable ranges from a value of 1 (strongly Republican) to 7 (strongly Democrat). Thus an overall shift in *Party ID* from "strong Democrat" to "strong Republican" would increase support for the decision to attack Iraq by -0.071×-6, or an average of just under one-half a unit. This is not a negligible shift. The impact of *Party ID* appears to be comparable to, though slightly smaller than, the impact of one's views about whether terrorism is the PPO of the Iraq War. Partisan divisions, however, did not by any means dominate the respondent's judgments about whether the Iraq war was the right thing to do. For example, the impact of party identification on attitudes toward the rightness of the war was dwarfed by the impact of perceived success. As figure 7.2 indicates, each one-unit increase in perceived success creates a total of slightly more than a one-unit increase in approval for the president's initial decision to attack. Thus a one-unit increase in perceived success has more than double the impact of shifting from strongly Democratic to strongly Republican party identification.

Interestingly, none of the demographic factors that was a direct cause of casualty tolerance has a statistically significant impact on respondents' judgments of the likelihood of success.[41] The impact of age and race do approach statistical significance, but neither achieves traditional thresholds of significance. Nonetheless, our results suggest that older respondents may tend to be slightly more pessimistic about the mission, while minority respondents may tend to be more optimistic. Both of these results, however, should be viewed as tentative, especially because the substantive effects are also not very strong. Unlike our results in chapter 5, education has no impact on attitudes toward the rightness and likely success of the war. This suggests that education influences attitudes toward the war through its impact on how respondents think about and weigh the human costs of the war. It does not seem to shape these other underlying attitudes.

Finally, *Party* ID did *not* have a significant impact on perceptions of the likelihood of success. The estimated coefficient for this variable is about as close to zero as one can obtain, and the very small t-statistic indicates that this coefficient is effectively zero. Using a dummy variable for presidential approval reveals similar results. This is an important result because while perceptions of success appear to be the dominant factor in deter-

[41] Multicolinearity was also not an issue in our analysis of perceptions of success. The two variables with the highest correlations with other variables were the perceptions of whether Bush did the right thing and "confidence" in the Bush administration. Auxiliary regressions revealed r-squared values of approximately 0.6. This level is reasonable given the number of respondents in our survey. Moreover, both of these variables were highly statistically significant, rendering the issue of multicolinearity moot. Auxiliary r-squared values for all the other variables in the analysis of success were below 0.4.

mining both casualty tolerance (as we discussed in chapter 5) and perceptions of the rightness of the war, perceptions of success are not directly a function of partisan differences. Thus to the extent that attitudes toward the war in Iraq hinge primarily on public perceptions of the likely success of the mission, this represents evidence that differences of opinion over the war are not primarily a function of partisanship per se. Once again, these results reveal an American public that is focused on whether and how the United States can move forward toward a successful mission in Iraq rather than being focused retrospectively on partisan debates over what the president should or should not have done a year or two earlier.

The Structure versus the Substance of Public Opinion

Our analysis of attitudes toward whether President Bush did the right thing by attacking Iraq and whether the United States would succeed in this war indicated that public attitudes were well structured and organized. That is, respondent's opinions on various issues were related to one another in systematic and reasonable ways. Well-structured and organized opinions, however, are not the same thing as well-informed opinions. Despite our robust findings of well-structured attitudes, our survey results also indicated that the factual knowledge that many respondents had about foreign affairs was limited. For example, in our October 2003 survey discussed in chapters 3 and 4, we asked our respondents "Do you happen to know who Donald Rumsfeld is?" If the respondent answered "yes," then we probed further by asking, "Can you tell me what office he holds?" We then asked the same two questions about Kofi Annan. More than 78 percent of our respondents stated that they knew who Donald Rumsfeld was, but, when pressed further, only 48 percent could correctly identify the office that he held, despite our acceptance of any answer that generally placed him in charge of the U.S. military as "correct." Not surprisingly, Kofi Annan was even less well known than Rumsfeld. Slightly less than 44 percent of our respondents stated that they knew Annan, and 33 percent were able to place him in a leadership role at the United Nations. Almost 45 percent of our respondents could not correctly identify either Rumsfeld or Annan, while only 26 percent correctly identified both figures. Thus our survey data is quite consistent with other studies that conclude that the public has limited knowledge of international affairs.[42]

Can respondents change their beliefs in response to real-world events if they lack such basic factual knowledge? Our answer is of the half-full/

[42] Lippmann (1922, 1955); Almond (1950); Converse (1964).

half-empty variety. On the one hand, our data do suggest an aggregate responsiveness to real-world events. In chapter 5, for example, we demonstrated that the capture of Saddam Hussein had a significant impact on perceptions that the U.S. mission in Iraq would succeed. Similarly, the aggregate data in chapter 2 consistently indicated that the public responded to battlefield events in Iraq, Korea, Vietnam, and elsewhere. These findings are consistent with those of Page and Shapiro (1992) and Nincic (1992), who contend that aggregate public opinion on foreign policy issues responds appropriately to real-world events.

On the other hand, as noted earlier, we find that a substantial minority of our respondents could not identify the offices held by either Donald Rumsfeld or Kofi Annan. Perhaps even more disturbing than the public's lack of knowledge, however, is the willingness of some respondents to cling to misinformation. Specifically, the questions we asked respondents about their beliefs regarding the extent of Saddam Hussein's WMD programs and the extent of his links to al-Qaeda offered a range of responses that differed in terms of the level of factual information that could support such a belief.

We would acknowledge, of course, that even at the time of our survey the true nature of Hussein's WMD programs and his links to al-Qaeda could not be fully known with complete certainty. In fact, they may never be fully known with complete certainty. A good deal of evidence, however, had come to light about these issues through the release of the Kay report, the Duelfer report, and the 9/11 Commission, which narrowed the range of views on these issues that could be supported by the available facts.

For example, with regard to Iraq's WMD programs prior to the U.S. invasion, we offered respondents four options to describe their views. These options, along with the distribution of public responses are displayed in table 7.5. By October 2004 the central piece of information that respondents had in forming their beliefs about prewar Iraqi WMD was the two reports of the Iraqi Survey Group: the interim Kay report released in January 2004 and the final Duelfer report released in late September 2004. Both reports clearly indicated two things: (1) Saddam Hussein did have some WMD programs and had a desire to pursue WMD, and (2) Iraq apparently did not have stockpiles of WMD immediately prior to the U.S. invasion, certainly not in the amount claimed by Western intelligence agencies.[43] Some reasonable difference of opinion could remain as to

[43] A transcript of Kay's 2 October 2003 testimony can be found on the Central Intelligence Agency website at http://cia.gov/cia/public_affairs/speeches/2003/david_kay_1002 2003.html. A transcript of Kay's 28 January 2004 testimony can be found on the Carnegie Foundation website at http://www.ceip.org/files/projects/npp/pdf/Iraq/kaytestimony.pdf.

TABLE 7.5.
Public Beliefs about Iraq's Prewar Terror and WMD Links, October 2004

Prewar Iraqi WMD programs		*Prewar Iraqi link to Al-Qaeda*	
Iraq had a WMD program and large stockpiles of weapons, but Hussein hid or destroyed them before U.S. forces arrived.	349 32%	Hussein helped plan and carry out the 9/11 attacks, and was planning future attacks against the U.S. with al-Qaeda, possibly including the use of Iraqi WMD.	345 32%
Iraq had a WMD program and could produce these weapons, but did not have stockpiles of weapons.	372 34%	Hussein did not help carry out the 9/11 attacks, but he was willing to help al-Qaeda in future attacks against the U.S., possibly including the use of Iraqi WMD.	472 43%
Iraq had a small program researching WMD, but could not produce them and did not have stockpiles of weapons.	290 26%	Hussein met with al-Qaeda but was not willing to help them in future attacks against the U.S. or give them WMD.	145 13%
Iraq did not have any activities related to researching or producing WMD.	94 9%	Hussein's government had no connection whatsoever with al-Qaeda and was not likely to help them in the future or give them WMD.	128 12%
N	1,105		1,090

the extent of those programs and the ability of Hussein's regime to produce WMD, but it seems clear that even though there were programs and desire, no substantial stockpiles of weapons actually existed. The findings of the Kay report were widely discussed across the mainstream U.S. media. For example, the three major networks spent more than an hour of their nightly news broadcasts on the results of the Kay report over the two weeks following its release. More than 100 stories appeared in the *New York Times* and *Washington Post* on the subject between January and November 2004, not to mention the massive coverage of the topic on cable news networks, Sunday morning talk shows, and elsewhere. It would be difficult to argue that the coverage of the Kay report's findings was not thorough and extensive. The Duelfer report was released after most of our waves of surveys were complete, though not before the final wave. It, too, was widely covered and so should have been accessible to participants in our final survey

Yet the responses in table 7.5 indicate that only about 60 percent of the respondents in the October 2004 survey gave answers that we would construe as consistent with the findings of the Kay and Duelfer reports. Specifically, we would argue that the second and third response categories are both plausibly consistent with the Kay and Duelfer reports because both responses acknowledge the existence of Iraqi WMD programs and the absence of any stockpiles of weapons. The two responses differ in terms of their judgments about the ability of Hussein's government to produce WMD—a fact that could not be definitively established by the Kay and Duelfer reports. But 32 percent of the respondent's stated their belief that Saddam Hussein did have stockpiles of WMD and hid them immediately prior to the U.S. invasion, while 9 percent of respondents denied that Hussein had any WMD activities. The latter of these beliefs would seem to be directly contradicted by the findings of the Kay report, and the former belief goes well beyond what the facts, as they were then known, support. Of course, one cannot prove that Hussein did not hide his WMD stockpile, since if he hid it successfully it would leave no trace. We can say, however, that at of the time of our surveys, extremely thorough searching by officials selected by the Bush administration yielded no evidence that Saddam had WMD stockpiles immediately prior to the U.S. invasion and uncovered substantial evidence to suggest that he did not have any such stockpiles.[44]

Similarly, we found that a substantial minority of the public had beliefs regarding Saddam Hussein's links to the al-Qaeda terrorist network that were at odds with the available facts on that issue. In this case, the critical factual evidence was provided by the 9/11 Commission, which re-

[44] In June 2006, the Bush administration released declassified intelligence reports that described the discovery (subsequent to the Kay and Duelfer reports) of various caches totaling some 500 chemical warheads. The weapons dated from before the first Gulf War and were part of Iraq's arsenal that was supposed to be destroyed under various U.N. resolutions. They were not the new WMD that the Bush administration alleged Hussein was building, but they were part of preexisting stockpiles—now badly degraded—that the Bush administration alleged Hussein had falsely claimed to have destroyed. Whether these were the Iraqi WMD that the "Bush administration was looking for" is a matter of interpretation, though clearly the publicly known findings as of press time are far more modest than what the administration's prewar rhetoric warned. In any case, these findings were not known during the period of our surveys and so do not influence the foregoing analysis. Interestingly, however, the attention brought to these weapons by Senator Rick Santorum did appear to alter public beliefs about whether Iraq possessed WMD at the time of the U.S. invasion. A Harris poll reported an increase in the percentage of the population expressing this view from 36 to 50 percent between February 2005 and July 2006. See Jennifer Harper, "50 Percent of U.S. Says Iraq Had WMDs," *Washington Times*, 25 July 2006.

leased its report in July 2004. Similar to the groups that prepared the Kay and Duelfer reports, the 9/11 Commission was a bipartisan panel. It had sharp criticisms of both the Bush and Clinton administrations' strategies for coping with al-Qaeda. It is difficult to dismiss their conclusions as a partisan critique. Once again, the 9/11 Commission's report reached at least two clear conclusions regarding potential ties between Saddam Hussein's government and the al-Qaeda terrorist network: (1) members of al-Qaeda did meet with representatives of Hussein's government; and (2) there is no evidence that Saddam Hussein had any connection to the planning of the attacks of 11 September 2001. The extent and meaning of the contacts between Hussein and al-Qaeda remained a matter of considerable debate, and Hussein's potential willingness to help al-Qaeda in the future, of course, could not be determined with certainty. Strong opinions were held on both sides of this issue, but they could not be resolved as matters of fact. As with the Kay and Duelfer reports, the 9/11 Commission's report received massive media attention upon its release. Surprisingly, the report actually became a bestseller, with more than 150,000 copies sold on its first day. Norton Publishers had to order a second print run of 200,000 books almost immediately because the initial printing of 600,000 copies sold so quickly. Nearly 100 stories ran between July and November in the *Washington Post* and the *New York Times* that mentioned the commission's findings regarding Saddam Hussein and his (lack of) connection to 9/11.

Once again, we would argue that the second and third response categories to this question (highlighted in gray) in table 7.5 would potentially be consistent with the facts established by the 9/11 Commission. Both of these responses allow that Hussein had contact with al-Qaeda, but neither alleges any link to 9/11. They differ, however, on the question of whether Hussein was willing to help al-Qaeda in the future. Nonetheless, only 58 percent of the responses we received were compatible with the factual findings of the 9/11 commission. Specifically, 32 percent of the respondents in the October 2004 survey stated that they believed Saddam Hussein participated in planning and carrying out the 9/11 attacks, while 12 percent of the respondents insisted that there had been no connection between Hussein and al-Qaeda at all. Once again, the latter view is contradicted by the facts presented by the 9/11 Commission report, while the former position goes well beyond the facts and, indeed, flies in the face of the well-publicized conclusions of the 9/11 Commission.[45]

[45] Interestingly, there is clearly some overlap between the respondents who take the more extreme positions on these two questions, but the match-up is far from perfect. Just over 15 percent of respondents believed that Saddam had stockpiles of weapons and had planned 9/11, but only 3 percent stated that Hussein had no WMD programs and no contact with al-Qaeda.

Our survey is hardly the only study to find that many Americans believe that Saddam Hussein had stockpiles of WMD and participated in the 9/11 attacks. For example, a CBS/*New York Times* poll in September 2002 revealed that 52 percent of the public believed that Saddam Hussein was personally involved in the 11September 2001 terrorist attacks against the World Trade Center and the Pentagon."[46] In February of 2003 this number had slipped to 42 percent. Similarly, in February 2003 two separate ABC /*Washington Post* surveys indicated that approximately 70 percent of the public believed that Iraq possessed chemical or biological weapons. By June of 2003, after the U.S. invasion and occupation, 25 percent believed that Iraq had WMD stockpiles that had not yet been found, and 50 percent believed that Hussein had hidden or destroyed the weapons prior to the U.S. invasion.[47]

To be fair to the respondents in our October 2004 survey we should emphasize that very few of them were stating beliefs that were directly contradicted by the available facts. Rather they were continuing to express beliefs after extensive searches had failed to produce convincing evidence to support them. As we noted earlier, we could not prove that Saddam Hussein did not have stockpiles of WMD because if he was successful at hiding them, then we should have *expected* to find none. Likewise, it is always possible that new evidence will turn up about collaborations between al-Qaeda and the Hussein regime.[48]

Moreover, as we've already noted, aggregate public opinion tended to respond accurately and appropriately to new evidence regarding Hussein's WMD capabilities and ties to al-Qaeda. After all, prior to the outbreak of the war, an overwhelming majority of the public believed that Iraq had stockpiled WMD, and by October 2004 less than one-third of the public held this view. Similarly, prior to the outbreak of the war, a majority of the public believed that Hussein was involved in planning the 9/11 attacks, and by October 2004 this number had dropped to just under one-third.

Nonetheless, it appears that a substantial minority of the public resisted changing their beliefs about these issues despite the increasingly prominent lack of evidence to support them. What can explain this resistance? Our study was not constructed to answer this question. As we noted in chapter 1, our central goal in this research is to understand the structure of American attitudes toward military conflict. Our research design was not structured to examine the manner in which individuals process informa-

[46] See http://www.pollingreport.com.

[47] Ibid.

[48] Indeed, this is precisely the claim of a series of articles by Stephen Hayes. See, for example, his "Case Closed," *Weekly Standard* 9 no. 11 (November 24. 2003).

tion so as to form beliefs about the "reality" of a military conflict. We hope that our research has highlighted the importance of understanding such information processing, since the beliefs that are formed relate systematically to other attitudes and behaviors like casualty tolerance and vote choice. Definitive answers regarding the cognitive and emotional mechanisms underpinning the formation of beliefs about "reality" will have to await further theoretical and empirical research in political psychology. We can only offer some speculation that we hope will be useful to those who will tackle these interesting questions more directly.

Specifically, we would offer four possible explanations for the persistence of public beliefs that, in retrospect, appear not to be supported by the facts. The first possible explanation draws on insights from cognitive psychology to explain the persistence of public attitudes. As we have noted, respondents appeared to be more likely to hold a view that lacked empirical support but was not (and perhaps could not be) conclusively proved false than they were to express a belief that was directly contradicted by evidence. Numerous psychological studies argue that humans tend to be "cognitive misers" who like to maintain the stability of their belief systems and change their beliefs and opinions only when they are vividly and overwhelmingly contradicted by the evidence.[49] Prior to the outbreak of the war, the belief that Saddam Hussein had WMD was almost a consensus position. Even the leaders of governments that opposed America's decision to use force did not dispute the claim that Saddam was not complying with U.N. WMD inspections and possibly was concealing a WMD capability.[50] Since it is virtually impossible to prove that Hussein did not successfully hide his WMD, cognitive psychological arguments would expect many people to cling to what was a widely held belief simply because they could do so without causing themselves too much psychological stress.

A second possible explanation draws from the psychological literature on motivated rather than cognitive misperceptions. According to this view, people construct their beliefs to support their self-esteem. One of the key elements in maintaining one's self-esteem is continuing to feel good about the decisions that one makes. This argument would suggest that respondents maintained their beliefs about Hussein's links to al-Qaeda and stockpiles of WMD so they could feel good about their initial decision to support or oppose the use of force. Admitting that their beliefs about

[49] Kaufmann (1994). See also Jervis (1976) among many others.

[50] Hans Blix's reports to the U.N. Security Council, for example, identified a number of "unresolved issues" regarding Iraq's record of its pre-1991 stockpiles of WMD. Blix's reports to the Security Council are archived at http://www.un.org/Depts/unmovic/new/pages/security_council_briefings.asp#2.

Hussein may have been incorrect would have led them to the uncomfortable position that they had supported or opposed the use of force based upon incorrect information.

Third, much of the popular coverage of public attitudes toward Iraqi WMD and links to al-Qaeda focused on the diversification and politicization of media outlets as the source of the public's failure to update its beliefs.[51] Fox News, for example, is often viewed as providing a more conservative perspective on events that tends to support the Bush administration's views, while networks such as PBS are viewed as providing a more liberal perspective. Perhaps—consistent with both the aforementioned cognitive and motivational arguments—respondents maintained the stability of their beliefs by seeking out media sources that supported their views. While we cannot definitively address this argument, our data do appear to be consistent with this view. Four hundred and ninety-five of the 1,125 respondents in our survey had also participated in a media usage panel for Knowledge Networks. Knowledge Networks generously provided us with these responses, and we discovered that more than 50 percent of the eighty respondents who stated that they turned to Fox News as their first choice for news also stated that they still believed that Saddam Hussein had stockpiles of weapons that he hid or destroyed prior to the U.S. invasion. *None* of these eighty respondents stated that Hussein never had any WMD programs. By way of comparison, only about 28 percent of ABC, NBC, and CBS viewers believed that Hussein had hidden his stockpiles and about 9 percent stated that Iraq never had WMD programs. Only thirteen of these 495 respondents stated that they turned to PBS News first, making it impossible to draw reliable comparisons between Fox News and PBS viewers. Even these few data points, however, are consistent with the data usage argument. None of the thirteen PBS viewers stated that Saddam Hussein had hidden stockpiles of WMD and four of them (30 percent) stated that Hussein never had any WMD programs.[52] While these data clearly indicate that respondent beliefs and media usage do correlate with one another, we cannot reliably establish whether media usage caused the beliefs or whether the beliefs shape media usage.

A fourth possible explanation may point to the role of elite rhetoric—especially that of the Bush administration—or, more precisely, to the pub-

[51] Steven Kull, "The Separate Realities of Bush and Kerry Supporters," PIPA/Knowledge Networks Study, 21 October 2004; available at www.pipa.org.

[52] These results are consistent with the more extensive study of media usage and opinions toward Iraq as discussed in the PIPA poll (Kull et al. 2004). The PIPA study on media usage, however, focused only on "conservative" misperceptions and did not examine questions on which there were "liberal"misperceptions. Thus we reexamined this question with the data we had available on media usage, because our questions on Hussein's WMD and links to al-Qaeda allow for both liberal and conservative "errors."

lic perception of that rhetoric. Substantial literatures on the priming and framing of issues emphasize the influence of elite rhetoric on public opinion (see, for example, Kinder and Iyengar 1987; Krosnick and Kinder 1990; Iyengar and Simon 1990; Berinsky and Kinder 2006). Arguments about the influence of elites on the public represent a promising avenue for future research on both the ability of the public's ability to hold well-structured belief systems despite a relatively low level of factual knowledge and the tendency to retain certain beliefs despite a lack of factual evidence to support them. Some of this literature suggests that the White House should be in a position to influence opinion by dominating public discourse (Entman 2004; Paletz and Entman 1981), while other works emphasize competing elites and partisan divisions as the mechanisms for shaping public attitudes (Zaller 1992; Berinsky and Druckman 2007; Berinsky 2007). We turn now to an examination of Bush administration rhetoric to evaluate ways in which public perceptions of their words may have created some of the public's resistance to new information about Iraqi WMD and links to al-Qaeda.

Prior to the release of the Kay and Duelfer reports, the administration clearly conveyed the idea that Hussein had WMD stockpiles and that they would eventually be found. The administration stopped explicitly making this claim once the interim Kay report was released, but the president continued to insist on the possibility that the weapons stockpiles existed and that this might be confirmed when the final report of the Iraqi Survey Group was issued. In an 8 February 2004 interview with Tim Russert on *Meet the Press*, for example, President Bush argued, "Now, when David Kay goes in and says we haven't found stockpiles yet, and there [are] theories as to where the weapons went. They could have been destroyed during the war. Saddam and his henchmen could have destroyed them as we entered into Iraq. They could be hidden. They could have been transported to another country, and we'll find out."[53]

Moreover, as the administration backed off of its claims regarding stockpiles of weapons, it began focusing on the existence of WMD programs and on the findings of the Kay and Duelfer reports that Hussein intended to reinvigorate the programs once U.N. sanctions were lifted. For example, in October 2004, the president argued, "There was a risk, a real risk, that Saddam Hussein would pass weapons or materials or information to terrorist networks, and in the world after September the 11th, that was a risk we could not afford to take."[54] In the strict sense, this statement is consistent with the findings of the Kay and Duelfer reports because it

[53] Transcript available at http://www.msnbc.msn.com/id/4179618/.

[54] Wayne Drash, "Iraq WMD Report Enters Political Fray," 8 October 2004; available at: http://www.cnn.com.

pools together the risks of sharing weapons, materials, and information, and it is vague on when Iraq might have been able to share these things with terrorists. Nonetheless, one could also infer from the statement that the president still believed there to be a risk that Hussein could have shared weapons with terrorist groups prior to the U.S. invasion.

In light of our findings regarding knowledge of Donald Rumsfeld and Kofi Annan, it should not be too surprising that many members of the public did not parse out the distinctions between Iraqi weapons, Iraqi weapons programs, and the possible intention to renew those weapons programs. It is worth noting that the failure to draw these fine-grained distinctions was not due to partisan bias. A PIPA/Knowledge Networks poll released in October 2004 revealed that substantial majorities of both Kerry and Bush supporters believed that the Bush administration was arguing to voters that Hussein had stockpiles of WMD prior to the U.S. invasion.[55] Republicans tended to believe this claim while Democrats did not, but members of both parties seemed to agree that the president believed Iraq to have stockpiles of WMD.

The phenomenon is even more striking with regard to the Iraqi links to al-Qaeda. The Bush administration clearly linked Iraq to the larger war on terror, but never directly claimed that Hussein was behind the 9/11 attacks. Indeed, in September 2003 the president explicitly acknowledged that Hussein was not involved in the 9/11 attacks.[56] The Bush administration did hint, however, that they thought the Iraqi links to al-Qaeda were stronger than the limited contacts claimed by the 9/11 Commission. In a 14 September 2003 interview with Tim Russert on *Meet the Press*, for example, Vice President Dick Cheney highlighted some of these alleged links:

> RUSSERT: The *Washington Post* asked the American people about Saddam Hussein, and this is what they said: 69 percent said he was involved in the September 11 attacks. Are you surprised by that?
>
> CHENEY: No. I think it's not surprising that people make that connection.
>
> RUSSERT: But is there a connection?
>
> CHENEY: We don't know. You and I talked about this two years ago. I can remember you asking me this question just a few days after the original attack. At the time I said no, we didn't have any evidence of that. Subsequent to that, we've learned a couple of things. We learned more and more that there

[55] See Steven Kull, "The Separate Realities of Bush and Kerry Supporters," PIPA/Knowledge Networks Study, 21 October 2004; available at www.pipa.org. It is especially interesting that in a study that finds so many differences of opinion between Bush and Kerry supporters, there seems to be a broad consensus on the arguments being made by the Bush campaign.

[56] See "Remarks by the President after Meeting with Members of the Congressional Conference Committee on Energy Legislation"; transcript available at http://www.whitehouse.gov/news/releases/2003/09/20030917-7.html.

> was a relationship between Iraq and al-Qaeda that stretched back through most of the decade of the 90s, that it involved training, for example, on BW and CW, that al-Qaeda sent personnel to Baghdad to get trained on the systems that are involved. The Iraqis providing bomb-making expertise and advice to the al-Qaeda organization.
>
> We know, for example, in connection with the original World Trade Center bombing in '93 that one of the bombers was Iraqi, returned to Iraq after the attack of '93. And we've learned subsequent to that, since we went into Baghdad and got into the intelligence files, that this individual probably also received financing from the Iraqi government as well as safe haven.
>
> Now, is there a connection between the Iraqi government and the original World Trade Center bombing in '93? We know, as I say, that one of the perpetrators of that act did, in fact, receive support from the Iraqi government after the fact. With respect to 9/11, of course, we've had the story that's been public out there. The Czechs alleged that Mohamed Atta, the lead attacker, met in Prague with a senior Iraqi intelligence official five months before the attack, but we've never been able to develop anymore of that yet either in terms of confirming it or discrediting it. We just don't know.[57]

Vice President Cheney was careful not to claim that Iraq was directly and operationally linked to al-Qaeda's 9/11 attack. Some of the press coverage of this interview argued, however, that Cheney was actually trying to make such a claim, and it was likely that it was this sort of coverage that led President Bush to deny explicitly any such claim a few days later. While the 9/11 Commission did find that there had been some contact between al-Qaeda and Saddam Hussein's regime, it rejected the notion of explicit collaboration between the two. Vice President Cheney persisted, however, and famously claimed that the 9/11 Commission may not have seen all the evidence. This claim was not reinforced in subsequent administration statements, but neither did the vice president disavow his claim.[58]

More often, however, the linkages that the Bush administration drew between Iraq and al-Qaeda were more diffuse than those raised by Cheney. Often Bush's officials emphasized that the lesson they drew from 9/11 was that threats had to be dealt with before they culminated. They suggested that Hussein's opposition to the United States might have led him to cooperate with others who hate our country, like al-Qaeda. They argued that Hussein's support of terrorism in the Middle East would give him few reasons to eschew cooperating with terrorists in the future, and that Hussein's exploratory contacts with al-Qaeda showed the possibility of future cooperation, and so on. Finally, perhaps the strongest rhetorical

[57]Transcript available at http://www.msnbc.msn.com/id/3080244/

[58]The 9/11 Commission chair subsequently endorsed Cheney's claim that there were contacts between the Hussein regime and al-Qaeda. Thus the commission's conclusion of "no active collaboration" should not be interpreted as "no contact whatsoever."

link that the Bush administration made was the repeated claim that Iraq was the central front in the broader war on terror that began with the 9/11 attacks. In making the case for American involvement in Iraq during a radio address on 18 May 2005, for example, the president argued, "We went to war because we were attacked, and we are at war today because there are still people out there who want to harm our country and hurt our citizens. Some may disagree with my decision to remove Saddam Hussein from power, but all of us can agree that the world's terrorists have now made Iraq a central front in the war on terror."[59] Nothing in this statement directly claims that Saddam Hussein contributed to the 9/11 attacks, but it does state that we attacked Iraq because of those attacks.

Once again, at least a portion of the public appeared to miss the subtle distinctions being drawn by the Bush administration and connected the dots directly from Saddam Hussein to 11 September. The same October 2004 PIPA poll cited earlier found that one-quarter of the public believed that the Bush administration was claiming that Iraq was "directly involved in carrying out the 11 September attacks," while another 52 percent believed the Bush administration was claiming "Iraq gave substantial support to al-Qaeda, but was not involved in the 11 September attacks."

Supporters and opponents of the president have argued vigorously over whether the Bush administration deliberately misled the public about stockpiles of Iraqi WMD and links between Hussein and al-Qaeda. Critics of the president claimed that these public misperceptions were the result of a careful campaign of misinformation, while presidential supporters contend that the administration was honest in its communications with the public and that any misperceptions were due to popular misreadings of the more subtle and nuanced claims that the administration was making. We are not in a position to settle such arguments. Indeed, we disagree among ourselves on these points. They are not central, however, to our concerns in this work. Regardless of their intentions, the record of Bush administration rhetoric suggests that the public may have responded to their words in ways that led them to hold attitudes that lacked factual support. Documenting the scope and nature of this influence as well as the mechanisms by which it may have occurred must await future research. The initial evidence that we can gather from our data, however, suggests that the impact of elite rhetoric is highly varied and conditional.

Some of our data seem consistent with the notion that the White House has wide discretion in shaping public beliefs. In our experiment regarding a hypothetical intervention in Yemen in chapter 4, for example, we were able to reframe the bases of public support for using force regardless of the partisanship of the respondent. Similarly, the public's definitions of "success" in Iraq, discussed earlier in this chapter, seem to be highly con-

[59] Transcript available at http://www.whitehouse.gov/news/releases/2005/06/20050618.html.

sistent with administration rhetoric. Moreover, these definitions were widely and consistently held across the public with virtually no variation according to party identification. Public misperceptions of Iraqi links to al-Qaeda and 9/11 were similarly broad based. Specifically in October 2004, 33 percent of Republicans and 30 percent of Democrats believed that Saddam Hussein was involved in planning the 9/11 attacks.

Other pieces of evidence, however, are more consistent with the notion that competing elites influence the segments of the public that look to them for cues about how to structure their opinions (Zaller 1992; Lupia 1994; Lupia and McCubbins 1998; Berinsky and Druckman 2007; Berinsky 2007). For example, we do find that party identification has a significant impact on whether one believes that President Bush did the right thing by attacking Iraq. Similarly, the data discussed in chapter 2 indicate that Republicans were about 10 percent more likely to believe that America's mission in Lebanon under President Ronald Reagan was morally justified, while Democrats were about 10 percent more likely to believe that America had a "moral obligation" to help the people of Kosovo under President Bill Clinton. Furthermore, our experiment on elite endorsements of a hypothetical intervention in East Timor indicated that such cues can interact strongly with partisan identification in shaping support for the use of force. Finally, we do find significant partisan divisions regarding the (mis)perceptions of Iraqi WMD. Specifically, 51 percent of Republicans believed that Saddam held stockpiles of WMD prior to the U.S. invasion, while only 15 percent of Democrats held this view. Conversely, 15 percent of Democrats believed that Hussein had no WMD activities whatsoever while less than 1 percent of Republicans believed this to be true.

Some of our data suggest that citizens respond to "battlefield events" in shaping their attitudes toward military conflict without much mediating influence by elites. For example, our natural experiment regarding the capture of Saddam Hussein asked respondents about their perceptions of success before they were likely to have heard any elite interpretation of its about the impact. Similarly, negative events such as the Chinese intervention in the Korean War seemed to have an impact on public opinion that overwhelmed any elite or partisan framing of the event. Media and elites are, of course, still important in transmitting information about these events to the public. The public has little direct contact with such foreign military conflicts, and so their impact on public opinion must be mediated. These examples, though, do suggest that elites may sometimes have limited leeway in interpreting the meaning of events for the public.[60]

[60]The Tet Offensive is a counter-example of a battlefield event that had great impact on public opinion but was open to widely varying elite interpretations (Johnson and Tierney 2006).

While conclusive evidence on the interplay of elite rhetoric and battlefield events in shaping public attitudes must await future research, we may be able to gain some tentative insight in the intersection of these variables by observing the public's reaction to major communication efforts by the Bush administration that have been associated with our research (Baker and Balz 2005; Shane 2005).

In December 2005, President Bush gave a series of speeches leading up to the parliamentary elections in Iraq. We recognize that key elements of those speeches and the accompanying National Strategy for Victory in Iraq (NSVI) contained rhetorical approaches consistent with our research findings that give explanatory power to perceptions of success.[61] Specifically, the speeches and the NSVI sought to gain credibility with the public by acknowledging setbacks and mistakes more candidly than previous administration statements on the war. Moreover, they sought to bolster public support for continuing to fight by describing the assumptions behind the administration's strategy, discussing how the various elements of the strategy fit together, and explaining why they believed that this approach might lead to success. In other words, the effort assumed that the public would respond supportively to arguments about why the mission could still succeed despite rising U.S. casualties.[62] While we do not have definitive data available to us at the individual level on the impact of this elite rhetoric, we do have some aggregate data that can at least tentatively speak to this issue.[63]

The president began rolling out this communication effort on 30 November 2005 with a much-publicized speech in Annapolis, Md., and concluded it with a prime-time televised address from the Oval Office on 18 December 2005, in which he reflected upon the success of the Iraqi elections. The rhetorical effort was dramatized by the sharp contrast with the most salient Democratic alternative—Congressman Jack Murtha's proposal for complete withdrawal within six months. Interestingly, Murtha's opinion is also consistent with our model—he once supported the war, but when he became convinced that success was impossible, he was unwilling for the United States to incur additional costs.

[61] We would note, however, that those who might seek to increase public pressure to withdraw from Iraq could just as easily make extrapolations from our research to craft a communication strategy that seeks to demonstrate why prospects for success in Iraq are dim.

[62] We do not accept the interpretation—given in much of the commentary surrounding these events—that the link to our research could be found in the prominence and repetition of the word *victory* in the rhetoric. Nothing in our research suggests that the public can be won over by such ritual incantations.

[63] For the claim that perceptions of success do not matter, we would actually have to know whether elites were incorporating judgments of success or failure in their rhetoric. Our argument would still have substantial merit if appeals to success could persuade the public better than other appeals. Our argument would be even stronger (and be normatively more appealing) if the persuasive power of appeals to success are contingent on actual signs of success or progress.

Prior to Bush's speeches, public approval of his administration was at a low point. ABC news found that approval of Bush's handling of the Iraq War was at 36 percent on 2 November, and his overall presidential approval rating was at 39 percent. Just a few weeks later, on 18 December, in the wake of the "victory" speeches and the successful Iraqi election, approval of Bush's handling of Iraq jumped to 46 percent and his overall approval moved up to 47 percent. This ten-point bounce was not the result of a few isolated polls but represented an upward shift across the board that lasted for several weeks. Our own data in chapter 2 demonstrated that its impact was statistically significant. In addition to our data, Charles Franklin's compilation of presidential approval polls also shows a clear bounce of about ten points lasting through the month of December and into January 2006.[64]

By March of 2006, however, President Bush found his approval numbers sagging again and he gave another series of speeches on 13, 20, and 29 March emphasizing the progress he saw in Iraq. The president also held a press conference on 21 March that focused largely on Iraq. This time, however, the president lacked a "real-world" successful event to which he could anchor his speeches. On the contrary, the violence in Iraq was spiraling up after the bombing of the al-Askiriya mosque, while political progress stalled with the inability of Iraqi political leaders to form a unified government. As a result, the presidential rhetoric had no perceptible impact on public attitudes toward the war whatsoever. In early March the president's approval ratings—both on Iraq and overall—were at approximately 35 percent, and they remained unchanged throughout early April.

These contrasting events suggest that elite rhetoric matters in some circumstances and not in others. We cannot say with confidence what these circumstances might be, nor can we say with certainty what the mechanism is by which elite messages matter. The foregoing examples suggest that elite messages matter in combination with events in the "real world" and that they may have little influence absent such anchors.

Conclusion

Our analyses confirm that public perceptions of whether President Bush did the right thing by attacking Iraq tend to be retrospective judgments that are caused by beliefs about past events. Beliefs about the extent of Saddam Hussein's WMD programs, his alleged links to al-Qaeda, the legitimacy of preemptive military strikes, and the importance of U.N. approval before using force are all judgments about events prior to October

[64] Data available at http://www.pollster.com/presbushapproval.php.

2004 that have a significant impact on respondents' beliefs as to whether the president did the right thing by attacking Iraq. The one exception to the retrospective character of judgments about the attack is the powerful feedback loop between perceptions of rightness of the war and perceptions of the prospects for success. While many retrospective judgments influenced support for Bush's decision to attack, the largest single cause of this support was the prospective judgment about whether the mission would succeed.

Moreover, our analyses indicate that respondents' beliefs about whether the U.S. would succeed in Iraq tend to be prospective in nature. The retrospective judgments about WMD and Hussein's links to al-Qaeda were not causes of respondents' beliefs about the likelihood of success. Nor was partisanship a cause of optimism or pessimism about the success of the Iraq War. Moreover, our results clearly indicate that the vast majority of respondents did *not* judge the likelihood of success by looking backward at the number of American soldiers that had been killed. This is particularly important because it demonstrates that our argument about the importance of success in determining casualty tolerance is not tautological. Instead, during the crucial 2004 time period, respondents appeared to have formed their attitudes about the prospects for success by making judgments about whether the United States could build a stable, self-reliant, and democratic government in Iraq that could provide for the needs of its own people. In forming their views on this question, respondents appear to have focused most closely on the extent to which they believed Iraqi citizens were cooperating with coalition forces against the insurgents.

Our analysis also indicates the presence of a strong feedback loop between attitudes toward approval for attacking Iraq and optimism about eventual success. While each of these two attitudes has a substantial effect in causing the other, the causal influence in our study appears to have flowed more powerfully from beliefs about success to attitudes about the rightness of the war than the other way around. To the extent that this feedback loop emphasizes the impact of success over rightness, our analyses in chapters 4 and 5 tended to underestimate the importance of perceptions of success relative to other factors.

We feel confident, in concluding, that respondents appear to be forming attitudes about success that are distinct from many of the factors that have been emphasized in popular accounts of attitudes toward the war, such as partisan divisions and the number of U.S. military deaths. As our natural experiment surrounding the capture of Saddam Hussein indicated, these attitudes do appear to have moved in sensible ways in response to events on the ground. Thus our results continue to be consistent with the notion of a sensible and "prudent" public that responds in reasonable ways to issues that arise. Moreover, we have shown that individual members of the public structure and organize their attitudes toward the Iraq War in sensible and systematic ways. All of these findings are consistent with a "good news" story of a public that is capable of demanding a "democratic" American foreign policy that represents the will of the American people.

We want to be clear, however, in stating that having well-organized views that are "responsive" in the aggregate to real-world events is not the same thing as being accurate or knowledgeable. As we noted in chapter 1, the overwhelming consensus in the public opinion literature contends that the public's grip on factual specifics of foreign policy events is tenuous. We do not dispute this view, and we find that this lack of factual specifics does create challenges to a "representative" foreign policy.

Chapter Eight

CONCLUSION

THE AMERICAN PUBLIC does not give the president a blank check of unqualified support for costly military operations. In this book we have argued that the public weighs the costs of a war against the expected benefits when making judgments about the use of force. Surveys taken before military operations frequently show that a majority of the public might oppose a proposed military venture, or set very stringent criteria on their support. Yet these ex ante surveys tend to understate the level of support that military operations eventually enjoy. When the military is engaged in combat, the "rally-'round the flag" effect creates a reservoir of support for virtually every military operation in the short run. Surveys conducted concurrent with the start of a military campaign, however, are likely to overstate the level of support that the operations will eventually enjoy since, unless the conflict ends quickly, the rally gives way to an ongoing cost-benefit calculation that can cause support to erode over time. Contrary to the received wisdom among pundits and even most U.S. adversaries, however, the public's stomach for costly military ventures can be strong. Determined political leaders can make the use of force a credible option. Public qualms about casualties do not render the United States a paper tiger.

Many factors shape the cost-benefit calculation, but the primary factor appears to be the public's expectation that the mission will be successful. People who believe that the mission will be successful will continue to support the mission, even if they had initial doubts about the wisdom of using force in the first place. People who believe that the mission will not be successful are unwilling to continue to support the mission, even if they initially believed that the resort to military force was the right thing to do.[1] Most Americans are not willing to pay any price or bear any burden, but the willingness to pay a price increases when they expect a military venture ultimately to be successful. The American public, taken as a whole, is far from being casualty phobic and is best viewed as being defeat phobic. Political leaders who credibly promise and deliver military victory are likely to have sufficient public support behind a military operation.

[1] Sachs (2006) makes a corollary argument about the importance of perceptions of success in nonmilitary foreign policy initiatives, especially the opinion toward development policies held by the citizens of the developing nations.

When we say that the public, taken as a whole, is best viewed as being defeat phobic, we do not mean to imply that every single member of the public is defeat phobic. Building from prior work (Feaver and Gelpi 2004), we show in chapter 3 that the public can be roughly divided into four distinct groups: doves (who essentially oppose all use of force), hawks (who support force even when it comes with significant human costs), casualty-phobics (those who support force as long as the human costs are minimal to none), and defeat-phobics (those who support the mission as long as it is seen as terminating in success). Of these four groups, we argue that the defeat-phobics are the key swing constituency. Just as elections are decided by swing voters, support for military missions is decided by this swing constituency. Doves will continue to oppose war no matter the costs, hawks will support it almost regardless of cost, and the casualty-phobics will oppose war once the United States has experienced even minimal human costs. Thus, the support of these three groups is determined very early in a campaign, and it is hard to move or persuade these groups in response to events on the battlefield. The defeat-phobics, however, are sensitive to the progress of the war. Because the others are fairly set in their support early on in a conflict, in longer military campaigns it is the defeat-phobic group that moves aggregate public opinion—and this movement comes in response to the progress of the war (or at least in response to perceptions of the war's progress).

Persuading the public that a military operation will be successful may be the linchpin of public support for that operation, but it is not the linchpin of public support for reelecting the leader who initiated that military operation. On the contrary, the vote choice appears to turn more on the public's retrospective judgment about the wisdom of going to war in the first place. Incumbents, then, must convince the public that they made the right choice in going to war (to shore up support in the ballot box) and convince the public that the operation eventually will be successful (to shore up support for the military operation itself). Challengers must convince the public that the war was a mistake (so the public will want a change in political leadership), but if in so doing they also convince the public that the war is hopelessly headed to defeat, the challengers will undermine public support for the military operation itself—the very operation they would inherit upon winning the election.

Since public expectations of success are so central to public support for military operations, it is important to understand the factors that shape it. Here the evidence is ambiguous, and so our conclusions are mixed. We know that the public does not measure and track success by counting body bags of U.S. servicemen; our argument is not circular, as in "The public is defeat phobic not casualty phobic, but defeat is measured in casualty counts." At the same time, expectations of victory are a function of other factors, including judgments about whether the war was a mistake in the first place, which otherwise stand as partial rival explanations for explaining the public's tolerance for paying the costs of war.

The public's definitions of victory, and the metrics identified as the best way to track whether victory is more or less likely, are themselves shaped by presidential rhetoric. The answers that the public gave when we asked them in the spring/summer/fall of 2004 "How do you define success in Iraq" bore a striking resemblance to the Bush administration's public rhetoric on this subject at the time. While we cannot be certain since we do not have survey evidence from other periods, it is likely that factors that were emphasized in the run-up to the war—the WMD threat and Iraq's possible links to terrorism—would have featured more prominently in public definitions of success than they did by mid-2004, by which time the failure to find WMD stockpiles had shifted the frame substantially.

We developed this argument in stages. Chapter 2 presented a series of analyses of aggregate opinion data collected during military operations in Korea (1950–52), Vietnam (1965–71), Lebanon (1983), Somalia (1993), Kosovo (1999), and the recent conflict in Iraq (2003–06). We examined the relationship between mounting casualties and the public's expressed approval of the president, and in so doing proposed a modification to the familiar model presented by Mueller. In each of these conflicts, mounting casualties did not produce a reflexive, logarithmic drop in public support. Rather, the corrosive effect of mounting casualties depended on the larger context of the fighting: If the casualties happened during phases when the U.S. military appeared to be winning the fight, the casualties were not associated with dramatic drops in public support, but they were when casualties happened during phases in which the U.S. military appeared to be losing the fight. Casualties even during a lengthy stalemate, such as what we saw in Korea, were not so corrosive. This pattern is clear, but dependent on post-hoc analytical judgments about when the public was likely to shift its expectations of victory, hence the need to go beyond aggregate data and look more closely at the makeup of individual opinion, which we did in subsequent chapters.

While most of the research on public opinion and casualties in war has relied on aggregate data to test its hypotheses, we believe that examining individual attitudes may shed more light on the causal mechanisms behind the aggregate shifts that we observed in chapter 2. Thus chapter 3 presented analyses of some of the individual-level data collected in our own polls. Here we focused on investigating the structure of individual attitudes toward the use of military force and on developing a measure of support for war that captured the critical theoretical and political issues outlined in chapter 1. These analyses led to three main findings: First, individuals structure their attitudes toward the use of force in coherent ways along at least two distinct dimensions—support for security-oriented missions and support for humanitarian missions. Second, individuals construct their attitudes toward paying the cost of military conflict in consistent ways. In particular, respondents are capable of facing up to the difficult and sometimes disturbing trade-offs involved in deciding whether the human costs of a military mission are too high. We label this underlying attitude "casualty tolerance." Third, we find that casualty tolerance is distinct from generalized support for the use of military force for security or humanitarian purposes, but is related to those more general attitudes in sensible ways.

Having demonstrated that individual attitudes represent a solid foundation for studying casualty tolerance and public support for military force, we focused on testing the various factors identified in the literature as plausible mechanisms driving the casualty tolerance of the general public. Through a series of innovative survey experiments involving hypothetical but plausible uses of force, we were able to probe the effect of different cues—for example, different rationales, different degrees of domestic or international support, different levels of casualties, and different expectations of success—on the public's expressed support for the mission. We show that the most prominent alternative explanations of casualty sensitivity in the scholarly literature all have merit; that is, factors that scholars have speculated to "matter," based on evaluations of aggregate-opinion data, do in fact "matter" when assessed with individual-level data on hypothetical scenarios.

As Jentleson proposed, casualty tolerance varies with the type of military mission envisioned; as Larson proposed, casualty tolerance is greater for those individuals who are told that an elite consensus exists in support of the mission; as Kull proposed, casualty tolerance is greater for those individuals who are told that a multilateral coalition supports the mission. Our key factor, expectations of success, also mattered consistently across our various experiments and its substantive impact was always large.[2] Expectations of casualties, on the other hand, seem to vary substantially in their impact on public opinion. When we asked respondents about their expectations of casualties after asking about their support for a military mission—as we did in our Yemen and East Timor experiments—we found little association between expected casualties and war support. When we prompted respondents with expert opinions on the likely number of casualties prior to asking about support for a military mission—as we did in the Joint Chiefs of Staff (JCS) experiment—messages about expected casualties had a large impact on public support.

Chapter 5 extended these findings on casualty tolerance to the context of a real war with actual combat deaths—the current conflict in Iraq. We developed a model explaining how ongoing public support for U.S. military

[2] Jentleson (1992); Jentleson and Britton (1998); Larson (1996); Kull and Destler (1999); Kull and Ramsay (2001); Feaver and Gelpi (2004).

operations in Iraq is a function of casualty tolerance, which is itself a function of two key underlying attitudes: (1) did we do the right thing in invading Iraq and (2) are we going to be successful in Iraq. We explored how that support shifts in response to mounting casualties, and thus assessed the public's elasticity of demand for war. These analyses showed that expectations of success trumped other considerations in determining the public's casualty tolerance.

Chapter 6 linked our findings to the 2004 presidential election. We showed the role that attitudes about Iraq played in determining individual voters' choice between President Bush and Senator Kerry. We further showed that our basic model explaining casualty tolerance also applies, but with some crucial differences, to vote choice. Specifically, the relative importance of the contributing factors reversed. With vote choice, "did we do the right thing" trumps "expectations of success." Crucial to President Bush's electoral victory, then, was his ability to persuade a majority of the voters that his initial decision to use military force against Iraq was correct. The public likely agreed with President Bush in part because they accepted his argument that the war in Iraq was linked to the broader (and less controversial) war on terror. Our data shed light on the predicament facing Senator Kerry, or indeed any political challenger in war time. Senator Kerry wanted to convince the American public that the war in Iraq was a mistake, but he did not want to undermine public support for a war that he would have to continue waging if he won the presidency. Our data suggest that there was a "sweet spot" message available to Senator Kerry that would, in theory, accomplish both ends: the "Pottery Barn" message that the war was wrong, but we could (and would) win it. Senator Kerry was unable to make that point persuasively to the electorate, perhaps in part because his initial vote authorizing the use of force complicated his ability to declare the war a mistake while his vote against funding part of the ongoing operation (albeit after voting in favor of an earlier version of the funding bill) complicated his ability to declare that the war would be won.

Chapter 7 addressed several questions left hanging by the preceding analyses. If the perceived rightness or wrongness of the war and expectations of success are the crucial factors driving public attitudes toward casualties, the war, and President Bush's reelection, what deeper factors explain *those* attitudes? We used other questions from our survey and different model specifications to probe these issues. We showed that there is likely some mutual cause-and-effect going on: that optimism about victory props up a conviction that we did the right thing, while at the same time a conviction that we did the right thing in going to war props up optimism about eventual victory. We also showed that arguments that were prominent in the public debate before the war—the threat of Iraqi WMD and possible Iraqi links to terror organizations—were not prominent in public definitions of success a year into the war itself. There was, in fact, little evidence in the data to support the idea that the public was willing to "declare victory and go home" once no stockpiles of WMD were found. Nor were body counts, tragic as they were, dominating the public's view of success in Iraq. On the contrary, the public embraced a view that bore a striking resemblance to the argument that the Bush administration was itself making in 2004: Success in Iraq meant that "An Iraqi government that is stable and democratic is established" and "Iraqis are able to live peaceful, normal everyday lives," as well as "Iraqis provide for their own security and maintain order." Success did *not* mean that "The Iraqi government is prevented from producing weapons of mass destruction," nor "The Iraqi government is prevented from supporting international terrorist organizations." Moreover, the public gauged that success according to a metric that the Bush administration itself emphasized: "Whether Iraqis are cooperating with U.S. authorities and not protecting terrorists or insurgents," and not according to the metric implied by the casualty-phobia thesis, "How many U.S. soldiers are killed or wounded."

In sum, despite their lack of factual knowledge about international affairs, members of the American public can and do form reasonable and coherent attitudes about the use of military force, and even about complex and difficult issues like bearing the human costs of war. Suffering casualties in wartime is undoubtedly a difficult and troubling experience. One could understand if the public would shy away from such experiences and simply say "no!" This has been the expectation of the conventional wisdom that the American public is "casualty phobic"—willing to use force, but only if no Americans get killed.

Our analysis strongly indicates that members of the American public are willing to face up to these difficult decisions. Not only to they face up to them, but they also make reasoned and reasonable judgments about the level of human costs that they are willing to tolerate. By listening to elite cues about the primary objectives of the military operation, the breadth of elite support for the mission, and the likelihood that the mission will succeed, members of the public make plausible judgments about tolerable costs. As a result, the public does not simply abandon a mission whenever the human costs begin to mount. Instead they make judgments about the importance of the mission and its likelihood of success and offer their support accordingly.

Public Attitudes toward Iraq after the Election of 2004

The conclusion that the public is not casualty phobic may be jarring to some readers in light of the erosion of support for the president and the war beginning in 2005 and intensifying in 2006 and 2007. Purveyors of the conventional wisdom such as Mueller (2005) and Klarevas (2006) invoked declining support for war as new evidence for the "simple association" of casualties and public opinion: as casualties go up, public support goes down. As we have shown throughout this book, the conventional wisdom simply cannot account for the actual movements of public opinion as well as our argument can. Our argument is not, however, that public support will never erode. Rather, our argument states that the cause of declining support is more likely because expectations of victory have eroded rather than because casualties have mounted. The movement of public support from January 2005 through to summer 2007 fits this pattern well. Casualties did mount, but not as dramatically as public support declined. Importantly, public support dropped faster than the Mueller logarithmic rule-of-thumb would predict.

We did not continue to field our survey, and so we do not have as rich a source of data to evaluate opinions from 2005 to 2007. Nevertheless, the patterns we have identified from the first three years of the war—and from the Cold War experience—likely account for the movement. Progress in Iraq was slow at best, with political achievements like the January 2005 vote (the famous "purple finger" moment) followed by months of violence and political stalemate, first in seating the interim government, then in securing a constitution, then in forming a unity government. The political progress never seemed to accelerate with success compounding success. Just as importantly, prominent milestones in the development of a functioning government did not result in a dramatic lessening of violence. While U.S. casualty rates ebbed and flowed, the overall violence in Iraq seemed fairly steady. If anything, the violence appeared to worsen with countless warnings that Iraq was slipping into uncontrollable sectarian civil war. Groups like "Iraq Body Count," for example, reported that the number of Iraqi civilians killed in Iraq increased rather than decreased over each of the first three years of the war and reached new highs in the summer of 2006.[3]

These events unfolded against a backdrop of relentless criticism from Democrats (and even some Republicans) that the Bush team lacked a "plan for success" in Iraq. The criticism matched the intensity of the 2004 election, and had a telling effect on public opinion despite efforts by the Bush administration to advance its message. Disapproval of the president's handling of Iraq drifted up after the election from about 50 percent to more than 60 percent by the summer of 2006, and, in June 2006, an ABC News poll revealed that some 64 percent of the public stated that the administration did not have "a clear plan for handling the situation

[3] See Iraq Body Count Press Release 13, "Iraq Death Toll in Third Year of Occupation Is Highest Yet"; available at http://www.iraqbodycount.net.

in Iraq." Similarly, in June of 2006 a Pew Research Center for the People and the Press survey revealed that only about 55 percent of the public expected that the United States would probably or definitely succeed in Iraq. That result represents a 10 percent decline in optimism since our last poll in October 2004 and a 20 percent decline since our first survey in October 2003. Thus the ten-percentage-point change in disapproval from October 2004 to June 2006 closely matches the ten-percentage-point change in perceptions of success over that period. Contrary to the conventional view, however, the decline in public support was neither constant nor monotonic. Public support revived briefly when the administration made a focused effort to answer the charges of the critics in late 2005, but the six-month delay in finalizing a unity government undermined these gains.

Dissatisfaction with the lack of progress in stabilizing Iraq helped sweep the Democratic Party to control of both the House of Representatives and the Senate in the fall of 2006. In response, President Bush announced changes in the personnel responsible for overseeing the conflict along with a new strategic approach, dubbed "The New Way Forward," which involved change in military tactics, new diplomatic and economic initiatives, and, most prominently, an increase in the number of American troops in Iraq. By the summer of 2007, however, authorities in the Pentagon were conceding that little progress had been made, though they emphasized that it was still too early to tell whether the New Way Forward would succeed or fail.[4] The Baghdad clock was moving too slowly for the Washington clock, however, and, as a consequence, political elites sharply criticized the conduct of the Iraq war and a growing proportion of the public expressed similar doubts. While no option enjoyed a clear majority, a plurality was forming behind the option of a phased, gradual de-escalation of U.S. involvement in Iraq. This erosion of support is exactly as our theory would predict. In other words, the fluctuation and eventual drop in public war-support that we observed from 2005 through 2007 is consistent with our argument, not a challenge to it.

Scope Conditions: Technology and American Exceptionalism

Thus we remain confident that our understanding of American support for the Iraq War and the public's tolerance for the human costs of war more generally is quite robust across both time and space. There are, however, at

[4]David S. Cloud and Damien Cave, "Commanders Say Push in Baghdad Is Short of Goal." *New York Times*, 5 June 2007, p.1.

least two important scope conditions that we believe may limit the generalizability of our argument. First, the raw statistics on over one hundred years of U.S. combat fatalities do indicate that something has changed. Adding together all of the combat fatalities that the United States has suffered since the fall of Baghdad amounts to roughly 3,000 dead—at the time of this writing. That number roughly matches the five-week death toll during the height of the Vietnam War in 1968, or five months during most of the rest of that conflict.[5] The death toll in Iraq today is roughly comparable to the fatalities suffered in some of the major battles of World War II or the Civil War. It is indisputably true that the casualties from recent conflicts such as the Iraq War have generated levels of political controversy comparable to those of earlier wars such as Korea or Vietnam, despite the fact that casualty rates in Iraq have been an order of magnitude lower than those in Korea or Vietnam. In that minimal sense, the public has indeed become more casualty sensitive, and readers might wonder if this cuts against our basic thesis.

We would reply that it doesn't, because something else has been changing over the same time period: the technology of warfare. The underlying logic of our argument is that the public views the human cost of war as a necessary evil; it may be perceived as an evil that should be minimized, but a necessary one that should be tolerated provided other greater goods (the goods that come from victory) are achieved. The rapid evolution of technology—what many call the technology revolution—has drastically changed the terms of what level of casualties are, in fact, necessary for victory. Over the course of a few weeks in March and April of 2003, the United States military invaded Iraq and toppled a regime that boasted roughly 300,000 to 400,000 armed men and women, and more than 2,000 armored tanks. The United States accomplished all this, while suffering less than 150 deaths. In World War II, a comparable campaign (for example, the invasion and defeat of Italy) took more than a year and cost more than 100,000 Allied dead.

Of course, many factors were different, but chief among them were the new technologies and doctrines shaping the new American way in war. In other words, the U.S. military has recently been able to accomplish more at a significantly lower human cost and this has doubtless changed the basic frame through which the public evaluates military missions. This hypothesis is not testable through survey research, but it is plausible and is consistent with the overall logic we present here. Moreover, recent research on the impact of medical technology on casualty rates suggests that the intensity of combat in Iraq today is roughly comparable to that

[5] See Gartner (1998).

experienced during the Vietnam War.[6] The casualty burden has been lighter not because the combat is less intense in Iraq but because our medical technology has improved. Specifically, the lethality rate of combat wounds has dropped from 42 percent during the Revolutionary War, and 24 percent during Vietnam, to only 10 percent in the current conflict. Other analysts suggest that once we account for these changes in military and medical technology, the combat in Fallujah has been roughly comparable in its intensity to the combat in Hue—one of the more intense battles of Vietnam.[7] Thus the public would probably not tolerate casualty rates on the order suffered even forty years ago in Hue, let alone 140 years ago in Antietam, but that is because these same casualty rates would have drastically different meanings, not because the public shies away from intense fighting.. Military historians can debate endlessly whether these rates were in fact *necessary* in earlier wars; it is beyond debate that they are unnecessary today, at least for the United States in the kinds of missions currently envisioned. The public will not tolerate unnecessary casualty rates, but the public will continue to tolerate casualties that are necessary to achieve victory.[8]

Our argument thus links up with the now-standard argument about the technological revolution and its impact on military affairs. As many have observed, Western societies, especially the United States, have pursued advanced military technologies in a quest to manage and mitigate the human costs of war.[9] This is, in some sense, the very definition of casualty aversion: pursuing policies designed to minimize casualties. We depart from this traditional interpretation of technology, however, when the American embrace of technology is cited as evidence that the public no longer can tolerate the costs of war. From a policy-making perspective, there is a world of difference between leading a public that wants you to use the

[6] See Atul Gawande, "Casualties of War: Military Care for Wounded from Iraq and Afghanistan," *New England Journal of Medicine* 351, no. 24 (2004):2471–75.

[7] Phillip Carter and Owen West, "Iraq 2004 Looks Like Vietnam 1966," *Slate Magazine*, 2004; at http://www.slate.com/id/2111432/, accessed 9 August 2006.

[8] This is the flip-side of the argument advanced by Alexander Downes (2004) about the willingness of countries to target civilians and thus deliberately to inflict casualties on noncombatants. He argues that democratic states will be willing to target the civilians in opposing states if the war has become stalemated or if the opponent is engaging in guerilla war tactics.

[9] Toffler and Toffler (1993); Sapolsky and Weiner (1994); Morehouse (1996); Sapolksy and Shapiro (1996); Eikenberry (1996); Ignatieff (2000); Coker (2001, 2002); Mueller (2002); Wrage (2003); Mandel (2004). Interestingly, Ralph Peters (1996) and Colin McInnes (2002) make almost the opposite argument, claiming that we have so distanced ourselves from killing that it no longer looks serious to us. Gartzke (2001) argues that the march of technology is more a function of the availability of capital than it is a political response to public concerns about casualties.

best technology and techniques to minimize unnecessary deaths and leading a public that believes technology has eliminated all human costs of war whatsoever, and whose morale, therefore, would collapse quickly in a bloody conflict.

The "necessary casualties" scope condition likely operates across different scenarios as well. The number of casualties that the United States would need to suffer to defeat the Haitian military is very different from the number that it would need to defeat the Iraqi military or the North Korean military or, indeed, the Chinese military. Of course, other factors that shape public support for military operations also vary across those scenarios, chief of which would be the public's estimation of the importance of the interests at stake. But even if in theory the stakes might be considered comparable and technology was likewise held constant—say comparing Iraq 2003 to a possible war with North Korea—the sheer difference in military capabilities means that it is likely that very different rates of casualties would be "necessary." Our argument suggests that the public likewise adjusts its tolerance of casualties accordingly; that the public might deem as necessary (and therefore tolerable) a higher level of casualties in a conflict with North Korea than it would against Iraq, simply because the military challenge is far more daunting in North Korea.

In other words, technological necessity is an important scope condition that serves as a caveat for everything else we have argued in this book. The public will tolerate mounting casualties if it believes that the United States is still likely to win, *provided that the casualties are themselves deemed necessary for success*. In this way, the controversy over the adequacy of armor plating on military transports in Iraq—a controversy that bubbled into a full-blown crisis for the Bush administration in the months immediately after the 2004 presidential election and likely caused much of the post-election bounce to dissipate—is entirely consistent with an overall bullish judgment about the public's stomach for the war.[10] The possibility of reducing casualties through relatively modest technological fixes—and especially the fact that some units had well-armored vehicles while others did not—made at least some of the casualties appear to be unnecessary, a result of carelessness or worse. The public's stomach for that sort of cost is minimal.

The second major scope condition for our argument is important: we are making claims only about the attitudes of the U.S. public.[11] We be-

[10] Brown (2004); Ricks (2004); Schmitt (2004); Shanker and Schmitt (2004); Moss (2005).

[11] A related scope condition is that we are making claims only about U.S. public attitudes concerning U.S. military casualties. As we discuss later in this chapter, extending the analysis to attitudes about civilian casualties is an important priority for future research.

lieve that it is plausible that the patterns evident in U.S. public opinion data extend to other countries, perhaps other modern democracies, but we view that as a hypothesis worthy of further testing. The conventional wisdom on the casualty sensitivity of other publics is harder to pin down. On one end of the spectrum, some analysts unfavorably compared the American force protection "fetishism," with the more risk-tolerant and putatively more effective approach of allies like the British.[12] Somewhere in the middle is the observation that the casualty-phobia thesis invokes trends that extend beyond American society to other advanced industrial democracies, and so logically would hold in those societies as well.[13] At the opposite end is the "U.S. from Mars, Europe from Venus" view, which holds that the United States is uniquely martial in its approach to foreign policy and thus willing to accept casualties, whereas our European allies have increasingly adopted an approach that might be characterized as beyond casualty phobia into combat phobia—a deep reluctance to use force at all.

Over the past decade, public opinion data in other countries, particularly in Europe and Japan, has become more abundant, thus allowing for systematic studies of casualty sensitivity of the kind that have been done on U.S. public opinion for decades. The best studies suggest that there is a fair degree of commonality across U.S. and European public opinion in this area. Philip Everts has done the most exhaustive comparative study of the casualty sensitivity issue and he largely concludes (1) that what he calls the "body bag syndrome" is a myth, and (2) that it is equally mythical in both U.S. and European contexts.[14] To be sure, there are differences across NATO publics, and these differences emerged both at a policy-making level and at a public opinion–survey level, especially during the Kosovo mission; the differences that did emerge generally conformed to the "U.S. from Mars, Europe from Venus" pattern, with more skeptical and casualty-sensitive publics found in Europe than in the United States.[15] The matter, however, is a fruitful field for further research, and, for our part, we make confident claims only about the nature of U.S. public opinion.[16]

[12] See, for instance, Caniglia (2001).

[13] Mack (1975); Luttwak (1994); Merom (2003); Smith (2003). Lee (2003/04) challenges the archetype of the doughty Brit in World War II, arguing that an earlier version of casualty phobia drove British policy during the 1938 Munich negotiations.

[14] Everts (2002: esp. 158–81; 2005). See also Isernia (2001).

[15] Everts does not frame the conclusions this way, but the inferences can be drawn from the data presented in Everts (2002: 134–57).

[16] One promising study uses some of the framework developed in this book to guide a systematic comparison of U.S., U.K., and French sensitivities to civilian casualties: see Richardson (in draft).

Implications for Future Research

The Role of the Media

We have presented earlier versions of these findings in scores of briefings, and have repeatedly encountered one common skeptical reaction: perhaps the public is casualty tolerant because the casualties have not been emphasized much, especially in media accounts. The reaction is usually framed as an assertion in the following manner: The public would become more casualty sensitive if only the public could [fill in the blank], where the blank might be filled in by any one of the following: see pictures of caskets coming into Dover Air Force base; see more bloody images of dead American soldiers in the streets of Iraq; see more front-page, top-of-the-news stories about U.S. casualties; hear more skeptical coverage about the futility of the war; or have more detailed coverage about wounded U.S. soldiers; and so forth.[17] At some level, this critique is inherently unanswerable. We cannot ex ante rule out the possibility that there would be changes in public opinion if there are dramatic changes in the way the war is reported to the public.

Still, within the limits of the available data, this line of critique seems unpersuasive for four reasons. First, the media has been reporting fairly vigorously on the costs of the war and arguably devotes more effort to parsing and tabulating the costs, especially casualties, than it does to calculating the benefits. A Lexis search reveals hundreds of articles mentioning casualties in Iraq in any month of reporting; the maxim "If it bleeds, it leads" aptly captures the prominence given to these tragic developments; every milestone of casualty threshold sparks another wave of critical analysis of the mounting toll.[18] It is simply not accurate to claim that, for example, a ban on photos of caskets at the Dover Air Force base is blocking the public's awareness of the human toll of the war.[19] Second, perhaps because of the extensive media coverage, polls show that the public actu-

[17] Often there is a certain wistfulness to the question as well, as if the questioner were really asking, "Why isn't the public as opposed to the war as I am? Perhaps they are not as aware of the costs of the war as I am? How can I make them more aware of the costs?"

[18] The major newspapers of record publish a daily log of U.S. casualties, amplified with photos and obituaries on their websites. One TV news show famously devoted an entire broadcast simply to reading the names of all the U.S. dead, and then did it a second time a year later: Carter (2004); De Moraes (2004); Jensen (2004); Gough (2005). Virtually every news outlet has run multiple human interest stories probing the deaths of "typical" soldiers or the grief of survivors: Harris and Arms (2004); Brown (2005); Gorney (2005). Prestige journals have likewise devoted extensive coverage to the topic: Baum (2004a,b,c); Carter and West (2004); Freedberg (2004).

[19] Brunt (2003); Harden and Milbank (2004); Griffin (2004); Ripley (2004); Jaffe (2004); Tyson (2005).

ally has a fairly good idea about some of the costs of the war, namely the death toll. [20] Third, while it is true that the public is not able to estimate accurately the toll of wounded, our polling as reported in chapter 5 showed that there was no difference in public responses when the prompts covered dead and wounded or just dead; in other words, it is likely that the public views wounded the way it views fatalities, an unavoidable evil that should be minimized but can be tolerated under the right circumstances. Fourth, graphic images of dead and wounded in Iraq are, in fact, widely available on the Internet, and so there is nothing antiseptic about the coverage of the war as a whole, even if the most gruesome images are not prominent in mainstream broadcasts.[21] Nevertheless, it is doubtful that graphic images would change our findings substantially since what matters the most is not the content of the image but the frame that is put around that image.[22] The same image of a dead American soldier can signify either "the costs of this war are too horrible to sustain" or "see what the enemy does to us, we need to avenge this death"; the alternate frames lead to very different levels of casualty tolerance. These frames may have uniform results across the population, but more likely frames vary across individuals with different individuals finding different meanings from the same pictures.[23]

While this superficial line of critique does not have much merit, it does point to an avenue of research that would be quite fruitful: probing further the role of the media in the casualty issue. In chapter 2, we incorporated the media in a rudimentary fashion: controlling for the quantity of coverage of the Iraq conflict, and the portion of that coverage that was devoted to high-intensity combat operations versus counter-insurgency and military occupation. More systematic content analysis of the media coverage would allow for more nuanced hypotheses about the relationship between public opinion and media coverage. Similarly, a research design that incorporated media experiments—for instance, constructed and controlled media reports given to focus groups—would be a priority for follow-up studies. These would be able to account for the way in which different frames put around the same images could adjust in substantial ways the "meaning" conveyed by the images. While the simplistic versions

[20] Kull et al. (2003b); Kull et al. (2004).

[21] Aday (forthcoming) argues otherwise, claiming that the mainstream media coverage of the Iraq War was jingoistic and minimized coverage of U.S. casualties. This study looked at media coverage only during the period of high-intensity combat, from 20 March to 9 April 2003; it is doubtful that the conclusions would hold if all of the years of war coverage were assessed. Rainey (2005) found that there were few photos of American dead and wounded in the mainstream newspapers on a week-to-week basis, but also noted that the leading papers of record had, in fact, run extensive photo-displays at key milestones during the war in Iraq.

[22] Dauber (2001) makes this point forcefully.

[23] See Reifler (2006).

of the "CNN effect" hypothesis have been debunked, the more sophisticated versions remain plausible.[24] The public gets information about foreign affairs, and especially casualties in war, from the media. Importantly, the public also gets information about how the rest of the public thinks—that is, information about the level of popular support for the Iraq war, the extent to which casualties are eroding public support, and so on—from the media, which is the chief conduit reporting on the extensive polling done during the Iraq War.[25] Understanding better the linkage between the content of that media coverage and the content of public attitudes is thus a logical next step in this research agenda.[26]

Such an effort would also be able to pick up on the intriguing implications of the findings reported in chapter 7, namely the role of presidential rhetoric.[27] We showed that the responses given by the public to questions about defining and measuring success in the ongoing Iraq war bore a striking resemblance to presidential rhetoric at the time. When the public received conflicting messages, one from the president and administration spokespersons and another from critical media coverage, which message prevailed and under what conditions? Did our surveys exaggerate the strength of presidential rhetoric because, at the time, no powerful alternative voice was presenting a comparably coherent message? Or was the press not sufficiently critical?[28] This last hypothesis is questionable, since we surveyed during an election year when partisan voices presented loud and sustained critiques of the administration's Iraq policy and during a season that included such dramatic and well-publicized adverse developments like the Abu Ghraib torture controversy, the Fallujah uprising, the 9/11 Commission hearings, and the official reports documenting the failure to find WMD stockpiles in Iraq. The alternative message may not have been coherent, but it certainly provided a counterweight to presidential statements on Iraq.

[24] McNulty (1993); Mermin (1997); Strobel (1997); Powlick and Katz (1998); Nacos, Shapiro, and Isernia (2000); Gowing (2003).

[25] See Mutz (1998) for an evaluation of how perceptions of various collective opinions can shape individual opinion.

[26] Entman (2003) provides an intriguing framework that could be applied to the casualty question. Similarly, Andrade's (2003) findings on the use of presidential rhetoric to divert attention from adverse domestic conditions use an innovative method for systematically linking presidential rhetoric to foreign policy. Going beyond mainstream media to look at local and cable news, as in Baum's (2003) path-breaking study, would also be important. The role of the Internet and blogging in this arena is also ripe for further study. Finally, disaggregating the national media to look at local effects, responding to local casualties, as in Gartner (2004), is likewise a fruitful next step.

[27] Shapiro and Jacobs (2000).

[28] Zaller and Chu (2000) claim that during the Cold War and post–Cold War crises, the press had a "hawkish" bias, reporting news in a fashion that reinforced consumer's hawkish reactions–just as political leaders would want them to.

Alternatively, perhaps the overall findings of fairly robust public support for the war despite mounting casualties in 2003 and 2004 are a function of "misperceptions" about the war. Some poll results do show the public holding views at odds with what the best expert opinion holds; for instance, a series of polls in 2003 conducted by the Program on International Policy Attitudes (PIPA) at the University of Maryland showed that portions of the American public believed that a majority of the people in the world supported the Iraq War and that investigators had found WMD in Iraq as well as evidence of close links between Iraq and Al Qaeda.[29] Moreover, the PIPA team speculates that these misperceptions are reinforced by a biased media that filters news according to partisan ideology. The findings are suggestive of a fruitful line of future research, though the initial results may be overdrawn. Much turns on the ambiguity of question wording and legitimate conflicting interpretations over ambiguous intelligence findings. Thus, the 9/11 Commission found evidence of several contacts between Iraq and representatives of al-Qaeda over the decade preceding the Iraq War, but concluded that these overtures never amounted to an operational alliance. If that is taken as "truth," then what is the correct response to the PIPA poll question that asks, "Is it your impression that the U.S. has or has not found clear evidence in Iraq that Saddam Hussein was working closely with the al-Qaeda terrorist organization?" The correct answer is probably, "Not exactly, but they have found evidence of some contact," a response option that the survey did not provide. Moreover, our own polling shows that when respondents are given a wider range of possible answers—from "Saddam Hussein's government had no connection whatsoever with al-Qaeda and was not likely to help al-Qaeda in the future or give weapons of mass destruction to al-Qaeda" all the way to "Saddam Hussein's government helped al-Qaeda plan and carry out the 9/11 attacks, and Iraq was actively planning future attacks against the United Stated with al-Qaeda that would possibly include the use of Iraqi weapons of mass destruction"—there is, in fact, a distribution of "misperceptions." Three times as many people, however, give the "wrong" answer that Hussein helped carry out the 9/11 attacks than give the other "wrong" answer that there was no connection whatsoever between the two (31 percent versus 11 percent). Nevertheless, these findings underscore the importance of probing further the linkages between presidential rhetoric, media, and public opinion.[30]

The difficulty that the administration faced in maintaining support in 2005 and 2006 further reinforces the point. The president even had trouble moving opinion on concrete issues like "Do you think the Bush administration does or does not have a clear plan for handling the

[29] Kull, Ramsay, and Lewis (2003/04).

[30] See, for example, Reifler (2006) for work addressing this issue.

situation in Iraq? " The administration released an unclassified version of its strategy to great fanfare, but in the immediate aftermath of this effort 60 percent of the public still stated that the administration had no clear plan.[31] In other words, models of public rhetoric that assume an all-dominant White House imposing its view upon an unsuspecting public are unlikely to withstand close scrutiny. Further research, however, may be able to tease out the conditions under which administration rhetoric prevails and under which outside critics succeed in framing public perceptions.

Probing the Psychology of Casualty Attitudes

Throughout we have characterized our findings as consistent with the "rational public" view: a public capable of making reasoned judgments about costs and benefits even when confronted with difficult and emotionally fraught issues.[32] It does not necessarily follow, however, that the rough cost-benefit calculation that we see in the data matches exactly a cold and inexorable economic logic. For one thing, the public may confront in survey questions about casualties precisely the kinds of "hard choice" questions that defy straightforward answers. Michael Alvarez and John Brehm, in analyzing earlier survey data on casualty attitudes, concluded that the general public showed great "equivocation," meaning that respondents held potentially contradictory positions but did not see these as contradictory, whereas the elite respondents showed "ambivalence," meaning that the more information the elites had the more variable their responses because the questions tapped into underlying attitudes that were truly irreconcilable.[33] Furthermore, our findings are suggestive of the possibility that the public embraces approaches to the calculation that have traditionally been presented as challenges to economic reasoning: loss aversion and sunk costs. Future research could profitably explore this possibility and in so doing probe the underlying psychology of public attitudes toward casualties.

Prospect theory, as advanced by Kahneman and Tversky, argues that humans tend to experience losses more intensely than gains.[34] Kahneman and Tversky show that framing choices presented as losses leads humans to risk aversion (opting for a guaranteed but lower payout over an uncertain but higher payout, even if the expected utility of the gamble is higher), whereas frames articulated as gains are likely to lead to risk acceptance (opting for an uncertain but possibly higher loss rather than the certain

[31] One of the co-authors, then working on the National Security Council staff, helped draft the public version of the strategy.

[32] Page and Shapiro (1992); Sniderman (1993).

[33] Alvarez and Brehm (2002).

[34] Kahneman and Tversky (1979); Jervis (1992); Levy (1992, 1997, 2000).

but smaller loss, even if the expected utility of the gamble is more negative). The crucial step in the analysis, however, is identifying the reference point, or the frame of reference, that the individual establishes and against which these options are compared. The usual reference point is the status quo, as perceived by the individual, but it can in some cases be an "aspiration point," a condition not yet achieved but hoped for.[35] As Levy has summarized it, "Because of loss aversion, people tend to value what they have more than comparable things that they do not have, and the psychological cost of relinquishing a good is greater than the psychological benefit of acquiring it.[36] An implication of loss-aversion theory is that individuals make a distinction between "uncompensated losses" or "dead losses" on the one hand, and the "costs of protection" on the other hand; and they are far more sensitive to the former than the latter. That is, negative outcomes that look like the inevitable costs of doing business (for example, premiums paid for insurance) are not viewed as negatively as losses that are perceived as just straight losses.[37] By extension, varying casualty tolerances across individuals and, in the aggregate, across different missions may be reflecting these dynamics from prospect theory. Perhaps casualty-acceptant individuals have adopted an aspiration point as their reference point, whereas casualty-phobic individuals have adopted the status quo; or perhaps casualty-acceptant individuals see casualties as "costs of protection," whereas casualty-phobic individuals view them as dead losses. Indeed, our general finding of a relatively casualty-acceptant American public in the aggregate can be recast as a general finding that the public, in the aggregate, views casualties as the inevitable cost of protecting American interests and security—a loss that is tragic but not overweighted. Well-designed experiments could tease out these issues and provide a clearer picture of underlying dynamics.[38]

Alternatively, or perhaps in tandem, the casualty issue may be a matter of sunk costs. Economists have long argued that when considering whether to persist in an endeavor rational consumers should ignore sunk costs—unrecoverable costs (whether time, money, or other value) that have already been made in the endeavor—and focus only on calculating the balance of future costs and benefits. In fact, many people do factor in sunk costs in weighing different courses of action and, as a consequence, continue an operation to "make good" on the costs that have already been

[35] Heath, Larrick, and Wu (1999).

[36] Levy (2000: 195).

[37] Kahneman and Tversky (1984); Levy (2000).

[38] One suggestive experimental study asked subjects to compare across various hostage rescue missions with varying numbers of hostages saved or killed in the rescue attempt; the results were mixed and underscored the difficulty of specifying the expectations of prospect theory giving the shifting contexts of experimental versus real-world conditions (Boettcher 2004).

incurred.[39] The prominence of "expectations of success" as the long pole undergirding public casualty tolerance may, in fact, reflect something of a sunk cost mentality; a desire to stick with the military operation in order to secure victory so that those who have already died will not have died in vain.

The sunk cost effect is less prominent when individuals employ a mental budget, one that set a priori a limit to the costs that one is willing to pay for a given endeavor.[40] Mental budgets, however, make individuals prone to a "reverse sunk cost effect," in which individuals give up on a project too soon as a result of resources already expended without giving due consideration to future costs and benefits.[41] The casualty issue seems prone to this sort of dynamic, especially in light of rhetoric in public debates that the war is "only worth so many lives." It may even be the case, as Donna Nincic and Miroslav Nincic have speculated, that governments and publics approach the cost-benefit calculation inherent in war in fundamentally different ways, each with a different internal logic that contradicts the other.[42] Perhaps the public approaches war with a "consumer" mindset, accepting an implied contract from the government for given benefits (goals of the war) in exchange for given costs (expectations of casualties); if the casualties go up, the effect on the consumer's cost-benefit calculation is adverse, and so support drops. By contrast, the government may approach the war with an "investor" mindset, deciding in advance what benefits to pursue and absorbing higher costs indefinitely until the environment changes so drastically that it requires a radical reassessment of the initial investment decision.

It is unclear how much the sunk costs effect has influenced the results that we present here. By making the costs explicit in our question—in the question stem we tell respondents the number of casualties already incurred (the sunk cost)—we reduce the likelihood that the effect is observed.[43] For that matter, factoring in sunk costs may not necessarily be the "irrational" behavior that traditional economics claims it to be—or rather, honoring sunk costs may produce other benefits that compensate for the intrinsic losses and thus shift the cost-benefit calculation; for instance, developing a reputation for resolve even in the face of mounting costs lowers the incentives that enemies have in challenging the established power.[44] Nevertheless, the unique circumstances of the survey context of our research—repeated measures of casualty tolerance in the con-

[39] Teger (1980); Arkes and Blumer (1985).

[40] Heath (1995).

[41] Zeelenberg and van Dijk (1997); Johnstone (2000).

[42] Nincic and Nincic (1995).

[43] Northcraft and Neale (1986).

[44] Kelly (2004).

text of an actual war with prominently rising costs—suggest that the data we have collected could be used to study the issue of casualty tolerance as a sunk cost effect.

Civilian Casualties

Our argument concerns only American public attitudes toward U.S. combat casualties. A logical next step is to extend the analysis to public attitudes toward civilian casualties, the so-called collateral damage of war. Polling data in this area is more sparse but not nonexistent, and, given the extensive coverage and speculation about civilian casualties, the time is ripe.

There are three working hypotheses that would merit closer scrutiny. The first, arguably the null hypothesis, is that the American public simply does not care about civilian casualties. John Mueller says as much in his review of polling from the first Gulf War: "[T]he American people were quite insensitive to Iraqi casualties, even though they appear to have harbored little ill will toward the Iraqi people. Also relevant is the public's bland reaction to early estimates suggesting that a hundred thousand or more Iraqis had died in the war."[45] The opposite hypothesis is at least plausible: Civilian noncombatants are *not* the enemy, and the prevailing ethical norms of just war theory, not to mention the laws of war, make clear that noncombatants are not legitimate targets of war, and therefore the public would not well tolerate civilian casualties. The third hypothesis, and the one that we find most plausible, is that the American public views civilian casualties much the same way they view military casualties—as a necessary evil to be minimized, but tolerable under the right conditions.

This third hypothesis, however, raises as many questions as it answers. What is the link between media coverage and public attitudes toward civilian deaths? For starters, a standard trope by critics of U.S. foreign policy is the claim that the U.S. media downplays civilian casualties (at least compared to other media)—not reporting on it, or, when they do report it, avoiding the kind of graphic and sensationalized coverage that would move public opinion significantly.[46] For that matter, the U.S. military goes to great pains to minimize collateral damage and, increasingly, it is the enemy that attempts to maximize collateral damage—both by exaggerating the number of civilians claimed to have died and by adopting tactics like fighting without uniforms and using civilians as human shields, which raise the toll beyond what it otherwise would be.[47] When

[45] Mueller (1994), p. 123.

[46] Conetta (2004). In fact, however, the media do give civilian casualties extensive coverage, even though that coverage accentuates the uncertainty of tabulating the toll precisely Morley (2004). For illustrative examples, see Epstein (2003); Ford (2003); or Hegland (2004).

[47] Zucchino (2002).

the American public sees the enemy taking these steps, does it increase Americans' willingness to accept civilian casualties? Finally, at some level there is an unavoidable trade-off between *their* civilian casualties and *our* military casualties; how does the public weigh that trade-off and what, to use an infelicitous metaphor from economics, is the exchange rate? For that matter, do different kinds of people (men versus women, for instance) weigh the trade-offs differently?

Our survey data offer tantalizing clues, but they are not dispositive. The survey we administered in October 2003 contained an experiment designed to compare the effects of different kinds of casualties in a hypothetical scenario involving a war with North Korea. The basic question stem did not mention casualties and was administered to one-fifth of our sample: "Now I am going to ask you about your views of other possible American military operations in different countries. Would you approve or disapprove of the United States taking military action to eliminate North Korea's nuclear weapons program?" Another fifth got the same question but with the additional condition, "if it resulted in 2,000 U.S. military deaths?" A third fifth was asked about a different condition, "if it resulted in 2,000 civilian deaths in North Korea?" A fourth fifth was asked, "if it resulted in 2,000 civilian deaths in South Korea?" And the last fifth, "if it resulted in 2,000 civilian deaths in America because, in response, North Korea helped terrorists carry out an attack in the United States?" The results are displayed in figure 8.1.

The results are intriguing. As we have seen in numerous other polls, mentioning U.S. military casualties drops overall public approval for a proposed hypothetical military mission by about sixteen percentage points—in this case, from a clear majority to a minority. Mentioning other civilian casualties, however, has roughly the same effect: North Korean civilians drops it seventeen points; South Korean civilians drops it the same amount. The one exception, surprisingly, is that mentioning U.S. civilian casualties drops support only by seven points, leaving a thin majority favoring military action. The inference—that the American public cares more about U.S. soldiers dying than U.S. civilians dying—is possible, though it should be pointed out that the question stem varies the stakes somewhat by mentioning a North Korean terrorist reprisal, which could account for the result. As far as *their* civilian casualties are concerned, however, whether "enemy" or "allied," the inference is clear that, in the abstract and under hypothetical scenarios, civilian and military casualties have roughly the same impact on U.S. public opinion.

When the public is asked directly about the trade-off between civilian and military casualties, a slightly different picture emerges. We asked, "In general, how would you rate the importance of limiting American military deaths as compared to limiting foreign civilian deaths? Is limiting U.S. military deaths much more important, somewhat more important,

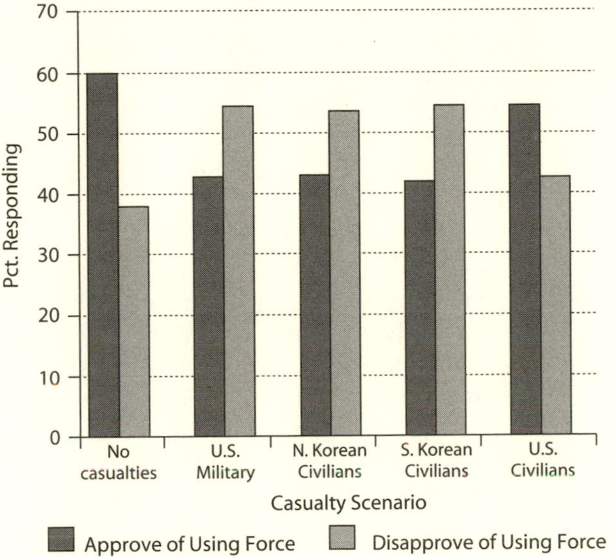

FIGURE 8.1. Predicted Casualties and Support for Eliminating North Korean WMD

about equally important, somewhat less important, or much less important than limiting foreign civilian deaths?" The response was split, but clearly tilted in favor of protecting the U.S. military over civilians: 52 percent said "much more" or "somewhat more important" (with nearly a third saying "much more"); 38 percent said "about equally important"; and only 6 percent said "somewhat less" or "much less important." On the other hand, when asked whether "[m]ilitary planners need to limit the danger to the civilians of the enemy nation during military operations, even if it means exposing U.S. soldiers to greater danger," 53 percent agreed (strongly or somewhat) and 43 percent disagreed (strongly or somewhat). Questions about favoring allied civilians produced an even greater gap: 60 percent agreeing versus 36 percent disagreeing. Not surprisingly, the public did not think enemy troops needed to be favored over U.S. soldiers (21 percent agreeing versus 75 percent); nor did they favor enemy electrical and water infrastructure over U.S. soldiers (35 percent versus 61 percent). In sum, there is ample evidence that the public is making a trade-off in its mind—at least in hypothetical scenarios—and that the public is not insensitive to civilian casualties.

How robust these sensitivities are in an ongoing conflict, however, is still subject to dispute. To begin with, just as hypothetical questions exaggerate the public's sensitivity to combat casualties, it is likely that these hypothetical questions exaggerate the public's sensitivity to civilian casualties. As noted earlier, Mueller claims that the American public seemed fairly unfazed by actual reports of civilian deaths in the first war in Iraq. Moreover, Alexander Downes has argued that democratic governments (and by extension the publics) want the military to avoid civilian deaths only so long as doing so does not jeopardize military success. When the war is going poorly, democratic regimes have not been reluctant about risking civilian deaths or, more tellingly, deliberately targeting civilians.[48] Strict observance of *jus in bello*, in other words, might be a luxury in which vastly superior militaries tend to indulge.

Another reason why public responses to civilian casualties may be more variable is that public information about civilian deaths are hard to come by; estimates of likely casualties before the war have wide error bands around them, and once the war starts the error bands do not narrow much. Here there is a sharp difference between military and civilian casualties. To be sure, ex ante estimates about likely *military* casualties are notoriously unreliable. During the Gulf War in the 1990s, "expert" opinion varied widely and most estimates were wildly off the mark.[49] Once the war started, however, the actual number of U.S. combat casualties was tracked and reported on a daily basis. The forecasting debacle of the Gulf War probably scared off predictions in the later war in Iraq, and so it is very difficult to find many estimates. One prominent exception is Michael O'Hanlon, who offered an estimate laden with caveats and provisos that said the war in Iraq could cost coalition forces "anywhere from 100 to 5,000 personnel. . . . The lower end of the range is only realistic if Iraq quickly capitulates, making an actual war very short in duration or even unnecessary, or if Iraqi forces can be drawn out of the cities to fight in the open. The upper ranges appear relatively unlikely to occur but cannot be dismissed."[50] As before, however, once the war started, the body count of coalition forces was meticulously documented and reported in near real-time, with reliable and elaborate summaries widely available.[51] Polls documented that the American public claimed to be paying relatively close attention to the war in Iraq, and was able to estimate fairly accurately the actual number of U.S. war fatalities incurred to date.[52]

Civilian casualties, on the other hand, are a different matter. Ex ante estimates of likely civilian casualties are at least as variable as estimates of military casualties, and perhaps even more so. Thus, O'Hanlon estimated that a war in Iraq would result in somewhere between 2,000 and 50,000 Iraqi civilian deaths.[53] Others warned about "hundreds of thousands of

[48] Downes (2004).
[49] Muravchik (1991).
[50] O'Hanlon (2003:23).
[51] For instance, see http://icasualties.org/oif.
[52] Kull et al. (2003b, 2004).
[53] O'Hanlon (2003:39).

civilian casualties in downtown Baghdad," and when the wildcard of possible WMD use was raised, the estimates grew still larger, with some speculating as many as 260,000 dead.[54] A U.N. contingency plan leaked in advance of the Iraq war speculated that 500,000 Iraqis might require medical treatment if the coalition invaded Iraq.[55]

But importantly, the uncertainty does not dissipate once the war begins.[56] Even years afterward, there are wide disputes about how many civilians died in the Gulf War or in the Kosovo conflict. Part of the confusion involves the lingering effects of war, whether in the form of disease or cluster bomblets, which can remain lethal even years after the war ends.[57] In the case of Kosovo, the confusion was partly political. Many estimates, based on claims by the Serbian government, ranged from 1,200 on up.[58] In contrast, the Human Rights Watch report, the most definitive study of civilian bombing fatalities in the Kosovo mission, estimated that between 488 and 527 civilians died as a result of the bombing; this estimate was possible, however, because the Kosovo conflict did not involve much ground action.[59]

Ongoing wars with considerable ground action, like the ones in Afghanistan and Iraq, are subject to extensive expert scrutiny, but analysts have not produced anything like a consensus on casualty estimates. One widely reported estimate of civilian casualties in the Afghanistan war gave a range of 3,100 to 3,600 killed as a direct result of hostile fire; the estimate's method, however, does not generate much confidence because it involves tabulating the second-hand reports made in the foreign press by enemy combatants who have a strong incentive to exaggerate the figures.[60] A more careful study put the Afghanistan civilian death toll at around 1300 for the first year of the war, but even this estimate came with strong caveats and uncertainties.[61] Civilian casualties in the ongoing Iraq War, with its protracted counter-insurgency and ground campaign, are even more difficult to track. The Iraq Body Count Database, using the suspect method of tabulating all claimed deaths, estimates that as of June 2006, the civilian death toll ranged from roughly 39,000 to 44,000.[62] A more rigorous estimate of civilian deaths, but one limited just to those incurred during the period of major combat operations, gave an estimate of roughly 3,200 to 4,300.[63] Estimating the wider human toll, that is the number of

[54] Boyer (2003); Cowley (2003).
[55] Preston (2003).
[56] Powers (2003).
[57] Contrast Arkin (2002) with Meilinger (2002).
[58] Conetta (2004).
[59] Human Rights Watch (2000).
[60] See Herold (n.d.); Chafetz (2003).
[61] Conetta (2002).
[62] http://www.iraqbodycount.net.
[63] Conetta (2003).

civilians who have died not just from the war's direct effects (errant bombs) but from the war's indirect effects (reduced health care, disease from contaminated water, and so forth) pushes the estimates into even greater zones of uncertainty. Thus, one widely quoted study estimated that the comprehensive civilian death toll attributable to the war was about 100,000, but with a great deal of uncertainty surrounding that figure (the 95 percent confidence interval ranged from 8,000 to 194,000).[64] The U.N. Development Program, however, claimed much lower casualty figures—estimating that 24,000 civilians and Iraqi military personnel died as a result of the war.[65] The U.S. military, for its part, is very reluctant to publicize any of its casualty estimates, and it is not clear whether the military has a more accurate handle on the issue than does the public punditry.[66]

With so much uncertainty about the actual figures, it is hard to make precise claims about how public opinion responds to the mounting civilian death toll. The public response to widely reported isolated incidents like a stray bomb can be tracked, but the kinds of close time-series analyses done on military casualties in this book cannot be applied to this other question. The situation becomes even murkier in "unconventional" wars like the Iraqi insurgency, where a significant portion of the civilian deaths are the result of suicide bombings by the enemy, not stray fire by U.S. forces. Indeed, who counts as a "civilian" in war is itself a murky subject that has increasingly preoccupied jurists and ethicists.[67] How the public unpacks all of these issues, and how the public deals with the uncertainty surrounding them, is not well understood and should be a priority for future study.[68]

Implications for Policy

The policy implications of our argument are clear. The U.S. public is not casualty phobic, and so U.S. foreign policy need not be seen as a paper tiger. At the same time, the U.S. public can be thought of as "defeat phobic," and so U.S. foreign policymakers must deliver results, especially when the costs of a policy mount. The public does appear to respond to elite cues, both presidential rhetoric and broader debates in the media, and so public argument pro and con about the war is consequential. Presidential rhetoric seems to play an important but by no means all-powerful

[64] Roberts et al. (2004). The study generated some skepticism, however, since the sampling procedures created wide confidence intervals and the data included some rather extreme outlier data points (see for example, Kaplan 2004).

[65] Jervis (2005).

[66] Cummins (2001); Conetta (2004).

[67] Chesterman (2001).

[68] Richardson (in draft) is one promising effort to address this lacuna.

role, especially concerning public attitudes about the likelihood of eventual success—the crucial factor undergirding the public's willingness to tolerate a mounting cost. Communicating presidential resolve is thus a critically important ingredient in preserving adequate public support for one's policies. Put another way, a president who signals that he is personally indecisive or conflicted about his willingness to tolerate the mounting casualty toll will find that the public is likewise abandoning its support for the administration's policies; but a president who effectively communicates resolve is likely to find adequate support from the public, even in the face of adverse news or short-term setbacks.[69] Resolve is a necessary ingredient, but our data suggest that the public is also responding to presidential cues about how to track success in Iraq, and thus, at some point, the issue is not simply a matter of spin. The public does look at reasonable indicators—in the present case, the extent to which the war's burden is being effectively and increasingly shouldered by the Iraqis themselves—and if these indicators trend sharply negative, then public support may well collapse; if they improve, however, the public can tolerate a mounting cost.

To shore up public support for a military operation that one wishes to buttress—or, for that matter, to undermine public support for an operation that one opposes—it is advisable to focus on the future rather than the past. That is, in the case of Iraq, the public's willingness to persevere owed more to public judgments about the ultimate "winnability" of the war, than it did to public judgments about the rightness of launching the war in the first place. Debates about the validity of the intelligence claims on which the original case for war rested are important, but not necessarily for affecting public willingness to continue to fight. If the policy object shifts, however, from war support/opposition to election support/opposition, the relative importance of the debate also shifts. Retrospective judgments about the wisdom of invading Iraq were decisive in the 2004 presidential elections. A president seeking both continued support for the Iraq war and reelection (or opponents seeking the opposite) must attend to both the retrospective and the prospective concerns.

In short, public opinion is best thought of as a constraint on policymakers, but it is not so limiting a constraint as to preclude even a fairly hawkish foreign policy—so long as that hawkish policy is perceived as successful.[70]

[69] In this regard, the contrast between the Bush and Clinton White Houses is quite stark. The Clinton team worried aloud about the resolve of its president and the public, far more than the Bush team has (York 2001).

[70] Sobel (2001). Baum (2004) notes that policymakers must pay closer attention to long-term public opinion than short-term public opinion; withstanding the volatile buffeting of short-term public opinion requires precisely the resolve discussed earlier.

Why does the conventional wisdom of an American foreign policy that is hamstrung by a public zero-tolerance for casualties persist, even when the evidence (ours and that of many other scholars) cuts so squarely against it? Philip Everts has raised this question and offers an intriguing and plausible answer:

> The fact is, incidentally, that it is a myth that serves politicians and military leaders well. It enables them to blame public opinion twice: first for forcing the politicians into (dangerous) action and then for its alleged unwillingness to face up to the consequences. It provides a useful alibi which they can employ in order to avoid taking responsibility themselves.[71]

The same logic, however, applies to the war protestor—that is, claiming the American public cannot bear the costs of the war, and then highlighting (and in some cases, exaggerating) those costs serves the political interests of those who oppose the use of force in American foreign policy.

The political utility of the conventional wisdom allows such thinking to enjoy a self-reinforcing cycle. Political leaders adopt casualty-averse policies because they believe that the public is casualty phobic. The historical record of this casualty phobia in action—Beirut, Somalia, Kosovo—serves to reinforce the idea that the public is indeed casualty phobic. Over time, this conventional wisdom can even shape individual opinions. We found that when asked to judge the casualty tolerance of the rest of the public, individuals were fairly bearish—the question was worded as follows: "Some people think that the American public will ONLY support military operations if the United States suffers a small number of deaths. Other people disagree. Would you strongly agree, somewhat agree, somewhat disagree, or strongly disagree with the statement that the American public will ONLY support military operations if the United States suffers a small number of deaths?" In response, 25 percent strongly agreed, 35 percent somewhat agreed, 16 percent somewhat disagreed, and 19 percent strongly disagreed.[72] In other words, it is possible that the public's aggregate casualty tolerance is itself dampened by concerns about casualty phobia, concerns that our (and others') analyses show are exaggerated.[73]

A Normative Observation

We have argued at some length that the American public is not as casualty phobic as is widely believed. In closing, however, we want to emphasize that whether or not the public is *willing* to bear the costs of war does

[71] Everts (2002: 181).

[72] Interestingly, even individuals who are themselves quite hawkish about accepting casualties express doubts about the tolerance of the public as a whole.

[73] This is akin to the dynamic identified in Mutz (1998).

not, by itself, settle the question of whether or not we *ought* to pay those costs. Much of the public commentary about American public opinion on foreign policy is, in fact, thinly masked debate over what American foreign policy ought to be. Throughout this book, we have taken pains to avoid that larger question, in part because as authors we disagree on some of the central policies in dispute. As analysts, we can reach a consensus on how casualties affect public opinion with regard to the ongoing war in Iraq without necessarily agreeing on the best course of action for the United States to take in Iraq or elsewhere.

Similarly, dealing dispassionately with opinion data about 500, or 5000, or 50,000 casualties is not a tacit dismissal of the human suffering that even one death can bring to friends and loved ones. Putting a human face on the numbers is an important and noble exercise, and we are encouraged that the media goes to such extraordinary lengths to document and report on the human costs of the war. The media and scholarly efforts to tabulate the costs of war far exceed the efforts to tabulate any benefits, and given the stakes this imbalance may actually be appropriate.[74] We probably will never see the human costs of war treated cavalierly—certainly there is little evidence that this is happening in the policymaking community, in popular commentary, or among the public themselves.

Taking the costs seriously, however, does not require that those costs swamp all other considerations. Furthermore, the findings that we present in this book show that the public is not, in fact, paralyzed by concerns about the costs. If the public is not hindered by such considerations in its support for military action, then neither should its policymakers be. To be sure, the costs of particular prospective military operations may well exceed the benefits and, in those cases, policymakers should not resort to force. Beyond this sensible calculus, however, policymakers need not fear that public indecisiveness will hamstring effective foreign policy.

[74] One speculative exception is Kristof (2002).

BIBLIOGRAPHY

Achen, Christopher. 1975. "Mass Political Attitudes and the Survey Response." *American Political Science Review* 69:1218–31.

Aday, Sean. Forthcoming. "The Real War Will Never Get On Television: An Analysis of Casualty Imagery in American Television Coverage of the Iraq War." In Philip Seib, ed., *Media and Conflict in the 21st Century*. New York: Palgrave.

Aldrich, John. 1995. "Why Parties?" in *The Origin and Transformation of Political Parties in America*. Chicago: University of Chicago Press

Aldrich, John, Richard Niemi, George Rabinowitz, and David Rohde. 1982. "The Measurement of Public Opinion about Public Policy: A Report on Some New Issue Question Formats."*American Journal of Political Science* 26, no. 2: 391–414.

Aldrich, John, John Sullivan, and Eugene Borgida. 1989. "Foreign Affairs and Issue Voting: Do Presidential Candidates 'Waltz before a Blind Audience?'" *American Political Science Review* 83, no.1: 123–41.

Allen, Mike. 2003. "Al-Qaeda at Work in Iraq, Bush Tells BBC; President Suggests Connection between Terrorist Group and Hussein Government." *Washington Post*, 16 November,p. A22.

Almond, Gabriel. 1950. *The American People and Foreign Policy*. New York: Praeger.

Althaus, Scott L. 2003. *Collective Preferences in Democratic Politics: Opinion Surveys and the Will of the People*. Cambridge: Cambridge University Press.

Alvarez, R. Michael, and John Brehm. 2002. *Hard Choices, Easy Answers*. Princeton: Princeton University Press.

Alvis, Michael W. 1999. "Understanding the Role of Casualties in U.S. Peace Operations." Landpower Essay Series, no. 99-1. Washington, D.C.: Institute of Land Warfare, Association of the United States Army.

Andrade, Lydia M. 2003. "Presidential Diversionary Attempts: A Peaceful Perspective." *Congress and the Presidency* 30, no. 1 (Spring):55–79.

Annand, Sowmya, and Jon Krosnik. 2003. "The Impact of Attitudes toward Foreign Policy Goals on Public Preferences among Presidential Candidates: A Study of Issue Publics and the Attentive Public in the 2000 U.S. Presidential Election." *Presidential Studies Quarterly* 20, no.10:1–41.

Arend, Anthony Clark. 2003. "International Law and the Preemptive Use of Military Force." *Washington Quarterly* 26, no. 2:89–103.

Arkes, Hal R., and Catherine Blumer. 1985. "The Psychology of Sunk Cost." *Organizational Behavior and Human Decision Processes* 35, no. 1:124–40.

Arkin, Bill. 2002. "Not Good Enough Mr. Rumfeld." *Washingtonpost.com,* 25 February 2002.

Arnold, James. 1990. *Tet Offensive 1968: Turning Point in Vietnam*. Oxford: Osprey.

Atkinson, Rick. 1996. "Warriors without a War: U.S. Peacekeepers in Bosnia Adjusting to New Tasks: Arbitration, Bluff, Restraint." *Washington Post*, 14 April, p. A1.

Bacevich, Andrew. 2004. *The New American Militarism: How Americans Are Seduced by War*. Oxford: Oxford University Press.

Baker Peter, and Daniel Balz. 2005. "Bush Words Reflect Public Opinion Strategy." *Washington Post*. June 30, p. A01.

Baker, William D., and John R. Oneal. 2001. "Patriotism or Opinion Leadership? The Nature and Origins of the 'Rally 'Round the Flag' Effect." *Journal of Conflict Resolution* 45, no. 5 (October):661–87.

Baron, R. M., and D. A. Kenny. 1986. "The Moderator-Mediator Variable Distinction in Social Psychological Research: Conceptual, strategic, and Statistical Considerations." *Journal of Personality and Social Psychology* 51:1173–82.

Baum, Dan. 2004a. "The Casualty: An American Soldier Comes Home From Iraq." *New Yorker*, 8 March 2004, pp. 64–73.

———. 2004b. "The Price of Valor," *New Yorker*. 12 July 2004.

———. 2004c. "Two Soldiers: How the Dead Come Home." *New Yorker*, 9 August 2004.

Baum M. 2002. "Sex, Lies, and War: How Soft News Brings Foreign Policy to the Inattentive Public." *American Political Science Review* 96:91–109.

Baum, Matthew A. 2003. *Soft News Goes to War: Public Opinion and American Foreign Policy in the New Media Age*. Princeton: Princeton University Press.

———. 2004. "How Public Opinion Constraints the Use of Force: The Case of Operation Restore Hope." *Presidential Studies Quarterly* 24, no. 2 (June): 187–227.

Becker, Elizabeth. 1999. "NATO Calls Transformers a Key Target in War Plan." *New York Times*, 25 May, p. 16.

Bendyna, Mary, Tamara Finucane, Lynn Kirby, John O'Donnell, and Clyde Wilcox. 1996. "Gender Differences in Public Attitudes toward the Gulf War: A Test of Competing Hypotheses." *Social Science Journal* 33, no. 1:1–22.

Berinsky, A., and D. Kinder. 2006. "Making Sense of Issues through Media Frames: Understanding the Kosovo Crisis." *Journal of Politics* 68, no. 3:640–56.

Berinsky, Adam. 2004. *Silent Voices: Public Opinion and Political Participation in America*. Princeton: Princeton University Press.

———. 2007. "Assuming the Costs of War: Events, Elites, and American Public Support for Military Conflict." Journal of Politics 69, 4:975–97.

Berinsky, Adam, and James Druckman. 2007. "The Polls—Review: Public Opinion Research and Support for the Iraq War." *Public Opinion Quarterly* 71, no.1:126–41.

Bernstein, Alvin, and Martin Libicki. 1998. "High-Tech: The Future Face of War? A Debate." *Commentary* (January):31.

Bernstein, Richard. 1993. "U.S. Presents Evidence to U.N. Justifying Its Missile Attack on Iraq." *New York Times*, 28 June, p. 7.

Betts, Richard K. 1995. "What Will It Take to Deter the United States." *Parameters* 25, no. 4: 70–79.

Bin Laden, Osama. 1996. "Declaration of War against the Americans Occupying the Land of the Two Holy Places." Originally published in *Al Quds Al Arabi*

(November). Accessible at http://www.pbs.org/newshour/terrorism/international/fatwa_1996.html.

Boettcher, William A. 2004. "The Prospects for Prospect Theory: An Empirical Evaluation of International Relations Applications of Framing and Loss Aversion." *Political Psychology* 25, no. 3:331–62.

Bowers, Jake, and Michael Ensley. 2003. "Issues in Analyzing Data from the Dual Mode 2000 American National Election Study." National Election Studies Technical Reports. Available at http://www.umich.edu/~nes.

Boyer, Peter. 2003. "The New War Machine." *New Yorker*, 30 June 2003, pp. 54.

———. 2004. "Paul Wolfowitz Defends His War." *New Yorker*, 1 November 2004.

Broder, John M. 1999. "Crisis in the Balkans: White House Memo: From Baptism of Fire to Kosovo: Clinton as Commander in Chief." *New York Times*, 8 April, p. 16.

Brody, Richard. 1984. "International Crises: A Rallying Point for the President?" *Public Opinion*, 6, no. 6:41–43.

Brown, Drew. 2004. "Rumsfeld in His Toughest Battle?" *Philadelphia Inquirer*, 18 December, p. 1.

Brown, DeNeen L. 2005. "A Portrait of Fallen Neighbors." *Washington Post*, 20 March, p. 1.

Brown, Justin. 2000. "Risks of Waging Only Risk-Free War." *Christian Science Monitor*, 24 May, p. 1.

Brunt, Martha. 2003. "Killed in Action." *Newsweek (Web exclusive)*, 17 October.

Burk, James. 1999. "Public Support for Peacekeeping in Lebanon and Somalia: Assessing the Casualties Hypothesis." *Political Science Quarterly*, 114, no. 1:53–78.

Burns, John, and Thom Shanker. 2004. "U.S. Officials Fashion Legal Basis to Keep Forces in Iraq." *New York Times*, 25 March, p. 10.

Byman, Daniel, and Matthew Waxman. 1999. "Defeating U.S. Coercion." *Survival*, 41, no. 2 (summer):107–20.

Cameron, Colin, and Pravin Trivedi. 2005. *Microeconometrics: Methods and Applications*. Cambridge: Cambridge University Press.

Campbell, Angus, Philip E. Converse, Warren E. Miller, and Donald E. Stokes. 1960. *The American Voter*. New York: Wiley.

Campbell, Kenneth J. 1998. "Once Burned, Twice Cautious: Explaining the Weinberger-Powell Doctrine." *Armed Forces and Society* 24, 3:357–74.

Caniglia, Richard R. 2001. "U.S. and British Approaches to Force Protection." *Military Review* 81, 4:73–81.

Carson, Jamie L., Jeffrey A. Jenkins, David W. Rohde, and Mark A. Souva. 2001. "The Impact of National Tides and District-Level Effects on Electoral Outcomes: The U.S. Congressional Elections of 1862–63." *American Journal of Political Science* 45, no. 4 (October):887–98.

Carter, Bill. 2004. "'Nightline' to Read off Iraq War Dead." *New York Times*, 28 April, p. 9.

Carter, Phillip, and Owen West. 2004. "Iraq 2004 Looks Like Vietnam 1966." *Slate*, 27 December 2004.

Caspary, William. 1970. "The 'Mood Theory': A Study of Public Opinion and Foreign Policy." *American Political Science Review* 64:536–47.

Chafetz, Josh. 2003. "Body Count: Inside the Voodoo Science of Calculating Civilian Casualties." *Daily Standard,* 16 April 2003.

Chang, LinChiat, and Jon Krosnick. 2002. "A Comparison of the Random Digit Dialing Telephone Survey Methodology with Internet Survey Methodology as Implemented by Knowledge Networks and Harris Interactive." Paper presented at the annual meeting of the American Political Science Association, Boston Marriott Copley Place, Sheraton Boston & Hynes Convention Center, Boston, 28 August. Available at http://www.allacademic.com/meta/p66294_index.html.

Chesterman, Simon, ed.. 2001. *Civilians in War*. Boulder, Colo.: Lynne Rienner.

Cho, Wendy, and Brian Gaines. 2004. "The Limits of Ecological Inference: The Case of Split-Ticket Voting." *American Journal of Political Science* 48, no. 1:152–71.

Clark, Richard, and Kenneth Dautrich. 2000. "Who's Really Misreading the Public? A Comment on Kull and Ramsay's 'Challenging U.S. Policymaker's Image of an Isolationist Public.'" *International Studies Perspectives* 1, no. 2:195–98.

Cockburn, Patrick. 1993. "Clinton Acclaims Iraq Strike." *The Independent*, 28 June, p. 1.

Coker, Christopher. 2001. *Humane Warfare*. New York: Routledge.

———. 2002. *Waging War without Warriors? The Changing Culture of Military Conflict*. Boulder, Colo.: Lynne Rienner,

Coll, Alberto R. 2001. "Kosovo and the Moral Burdens of Power." In Andrew Bacevich and Eliot A. Cohen, eds., "War over Kosovo: Politics and Strategy in a Global Age." New York: Columbia University Press.

Conetta, Carl. 2002. "Operation Enduring Freedom: Why a Higher Rate of Civilian Bombing Casualties." Project on Defense Alternatives Briefing Report #11, 24 January 2002.

———. 2003. "The Wages of War: Iraqi Combatant and Noncombatant Fatalities in the 2003 Conflict." Project on Defense Alternatives, Research Monograph #8, 20 October 2003.

———. 2004. "Disappearing the Dead: Iraq, Afghanistan, and the Idea of a 'New Warfare.'" Project on Defense Alternatives, Research Monograph #9, 18 February 2004.

Converse, Philip E. 1964. "The Nature of Belief Systems in Mass Publics." In David Apter, ed., *Ideology and Discontent*. New York: Free Press.

Conversino, Mark J. 1997. "Sawdust Superpower: Perceptions of U.S. Casualty Tolerance in the Post–Gulf War Era." *Strategic Review* 25, no. 1:15–23.

Cook, Martin L. 2000. "Immaculate War: Constraints on Humanitarian Intervention." *Ethics and International Affairs* 14:55–65.

Couper, Mick. 2000. Review: Web Surveys: A Review of Issues and Approaches. *Public Opinion Quarterly* 64, no. 4:464–94.

Cowley, Geoffrey. 2003. "Fallout: Gauging the Human Toll." *Newsweek*, 3 February, p. 40.

Cox, Matthew. 1999. "America Willing to Risk Your Life: Despite Possible Casualties, Most Surveyed Believe Ethnic Cleansing Must Stop." *Army Times*, 7 June, p. 10.

Cummins, Chip. 2001. "Military Avoids Estimating Civilian Deaths in Effort to Keep Focus off of Body Count." *Wall Street Journal*, 4 December, p. 20.

Cunningham, Henry. 2000. "Shelton Says Test Necessary: Death Potential Considered Factor." *Fayetteville Observer*, 27 January, p.1F.

Dauber, Cori. 2001. "The Role of Visual Imagery in Casualty Shyness and Casualty Aversion." In "Media and Education in the U.S. Civil-Military Gap," special edition of *Armed Forces and Society* 27, no. 2:205–30.

De Moraes, Lisa. 2004. "'Nightline' Ratings Rise for Roll Call of Iraq Dead." *Washington Post*, 4 May, p. C1.

Dennis, J. Michael, Cindy Chatt, Rick Li, Alicia Motta-Stanko, and Paul Pulliam. 2005. "Data Collection Mode Effects Controlling for Sample Origins in a Panel Survey: Telephone versus Internet." Unpublished manuscript, RTI International. Available at http://www.knowledgenetworks.com/ganp/docs/research0105.pdf.

Dixon, Paul. 2000. "Britain's 'Vietnam Syndrome'? Public Opinion and British Military Intervention from Palestine to Yugoslavia." *Review of International Studies* 26:99–121.

Downes, Alexander. 2004. *Targeting Civilians in War*. Ph.D. diss., University of Chicago.

———. 2006. "Desperate Times, Desperate Measures: The Causes of Civilian Victimization in War." *International Security* 30, no. 4: 152–95.

Doyle, Michael. 1986. "Liberalism and World Politics." *American Political Science Review* 80, 4:1151–69.

Drozdiak, William, and Dana Priest. 1999. "NATO's Cautious Air Strategy Comes under Fire." *Washington Post*, 16 May, p. 26.

Dunlap, Charles. 2000. "Kosovo, Casualty Aversion, and the American Military Ethos: A Perspective." *Journal of Legal Studies* 10:95–107.

Eichenberg, Richard. C. 2002. "Gender Differences and the Use of Force in the United States, 1990–2002." Paper prepared for the annual meeting of the American Political Science Association, Boston, 29 August–1 September.

———. 2004. "Victory Has Many Friends: The American Public and the Use of Military Force, 1981–2004." Working paper, Department of Political Science, Tufts University, 24 May 2004. Available at http://ase.tufts.edu/polsci/faculty/eichenberg/victory.pdf.

———. 2005. "Victory Has Many Friends: U.S. Public Opinion and the Use of Military Force, 1981–2005." *International Security* 33, no. 1:140–77.

Eikenberry, Karl W. 1996. "Take No Casualties." *Parameters* 26, no. 2:109–18.

Elder, Janet, and Adam Nagourney. 2003. "A Nation at War; POLL; Opinions Begin to Shift as Public Weighs Cost of War." *New York Times*, 26 March, p. B1.

Entman, Robert M. 2003. *Projections of Power: Framing News, Public Opinion, and U.S. Foreign Policy*. Chicago: University of Chicago Press.

Epstein, Edward. 2003. "How Many Iraqis Died? We May Never Know." *San Francisco Chronicle*, 3 May, p. 13

Erdmann, Andrew P. N. 1999. "The U.S. Presumption of Quick, Costless Wars." *Orbis* 43, no. 3:363–82.

Everts, Philip. 2000. "When the Going Gets Rough: Does the Public Support the Use of Force?" *World Affairs* 162:91–107.

———. 2001. "War without Bloodshed? Public Opinion and the Conflict Over

Kosovo." In Philip Everts and Pierangelo Isernia, eds., *Public Opinion and the International Use of Force*. New York: Routledge.

———. 2002. *Democracy and Military Force*. New York: Palgrave Macmillan.

———. 2005. "Casualty Aversion Hypothesis Revisited." Paper prepared for the "Agenda for Strategy and Policy Planning" Workshop, Triangle Institute for Security Studies, Duke University, and Woodrow Wilson International Center for Scholars, Washington D.C., 1–15 February.

Farer, Tom J. 2002. "Beyond the Charter Fame: Unilateralism or Condominium?" *American Journal of International Law* 96, no. 2:359–64.

Feaver, Peter. 2001. "To Maintain that Support, Show Us What Success Means." *Washington Post*, 7 October, p. B1.

Feaver, Peter D., and Christopher Gelpi. 1999. "How Many Deaths Are Acceptable? A Surprising Answer." *Washington Post*, 7 November, p. B3.

———Feaver, Peter D., and Chris Gelpi. 2004. *Choosing Your Battles: American Civil-Military Relations and the Use of Force*. Princeton: Princeton University Press.

Fiorina, Morris. 1981. *Retrospective Voting in American National Elections*. New Haven: Yale University Press.

Ford, Peter. 2003. "Surveys Pointing to High Civilian Death Toll in Iraq." *Christian Science Monitor*, 22 May, p. 1.

Franks, Tommy. 2004. "War of Words." *New York Times*, 29 October, p. 27.

Freedberg, Sydney J. 2004. "The Price." *National Journal* 36, no. 22:1688–93.

Friedlander, Saul. 1967. *Prelude to Downfall: Hitler and the United States, 1939–1941*. New York: Alfred A. Knopf.

Friedman, Thomas. 2001. "A Memo from Osama." *New York Times*, 26 June, p. A19.

Gardner, Richard N. 2003. "Neither Bush nor the 'Jurisprudes.'" *American Journal of International Law* 97, no. 3:585–90.

Gartner, Scott Sigmund. 2004. "Making the International Local: The Terrorist Attack on the USS *Cole*, Local Casualties, and Media Coverage." *Political Communication* 21, no. 2, pp. 139–59.

Gartner, Scott Sigmund, and Gary Segura. 1998. "War, Casualties, and Public Opinion." *Journal of Conflict Resolution* 42, no. 3:278–320.

———. 2000. "Race, Casualties, and Opinion in the Vietnam War." *Journal of Politics* 62, no. 1:115–46.

Gartner, Scott Sigmund, Gary Segura, and Michael Wilkening. 1997. "All Politics Are Local: Local Losses and Individual Attitudes toward the Vietnam War." *Journal of Conflict Resolution* 41, no. 5 (October):669–94.

Gartzke, Erik. 2001. "Democracy and the Preparation for War: Does Regime Type Affect States' Anticipation of Casualties?" *International Studies Quarterly* 45, no. 3:467–84.

Gelpi, Christopher, Peter Feaver, and Jason Reifler. 2005/06. "Success Matters: Casualty Sensitivity and the War in Iraq." *International Security* 30, no. 3:7–46.

Gentry, John. A. 1998. "Military Force in an Age of National Cowardice." *Washington Quarterly* 21, no. 4:179–92.

Giangreco, D. M. 2004. "'Spinning' the Casualties: Media Strategies during the

Roosevelt Administration." *Passport: The Newsletter of the Society for Historians of American Foreign Relations* 35, no. 3 (December):22–29.

Gifford, Brian. 2005. "Combat Casualties and Race: What Can We Learn from the 2003–2004 Iraq Conflict?" *Armed Forces and Society* 31, no. 2 (winter):201–26.

Gilbert, Marc Jason, and William Head. 1996. *The Tet Offensive*. Westport, Conn.: Praeger. Gordon, Michael R., and Bernard E. Trainor. 1995. *The Generals' War.* Boston: Little, Brown.

Gorney, Cynthia. 2005. "Mother's War." *New York Times Magazine*, 29 May, p. 32–42.

Gough, Paul J. 2005. "'Nightline' to Read 900 Names of War Dead." *Chicago Sun-Times*, 26 May, p. 54.

Gowing, Nik. 2003. "Real-Time Television Coverage of Armed Conflicts and Diplomatic Crises: Does It Pressure or Distort Foreign Policy Decisions?" Pp. 139–222 in Nancy Palmer, ed., *Terrorism, War, and the Press*. Cambridge: Harvard University Press.

Grieco, Joseph. 2003. "The American Public and the Future of NATO and American Multilateralism." Unpublished paper.

———. 2005 "Let's Get a Second Opinion: Allies, the U.N., and U.S. Public Support for War." Unpublished ms., Duke University.

Griffin, Ronald R. 2004. "Our Honor, Our Grief." *Wall Street Journal*, 26 April, p. 14.

Griffiths, William, R Carter Hill, and George Judge. 1993. *Learning and Practicing Econometrics*. New York: Wiley.

Hallion, Richard. 1999. "How Many Deaths?" *Washington Post*, 15 November, p. 22.

Hanushek, Erik, and John Jackson. 1977. *Statistical Methods for Social Scientists*. New York: Academic Press.

Harden, Blaine, and Dana Milbank. 2004. "Photos of Soldiers' Coffins Revive Controversy." *Washington Post*, 23 April, p. 10.

Harnden, Toby. 2003. "Democracy in Iraq Could 'Reshape the Middle East.'" *Daily Telegraph* (London), 7 February, p. 15.

Harris, Ron, and Charles Arms. 2004. "The Biggest Burdens of War Are Shouldered by Small Town, USA." *St. Louis Post-Dispatch*, 30 May.

Heath, Chip. 1995. "Escalation and De-escalation of Commitment in Response to Sunk Costs: The Role of Budgeting and Mental Accounting." *Organizational Behavior and Human Decision Processes* 62, no. 1:38–54.

Heath, Chip, Richard P. Larrick, and George Wu. 1999. "Goals as Reference Points." *Cognitive Psychology* 38:79–109.

Hegland, Corine. 2004. "The Civilian Death Toll." *National Journal* 36, no. 22: 1704–6.

Herold, Marc. N.d. "A Dossier of Civilian Victims of the United States' Aerial Bombing of Afghanistan." Unpublished manuscript, Departments of Economics and Women's Studies, University of New Hampshire. Available at http://pubpages.unh.edu/~mwherold/.

Herrmann, Richard K., Philip E. Tetlock, and Penny S. Visser. 1999. "Mass Public

Decisions to Go to War: A Cognitive-Interactionist Framework." *American Political Science Review* 93, no. 3:553–75.

Herron, Michael, and Kenneth Schotts. 2003. "Using Ecological Inference Point Estimates as Dependent Variables in Second-Stage Linear Regressions." *Political Analysis* 11, no. 1: 44–64.

Hinckley, Ronald H. 1992. *People, Polls, and Policymakers: American Public Opinion and National Security*. New York: Lexington.

Hodge, Carl Cavanagh. 2000. "Casual War: NATO's Intervention in Kosovo." *Ethics and International Affairs* 14:39–54.

Holsti, Ole. 1979. "The Three-Headed Eagle: The United States and System Change." *International Studies Quarterly 23:339–59.*

———. 1996. *Public Opinion and American Foreign Policy*. Ann Arbor: Michigan University Press.

Holsti, Ole, and James Rosenau. 1984. *American Leadership in World Affairs: Vietnam and the Breakdown of the Consensus*. Boston: Allen and Unwin.

Huelfer, Evan Andrew. 2003. *The 'Casualty Issue' in American Military Practice: The Impact of World War I*. Westport, Conn.: Praeger.

Human Rights Watch. 2000. "Civilian Deaths in the NATO Air Campaign." Human Rights Watch, February. Available at http://www.hrw.org/reports/2000/nato/.

Hurwitz, Jon, and Mark Peffley. 1987a. "How Are Foreign Policy Attitudes Structured? A Hierarchical Model." *American Political Science Review* 81, no.4:1099–120.

———. 1987b. "The Means and Ends of Foreign Policy as Determinants of Presidential Support." *American Journal of Political Science* 31, no. 2: 236–58.

Hyde, Charles. 2000. "Casualty Aversion: Implications for Policy Makers and Senior Military Officers." *Aerospace Power Journal* 14, no. 2:17–27.

Ignatieff, Michael. 2000. *Virtual War: Kosovo and Beyond*. New York: Holt.

Isernia, Pierangelo. 2001. "Conclusions: What Have We Learned and Where Do Go from Here?" Pp. 260–72 in Philip Everts and Pierangelo Isernia, eds., *Public Opinion and the International Use of Force*. New York: Routledge.

Iyengar, Shanto, and Simon Adam. 1993. "News Coverage of the Gulf Crisis and Public Opinion: A Study of Agenda-Setting, Priming, and Framing." *Communication Research* 20, no. 3:365–84.

Jacobson, Gary. 2005. "The Public, the President, and the War in Iraq." Paper presented at the annual meeting of the Midwest Political Science Association, Palmer House Hilton, Chicago, 7 April. Available at http://www.allacademic.com/meta/p85348_index.html.

Jaffe, Greg. 2004. "Private Duty: Army Brings Home Its Dead without Fanfare." *Wall Street Journal*, 27 May, p. 1.

Jehl, Douglas. 1993. "U.S. Says It Waited for Certain Proof before Iraq Raid." *New York Times*, 29 June, p. A1.

Jensen, Elizabeth. 2004. "'Nightline' Fuels Iraq Images Feud." *Los Angeles Times*, 29 April, p. A8.

Jentleson, Bruce W. 1992. "The Pretty Prudent Public: Post-Vietnam American Opinion on the Use of Military Force." *International Studies Quarterly* 36, no. 1:49–74.

Jentleson, Bruce W., and Rebecca L. Britton. 1998. "Still Pretty Prudent." *Journal of Conflict Resolution* 42, no. 2:395–417.

Jervis, Rick. 2005. "Quality of Life for Many Iraqis Still Poor, U.N. Says." *USA Today*, 13 May, p. 8.

Jervis, Robert. 1976. *Perception and Misperception in International Politics*. Princeton: Princeton University Press.

———. 1992. "Political Implications of Loss Aversion." *Political Psychology* 13, no. 2:187–204.

———. 2003. "Understanding the Bush Doctrine." *Political Science Quarterly* 118, 3:365–88.

Johnson, Dominic, and Dominic Tierney. 2006. *Failing to Win: Perceptions of Victory and Defeat in International Politics*. Cambridge: Harvard University Press.

Johnstone, David. 2000. "The 'Reverse' Sunk Costs Effect and Explanations Rational and Irrational." Unpublished manuscript, Department of Accounting and Finance, University of Wollongong.

Jones, Charisse. 2005. "Soldiers' Families to Hold Anti-War Rally." *USA Today*, 18 March, p. 6.

Kagan, Robert. 2003. *Of Paradise and Power: America and Europe in the New World Order*. New York: Knopf.

Kahneman, Daniel, and Amos Tversky. 1979. "Prospect Theory: An Analysis of Decision under Risk." *Econometrica* 47:263–91.

———. 1984. "Choices, Values, and Frames." *American Psychologist* 39, 4:341–50.

Kaplan, Fred. 2004. "100,000 Dead—or 8,000." *Slate*, 29 October.

Karol, David, and Edward Miguel. 2007. "The Electoral Cost of War: Iraq Casualties and the 2004 U.S. Presidential Election." *Journal of Politics* 69, no. 3:633–648.

Kaufmann, Chaim. 1994. "Out of the Lab and into the Archives: A Method for Testing Psychological Explanations of Political Decision-Making." *International Studies Quarterly* 38, no. 4:557–86.

Keller, Bill. 2002. "The Year in Ideas; Preemption." *New York Times*, 15 December, p. 114.

Kelly, Thomas. 2004. "Sunk Costs, Rationality, and Acting for the Sake of the Past." *Nous* 38, no. 1:612–40.

Kiewiet, D. Roderick. 1983. *Macroeconomics and Micropolitics: The Electoral Effects of Economic Issues*. Chicago: University of Chicago Press.

Kilian, Michael. 2002. "A Question of Casualties in Iraq." *Chicago Tribune*, 30 December, p. 1.Kinder, Donald, and Shanto Iyengar. 1987. *News That Matters: Television and American Opinion*. Chicago: University of Chicago Press.

Kinder, Donald, and D. Roderick Kiewiet. 1979. "Economic Grievances and Political Behavior: The Role of Personal Discontents and Collective Judgments in Congressional Voting." *American Journal of Political Science* 23:495–527.

———. 1981. "Sociotropic Politics: The American Case." *British Journal of Political Science* 11:129–61.

King, David C., and Zachary Karabell. 2003. *The Generation of Trust: Public Confidence in the Military since Vietnam*. Washington, D.C.: American Enterprise Institute.

King, Gary, Robert Keohane, and Sidney Verba. 1994. *Designing Social Inquiry.* Princeton: Princeton University Press.

Kitfield, James. 1998. "Standing Apart." *National Journal* 30, no. 24 (13 June):1350–58.

Klarevas, Louis. 2000. "Trends: The United States Peace Operation in Somalia." *Public Opinion Quarterly* 64, no. 4 (winter): 523–40.

———. 2002. "The 'Essential Domino' of Military Operations: American Public Opinion and the Use of Force." *International Studies Perspectives* 3, no. 4 (November):417–37.

———. 2003. "How Many Deaths Can Americans Take?" *Newsday*, 12 November, p. 23.

———. 2006. "Casualties, Polls, and the Iraq War." *International Security* 31, no. 2:186–98.

Knickerbocker, Brad. 2003. "Pentagon's Quietest Calculation: The Casualty Count." *Christian Science Monitor*, 28 January, p. 1.

Kober, Avi. 2003. "Western Democracies in Low Intensity Conflict: Some Postmodern Aspects." Pp. 3–21 in Efraim Inbar, ed., *Democracies and Small Wars.* London: Frank Cass.

Kornblut, Anne E. 2003. "Bush Talks of 'Real Threat' of Al-Qaeda, Voices Confidence in Weapons Hunt and Again Defends Case for War in Iraq." *Boston Globe*, 31 July, p. A2.

Kretchik, Walter E. 1997. "Force Protection Disparities." *Military Review* 77, no. 4:73–78.

Kristof, Nicholas D. 2002. "A Merciful War." *New York Times*, 1 February, p. A25.

Kull, Steven. 1995/96. "What the Public Knows that Washington Doesn't." *Foreign Policy* 101 (winter):102–5.

———. 1997. "Review of Eric Larson's *Casualties and Consensus.*" *Public Opinion Quarterly* 61, no. 4 (winter):672–74.

Kull, Steven, and I. M. Destler. 1999. *Misreading the Public: The Myth of a New Isolationism.* Washington, D.C.: Brookings.

Kull, Steven, I. M. Destler, and Clay Ramsay. 1997. *The Foreign Policy Gap: How Policymakers Misread the Public.* Center for International and Security Studies at Maryland, University of Maryland.

Kull, Steven, and Clay Ramsay. 2000. "A Rejoinder from Kull and Ramsay." *International Studies Perspectives* 1, no. 2:202–5.

———. 2001. "The Myth of the Reactive Public: American Public Attitudes on Military Fatalities in the Post–Cold War Period." Pp. 205–29 in Philip Everts and Pierangelo Isernia, eds., *Public Opinion and the International Use of Force.* London: Routledge, 2001.

Kull, Steven, Clay Ramsay, and Evan Lewis. 2003/04. "Misperceptions, the Media, and the Iraq War." *Political Science Quarterly* 118, no. 4:569–98.

Kull, Steven, et al. 2002. "Americans on the Conflict with Iraq." The PIPA/Knowledge Networks Poll, 2 October.

———. 2003a. "Americans on Iraq and the U.N. Inspections II." The PIPA/Knowledge Networks Poll, 21 February.

———. 2003b. "Americans on Iraq: WMD, Links to Al Qaeda, and Reconstruction." The PIPA/Knowledge Networks Poll, 1 July.

———. 2003c. "Americans Reevaluate Going to War with Iraq." The PIPA/Knowledge Networks Poll, 13 November.

———. 2004. "Americans and Iraq on the Eve of the Presidential Election." The PIPA/Knowledge Networks Poll, 28 October.

Lacquement, Richard A. 2004. "The Casualty-Aversion Myth." *Naval War College Review* 37, no. 1:39–57.

Lane, Charles. 1998. "Casualty Attitude." *New Republic* 219, no. 17 (October):6, 41.

Larson, Eric V. 1996. *Casualties and Consensus: The Historical Role of Casualties in Domestic Support for U.S. Military Operations.* Santa Monica, Calif.: Rand.

———. 2000. "Putting Theory to Work: Diagnosing Public Opinion on the U.S. Intervention in Bosnia." Pp. 174–233 in Miroslav Nincic and Joseph Lepgold, eds., *Being Useful: Policy Relevance and International Relations Theory.* Ann Arbor: Michigan University Press.

Lau, Richard L., and David P. Redlawsk. 1997. "Voting Correctly." *American Political Science Review* 91, no. 3:585–599.

Lee, Gerald Geunwook. 2003/04. "'I See Dead People': Air-Raid Phobia and Britain's Behavior in the Munich Crisis." *Security Studies* 13, no. 2 (winter):230–72.

Levy, Jack S. 1992. "An Introduction to Prospect Theory." *Political Psychology* 13, no. 2:171–86.

———. 1997. "Prospect Theory, Rational Choice, and International Relations." *International Studies Quarterly* 41, no. 1:87–112.

———. 2000. "Loss Aversion, Framing Effects, and International Conflict." Pp. 193–221 in Manus I. Midlarsky, ed., *Handbook of War Studies II.* Ann Arbor: University of Michigan Press.

Lewy, Gunter. 1978. *America in Vietnam.* New York: Oxford University Press.

Lippmann, Walter. 1922. *Public Opinion.* New York: Macmillan.

———. 1955. *Essays in the Public Philosophy.* Boston: Little Brown.

Livingston, Steven. 1997. "Clarifying the CNN Effect: An Examination of Media Effects According to Type of Military Intervention." Joan Shorenstein Center on Press, Politics, and Public Policy, Research Paper R-18 (June). Cambridge: Harvard University.

Lorell, Mark, and Charles Kelley. 1985. *Casualties, Public Opinion, and Presidential Policy during the Vietnam War.* R-3060-AF. Santa Monica, Calif.: RAND.

Lupia, A. 1994. "The Effect of Information on Voting Behavior and Electoral Outcomes: An Experimental Study of Direct Legislation." *Public Choice* 71, no. 1:65–86.

Lupia, Arthur, and Matthew D. McCubbins. 1998. *The Democratic Dilemma: Can Citizens Learn What They Need to Know?* New York: Cambridge University Press.

Luttwak, Edward N. 1994. "Where Are the Great Powers?" *Foreign Affairs* 73, no. 4:23–29.

———. 1995. "Towards Post-Heroic Warfare." *Foreign Affairs* 74, no. 3:109–22.

———. 1996. "A Post-Heroic Military Policy." *Foreign Affairs* 75, no. 4:33–44.

———. 1999. "From Vietnam to Desert Fox: Civil-Military Relations in Modern Democracies." *Survival* 41, no. 1:99–112.

Mack, Andrew. 1975. "Why Big Nations Lose Small Wars: The Politics of Asymmetric Conflict." *World Politics* 27, no. 2 (January):175–2000.

Mandel, Robert. 2004. *Security, Strategy, and the Quest for Bloodless War*. Boulder, Colo.: Lynne Rienner.

Mao, Tse-Tung. 1977. *Selected Works of Mao Tse-Tung*, vol. 5. New York: Pergamon.

Matthews, Mark, and Tom Bowman. 2004. "Fears of Another Somalia Stir." *Baltimore Sun*, 1 April, p. A1.

McGraw, Kathleen M., and Zachary M. Mears. 2004. "Casualties and Public Support for U.S. Military Operations: An Experimental Investigation." Unpublished paper, Department of Political Science, Ohio State University.

McInnes, Colin. 2002. *Spectator-Sport War: The West and Contemporary Conflict*. Boulder, Colo.: Lynne Rienner.

McManus, Doyle. 2003. "Public's High Expectations Might Lead to a Hard Crash." *Los Angeles Times*, 24 March, p. A7.

McNulty, Timothy J. 1993. "Television's Impact on Executive Decision-making and Diplomacy." *Fletcher Forum on World Affairs* (Winter):67–83.

Mearsheimer, John. 2001. "Guns Won't Win the Afghan War." *New York Times*, 4 November, p. 13.

Meilinger, Phillip. 2001. "A Matter of Precision." *Foreign Policy* (March/April 2001):78–79.

———. 2002. "More Bogus Charges against Airpower." *Air Force Magazine* 85, no. 10:52–56.

Mermin, Jonathan. 1997. "Television News and American Intervention in Somalia: The Myth of a Media-Driven Foreign Policy." *Political Science Quarterly* 112, no. 3:385–403.

Merom, Gil. 2003. *How Democracies Lose Small Wars*. Cambridge: Cambridge University Press.

Milstein, Jeffrey. 1969. "Changes in U.S. Domestic Support and Alternative Military Actions in the Vietnam War 1965–1968." Paper delivered to the 23rd Annual Meeting of the Western Political Science Association, 3 April 1969, Honolulu, Hawaii.

———. 1973. "The Vietnam War from the 1968 Tet Offensive to the 1970 Cambodian Invasion." In H. R. Alker, Jr., K. W. Deutsch, A. H. Stoetzel, *Mathematical Approaches to Politics*. New York: Elsevier Scientific.

———. 1974. *Dynamics of the Vietnam War: A Quantitative Analysis and Predictive Computer Simulation*. Columbus: Ohio State University Press.

Milstein, Jeffrey, and William C. Mitchell. 1968. "Dynamics of the Vietnam Conflict: A Quantitative Analysis and Predictive Computer Simulation." Peace Research Society (International) Papers, 10.

Morehouse, David A. 1996. *Nonlethal Weapons: War without Death*. Westport, Conn.: Praeger.

Morin, Richard, and Claudia Deane. 2003. "Support for Bush Declines as Casualties Mount in Iraq." *Washington Post*, 12 July, p. A1.

Morley, Jefferson. 2004. "The Trouble with Civilian Casualty Stories." *Washingtonpost.com*, 15 April 2004. Accessed on 15 April 2004.

Moskos, Charles. 1995. "Grave Decision: When Americans Accept Casualties." *Chicago Tribune*, 12 December, p. 25.

———. 1996/97. "Casualties and the Will to Win." *Parameters*. 26, no. 4 (Winter):136–39.

Moss, Michael. 2005. "Many Actions Tied to Delay in Armor for Troops in Iraq." *New York Times*, 7 March, p. 1.

Mueller, John. 1971. "Trends in Popular Support for the Wars in Korea and Vietnam." *American Political Science Review* 65, no. 2 (June):358–75.

———. 1973. *War, Presidents, and Public Opinion*. New York: Wiley.

———. 1994. *Policy and Opinion in the Gulf War*. Chicago: Chicago University Press.

———. 2002. "Public Support for Military Ventures Abroad: Evidence from the Polls." In John Norton Moore and Robert F. Turner, eds., *The Real Lessons of the Vietnam War: Reflections Twenty-Five Years after the Fall of Saigon*. Durham, N.C.: Carolina Academic Press.

———. 2005. "The Iraq Syndrome." *Foreign Affairs* 84, no 6.

Mueller, Karl. 2000. "Politics, Death, and Morality in U.S. Foreign Policy." *Aerospace Power Journal* 14, 2:12–16.

Muravchik, Joshua. 1991. "The End of the Vietnam Paradigm?" *Commentary* 91, no. 5 (May): 17–23.

Murray, Alan. 2003. "Political Capital: Bush Officials Scramble to Push Democracy in Iraq." *Wall Street Journal*, 8 April, p. 4.

Murray, Shoon Kathleen. 2000. "Bringing the Majority Back In." *International Studies Perspectives* 1, no. 2:198–202.

Mutz, Diana C. 1998. *Impersonal Influence: How Perceptions of Mass Collectives Affect Political Attitudes*. Cambridge: Cambridge University Press.

Nacos, Brigitte L., Robert Y. Shapiro, and Pierangelo Isernia, eds. 2000. *Decisionmaking in a Glass House: Mass Media, Public Opinion, and American and European Foreign Policy in the 21st Century.* Lanham, Md.: Rowman and Littlefield.

Neuman, Johanna. 1996. *Lights, Camera, War: Is Media Technology Driving International Politics*. New York: St. Martin's.

Nickelsburg, Michael J., and Helmut Norpath. 2000. "Commander-in-Chief or Chief Economist? The President in the Eye of the Public." *Electoral Studies* 19:313–22.

Nincic, Donna J., and Miroslav Nincic. 1995. "Commitment to Military Intervention: The Democratic Government as Economic Investor." *Journal of Peace Research* 32, no. 4:413–36.

Nincic, Miroslav. 1992. "A Sensible Public: New Perspectives on Popular Opinion and Foreign Policy." *Journal of Conflict Resolution* 36, no. 4:772–89.

Nincic, Miroslav, and Barbara Hinckley. 1991. "Foreign Policy and the Evaluation of Presidential Candidates." *Journal of Conflict Resolution* 35, no. 2: 333–55.

Nincic, Miroslav, and Donna J. Nincic. 2002. "Race, Gender, and War." *Journal of Peace Research* 39, no. 5:547–68.

Noonan, Michael. 1997. "The Illusion of Bloodless Victories." *Orbis* 41, no. 2: 308–20.

Northcraft, Gregory B., and Margaret A. Neale. 1986. "Opportunity Costs and the Framing of Resource Allocation Decisions." *Organizational Behavior and Human Decision Processes* 37, no. 3:348–56.

Oberdorfer, Don. 2001. *The Two Koreas: A Contemporary History*. New York: Basic Books.

O'Hanlon, Michael. 2003. "Estimating Casualties in a War to Overthrow Saddam." *Orbis* 47, no. 1:21–40.

Oneal, John R., and Anna Lillian Bryan. 1995. "The Rally 'Round the Flag Effect in U.S. Foreign Policy Crises, 1950–1985." *Political Behavior* 17:379–401.

Ostrom, Charles W., and Brian L. Job. 1986. "The President and the Political Use of Force." *American Political Science Review* 80, no. 2:541–66.

Page, Benjamin I., and Robert Y. Shapiro. 1982. "Changes in Americans' Policy Preferences, 1935–1979." *Public Opinion Quarterly* 46, no. 1:24–42.

———. 1988. "Foreign Policy and the Rational Public." *Journal of Conflict Resolution* 32, no. 2:211–47.

———. 1992. *The Rational Public: Fifty Years of Trends in Americans' Policy Preferences*. Chicago: University of Chicago Press.

Paletz, David L., and Robert M. Entman. 1981. *Media Power Politics*. New York: Free Press.

Parish, Peter J. 1975. *The American Civil War*. New York: Holmes and Meier.

Parker, Suzanne L. 1995. "Toward Understanding of 'Rally' Effects: Public Opinion in the Persian Gulf War." *Public Opinion Quarterly* 5, no. 9:526–46.

Peffley, Mark, and Jon Hurwitz. 1993. "Models of Attitude Constraint in Foreign Affairs." *Political Behavior* 15, no. 1:61–90.

Peffley, Mark, Ronald E. Langley, and Robert Kirby Goidel. 1995. "Public Responses to the Presidential Use of Military Force: A Panel Analysis." *Political Behavior*17, no. 3: 307–36.

Peters, Ralph. 1996. "A Revolution in Military Ethics?" *Parameters* 26, no. 2:102–8.

Pomfret, John. 2001. "In Beijing's Moves, A Strategy on Taiwan." *Washington Post*, 6 April, p. A1.

Popkin, Samuel L. 1991. *The Reasoning Voter: Communication and Persuasion in Presidential Campaigns*. Chicago: University of Chicago Press.

Powell, Colin, and Joseph E. Persico. 1995. *My American Journey*. New York: Ballantine.

Powers, William. 2003. "Civilian Casualties: A Media Primer." *National Journal* 35, no. 11:802.

Powlick, Philip J., and Andrew Z. Katz. 1998. "Defining the American Public Opinion/Foreign Policy Nexus." *Mershon International Studies Review* 42, no. 1 (May):29–61.

Preston, Julia. 2003. "U.N. Study Sees 500,000 Facing Injury in Case of War." *New York Times*, 8 January, p. A11.

Purdum, Todd S. 2003. "A Nation at War: The Casualties; Delicate Calculus of Casualties and Public Opinion." *New York Times*, 27 March, p. B1.

Rainey, James. 2005. "Unseen Pictures, Untold Stories." *Los Angeles Times*, 21 May, p. 1.

Rangel, Charles. 2003. "Military Conscription: Mandatory Service Might Make Hawks Think Twice." *Atlanta Journal-Constitution*, 14 January, p. 21A.

Ray, James Lee. 1995. *Democracy and International Conflict: An Evaluation of the Democratic Peace Proposition*. Columbia: University of South Carolina Press.

Record, Jeffrey. 2000. "Failed States and Casualty Phobia: Implications for Force Structure and Technology Choices." Occasional Paper No. 18. October,. Center for Strategy and Technology, Air University.

Reiter, Dan, and Allan C. Stam. 2002. *Democracies at War*. Princeton: Princeton University Press.

Richardson, Renee. In draft. "Managing Coalition Warfare: Herding Lions . . . and Kittens." Ph.D. diss., Duke University.

Richburg, Keith B. 1993. "Rangers Net 17 but Miss Aideed Again; Mogadishu Warlord Frustrates Elite GIs." *Washington Post,* 8 September, p. A1.

Richman, Alvin. 1995. "When Should We Be Prepared to Fight?" *Public Perspective* 6, no. 3 (April/May):44.

Ricks, Thomas E. 2003a. "Duration of War Key to U.S. Victory." *Washington Post,* 19 March,p. A19.

———. 2003b. "U.S. Casualties Expose Risks, Raise Doubts about Strategy." *Washington Post*, 24 March, p. 1.

———. 2004. "Rumsfeld Gets Earful from Troops." *Washington Post*, 9 December, p. 1.

Ripley, Amanda. 2004. "An Image of Grief Returns." *Time*, 3 May.

Roberts, Les, Riyadh Lafta, Richard Garfield, Jamal Khudhairi, and Gilbert Burnham. 2004. "Mortality Before and After the 2003 Invasion of Iraq: Cluster Sample Survey." *Lancet* 29 October.

Rohde, David. 1991. *Parties and Leaders in the Post-Reform House*. Chicago: University of Chicago Press.

Rugg, Donald, and Hadley Cantril. 1940. "Analysis of Poll Results; War Attitudes of Families with Potential Soldiers." *Public Opinion Quarterly* 4, no. 2 (June):327–30.

Russett, Bruce. 1990. *Controlling the Sword: The Democratic Governance of National Security*. Cambridge: Harvard University Press.

Russett, Bruce, and John Oneal. 2001. *Triangulating Peace: Democracy, Interdependence, and International Organizations*. New York: Norton.

Sachs, Jeffrey. 2005. *The End of Poverty: Economic Possibilities for Our Time*. New York: Penguin.

Sapolsky, Harvey, and Jeremy Shapiro. 1996. "Casualties, Technology, and America's Future Wars." *Parameters* 26, no. 2:119–27.

Sapolsky, Harvey, and Sharon Weiner. 1994. "War without Casualties." *Across the Board* 31, no. 9 (October):39–42.

Schmitt, Eric. 1999a. "What Price Civilian Deaths?" *New York Times*, 15 April, p. 13.

———. 1999b. "It Costs a Lot to Kill Fewer People." *New York Times*, 2 May, p. 5.

———. 2003. "The Struggle for Iraq: Greenwich Village." *New York Times*, 23 September, p. 8.

———. 2004. "Troops' Queries Leave Rumsfeld on the Defensive." *New York Times*, 9 December, p. 1.

Schmitt, Eric, and Thom Shanker. 2002. "U.S. Refines Plan for War in Cities." *New York Times*, 21 October, p. A1.

Schwarz, Benjamin C. 1994. *Casualties, Public Opinion, and U.S. Military Intervention: Implications for U.S. Regional Deterrence Strategies*. Santa Monica, Calif.: RAND.

Schwarzkopf, H. Norman. 1992. *It Doesn't Take a Hero*. New York: Bantam.

Shane, Scott. 2005. "Bush's Speech on Iraq War Echoes Voices of an Analyst." *New York Times*, 4 December.

Shanker, Thom. 2004. "Regime Thought War Unlikely, Iraqis Tell U.S." *New York Times*, 12 Feb,p. A1.

Shanker, Thom, and Eric Schmitt. 2004. "Armor Scarce for Big Trucks Serving in Iraq." *New York Times*, 10 December, p. 1.

Shapiro, Robert Y., and Lawrence R. Jacobs. 2000. "Who Leads and Who Follows? U.S. Presidents, Public Opinion, and Foreign Policy." Pp. 223–45 in Brigitte L. Nacos, Robert Y. Shapiro, and Pierangelo Isernia, eds., *Decision-making in a Glass House: Mass Media, Public Opinion, and American and European Foreign Policy in the 21st Century*. Lanham, Md.: Rowman and Littlefield.

Shapiro, Robert Y., and Benjamin I. Page. 1988. "Foreign Policy and the Rational Public." *Journal of Conflict Resolution* 32, no. 2:211–47.

Shelton, Henry H. 2000. "National Security and the Intersection of Force and Diplomacy." Remarks to the ARCO Forum, Kennedy School of Government, Harvard University, 19 January.

Slevin, Peter. 2003. "U.S. Says War Has Legal Basis; Reliance on Gulf War Resolutions Is Questioned by Others." *Washington Post*, 21 March, p. A14

Smith, Hugh. 2003. "The Casualty Factor: What Costs Will Democracies Bear?" Paper presented at the Inter-University Seminar on Armed Forces and Society Biennial Conference, Chicago, 24-26 October.

Smith, Michael. 2001. "American 'Body-Bag Syndrome' Is Holding Back NATO." *London Daily Telegraph*, 21 March, p. 15.

Sniderman, Paul M. 1993. "The New Look in Public Opinion Research." In Ada Finifter, ed., *The State of the Discipline II*. Washington, D.C.: American Political Science Association.

Sobel, Richard. 2001. *The Impact of Public Opinion on U.S. Foreign Policy Since Vietnam*. New York: Oxford University Press.

Stech, Frank J. "Winning CNN Wars." *Parameters* 14, no. 3 (Autumn):37–56.

Stokes, Donald E. 1966. "Some Dynamic Elements of Contests for the Presidency." *American Political Science Review* 60, no. 1 (March):19–28.

Strobel, Warren. 1997. *Late-Breaking Foreign Policy: The News Media's Influence on Peace Operations*. Washington, D.C.: United States Institute of Peace Press.

———. 2001. "Public Shows Support for U.S. Aggression; But Sentiments Could

Change over Time, Analysts Say." *Milwaukee Journal Sentinel*, 28 October, p.A10.

Tarzi, Shah. 2001. "The Threat of the Use of Force in American Post–Cold War Policy in the Third World." *Journal of Third World Studies* 18, no. 1 (spring):39–64.

Teger, Al. 1980. *Too Much Invested to Quit*. New York: Pergamon.

Toffler, Alvin, and Heidi Toffler. 1993. *War and Anti-War: Making Sense of Today's Global Chaos*. New York: Warner.

Toner, Robin, and Jim Rutenberg. 2006. "Partisan Divide on Iraq Exceeds Split on Vietnam." *New York Times*, 30 June, p. 1.

Tyson, Ann Scott. 2005. "Hundreds of Photos of Caskets Released." *Washington Post*, 29 April, p. 10.

Unattributed. 1993. *FM 100-5: Operations*. Washington, D.C.: Department of the Army.

Unattributed. 2000. "What Will America Risk." *Wilson Quarterly* 24, no. 4:97–98.

Unattributed. 2002. "Excerpts from Iraqi President Saddam Hussein's speech on Thursday, the anniversary of the end of the 1980–88 Iran-Iraq War, as provided by the official Iraqi News Agency." Associated Press. 8 August.

Van der Meulen, Jan, and Marijke de Konink. 2001. "Risky Missions: Dutch Public Opinion on Peacekeeping in the Balkans." Pp. 116–38 in Philip Everts and Pierangelo Isernia, eds., *Public Opinion and the International Use of Force*. New York: Routledge.

Verba, Sidney, et al. 1967. "Public Opinion and the War in Vietnam." *American Political Science Review* 61, no.1 (June):317–33.

Waltz, Kenneth. 1967. *Foreign Policy and Democratic Politics: The American and British Experience*. New York: Little, Brown.

Washington, George. 1937. "To Lieutenant Colonel John Laurens." Chapter 4, no. 61, in *George Washington: A Collection,* compiled and edited by W. B. Allen. Indianapolis: Liberty Fund, 1988), Chapter 4, No. 61. Accessed from http://oll.libertyfund.org/title/848/101682 on 29 May 2008.

Watson, Paul. 1993. "Aideed Hunt's Still On, Peacekeepers Insist." *Toronto Star,* 29 September, p. A4.

Weigley, Russell. 1973. *American Way in War*. New York: Macmillan.

Wilcox, Clyde, and Dee Allsop. 1991. "Economic and Foreign Policy as Sources of Reagan Support." *Western Political Quarterly* 44, no. 4:941–58.

Witko, Christopher. 2003. "Cold War Belligerence and U.S. Public Opinion toward Defense Spending." *American Politics Research* 31, no. 4:379–403.

Wittkopf, Eugene R. 1986. "On the Foreign Policy Beliefs of the American People: A Critique and Some Evidence." *International Studies Quarterly* 30, no. 4:425–45.

———. 1990. *Faces of Internationalism: Public Opinion and American Foreign Policy*. Durham, N.C.: Duke University Press.

Wlezien, Christopher. 1995. "The Public as Thermostat: Dynamics of Preferences for Spending." *American Journal of Political Science* 39, no. 4:981–1000.

———. 1996. "Dynamics of Representation: The Case of U.S. Spending on Defense." *British Journal of Political Science* 26, no. 1:81–103.

Wrage, Stephen D., ed. 2003. *Immaculate Warfare: Participants Reflect on the Air Campaigns Over Kosovo, Afghanistan, and Iraq*. New York: Praeger.

York, Byron. 2001. "Clinton Has No Clothes." *National Review* 53, no. 24: 34–38.

Zaller, John. 1992. *The Nature and Origin of Mass Opinion*. New York: Cambridge University Press.

———. 1994. *The Nature and Origins of Public Opinion*. New York: Cambridge University Press.

Zaller, John, and Dennis Chu. 2000. "Government's Little Helper: U.S. Press Coverage of Foreign Policy Crises, 1946–1999." Pp. 61–84 in Brigitte L. Nacos, Robert Y. Shapiro, and Pierangelo Isernia, eds., *Decision-making in a Glass House: Mass Media, Public Opinion, and American and European Foreign Policy in the 21st Century.* Lanham, Md.: Rowman and Littlefield.

Zeelenberg, Marcel, and Eric van Dijk. 1997. "A Reverse Sunk Cost Effect in Risky Decision-making: Sometimes We Have Too Much Invested to Gamble." *Journal of Economic Psychology* 18, no. 6 (November):671–91.

Zucchino, David. 2002. "In the Taliban's Eyes, Bad News Was Good." *Los Angeles Times*, 3 June, p. A1.

———. 2003. "Iraq's Swift Defeat Blamed on Leaders." *Los Angeles Times*, 11 Aug., p. A1.

INDEX